Edwin J. Sanow

Published by

**krause
publications**

700 E. State Street • Iola, WI 54990-0001
Telephone: 715/445-2214

Please call or write for our free catalog.
Our toll-free number to place an order or obtain a free catalog is 800-258-0929 or
please use our regular business telephone 715-445-2214 for editorial comment and further information.

ISBN: 0-87341-483-7

Printed in the United States of America

Table of Contents

Acknowledgments 4

Foreword by 1/Lt. Curt VanDenBerg, Michigan State Police (ret.)................................. 5

Introduction 6

Chapter 1   1955: 265-cid Small-Block V-8 7

Chapter 2   1956: Chevrolet's First Police Package 11

Chapter 3   1957: 283-cid Small-Block V-8 14

Chapter 4   1958: Turbo-Thrust 348-cid Big-Block 18

Chapter 5   1959: Finned B-Body 22

Chapter 6   1960: Economy Turbo-Fire 283 26

Chapter 7   1961: Corvair Police Package 29

Chapter 8   1962: First 327-cid and 409-cid Engines 33

Chapter 9   1963: De-tuned 327-cid and 409-cid Engines 37

Chapter 10   1964: Chevelle Mid-Size Police Car 41

Chapter 11   1965: 396 cid and Turbo Hydra-Matic 45

Chapter 12   1966: 427-cid Big Block 50

Chapter 13   1967: Front Disc Brakes 54

Chapter 14   1968: 307 cid and Large Journal Small-Blocks 58

Chapter 15   1969: First 350-cid Mouse Motor V-8 61

Chapter 16   1970: First 454-cid Big-Block V-8 66

Chapter 17   1971: 400-cid V-8 and Longer Wheelbases 70

Chapter 18   1972: 402-cid Big-Block V-8 74

Chapter 19   1973: Leaner Carbs, Milder Cams, EGR 78

Chapter 20   1974: Malibu Mid-Size Police Car 81

Chapter 21   1975: Nova, *Motor Trend*, Los Angeles Sheriff 85

Chapter 22   1976: Last Long Wheelbase Big-Block Sedan 90

Chapter 23   1977: Downsized B-Body Impala 95

Chapter 24   1978: Nova Dominates in Last Year 100

Chapter 25   1979: CHP Special Purpose Vehicle Study.. 113

Chapter 26   1980: First V-6 Powered Re-Styled Impala 122

Chapter 27   1981: Malibu 9C1 Police Car of the Year 126

Chapter 28   1982: CHP Adopts Impala 9C1 130

Chapter 29   1983: Four-speed Overdrive Automatic 134

Chapter 30   1984: Year of the Celebrity 138

Chapter 31   1985: Fuel-injected Impala and Celebrity 142

Chapter 32   1986: First Caprice Police Car 146

Chapter 33   1987: Caprice Captures Michigan State Police....................................... 150

Chapter 34   1988: Last Carbureted Caprice 154

Chapter 35   1989: Fuel-injected 350-cid Caprice 158

Chapter 36   1990: Door-Mounted Seat Belt Blues 162

Chapter 37   1991: New Caprice, First Camaro... 166

Chapter 38   1992: Lumina Special Service Sedan.. 173

Chapter 39   1993: LT1-powered Camaro 178

Chapter 40   1994: LT1-powered Caprice 183

Chapter 41   1995: Totally New Police Lumina 188

Chapter 42   1996: Last Caprice Police Car... 192

Chapter 43   Chevy Cop Cars in California (by John Bellah) 200

Chapter 44   Police Car Collecting (by Jim Post) 206

Chapter 45   1990 Caprice 9C1 Daily Driver (by Bill Hattersley) 213

Contributors 217

Appendix A   Sources for Cars and Parts 218

Appendix B   Chevrolet Police Engines by Year 220

About the Author 221

Contributing Authors 222

Acknowledgments

A book that covers as many eras as this one requires the help of a great many people. A few of the many enthusiasts and collectors made such significant contributions to the book, that a special and individual thanks is in order.

First, a special thanks goes to the three men who wrote guest chapters. An investigator with the California State-Long Beach Police, John Bellah, gives us the perspective from the Los Angeles County Sheriff. From the LASD came Chevrolet's most significant police car: the 1975 Nova. A retired sergeant with the Kansas City, Missouri, police and founder of the PCOOA, Jim Post, explains the hobby of police car collecting. Post points out which used police cars are best to buy and tells how to show them. A contributing editor with *Fire Apparatus Journal*, Bill Hattersley, describes life with an ex-police car, in this case, a Washington State Patrol 1990 Caprice. This chapter gives the squad car enthusiast many valuable tips.

Special thanks also goes to a group of enthusiasts who opened up their massive photo collections for use in this book. Chicago police officer Greg Reynolds contributed photos from all 50 states. Some of his most important shots were of Chevrolets used by the Chicago Police. Special agent Ned Schwartz contributed photos of New York and New Jersey police cars. His most critical photos are of the 1970 to 1975 Chevrolets. Sunnyvale, California, communications officer and PCOOA Western States representative Darryl Lindsay contributed most of the photos of vintage California police cars. California does indeed set the trend for the rest of the country. Fire apparatus enthusiast Bill Hattersley crossed over to police cars with a large number of high quality photos from the Northwest. Sparta, Illinois, police officer Dave Dotson also contributed photos from all 50 states. His most significant photos come from the Midwest, especially Missouri. Finally, John Bellah made the arrangements for me to access the photo archives in the Los Angeles Police Department and the Los Angeles County Sheriffs Department.

Each of these photo collections number in the thousands, and photo swapping among enthusiasts is quite informal. As a result, the identity of the original photographer is sometimes lost. The photo credits in this book indicate the photos are from the "collection" of the contributor. However, the work of two other photographers is also known to be a part of these collections. With this in mind, thanks for unknown photos goes to both Glenn Sokolofsky and Jay Weinstein.

Special thanks goes to all those who contributed police car literature, flyers, magazine articles, owner's manuals, shop manuals and other documents. Vintage factory police car literature is extremely rare, yet is also absolutely critical if a book on police cars is to be authoritative. Darryl Lindsay contributed the original literature for over half of the model years covered in this book. Many of the rest of the documents were purchased from Walter Miller. Patrick LeBlanc and Tom Utech filled in the gaps with mid-1950s and early-1980s literature, respectively.

Special thanks goes to Chevrolet's Special Vehicle police team: Harry Hammond, assistant manager, Police & Taxi, who was involved with the 1975 LASD Nova program, for his friendship and openness; Bob Hapiak, police car program manager, for his support in both fielding questions and providing test vehicles; and platform engineers Brian Tolen (Caprice), Larry Stout (Lumina) and Andy Lang (Camaro) who answered hundreds of questions over the past five years.

Special thanks goes to John Gunnell at Krause Publications, editor of *Old Cars Weekly News & Marketplace*. In addition to his encouragement on other police car projects, Gunnell's many books and articles were also the basis for the chapter covering the early years of Chevrolet.

Special thanks goes to Donna Rogers, editor of *Law Enforcement Technology* magazine and to Bruce Cameron, editor of *Law & Order* magazine. Rogers allowed me to start formal coverage of the influential Michigan State Police vehicle tests and arranged for me to attend Bill Scott's exclusive Tactical Driving School. Cameron assigned me to cover the Los Angeles County Sheriff vehicle tests and arranged for me to attend the Bob Bondurant School of High Performance Driving. The assignments from both editors gave me the network necessary for this book.

Special thanks goes to Sheriff Boston "Butch" Pritchett of the Benton County (Indiana) Sheriffs Office. He has given me authority to act on behalf of his office in areas where law enforcement connections were absolutely required. Pritchett has actively supported my writing and instructing for the past 10 years. A Chevy man at heart, he helped arrange my use of Chevrolet test vehicles including the very first 1993 Camaro B4C to roll off the production line.

Special thanks for writing the Foreword goes to retired First Lieutenant Curtis VanDenBerg of the Michigan State Police. VanDenBerg developed and refined MSP's annual patrol vehicle tests conducted since 1978. VanDenBerg's test protocol forced all police car manufacturers to improve performance every year. Police cars with the best performance were given a dollars-and-cents advantage come bid time under the MSP system. Chevrolet won these most-bang-for-the-buck performance tests 10 years in-a-row.

Special thanks goes to Cindy Sanow for typing all the text and tables and for the arduous task of proofing the final manuscript. She also helped with many of the photos. Raised in a Dodge-Plymouth-Chrysler family, Cindy has become quite the Chevrolet expert. Thanks, Cindy.

Finally, special thanks goes to all those who supplied individual photos or individual car owners who allowed their police cars to be photographed.

Foreword

I guess like most kids of the male persuasion who reached their teen years during the Fifties, I had a real thing for cars. What pushed me even more in that direction was that my dad was a wholesale auto parts distributor, and my older brother built his first hot rod out in the family garage when I was 10 or 11. I didn't have a chance. Being a car enthusiast was in my blood.

My first personal exposure to police cars was when my hot rodding older brother bought a decommissioned (retired) Michigan State Police patrol car. It was a 1958 Chevy '348' with triple carbs, still painted the distinctive MSP royal blue that is used to this day...and it was *fast*! That car made a huge impression on me at age 15, and I'm not sure that it didn't ultimately influence my career choice a few years later.

When I enlisted in the Michigan State Police in 1966, I quickly discovered that the patrol car played an important role in my everyday work. The patrol car proved to be much more than mere transportation. To patrol officers, then and now, it is nothing less than a multifunctional tool upon which they depend every hour of their workday, and which they use far more regularly than the handgun on their hip.

During the early years of my MSP career I spent literally thousands of hours behind the wheel of patrol cars of all major marques and models. Later, with my promotion to sergeant and the ensuing transfer to the Planning and Research Section at Headquarters I found myself in a position that was directly involved in the patrol car selection process. As a police officer and a car enthusiast, how could anyone ask for anything more. With all of that drooling over my hot rod brother's 1958 Chevy, I could never have guessed that I would be so fortunate.

Chevrolet had been producing true "police package" cars for about 20 years when I first became involved in police car testing in 1975. While my knowledge of Chevrolet police cars of the 20 years since then is substantial, when I received Ed Sanow's manuscript of this book I found that I had much to learn about the earlier Chevrolet police cars. There were, as you will find, a number of truly notable examples of excellent police cars for their time, and a few not so notable ones, too. This book contains such a wealth of information about Chevy's 40 years of building police cars that it could be subtitled, *Everything You Always Wanted to Know About Chevy Police Cars, But Didn't Know Enough to Ask.*

You will be taken through Chevy's early years, when it started with the old "straight Six," and ultimately moved into the modern era with the introduction of its first V-8 in 1955. Once into that first V-8, which had a displacement of 265 cubic inches and produced 180 hp @ 4600 rpm, the engines seemed to grow more powerful every year, and sometimes even mid-year. The zenith was reached in 1963 when Chevy offered a police engine that displaced 409 cubic inches and produced 425 hp @ 6000 rpm. Over the next several years, big-block engines producing massive amounts of horsepower continued to be available.

By the early Seventies, federally mandated emissions regulations began to erode power output and, ultimately, performance. As this trend continued, and mandated fuel economy standards were also enacted, the larger displacement engines were phased out. By 1979, the largest and most powerful police engine available from Chevrolet produced only 170 hp from 350 cubic inches. Interestingly, because engines from Ford and Chrysler were also down on power by 1979 because of the same federal regulations, the MSP ultimately purchased Chevrolets for that year. With the 1982 model, the 350 cubic

inch engine in the Impala hit its low point, in terms of power output, producing only 150 horsepower.

With the support of top level management, and through a concerted effort by Chevrolet engineers over the next five years, the power output of the 350 cubic inch V-8 was significantly improved. That, combined with chassis and brake improvements, made the 1987 Chevrolet Caprice (the name was changed from Impala to Caprice in 1986) the clear performance leader among the "police package" cars on the market. Because it was the overall top scorer in the evaluation process, it was the vehicle selected for use by Michigan State Police troopers. The next three years saw slow but steady improvements in performance, and consequently Chevrolet was selected by the MSP for each of those years.

The 1991 model year saw a major sheet metal change for the Chevrolet Caprice, although the chassis continued essentially unchanged except for the addition of ABS brakes. The new aerodynamic body shape, while controversial, was also slippery. From a performance standpoint, the car won all six categories of the annual MSP patrol car evaluation, and once again the Chevrolet Caprice was chosen by the MSP. With incremental improvements each year, and major drivetrain improvements in 1994 with the addition of the LT-1 engine, the Caprice continued to win the MSP evaluation until it went out of production during the 1996 model year.

Ed Sanow and I have known each other for a number of years, having met through the Police Patrol Vehicle Evaluation and Purchasing Program conducted by the Michigan State Police each year. Our mutual interest in police patrol cars has involved both of us in some rather interesting projects since we first met. Having read and enjoyed the previous two books that he and John Bellah collaborated on, *Dodge, Plymouth and Chrysler Police Cars 1956 - 1978* and *Dodge, Plymouth and Chrysler Police Cars 1979 - 1994*, I was pleased to learn that he was involved in a similar project related to Chevrolet police cars. Those two books have literally become the enthusiasts' bibles for Chrysler police products, and I predict this book will similarly serve Chevrolet police product enthusiasts.

Putting a book such as this together is a monumental task, and clearly requires a massive amount of time and dedication. I have a keen personal appreciation for the value of the information contained herein because of my own involvement with evaluating and reporting on police car performance over the past 20-plus years. The historical perspective this book provides for current and future enthusiasts, as well as law enforcement officers such as myself, either active or retired, will be appreciated even more as time passes and memories get cloudy.

Thank you Ed Sanow and team for another tour de force.

Curtis L. VanDenBerg
First Lieutenant (Retired)
Michigan State Police

First Lieutenant Curtis VanDenBerg who developed the Michigan State Police patrol vehicle testing program.

Introduction

The full-sized Chevrolet is the most popular product in automotive history. More than 38 million have been sold since 1946, making it the Number One, all-time, best-selling car line in the world. In fact, the bowtie B-body alone, introduced in 1959, was produced in larger numbers than any other vehicle, car or truck. According to General Motors officials at the Arlington, Texas, assembly plant, 24.8 million full-size Chevrolets were built between the B-body introduction in 1959 and the time the last Caprice rolled off the assembly line on December 13, 1996. In comparison, Volkswagen made 22 million Beetles and Ford built 15 million Model Ts.

The full-sized Chevrolet police car has been known by many different names and powered by many different engines. As a member of the Low Priced Three, Chevrolet has been a competitor in the police car market against Ford and Plymouth since the 1930s. From 1929 through 1955, Chevrolet police cars were powered by the famous "Stovebolt Six." From the mid-1940s to mid-1950s, the police drove retail versions of the Stylemaster, Styleline Special and Special 150.

In 1950, Chevrolet became the first of the Low Priced Three to offer a fully automatic transmission, the two-speed Powerglide. In 1953, Chevrolet released a brand new Blue Flame Six. For the first time, aluminum pistons were used instead of cast iron, and the new engine had a fully pressurized lubrication system.

Chevrolet had individual police, taxi and export components in the early 1950s. In 1955, the police-oriented components were grouped in one informal, but still long lead time "police package." In 1955, Chevrolet introduced the One Fifty nameplate in a totally redesigned 115 inch wheelbase car and its first V-8 in decades, the 265-cid small-block. Equipped with the four-barrel "power pack" the One Fifty ran in the same league as the Chrysler New Yorker and Buick Century. No Chevrolet had ever done that before.

For 1956, Chevrolet released its first, formal, standard lead time police package for the two-door and four-door One Fifty and Two Ten. In 1957, Chevrolet released the 283-cid V-8 and the new Turboglide automatic. In 1958, Chevrolet responded to the horsepower race with its 348-cid big-block. This was the first year for triple two-barrel carbs on a Chevy police engine. This was also the first Chevrolet engine to produce more than 300 horsepower.

For 1958, the ladder frame chassis from 1955-57 was replaced with a new X-frame 117.5 inch wheelbase chassis and a new four-wheel coil spring suspension. The One Fifty was replaced with the name Delray. The Two Ten became the Biscayne. Brand new for 1959 was the 119 inch General Motors B-body platform, which Chevrolet shared with Pontiac, Buick and Oldsmobile. For the first time, Chevrolet police cars were available with four-speed manual transmissions. The six-barrel version of the 348-cid W-block was the top cop mill for 1961 producing 350 hp. This was the first carbureted, official Chevrolet police engine to achieve "one horsepower per cubic inch of displacement."

In 1962, cops got two new engines: the 327-cid small-block and the 409-cid big-block. The 409 was the first Chevrolet police car engine to use dual four-barrel carbs. The 409 was also the only police engine from Chevrolet, Ford, Mercury, Dodge, Plymouth, Chrysler, Pontiac, Buick or Oldsmobile to ever produce over 400 hp.

The 1965 Biscayne was totally restyled including a new, "wide stance" frame. The famous 396-cid big-block with its "porcupine head"

valvetrain layout was introduced in mid-year along with the TurboHydraMatic three-speed automatic. In 1966, the 427-cid/390-hp big-block became a police pursuit engine. This was also the first year the Bel Air nameplate was widely available with the police package.

At the peak of the muscle car craze, 1969 was the first year for Chevrolet's longest lasting police engine, the 350-cid "mouse motor." The 350 would be the primary Chevrolet police engine from 1977 through 1996.

In 1970, the big news—literally—was a new big-block, the TurboJet 454. This was the largest police engine ever offered by Chevrolet. In 1971, Chevrolet increased the B-body wheelbase from 119 inches to 121.5 inches. This was as long as a Chevrolet four-door sedan would ever be. New for 1971, the Chevrolet police cars were available with the 400-cid "giant" small-block. The 1972 model year was the first time the Impala was specifically listed as a police package car. This was the only year for the TurboJet 402 engine.

In 1974, *Motor Trend* editor John Christy and the Los Angeles County Sheriff teamed up to develop a new breed of police car. The ideal urban police car turned out to be a specially modified Chevrolet Nova. The resulting 1975 Nova 9C1 is one of the most significant police cars ever made by Chevrolet.

The 1976 model year was the first year that the police package was based strictly on the Impala. However, it was the last year for the 400-cid small-block V-8 and the 454-cid big-block V-8. The 1976 model year was also the last for the 121.5-inch wheelbase full-size Chevrolet. The police Nova 9C1 continued to be the most popular urban police car through 1978 when the newly downsized Malibu 9C1 would take over through 1981.

In 1977, the B-body wheelbase was reduced to 116 inches where it would stay until the demise of the full-size Chevrolet after 1996. In 1979, the California Highway Patrol began its famous Special Purpose Vehicle Study. This involved both the Malibu and the Camaro. The 1979 CHP Camaro was the first police pursuit pony car, which eventually led to the more famous 1982 CHP Mustang.

In 1980, the Impala 9C1 received its first V-6. In 1983, the durable TurboHydraMatic was upgraded to four-speed overdrive. In 1984, Chevrolet introduced its first front-wheel drive police package car, the Celebrity. By 1986, the Impala nameplate was replaced with the name Caprice. The 1988 model year marked the last carbureted 350-cid police engine. The police V-6s were upgraded to fuel injection in 1985. In 1989, Chevrolet released its first fuel-injected V-8 police engine since the 283-cid of the late 1950s.

The Camaro police package was tested in 1979 but not released until 1991. This was the same year for the radically redesigned Caprice. The Lumina became Chevrolet's second front-wheel drive police car in 1992. The potent "LT1" 350-cid V-8 achieved police status in the 1993 Camaro B4C and then in the 1994 Caprice 9C1.

The 1996 model year was the last for the full-size, rear drive, V-8-powered Chevrolet police car. However, in 1996 Chevrolet gave us a glimpse of what to expect for future police cars: the four-door, four-wheel-drive Geo Tracker and the 350-cid-powered four-door, two-wheel-drive Tahoe. Neither of these, of course, replace the Caprice. To this, Chevrolet special vehicle specialists simply say, "Stay tuned."

Chapter 1

1955: 265-cid Small-Block V-8

Of the Low Priced Three, Ford held a dominating lead over Chevrolet and Plymouth in the early 1950s police market. While the three marques were priced competitively, the Chevrolet Six produced just "second best" vehicle performance behind the Ford flathead V-8. Ford had offered a V-8 since 1932. This performance reputation changed forever with the 1955 Chevy.

"Baseball and hot dogs, apple pie and Chevrolet." The 1955 model year was certainly the Year of the Chevrolet. Chevrolet introduced its famous 265-cid small-block V-8 in a totally redesigned car. The 1955 Chevys caught on with cops as well as they did with the general public. This was also the year of 12-volt electrical systems, tubeless tires, ball joint suspensions, and overdrive transmissions.

Many enthusiasts judge how different or unique any one model year is based on the number of new parts from the previous year. By this definition, the 1955 Chevrolet was one of the most redesigned Chevys ever. The 1955 Chevy was made up of roughly 4,500 different parts. Of these, 3,825 were new for 1955 and different from 1954.

The biggest news of the decade was the 265-cid small-block V-8. This was the first Chevrolet V-8 since the ill-fated and ill-received 288-cid, overhead valve V-8 of 1917-1919.

The small-block Chevrolet V-8 came about through the efforts of many, including project engineer Harry Barr and production engineer E.H. Kelley under the guidance of engineer Zora Arkus-Duntov and Chevrolet's chief engineer Ed Cole. Cole had previously worked on the new-for-1948 Cadillac overhead valve V-8.

The Chevrolet small-block V-8 is, in a word, small. Depending on the induction and exhaust, the V-8 is just 25 inches tall, 25 inches wide and 25 inches long. With all cast iron components, it weighs just 550 pounds.

From 1955 through 1996, the Chevrolet small-block has been available in 11 different engine sizes. This includes eight bore sizes from 3.500 to 4.126 inches, five stroke lengths from 3.000 to 3.750 inches and three sets of main and rod journal diameters. The 302-, 327- and 350-cid engines are considered to have the same bore. The 1955 265-cid V-8 and the 1994 265-cid V-8, however, have very different journal diameters. With the single exception of the 400-cid "giant" small-block with siamesed cylinders, the only major differences between all of these small-blocks are the combinations of bore and stroke and the journal diameters.

The small-block V-8 had three important design features. The first and most significant was the new green-sand, thin-wall, block casting process. This kept production costs low, but at the same time greatly improved the casting precision. For the first time, cylinder block jacket walls as thin as 5/32 inch could be used. The result was a 265-cid V-8 that weighed 40 pounds less than a 235-cid Six.

As designed, the 265-cid block would allow displacements up to 302 cubic inches by stroking, but mostly by boring. The 350- and 400-cid small-blocks, based on this original 265-cid block, were made possible only by continued casting technology advancements.

The second major advance with the new 265-cid small-block was stamped rocker arms. This was also a cost reduction effort that reduced the misalignment problems common with shaft-mounted rockers. This was the first Chevy engine to use stamped steel rocker arms. Stamped rockers allowed higher engine rpm. This was, of course, the first overhead valve Chevy V-8 in generations.

The third breakthrough in engine technology was the use of hollow hydraulic lifter pushrods. This particular engine advance was also shared with Pontiac.

In 1955, Chevrolet produced its first small-block V-8, rated at 265 cid. The formal police package was available, but it had a long lead time.

The 265-cid small-block V-8 used new thin-wall casting techniques, stamped rocker arms and hollow pushrods. The two-barrel engine produced 162 hp. (Charles Havelka)

The Turbo-Fire 265-cid Wedge V-8 was of the "over-square," short-stroke design. This meant the bore (3.75 inches) was much larger than the stroke (3.00 inches). The large bore allowed the use of larger diameter intake and exhaust valves than ever before. The short stroke allowed higher operating rpm, less piston travel per revolution and less piston ring wear. For its day, the 8.0:1 compression ratio was considered "high." This Rochester two-barrel carbureted engine produced 162 hp and was a $99 retail option. A small die-cast and chrome-plated "V" emblem indicated the squad car was powered by a V-8.

Even bigger news for lead-footed flat foots was the four-barrel option on the 265-cid engine. Few enthusiasts know that the famous "plus power package," also known as the "power pack," was originally released as a police car option only. It was not until the spring of 1955 that the power pack became a regular production option (RPO). This explains why the record setters at the Daytona Speed Weeks used police package vehicles.

The power pack was a $95 option that included a four-barrel carb, an intake manifold with larger diameter ports and dual exhaust. This boosted the output to 180 hp.

During the 1955 Daytona Speed Weeks, the police package, power pack-equipped Chevys were clearly the fastest of the Low Priced Three. Even more, they seriously challenged the best from Chrysler and Cadillac.

Flying mile:

Chrysler 300	127.58 mph
Cadillac	120.48 mph
Buick Century	116.35 mph
Chrysler New Yorker	114.63 mph
Chevrolet Two Ten	112.88 mph

Standing start mile:

Cadillac	80.43 mph
Chevrolet Two Ten	78.16 mph
Chrysler 300	77.44 mph
Ford	73.43 mph
Plymouth	72.07 mph

No Chevrolet had ever run up with the big Chryslers and Cadillacs. In its class, the Chevy set records for acceleration in both the standing quarter-mile and in the flying mile. In one event, the power pack police Chevy top ended the Ford by 11 mph and the Plymouth by 17 mph.

The top gun Chevy at the 1955 event was Duran County Police Chief Harold Tapscott with his two-door, police package Chevy Two Ten. Cops all over the country took notice. These One Fifty and Two Ten police cruisers with the 265-cid/180-hp, four-barrel carbureted V-8s and the three-speed or three-speed overdrive transmissions reached 60 mph in 9.6 to 9.7 seconds. With the non-power pack, two-barrel version of the 265-cid V-8, these 0-60 mph times were in the 12.5 to 13.5 second range.

The overdrive was also new for 1955. The Warner gear overdrive was a $108 option and was a first for any General Motors car. The overdrive could be coupled to either of the V-8s or to the Blue Flame Six. Operating on the planetary gear principle, this gave a cruising fourth gear to these three-speed manual units. When engaged, the overdrive unit would shift into fourth gear when the gas pedal was momentarily raised at any speed over 30 mph. Flooring the gas would downshift the transmission back to third gear. A dash-mounted pull-knob served as a lockout when the driver did not want to engage the overdrive.

For 1955, the "stovebolt" 235-cid Blue Flame Six with its Rochester one-barrel carb got a power boost over the 1954 version. The sol-

The 1955 265-cid V-8 with the "plus power package" was originally a police-only option. This four-barrel, dual exhaust, 180-hp engine pushed the Chevy Two Ten into the Chrysler performance bracket. (Dave Dotson)

Both the 1955 Chevrolet One Fifty and Two Ten were available with two versions of the 235-cid Six, two versions of the 265-cid V-8 and three different transmissions. (Bernard Veile)

id lifter engine used with the three-speed and three-speed overdrive manual transmission was increased from 115 hp to 123 hp. The hydraulic lifter version of the Six used only with the two-speed Powerglide automatic was bumped from 125 hp to 136 hp.

The '55 Chevy was available in three basic trim levels: the low-priced One Fifty, the middle-priced Two Ten, and the top-end Bel Air. Nearly all police components were installed on two-door and four-door sedan versions of the One Fifty trim level.

The wheelbase continued at 115 inches, however, the frame and suspension were greatly improved over the pre-1955 models. The new sheet metal had been bolted to a new frame. The frame was reported as being 50 percent more rigid and was more twist resistant even though it was 18 percent lighter. The '55 Chevy was also the first Chevy sedan to use a wraparound one-piece windshield. (The Corvette got this curved front glass in 1953.)

The new chassis sported a new ball joint front suspension and lengthened rear leaf springs. This improved both the ride and high speed handling. In addition, the front coil springs were tilted and the upper and lower control arm (A-arm) mounting points were angled. This front suspension geometry change reduced front end dive during heavy braking. Chevy claimed this anti-dive design was an industry first. Both *Motor Trend* and *Consumer Reports* took special notice of the improved handling from the '55 Chevy. *Motor Trend* called it one of the year's best handling vehicles.

Also new for 1955 was the 12-volt electrical systems for all Chevrolet sedans. This was a big deal when other car lines went from 6-volt to 12-volt systems. However, the new sheet metal and suspension and numerous new powertrain options totally overshadowed this electrical advance. The 12-volt systems allowed hotter engine spark and more reliable engine starts.

The Idaho State Police and North Dakota State Patrol used Chevrolet police cars in 1955.

Chevrolet Small-Block V-8 Engines (both police and retail)				
cid	Bore	Stroke	Main	Rod
262	3.671	3.100	2.45	2.10
265 (1955)	3.750	3.000	2.30	2.00
265 (1994)	3.750	3.000	2.45	2.10
267	3.500	3.484	2.45	2.10
283	3.875	3.000	2.30	2.00
302	4.000	3.000	2.30	2.00
302	4.000	3.000	2.45	2.10
305	3.736	3.484	2.45	2.10
307	3.875	3.250	2.45	2.10
327	4.001	3.250	2.30	2.00
327	4.001	3.250	2.45	2.10
350	4.001	3.484	2.45	2.10
400	4.126	3.750	2.65	2.10

Police Drivetrains for 1955			
Engine	Size & Carb	Compression	Horsepower
Blue Flame Six	235.5 cid, 1-bbl (solid)	7.5:1	123 @ 3800 rpm (manual)
Blue Flame Six	235.5 cid, 1-bbl (hydraulic)	7.5:1	136 @ 4200 rpm (Powerglide)
Turbo Fire V-8	265 cid, 2-bbl	8.0:1	162 @ 4400 rpm
Plus Power V-8	265 cid, 4-bbl	8.0:1	180 @ 4600 rpm

The 1955 Chevrolet was used by the Idaho State Police and North Dakota State Patrol. (Greg Reynolds)

Transmissions and axle ratios:

Three-speed Synchro-Mesh manual: 2.94 (1), 1.68 (2), 1.00 (3), 3.70 Fuel-Saver axle

Three-speed Touchdown Overdrive: 0.71 (OD), 4.11 Power-Master axle

Powerglide Automatic: 1.82 (1), 1.00 (2), 3.55 Econo-Miser axle

Suspension: coil spring (front), leaf spring (rear), 11-inch drums, 6.70x15 tubeless tires

References for 1955

75 Years of Chevrolet, George Dammann, Motorbooks International

"The High Performance Cars from Chevrolet," Robert Ackerson, *Standard Catalog of Chevrolet 1912-1990*

Standard Catalog of Chevrolet 1912-1990, Jim Wangers, Paul Zazarine

"Spiffy Styling...for Chevy," Perry Zavitz, *Standard Catalog of Chevrolet 1912-1990*

"Coral and Grey," Tim Howley, *Standard Catalog of Chevrolet 1912-1990*

Illustrated Chevrolet Buyers Guide, John Gunnell, Motorbooks International

Chapter 2

1956: Chevrolet's First Police Package

"They don't get away when you've got a Chevrolet," according to Chevy ads in August 1956 issues of *Law and Order* and *Michigan Police Journal* magazines.

Indeed, for 1956 the Chevy squads were available with stronger engines. As the model year opened, the Blue Flame Six was renamed Blue Flame 140. The compression ratio had been bumped from 7.5:1 to 8.0:1 and this increased the horsepower to 140 hp.

The Blue Flame Six from 1955 had solid lifters when teamed with a manual shift and hydraulic lifters when bolted to a Powerglide. For 1956, all Blue Flame engines had hydraulic lifters. The Six for the Powerglide used either a Rochester or Carter one-barrel carb while the Six teamed with the manual transmission used a different Rochester one-barrel carb.

The 1956 Turbo-Fire 265-cid, two-barrel carbureted V-8 came in two different horsepower ratings. The 162 hp version with a Rochester two-barrel carb was used with manual transmissions. A 170 hp version with a different Rochester two-barrel carb was used only with the Powerglide. Both engines used hydraulic lifters. Chevy sedans and station wagons with any V-8 wore a wide die-cast "V" under the front marque medallion.

For most of the model year, the top cop engine was the Super Turbo Fire V-8. The compression of this 265-cid V-8 was boosted from the 1955 power pack engine's ratio of 8.0:1 to 9.25:1. With a four-barrel carb, higher lift cam, special intake and dual exhausts, the power output was now 205 hp.

As a carry-over from 1955, three transmissions were available: three-speed manual, three-speed manual overdrive and the two-speed Powerglide automatic. Power brakes were optional but only on the Two Ten and Bel Air. This meant most '56 Chevy cop cars had manual brakes because they were largely based on the One Fifty.

The One Fifty with the 205 hp V-8 and the three-speed transmission with 3.70 rear gears was pretty quick for its day. Zero to 60 mph times were around 8.5 seconds and the top speed was 111 mph. Many

four-door police sedans in the early 1980s were not that fast. The 1956 Chevy slogan, "The Hot One's Even Hotter" seemed quite true.

The 1956 Chevy sedan suspension and brakes were basically a carry-over from 1955. Some tweaking may have been done on the spring rates. However, new for '56 was an optional tire size. The 6.70x15 four-ply was the standard police and retail tire; however a 7.10x15 is listed as an option and in police trim, this was a six-ply tire.

With their new V-8 engines, the Chevy squads were catching on. The 1956 One Fifty was used by the Military Police and a number of other government agencies such as fire departments. In 1956, Chevrolet also entered the taxi fleet business with both its One Fifty and Two Ten four-door sedans.

For their 1956 police cars, Chevy ad men claimed blazing performance with mountainous power, super control and trigger-quick acceleration. In an era where we now want heavy, reduced assist power steering for maximum road feel, Chevrolet bragged about "featherlight" precision steering. Naturally, the automaker emphasized the Unitized Body by Fisher for dependability and ruggedness.

As for its powertrains, Chevrolet boasted an "ultra short-stroke" engine that efficiently delivered extra performance miles per budget dollar. Justly proud of its 265-cid engine, Chevy pointed out it had the shortest piston stroke in the industry. Of the four-barrel carbureted Super Turbo-Fire, Chevy noted it had the most power per cubic inch displacement in its class. In fact, this engine did indeed set a new official Pikes Peak hill climb record.

For the record, the police package was again based on the One Fifty two-door and four-door sedans. Chevrolet made it clear that the special police equipment was also available on Two Ten sedans and station wagons and on One Fifty wagons but with a longer delivery time. No mention whatsoever is made of putting "special police car equipment" on a Bel Air.

Just before the 1956 Daytona Speed Weeks, Chevrolet made an engine availability announcement. The Corvette V-8 was now a regu-

Chevrolet's first official, standard lead time police package was available in 1956. Used by the St. Louis, Missouri, Police, the police package included heavy-duty brakes and suspension. (St. Louis Police)

Engines for 1956 Chevrolet police cars included the 235-cid six-cylinder and four versions of the 265-cid V-8 including one with dual four-barrel carbs and 225 hp. Transmissions available were a three-speed stick, three-speed Overdrive and two-speed Powerglide.

Most 1956 Chevrolets were used by city departments such as this Crazy Horse, South Dakota, Police unit. Most state police departments wanted a wheelbase longer than the 115-inch Chevrolet. (Greg Reynolds)

lar production option (RPO), meaning it was available on any Chevrolet. Copywriters at Chevy's ad agency, Campbell-Ewald Co., aggressively got that word out. In fact, while the '56 police literature does not list this 225 hp version as a police engine, it, indeed, was one by mid-year.

Called either the Plus Power package or more correctly the Corvette V-8, this solid lifter engine came with dual four-barrel carbs, twin air cleaners, a special version of the high-lift cam, high-power exhaust "headers" and dual exhaust. All this boosted the Super Turbo-Fire output from 205 hp to 225 hp.

During Speed Weeks, a Chevy sedan with the 225 hp Corvette V-8 hit 121.34 mph in the flying mile. This was nearly 10 mph faster than in 1955. In the standing start mile, the dual four-barrel carbureted Chevy reached 81.34 mph. This was faster than any car from 1955 and just one-half mph behind the dual-quad Dodge D-500-1.

At the time, the Dodge D-500 was the fastest police car available regardless of make or price range. And now the Chevy, a member of the Low Priced Three, was right on its bumper. This Dodge-like performance from the Chevy caught the eye of many state police officers and highway patrolmen. Chevys were not supposed to be that fast. And this was just Chevrolet's second year with a V-8.

In spite of "highway patrol" levels of performance, the hot Chevys were almost never allowed to bid on many of the more prestigious and performance-oriented state police and highway patrol contracts. From the mid-1950s through the early-1970s, fleet managers demanded heavy, long wheelbase police cars. The California Highway Patrol, for example, required a vehicle weight of 3,800 pounds minimum and a wheelbase of 122 inches minimum.

In comparison, the '56 One Fifty four-door sedan weighed 3,186 pounds and had a 115-inch wheelbase. Ironically, the 1994 Caprice used by more than 60 percent of all cops weighs 4,244 pounds and has a 115.9-inch wheelbase. It was a long time until cops realized that suspension design and not wheelbase nor weight was the key to "holding the road."

Police Drivetrains for 1956			
Engine	Size & Carb	Compression	Horsepower
Blue Flame 140	235.5 cid, 1-bbl	8.0:1	140 @ 4200 rpm
Turbo-Fire V-8	265 cid, 2-bbl	8.0:1	162 @ 4400 rpm (manual)
Turbo-Fire V-8	265 cid, 2-bbl	8.0:1	170 @ 4400 rpm (Powerglide)
Super Turbo-Fire V-8	265 cid, 4-bbl	9.25:1	205 @ 4600 rpm
Corvette V-8	265 cid, 2x4-bbl	9.25:1	225 @ 5200 rpm

Transmissions and axle ratios:

Three-speed Synchro-Mesh manual: 2.94 (1), 1.68 (2), 1.00 (3),
                    3.70 Fuel-Saver axle
Three-speed Touchdown Overdrive: 0.71 (OD), 4.11
          Power-Master axle
Two-speed Powerglide Automatic: 1.82 (1), 1.00 (2),
          3.55 Econo-Miser axle

Suspension:

Coil spring (front), front stabilizer bar, leaf spring (rear), 11-inch
          drums, 6.70x15 or 7.10x15 tires

References for 1956

"Speaking of Chevys," Pat Chappell, *Old Cars Weekly*, March 7, 1991
75 Years of Chevrolets, George Dammann, Motorbooks International
Chevrolet Police Cars, Chevrolet Motor Division.
"Why Drivers Like New Little Taxis," E.D. Fales, Jr. *Popular Science*, January 1956
"Coral and Grey," Tim Howley, *Standard Catalog of Chevrolet 1912-1990*
"High Performance Cars from Chevrolet," Robert Ackerson, *Standard Catalog of Chevrolet 1912-1990*
Illustrated Chevrolet Buyers Guide, John Gunnell, Motorbooks International

Chapter 3

1957: 283-cid Small-Block V-8

Yes, Chevrolet made 1957 Chevy police cars. To some, this is the ultimate Chevy collectible. It is where the paths of two enthusiast groups cross. The '57 Chevy is the definite classic Chevrolet in its own right. To the ever-growing number of police car enthusiasts, this has a double nostalgic value.

For 1957, the Chevy sedans were restyled slightly with a new grille and broad, flat tailfins. However, the big news for cops in 1957 was the new 283-cid V-8 and the new Turboglide automatic transmission. Indeed, the ads read: "Chevy with 220 hp V-8 shows IT'S THE HOT CAR FOR POLICE DUTY."

Once again, the '57 Chevy cop cars were advertised as having "hair-trigger handling and split-second steering." We were also told, "There will be a surge of civic pride when the sleek new Chevrolet Police Car joins the force!"

A Washington State Patrol 1957 One Fifty. Yes, indeed, Chevrolet's most nostalgic car was available with a police package. (WSP)

The 1957 Chevrolet One Fifty was used by the Military Police worldwide. This one has a Six. It was the first year for the 283-cid V-8. (Chuck Schroedel)

The famous fins of the classic 1957 Chevy. This was the first year for the Turboglide transmission, but this MP unit has the 3-speed stick. (Chuck Schroedel)

Some classic car enthusiasts have challenged the very existence of two-door police cars. In fact, this has resulted in a heated debate in the "Letters to the Editor" in collector vehicle periodicals such as *Old Cars Weekly*. Part of this confusion is the fact that police departments do not always use police "package" cars. A difference may exist between a car used by the police as a police car and a car equipped by the carmaker with a police package.

For 1957, "Chevrolet offers two special police car packages, available on minimum delivery." These are the Two Ten and One Fifty two-door police cruisers. Certainly, two-door police cars existed. In fact, with the '57 Chevys, their "standard" police cars were the two-doors. The police package was merely "also available" on four-door sedans and station wagons and it took longer to get these vehicles.

New for '57, the 265-cid V-8 block was bored out from 3.75 inches to 3.875 inches while keeping the same 3.00-inch stroke. The result was the potent 283-cid V-8. In fact, the 265-cid V-8 had been bored out to 283 cubic inches by racing enthusiasts as early as 1955! The 283-cid V-8 would remain a police engine for 11 years.

With an 8.5:1 compression, the base 283-cid V-8 with two-barrel carb produced 185 hp. This was called the Turbo-Fire 283. The Turbo-Fire 265 with 162 hp and the 140 hp Blue Flame Six were carry-overs from 1956 to 1957.

The only other "official" police engine was the Super Turbo-Fire 283. This Carter four-barrel version had 9.5:1 compression, hydraulic lifters and dual exhaust and produced 220 hp.

"You'll experience outstanding acceleration and take-off torque, products of Chevrolets' proven short-stroke design coupled with big bore displacement, four-barrel carburetion, full dual exhaust system and a new high 9.5:1 compression ratio."

The 1957 dual-quad and the fuel-injected Corvette 283-cid V-8s in both hydraulic and solid lifter versions were not officially used in police package cars.

Fuel-injection was indeed the talk of the enthusiasts. And, indeed, Chevy police cars would eventually get fuel-injected engines...but not until 1985! Fuel injection is historically important not because it was a police reality in 1957. Instead, this was Chevrolet's first production fuel injection and it serves as a benchmark. In the 1980s, police package Celebrities would get electronic fuel-injected V-6s and the Caprices got EFI V-6s and V-8s.

The fuel-injected 283 was *not* listed as an "official" police package engine. However, according to Chevrolet historian R. Perry Zavitz, "these engines were offered in any Chevrolet model from the One Fifty Utility to the Corvette, according to the catalog."

The reality, however, was that fuel injection in even the Corvettes was rare. Records indicate that only 43 Corvettes were equipped with fuel-injected 283s. Cops had the durable 220 hp V-8s available that nearly equaled the dual four-barrel carbureted 225 hp Corvette V-8 from 1956. It is highly unlikely that even one fuel-injected engine made its way into police service.

Most highway patrol and state police fleet managers even avoided multiple carburetor engines such as dual quads and three-twos. They were certainly not going to experiment with a brand new, unproven induction system such as fuel-injection. Police fleet managers are generally not performance enthusiasts. Instead, as a rule, they are reliability and cost-control enthusiasts.

The fuel-injected engines proved to be extremely powerful, extremely unreliable and extremely thirsty. That's okay for a drag race engine but cops need something more like an endurance race engine.

In 1957, Chevrolet introduced a brand new transmission design called the Turboglide. The ill-fated variable ratio transmission was also similar to the Buick Dynaflow. It was designed with three turbines, a variable pitch stator, two planetary gear sets and conventional torque converter. The Turboglide included a "Hill Retarder" to assist in downhill engine braking. This transmission was available only with the two 283-cid V-8s.

"Exclusive new Turboglide with triple-turbine takeoff. Turboglide is the greatest contribution to automatic driving in years and only Chevrolet has it. Turboglide's torque converter features three turbines working together with incredible smoothness: one for take-off, one for cruising, and a third for passing. It results in an unbroken flow of power without the slightest hint of a shift. It has a single forward Drive range, a new Hill Retarder that saves regular brakes, a two-position variable stator."

This replica White Settlement, Texas, Police 1957 Bel Air is powered by a 283-cid/220-hp four-barrel carbureted V-8 with a Powerglide transmission and 3.36 gears. (Ken Mason)

It is the Hill Retarder selection that gave a two-speed reputation to this transmission that was technically a one-speed. The Turboglide had an infinitely variable gear ratio range from 4.3:1 to 1:1. Like the Powerglide, the Turboglide had an oil cooler integrated into the engine cooling system.

Motor Life magazine reviewed the new Turboglide transmission:

"Turboglide is certainly one of the smoothest automatics on the market and is the ultimate of simplicity in operation. It has only one forward and one reverse drive position, together with Grade Retarder position which can be used for extra braking down hills.

"The three turbines with their variable-pitch blades completely eliminate feel of shift points in the torque converter unit. With the lever in drive position, the car starts from a standstill and accelerates up to any given speed in one smooth, continuous flow of power. There is never any lurch to indicate a shift point as there is with most automatics.

"Lack of ability to downshift manually to a lower gear for a corner was noticed during test runs, however. The Grade Retarder position is no help in this because it has been designed so the engine and transmission windmill almost uselessly if attempts are made to accelerate in this gear."

The Turboglide was a complex transmission. By design, it provided an infinitely variable torque ratio for smooth acceleration from a standstill to top speed. The unit worked well enough when new but it was prone to failure and hard to repair. It did not have the reliability of the Turbo Hydra-Matic, introduced in 1965 and as a result the Turboglide was dropped by 1961.

The four-barrel carbureted, dual exhaust Super Turbo-Fire 283 was available with all four transmissions: Turboglide, Powerglide, Synchro-Mesh three-speed and Synchro-Mesh Overdrive. The two-barrel carbureted, single exhaust Turbo-Fire 283 was only available in the police cars with one of the automatics. The two-barrel carbureted, single exhaust Turbo-Fire 265 was only available with one of the stick shift transmis-

sions in the police package. The Blue Flame Six, basically unchanged from 1956, was available with any transmission except the Turboglide.

Chevrolet did make one minor but notable change to the '57 suspension system, which also affected rear gearing. The 15-inch wheels from earlier years became 14-inch wheels for 1957. The tire selection size was also increased from 6.70x15 to 7.50x14. This change in rim diameter lowered the chassis slightly and also resulted in new rear gear ratios. The Turboglide and Powerglide automatics came with 3.36 gears instead of the 3.55 ratio used in 1956. The Synchro-Mesh three-speed cars used 3.55 gears for 1957 instead of the 3.70:1 ratio. The Overdrive cars however, retained their 4.11 gears.

Also new for 1957 with the 14-inch wheels was the "safety-contoured" rim flange that decreased the possibility of air loss during high speed cornering. The police tires were 7.50x14 four-ply rated blackwalls, while whitewalls and six-ply rated black or whitewalls were optional.

The 1957 Chevy was actually used by quite a few departments. These include: Chicago Police, Metro Toronto Police, St. Paul Police, Washington State Patrol and the U.S. Military Police worldwide.

Official Police Package Drivetrains for 1957			
Engine	Size & Carb	Comp.	Horsepower
Blue Flame Six	235.5 cid, 1-bbl	8.0:1	140 @ 4200 rpm
Turbo-Fire 265	265 cid, 2-bbl	8.0:1	162 @ 4400 rpm
Turbo-Fire 283	283 cid, 2-bbl	8.5:1	185 @ 4600 rpm
Super Turbo-Fire 283	283 cid, 4-bbl	9.5:1	220 @ 4800 rpm

Transmissions and axles

Turboglide one-speed automatic with 3.36 rear gears (283 only)
Powerglide two-speed automatic with 3.36 rear gears (not 265)
Synchro-Mesh three-speed stick with 3.55 rear gears (not 283, 2-bbl)
Touchdown Overdrive with 4.11 rear gears (not 283, 2-bbl)

The streets of Chicago were patrolled using 1957 One Fifty models. Many used the 235-cid Six. (Greg Reynolds)

The short wheelbase 1957 Chevy One Fifty made a good urban police car, such as this two-door sedan from Toronto, Canada. (Greg Reynolds)

References for 1957

"Speaking of Chevys," Pat Chappell, *Old Cars Weekly*, March 7, 1991

75 Years of Chevrolets, George Dammann, Motorbooks International

Chevrolet Police Cars, Chevrolet Motor Division

"High Performance Cars from Chevrolet," Robert Ackerson, *Standard Catalog of Chevrolet 1912-1990*

Illustrated Chevrolet Buyers Guide, John Gunnell, Motorbooks International

"A Collector Favorite Today, the '57 Chevrolets," R. Perry Zavitz, *Standard Catalog of Chevrolet 1912-1990*

Chapter 4

1958: Turbo Thrust 348 Big-Block

For 1958, Chevrolet had a brand new X-frame chassis with a longer wheelbase and four wheel coil springs. It had a series of new and more powerful 348-cid V-8 engines including one with three two-barrel carbs. The fuel-injected 283-cid became a standard cataloged police engine for 1958. The Blue Flame Six picked up horsepower after a boost in compression ratio. And the name "Impala" was added to the Chevy lineup. Some year!

The so-called "ladder frame" of the 1955-57 Chevys was replaced in 1958 with a new X-frame. This was similar to the Cadillac X-frame introduced in 1957. Instead of straight box rails on either side of the car connected with cross members, the X-frame had box rails in the shape of an X.

The frame was fastened together near the center of the chassis and box sections extended outward to the four corners of the car. The driver and passenger obviously had less side impact protection with the X-frame and this was a complaint from cops.

Beefy cross members joined the body to the X-frame in a new way that permitted lower feature lines and flatter floors. Compared to the '55-'57 models, the '58 Chevy was visibly lower, wider and longer.

The front coil and rear leaf suspension from 1957 was replaced with an all-coil suspension. The resulting A-body was longer, lower and wider. The wheelbase was bumped from 115 to 117.5 inches. That was significant.

Motor Life magazine road tested the '58 Chevrolet. Here is how they described the new suspension:

"The familiar semi-elliptic leaf spring setup has been replaced by a four-link trailing arm design using either coil springs or air bags. Lower control arms run from each side of the rear axle to mounting hangers set on frame side rails just back of the pinch-in center frame section. These arms receive both the vertical force of highway bumps and braking and driving thrust of the axle.

"A single U-shaped upper control arm is pivotally mounted at the rear axle housing and curves up to frame attaching points. This arm controls lateral stability, restricts driveline and axle windup. The new frame and suspension design results in a higher roll center of gravity, so Chevrolet was able to soften ride without loss of stability."

Chevrolet called its new Body by Fisher the "sound-barrier" body. The automaker claimed the "safety-girder frame gives almost 30 percent greater rigidity to body and chassis members," and that the "X-design withstands twisting forces more effectively."

Chevrolet was proud of the "boulevard" ride on any road surface from its full coil spring suspension. The four-link rear suspension was said to absorb driving and braking forces, which increased high speed stability. The V-8-powered cars got front stabilizer bars. Also new for 1958 were a two-piece driveshaft and a foot-operated parking brake.

One of the new options for 1958 was the Level Air suspension. This air suspension used a system of inflated rubber bags replacing the coil springs. The theory was this suspension would keep the car level under any load. This new suspension was important to cops, not because they used it but because they watched for it on retail cars.

The Chevy sedans with the Level Air suspension were popular with moonshiners. The rum-running cars would stay level even

In 1958, Chevrolets such as this Ankeny, Iowa, Police unit got a new X-frame and the 348-cid big-block engine. (Robert Parks)

This Los Angeles County Sheriff Delray was powered by a 348-cid engine. Triple two-barrel carburetion was available, as was a fuel-injected 283-cid small-block. (LASD)

with a trunk full of alcohol. For a while the level appearing load hid the tell-tale drooping tail of a moonshiner. The cops finally caught on and then started looking specifically for this kind of car. The Level Air suspension was, however, failure prone and was eventually discontinued.

Along with the new body styles, Chevrolet introduced new nameplates. The low-priced One Fifty was replaced with the name Delray. The mid-priced Two Ten became the Biscayne. The two-door and four-door versions of the Delray and Biscayne received the police packages. As a side note, even though some literature used the term Del Ray, the correct spelling is Delray. The top-priced Chevy remained the Bel Air; however, a new Bel Air sub-series was introduced in 1958: Impala.

This 1958 Delray was used by a Los Angeles Police detective. Most of these cars used the 235-cid Six with a three-speed stick. (LAPD)

The Impala name itself originated from a 1956 Corvette concept show car. While the Impala was a trim option on the Bel Air, it involved different trim and sheet metal from the cowl back. The first Bel Air Impala was introduced on October 31, 1957.

Big news for 1958 was the W-engine 348-cid, big-block V-8. Chevrolet engineers felt the small-block 283 was not big enough to handle the projected car weights and performance needs of the late 1950s. They knew about the new 350 and 361 Mopar V-8s and the new 332 and 352 Ford V-8s. Chevy also needed a beefier engine for its truck lines. The result was the Turbo Thrust 348.

The new Chevy big-block was a full 100 pounds heavier than the 283 small-block. The 348-cid V-8 featured wedge combustion chambers built directly into the block. This was a radical block design. Wedge combustion chambers are normally built into the head as the 283-cid engine had been designed. The 348 also had a staggered valve train to take advantage of the new engine layout. All 348-cid engines used dual exhaust.

Motor Life magazine described the unconventional W-block:

"Combustion chambers are formed in the block, not the head. Top face of each cylinder bank is cut at a 16 degree angle, not machined perpendicular to the bore. Piston tops are also made with 16 degree sloping surfaces, giving them an arrow-like appearance.

"This permits use of large valves (1.94-inch diameter for intakes, 1.66-inch diameter for exhausts) and placement of plugs near the center of the chambers for short flame travel and minimum possibility of detonation.

"Bore spacing is a comfortable 4.84 inches center to center, leaving room for larger bores and greater displacement from this block in the future." (This future displacement would be the famous 409-cid big-block.)

At the beginning of the 1958 model year, the 348-cid V-8 was available in two police power levels. Both had hydraulic lifters, dual exhaust and a 9.5:1 compression. The four-barrel version, called the Turbo Thrust, produced 250 hp. The Super Turbo Thrust with three two-barrel carbs generated 280 hp. The result from either engine was

In 1958, the Ames, Iowa, Police patrolled in Ford, Chevrolet and Edsel police cars. (Robert Parks-Tribune)

The Michigan State Police used this 1958 Delray powered by a 348-cid/250-hp V-8 engine. The big-block Chevrolet was also used by the state patrol in Ohio and Nebraska. (MSP)

"a silk-smooth idle, sensational mid-range acceleration and an avalanche of torque."

Mechanical fuel injection was back in 1958 on the 283 small-block. Chevrolet produced two versions, however, only one was a police engine. The cops got a 9.5:1, hydraulic lifter Ramjet Fuel Injection V-8 producing 250 hp. The other fuel-injected engine used 10.5:1 compression and solid lifters to produce 290 hp.

The police-spec 283 was also available in two carbureted versions. The Super Turbo Fire V-8 with four-barrel cranked out 230 hp while the two-barrel Turbo Fire V-8 was rated at 185 hp.

At the urban patrol end, the 265-cid V-8 was no longer available. However, the durable 235-cid Blue Flame Six received a power increase. The compression was boosted from 8.0:1 to 8.25:1. This engine was now good for 145 hp.

All V-8 engines could be teamed with the Turboglide transmission. The 348-cid V-8 with four-barrel carb, the carbureted 283-cid engines and the Blue Flame Six were available with the Powerglide. The carbureted small-blocks and the Six could have the optional Overdrive. All engines could be mated to the three-speed stick, and in each case the gear ratios were specifically matched to the engine's

power band. The 348 V-8 got one three-speed, the 283 V-8 got another and the 235 Six got yet another.

Positraction rear axles are listed as a RPO for the 3.36 or 3.55 ratios in the general retail literature. However, no mention of this limited-slip rear end is made in the 1958 police catalogs. It made its first appearance in the police flyers in 1959.

Advertised horsepower figures are one thing but street results are quite another. The new Chevy with the 348-cid V-8 was not as fast as anyone had hoped. The 283-powered '57 Chevys were quicker. Worse yet, the 1958 Chevys with the fuel-injected 283 were faster than the same car with a triple two-barrel carbureted 348.

A mid-year police option for the 348 solved this problem. Called the Maximum Performance Super Turbo Thrust, this 348 V-8 was bad-to-the-bones. It featured solid lifters, a special performance cam, 11.0:1 compression, three two-barrel carbs and dual exhaust. The result was 315 hp. This was more powerful than any engine available in even the Corvette. The only transmissions available with this Maximum Performance 348 were the three-speed stick and "close ratio" three-speed stick.

Even with all this prowl-power, Chevrolet was still not permitted to quote on many state police contracts. The California Highway Patrol required V-8 engines of at least 350 cubic inches. The hot Chevy was only 348 cubic inches. The CHP demanded 122-inch wheelbases. Even the longer '58 Chevy only measured 117.5 inches.

In 1958, the CHP also required a minimum compression ratio of 10.0:1. Until the mid-year release of the Maximum Performance 348 with 11.0:1 compression, the top Chevy engine had merely 9.5:1 compression. Of course the 3,432 pound four-door Delray was a long way from the 3,800 pound CHP minimum vehicle weight. That year, a Dodge took the CHP tests from the best from Pontiac, Mercury, Buick and Oldsmobile.

In 1958, the CHP also required 15-inch wheel diameters to get plenty of air to the brake drums. At least Chevy had this demand covered. While nearly all of the '58 Chevy literature discussed 14-inch wheels, the police LPO 1108 includes 6.70 four-ply tires mounted on 15x5-inch steel wheels. These 15-inch diameters are the mark of a '58 Chevy squad car.

While none of the Low Priced Three were eligible to bid on police contracts such as the CHP, the Chevys did well in the retail sector. In 1958, Chevy took 29.5 percent of the market compared to 22.3 percent for Ford and just a 9.6 percent share for Plymouth.

While the Chevrolets did not meet the wheelbase and weight minimums for some state police contracts, Chevy was indeed qualified to bid on many city police contracts. In 1958, the Chevrolet Delray was the choice of both the Los Angeles Police and the Los Angeles County Sheriffs Department. That was as big a deal then as it is now. It was also used by the Ohio State Highway Patrol, Nebraska Safety Patrol, Michigan State Police and Iowa State Patrol.

Chevrolet Acceleration Comparison		
Vehicle	1958 Chevy Impala*	1988 Chevy Caprice**
Engine	348 cid	350 cid
Induction	3x2-bbl carbs	4-bbl carb
Horsepower	280 brake hp	180 net hp
Wheelbase	117.5 in	116.0 in
Weight	3,442 lbs	3,982 lbs
0-60 mph	9.1 sec	10.6 sec
Quarter-Mile	16.5 sec @ 83.5 mph	18.0 sec @ 77.6 mph
* police engine but not police package		
** last carbureted police V-8		

1958 Chevrolet Delray	
Engine	348 cid
Carb	4-bbl
Horsepower	250 hp
Transmission	Turboglide
Axle	3.36:1
Wheelbase	117.5 inches
Weight	3,684 lbs
0-60 mph	10.1 seconds

Police Drivetrains for 1958			
Engine	Size and Carb	Compression	Horsepower
Blue Flame Six	235 cid, 1-bbl	8.25:1	145 @ 4200
Turbo Fire V-8	283 cid, 2-bbl	8.5:1	185 @ 4600
Super Turbo Fire V-8	283 cid, 4-bbl	9.5:1	230 @ 4800
Ramjet Fuel Injection V-8	283 cid, f.i.	9.5:1	250 @ 5000
Turbo Thrust V-8	348 cid, 4-bbl	9.5:1	250 @ 4400
Super Turbo Thrust V-8	348 cid, 3x2-bbl	9.5:1	280 @ 4800
Super Turbo Thrust V-8 (Max. Performance)	348 cid, 3x2-bbl	11.0:1	315 @ 5600

Transmissions and Axles

Turboglide (3.36 gear)
Powerglide (3.36 gear)
Overdrive (4.11 gear)
Three-speed Synchro-Mesh (3.55)
    348: 2.21 (1), 1.32 (2), 1:1 (3)
    283: 2.47 (1), 1.53 (2), 1:1 (3)
    Six: 2.94 (1), 1.68 (2), 1:1 (3)

References for 1958

"Final Exam Day for Patrol Cars," Ewart Thomas, *Popular Mechanics*, June 1958

75 Years of Chevrolet, George Dammann, Motorbooks International

"Power," Phil Hall, *Car Exchange*, July 1979

"'58 Dodge on Trial," James Potter, *Motor Trend*, March 1958

"Ready For Any Call," *1958 Police Cars*, Chevrolet Motor Division

Illustrated Chevrolet Buyers Guide, John Gunnell, Motorbooks International

"1958 Chevy Impala," Pat Chappell, *Standard Catalog of Chevrolet 1912-1990*

Chevrolet Impala and SS 1958-1971, R.M. Clarke, Motorbooks International

Chapter 5

1959: Finned B-Body

The 1959 Chevrolet was the third totally redesigned Chevy in five model years. The wheelbase grew from 117.5 inches to the "big car" length of 119 inches. The new Chevy was now the longest car of the Low Priced Three. The '59 Chevy was wider by more than two inches and lower in profile by an inch-and-a-half.

Model	One Fifty, 4-dr	Delray, 4-dr	Biscayne, 4-dr
Year	1957	1958	1959
Wheelbase	115.0 in	117.5 in	119.0 in
Length	200.0 in	209.1 in	210.9 in
Width	73.9 in	77.7 in	79.9 in
Height	59.9 in	57.4 in	56.0 in
Weight	3,232 lbs	3,432 lbs	3,600 lbs

The new Chevy had headlights placed in the front sheet steel as low as the law allowed. The '59 Chevy had all new sheet metal and a new undercarriage.

Brand new for 1959 was the General Motors B-body platform replacing the so-called A-body from 1958. The B-body would be dramatically changed a couple of times, such as for the 1977 model year, but would otherwise remain Chevy's four-door police platform through 1996.

The '59 Chevy was indeed, "All New All Over Again." The superficial styling changes Chevy had planned to make on the '58 Chevy for the '59 model year were abandoned. Instead, for 1959 Chevrolet went to a shared platform along with Pontiac, Oldsmobile and Buick. These four GM divisions shared the same basic frame, suspension and body to save money corporate-wide.

The outer surfaces of these B-body cars were different enough so that no one would know they shared the same platform. However, underneath, where the major cost is, this would be shared. This change

allowed great economies of scale at Fisher Body while permitting different sheet metal for the four marques. Called "nameplating," General Motors became an industry expert at distinct product differentiation on otherwise similar vehicles.

The '59 Chevys had 34 percent more glass area and all the windows were now "safety plate glass."

For 1959, the same basic "Safety Girder X-frame" was retained. However, the suspension mounting points were relocated, which resulted in the longer wheelbase. The rear suspension was also attached at a lower point on the frame, which produced greater high-speed stability. The rear end also had a new four-link suspension geometry. The new platform featured a new steering gearbox and improved steering linkage.

In 1959, Chevrolet shuffled its own nameplates from 1958. The Delray was gone and now the Biscayne was the low-priced model. The Bel Air became the mid-priced Chevy. The LPO 1105 body police package or LPO 1108 chassis police package were only available on the Biscayne and Bel Air two-door and four-door and the Brookwood station wagon. The top-of-the-line retail Chevy in 1959 was the Impala.

The body police package included options such as heavy-duty seats, all-vinyl interiors and right-side sun visor. The chassis police package included options such as heavy-duty springs, shocks, brakes, stabilizer bars, wheel bearings, battery, generator and special 15-inch wheels with "Tyrex cord tires that ride better, roll easier and last longer."

A hood ornament identified the powerplant in the '59 Chevys: The word, Chevrolet, in script by itself designated a six-cylinder engine. The Chevrolet script plus a "V" meant one of the 283-cid small-block engines. The script, "V" and crossed flags indicated one of the 348-cid big-block engines.

Chevrolet's 1959 police performance engine lineup was based around the 348-cid W-engine. The 250 hp, four-barrel carbureted Turbo-Thrust and the 280 hp, triple two-barrel carbureted Super Turbo

This 1959 Biscayne used by the North Dakota State Patrol is powered by the 348-cid/300-hp big-block engine. The state police in Indiana and Alabama also used the Biscayne. (Jim Benjaminson)

In 1959, the police package came on the two-door and four-door Biscayne and Bel Air (pictured).

Thrust produced enough power for most enforcement activities. Yet with hydraulic lifters and 9.5:1 compression, these were tame and tolerant engines.

In 1959, each of these 348-cid powerplants was available in a "Special" version. These Special versions used the same carburetion and fully separated dual exhaust. However, the compression was bumped to 11.0:1 and the engines had heavy-duty main and connecting rod bearings. The coil, distributor and spark plugs were also special for positive ignition at high engine speeds.

These Special engines used solid lifters and a special Duntov grind high-lift camshaft. The high compression engines used different pistons than the stock "pent-roof" design. The pistons on the Special versions were relieved for extreme valve duration overlap. These engines were topped off with large port intake manifolds.

These changes boosted the four-barrel version from 250 hp to 300 hp. Likewise, the triple two-barrel carbureted engine was increased from 280 hp to 315 hp. The "three deuce" version was available only with a three-speed or four-speed manual, while the four-barrel carbureted Special could also be teamed with the newly beefed-up Powerglide.

Motor Trend tested a 315 hp Super Turbo Thrust Special V-8-powered police package Biscayne and posted the following results:

0-60 mph	7.4 sec
0-100 mph	18.8 sec
Top speed, 3.70 axle	129 mph
Top speed, 3.36 axle	135.5 mph

In 1959, the four-door police Biscayne with the 348-cid, triple two-barrel carbureted Special V-8 could chase down the Ferrari 250 Gran Turismo, which was the fastest sports car available.

"For an extra dash of emergency performance, still with excellent overall fuel economy, Ramjet Fuel Injection and Ramjet Special V-8s are also available. The Ramjet Special combines fuel injection with a special camshaft and high-speed valve train, plus many other special-duty features."

Fuel injection was back in police cars for 1959. The 9.5:1 engine with hydraulic lifters cranked out 250 hp. The Ramjet Special with special bearings, pistons, solid lifters, Duntov cam and a 10.5:1 compression produced 290 hp at a screaming 6200 rpm.

It is unknown how many fuel-injected police package cars were produced. However, the demand carried over from 1958 was obviously strong enough to result in two injected versions for 1959.

At the other end of the powerband, Chevrolet re-engineered its 235-cid police Six. The urban patrol engine received a new, economy-contoured camshaft, valve lifters and carburetor calibration. The engine produced less peak horsepower but more torque at lower engine speeds. The result was more usable power under normal traffic conditions with better fuel economy. Even the fuel consumption during idling was greatly reduced. With reasonable performance from an absolute minimum of fuel, this engine was renamed, Hi-Thrift Six.

New for 1959, Chevy police cars were available with the close-ratio, four-speed Synchro-Mesh transmission. This was available with both the fuel-injected 283-cid engines and with all of the 348-cid big-blocks. It was the same transmission used in the Corvette, the gearbox controlled by a floor-mounted, short-throw stick shift lever. The gear ratios were 2.20, 1.66, 1.31 and 1.00.

The rest of the drivetrain was also perked up for 1959. The Turboglide got stronger internal gears, increased bearing areas and multiple-disc clutches throughout. A special (Corvette) heavy-duty Powerglide was now used on the 348-cid engines. The Chevy police cars were also available in five different axle ratios depending on the engine and transmission: 3.08, 3.36, 3.55, 3.70 and 4.11

Brake problems in the past, and more powerful engines and greater vehicle weight for 1959 resulted in better brakes. The improvement in stopping power for 1959 included wider, air-cooled drums with 27 percent more bonded area. The LPO 1108 police-package included sintered-metallic linings for greater fade resistance after a series of panic stops and better effectiveness after driving through water.

The new "Safety-Master" brakes had 27 percent more lining area. This, combined with new drums with wide cooling flanges better exposed to the air stream, were supposed to greatly increase brake shoe life. The wheel webs were also vented for better brake cooling.

Motor Trend tested a police '59 Biscayne developed by none other than Zora Arkus-Duntov, of Corvette chief engineer fame. Duntov was a 1946 Indy 500 entrant, 1955 Pikes Peak record-holder and two-time LeMans endurance race class winner.

23

For 1959, cops had their choice of 10 police engines from the 235-cid/135-hp Six to the 348-cid/335-hp triple two-barrel carbureted V-8. (Chevrolet)

In 1959, Chevrolet police cars were based on the 119 inch wheelbase B-body. This remained the police sedan platform through 1996. (Chevrolet)

Cops had been critical of the Chevy brakes in the previous years. Duntov put a "stop" to that forever. To this day, the police cars with consistently the best brakes have been the Chevrolets. In addition to the 15-inch diameter police wheels (retail cars all had 14-inch wheels) for better air flow around the drums, Duntov pioneered the use of sintered brake pads. Here is what *Motor Trend* had to say about the '59 Biscayne brakes:

"Further changes included in the police option are the same sort of heavy-duty suspension as has been used for some time on police and export models, and those great sintered metal brakes—which are well worth getting excited about.

"Released by Chevrolet last winter—still only for use on police cars—the sintered metal linings make these brakes virtually non-fade. *Any number* of panic stops can be made without any sign of fade at all. Using the brakes brutally over and over and over again from very high speeds eventually may produce some signs of wear, but you'll end up with a dragging brake because the return spring has suffered from heat before you'll get even a hint of brake fade.

"Duntov mentioned that even though the brakes were power-assisted, I might find they had a somewhat different "feel" than I was used to. Actually the differences were so slight—no more than between two different makes of American cars—as to be barely noticeable. What was noticeable was the absolute reliability and effectiveness of braking in every way we could think to try. Detroit-car brakes can be criticized with justification, but these sintered metal linings make a tremendously impressive set of brakes. I asked why they weren't used for all Chevy passenger cars. Duntov explained that they were capable of being uneven before they were warmed up by a little use. It was so hot in Detroit that week-in the 90s-that perhaps outside temperature prevented the brakes from ever getting "cold" —though of course this is not the kind of cold Duntov meant. For whatever reason, at no time that I had the car did the brakes show any unevenness. (These iron brake linings came from Corvette competition experience, and are a milder version of the fiercely effective shoes that first showed their "metal" at Sebring 1956.)"

The February Daytona Speed Weeks, now called International Safety & Performance Trials because of the AMA racing ban, still had a profound influence on all carmakers. All of the mid-year engines and options were released in time for Speed Weeks. Chevrolet indeed, made one such mid-year release: The Super Turbo Thrust Special V-8 with its compression bumped from 11.0:1 to 11.25:1 among other changes. This triple two-barrel carbureted, dual-exhaust, 348-cid V-8 now pumped out an honest 335 hp.

In 1959, Chevrolet was used by the Pennsylvania State Police. The so-called Pennsylvania State Police "package" became a popular setup for many police departments wanting a pursuit car. In addition to the two Limited Production Option (LPO) packages that make up a police package (1105, body and 1108, chassis), the informal Pennsylvania State Police Package included a number of Regular Production Options (RPO). These included the heavy-duty 70 amp battery and the positraction rear end. The Posi-Traction (limited slip) axle was available with 3.36, 3.55 or 4.11 rear gears. These cars were all based around the mid-year release, 335 hp, 348-cid, triple two-barrel carbureted Super Turbo-Thrust Special V-8.

As a late-year offering, Chevrolet released yet another version of the 348-cid, "three deuce" engine. Starting with the mid-year release 335 hp version, the automaker changed the camshaft, cylinder heads and valves. The result was a rare and extremely limited 350 hp version of the 348 Turbo Thrust engine.

In addition to the Pennsylvania State Police, the 1959 Biscayne was used by the North Dakota State Patrol, Alabama Highway Patrol and the Indiana State Police.

1959 Chevrolet Biscayne		
Engine	348 cid	348 cid
Carb	4-bbl	4-bbl
Horsepower	250 hp	300 hp
Compression	9.5	11.0
Transmission	Turboglide	3-spd
Axle	3.08:1	3.70:1
Wheelbase	119.0 in	119.0 in
Weight	3,606 lbs	3,606 lbs
0-60 mph	10.7 sec	7.4 sec
0-100 mph	n/a	18.8 sec
Quarter-mile E.T.	18.5 sec	n/a
Quarter-mile Speed	80 mph	n/a
Top Speed	123 mph	129 mph

1959 Full Size Acceleration Performance

Car	Engine/HP/Trans	0-60 mph (sec)	Quarter-Mile	
			E.T. (sec)	Speed (mph)
Plymouth Fury	361 cid/305 hp/auto	8.5	16.4	83.3
Chevrolet Impala	348 cid/280 hp/auto	9.0	16.3	83.1
Mercury Montclair	383 cid/322 hp/auto	10.2	17.6	81.0
Chrysler Windsor	383 cid/305 hp/auto	10.8	17.4	77.0
Pontiac Catalina	389 cid/300 hp/auto	10.8	18.2	77.0
Oldsmobile Super 88	394 cid/315 hp/auto	11.0	17.7	74.7
Dodge Custom Royal	361 cid/305 hp/auto	11.3	17.9	77.0

1959 Police Drivetrain Combinations

Duty	Engine	Transmission	Axle
All-purpose special police car power team	Turbo-Thrust Special V-8	Special HD Powerglide	3.08 3.36 3.55 3.70
Turnpike & highway pursuit	Super Turbo-Thrust Spl V-8, Turbo-Thrust Spl V-8, Ramjet Spl V-8	3-speed Synchro-Mesh 4-speed Synchro-Mesh	3.36 3.55 3.70
Highway pursuit	Super Turbo-Thrust V-8, Turbo-Thrust V-8, Ramjet Fuel Injection V-8	3-speed Synchro-Mesh 4-speed Synchro-Mesh	3.36 3.55
Highway cruising	Super Turbo-Thrust V-8, Turbo-Thrust V-8, Ramjet Fuel Injection V-8	Turboglide Powerglide	3.08 3.36
Urban pursuit, cruising, patrol	Super Turbo-Fire V-8	3-speed Synchro-Mesh Overdrive Turboglide Powerglide	3.55 4.11 3.36
Urban economy pursuit, cruising, patrol	Turbo-Fire V-8	3-speed Synchro-Mesh Overdrive Turboglide Powerglide	3.55 4.11 3.36
Economy & convenience utility	Hi-Thrift Six	3-speed Synchro-Mesh Overdrive Powerglide	3.55 4.11 3.36

Police Engines for 1959

Engine	Size & Carb	Compression	Horsepower
Hi-Thrift Six	235 cid, 1-bbl	8.25	135 @ 4000
Turbo Fire V-8	283 cid, 2-bbl	8.5	185 @ 4600
Super Turbo Fire V-8	283 cid, 4-bbl	9.5	230 @ 4800
Ramjet Fuel Injection V-8	283 cid, f.i.	9.5	250 @ 5000
Turbo Thrust V-8	348 cid, 4-bbl	9.5	250 @ 4400
Super Turbo Thrust V-8	348 cid, 3x2-bbl	9.5	280 @ 4800
Ramjet Special V-8	283 cid, f.i.	10.5	290 @ 6200
Turbo Thrust Special V-8	348 cid, 4-bbl	11.0	300 @ 5600
Super Turbo Thrust Special V-8	348 cid, 3x2-bbl	11.0	315 @ 5600
Super Turbo Thrust Special V-8 (mid-year release)	348 cid, 3x2-bbl	11.25	335 @ 5600

References for 1959

75 Years of Chevrolet, George Dammann, Motorbooks International

Illustrated Chevrolet Buyers Guide, John Gunnell, Motorbooks International

"Chevy for '59," Pat Chappell, Standard Catalog of Chevrolet 1912-1990

1959 Chevrolet Police Cars, Chevrolet Motor Division

"I Drove a Stock Chevrolet 135 mph," D.M. Bartley, Motor Trend, December 1958

"The World's Newest 1959 Impala," staff report, Special Interest Autos, June 1988

"Power," Phil Hall, Car Exchange, July 1979

"The Impala Look," Wick Humble, Standard Catalog of Chevrolet 1912-1990

Chapter 6

1960: Economy Turbo-Fire 283

This Indiana State Police 1960 Biscayne was powered by a 348-cid/250-hp engine. It reached 60 mph in 10 seconds. (Ed Moody)

For 1960, Chevrolet made only subtle changes to sheet metal and drivetrains. After all, for two years in a row, it had introduced totally new vehicles. As a side note, in late 1959 Chevrolet introduced the rear-engine Corvair as a 1960 model year vehicle. Unknown to most enthusiasts, the Corvair became available with a police package in 1961.

For 1960, the LPO 1105 and 1108 police packages were available only on the Biscayne two-door and four-door and the Brookwood station wagon.

A new sub-series was added to the low-price Biscayne, called the Biscayne Fleetmaster. This low-price model was intended to compete with the Plymouth Savoy Fleet Special. These cars were aimed at the commercial, taxi, police and government fleet sales.

While the Fleetmaster had the trim of a Biscayne, it came without cigarette lighter, without front seat armrests, without electric windshield wipers and with only a driver's side sun visor. Ironically, the Fleetmaster nameplate selected for this stripped, no-frills Biscayne was the name once used for Chevrolet's most prestigious car.

Only a few engine option changes were made and no changes were made to transmissions or rear gear ratios. For one, fuel injection was no longer offered on the sedans. The Corvette would, however, retain fuel injection through 1965. In the late-1950s and early-1960s, mechanical fuel injection proved to be both complicated and fuel-

Police package station wagons have been available nearly as long as police package sedans. This V-8-powered Indiana State Police unit was used for truck regulation enforcement. (Rick Hammer)

26

The 1960 police sedans, such as this Clinton County, Indiana, Sheriff unit, were available with eight police engines including triple two-barrel carburetion.

The 1960 Chevrolet police cars had these "seagull" rear fins. An "economy" version of the 283-cid was the new police engine for 1960.

hungry. As it turned out, the loss of fuel-injected engines did not affect police sales or police car performance at all. Other engines with equal and even greater power were available in the police sedans.

For 1960, the 283-cid engines came standard with single exhaust. Dual exhaust was RPO 220.

In 1959, the Turbo-Fire 283-cid engine with two-barrel carb produced 185 hp. For 1960, this engine was actually de-tuned for police use. The new version, called the Economy Turbo-Fire, was fitted with a specially calibrated and jetted two-barrel carb.

The documents are a little unclear on this. Some literature states that this de-tuned two-barrel carbureted engine was the only two-barrel-equipped engine available. Other information indicates the fuel-miser carb was an $8.00 RPO, which means two versions were avail-

able at least to the retail public. Regardless, for police package vehicles, only the de-tuned version was available.

The de-tuned 283-cid V-8 produced just 170 hp. For police use in roles where horsepower is not important, such as detective units and crime scene investigators, this engine made sense and cents. They got 1 to 2 mpg better gas mileage under normal driving conditions, but had a real V-8 under the hood—instead of a Six—when emergency driving was required.

Some 348-cid engines were restricted to certain transmissions for 1960. For example, the solid lifter, 320 hp version required either a three-speed or four-speed Synchro-Mesh. The milder, hydraulic lifter, 305 hp version was teamed only with the heavy-duty (Corvette) Powerglide automatic.

Only one version of the Super Turbo Thrust "Special" was available for 1960. This was the 335 hp version of the 348-cid V-8 with three two-barrel carbs. Recall that in 1959, this Special came as a 315 hp new model year engine, then a 335 hp version was available mid-year, then a 350 hp version was available late in the year. A 280 hp "non-Special" version of this "three deuce" Super Turbo Thrust engine was also available in 1960. For this engine the term Super meant three two-barrel carbs, while Special meant solid lifters, high lift cam, high compression and beefier bearings.

In 1960, Chevrolet was a major factor among the Low Priced Three when it came to city police and sheriffs department contracts. The Los Angeles Police, in conjunction with the Pomona Police and Los Angeles County Sheriffs Department, had conducted vehicle tests since 1956. These tests were performed at the Los Angeles County fairgrounds, the current site of the National Hot Rod Association's (NHRA) Winternationals.

The LAPD had a 2.1-mile road course set up on the massive parking lot. Each squad car was given a preliminary high-speed handling test around this course. The cars were then run down the quarter-mile for time and then put through a series of 90 mph to zero brake tests. Once the police package car passed these subjective tests, it was considered "qualified" and eligible to bid.

In 1960, the Los Angeles-area Police tests included the Chevrolet Biscayne along with the Plymouth Savoy, full-size Dodge, Dodge Dart, Pontiac Catalina and Ford. The Biscayne had the performance to qualify, of course. However, the low bid for the LAPD that year was the Plymouth Savoy and the low bid for the L.A. Sheriffs Department was the Dodge Dart. Not to worry. Chevy would capture the Los Angeles County Sheriffs Department police car business for 1961. However, in 1960 both the Indiana State Police and the Ohio State Highway Patrol ran Chevrolets.

1960 Chevrolet Biscayne	
Engine	348 cid
Carb	4-bbl
Horsepower	250 hp
Transmission	Turboglide
Axle	3.08
Wheelbase	119 in
Weight	3,840 lbs
0-60 mph	10.7 sec

Police Engines for 1960			
Engine	Size & Carb	Compression	Horsepower
Hi-Thrift Six	235 cid, 1-bbl	8.25	135 @ 4000
Economy Turbo-Fire V-8	283 cid, 2-bbl	8.5	170 @ 4200
Super Turbo-Fire V-8	283 cid, 4-bbl	9.5	230 @ 4800
Turbo Thrust V-8	348 cid, 4-bbl	9.5	250 @ 4400
Super Turbo Thrust V-8	348 cid, 3x2-bbl	9.5	280 @ 4800
Turbo Thrust Special V-8*	348 cid, 4-bbl	11.0	305 @ 5600
Turbo Thrust Special V-8**	348 cid, 4-bbl	11.25	320 @ 5600
Super Turbo Thrust Special V-8	348 cid, 3x2-bbl	11.25	335 @ 5800
*Heavy-duty Powerglide transmission only			
**Synchro-Mesh manual transmission only			

1960 Acceleration Times				
			Quarter-Mile	
Car	Engine & HP	0-60 (sec)	E.T. (sec)	Speed (mph)
Chrysler 300 F	413 cid, 375 hp	7.1	16.0	85.0
Dodge Dart Phoenix	383 cid, 340 hp	8.5	16.3	86.0
Plymouth Fury	361 cid, 310 hp	9.0	16.9	85.0
Dodge Polara	383 cid, 330 hp	9.3	17.1	88.0
Chevrolet Bel Air	348 cid, 280 hp	9.9	17.2	80.5
Pontiac Bonneville	389 cid, 348 hp	11.5	18.6	76.0
Ford Starliner	352 cid, 300 hp	11.7	20.7	80.0
Mercury Montclair	430 cid, 310 hp	12.0	17.7	76.0
Oldsmobile Dynamic 88	371 cid, 240 hp	12.7	18.3	75.0
Chevrolet Biscayne	235 cid, 135 hp	18.6	20.4	63.0

References for 1960

Illustrated Chevrolet Buyers Guide, John Gunnell, Motorbooks International

75 Years of Chevrolet, George Dammann, Motorbooks International

Standard Catalog of Chevrolet 1912-1990, Pat Chappell, Krause Publications

"Power," Phil Hall, *Car Exchange*, July 1979

"Torture Testing Cars for Police Patrol," Bill Carroll, *Popular Science*, June 1960

1960 Chevrolet Police Cars, Chevrolet Motor Division

Chapter 7

1961: Corvair Police Package

In 1961, the full-size Chevrolet had a totally new chassis and totally new sheet metal. The Safety Girder X-frame was retained and so was the "big car" 119-inch wheelbase. Overall, however, the Chevrolet was downsized slightly. The four-door '61 Biscayne was 1.5 inches shorter and 65 pounds lighter than the '60 version.

For 1961, the LPO 1105 and 1108 police packages were available only on the Biscayne and Biscayne Fleetmaster two-door and four-door sedan and Brookwood station wagon. The two retail-only lines were Bel Air and Impala. This was the last year for the stripper Fleetmaster.

This was basically the 1960 348-cid/335-hp engine with the larger diameter valves. With mechanical lifters, special Duntov-grind cam, premium bearings, dual-point distributor and a true dual exhaust, this was the first carbureted, official Chevrolet police engine to achieve "one horsepower per cubic inch of displacement."

The five transmissions (three-speed Synchro-Mesh, four-speed Synchro-Mesh, three-speed Overdrive, Turboglide and Powerglide) were carried over for 1961. Also a carry-over were the four powerteam-matched axle ratios (3.08, 3.36, 3.55 and 3.70). All were available with positraction.

The Biscayne, such as this Iowa Highway Patrol unit, was downsized slightly for 1961. (Robert Parks)

A new addition to the LPO 1108 suspension package was the heavy-duty rear axle. This was a high torque capacity unit with the upper control arm bracket specially welded to the housing. Engineered for the severest police duty, this axle used heavy-duty, roller-type wheel bearings.

Some horsepower shuffling took place on some of the 348-cid V-8s for 1961. The Turbo Thrust Special version that was available with the Corvette Powerglide was backed off in compression from 11.0:1 to 9.5:1. It still retained its 305 hp rating thanks to an aluminum intake manifold and larger diameter valves, however, it had the regular cam and hydraulic lifters. Very strange.

The Turbo Thrust Special available only with a manual transmission retained the 11.25:1 compression, special cam and solid lifters. With the larger valves and special aluminum intake manifold, the horsepower jumped 20 hp to a 340 hp rating.

For 1961, the Super Turbo Thrust Special V-8 fed by three two-barrel carbs and pumping out 350 hp was an official police engine.

In mid-year 1961, Chevrolet released one of its most famous engines, the 409-cid Turbo Fire. The 409 was a bored and stroked 348-cid big-block V-8:

Engine	348 cid	409 cid
Bore	4.125 in	4.313 in
Stroke	3.25 in	3.50 in

In 1961, the 409-cid V-8 was not an optional police engine. In fact, only 142 of these engines were built until production problems stopped the output. The ones that were produced were all single Carter AFB four-barrel versions rated at 360 hp. This big, bad Turbo Fire would be back in 1962 with a vengeance.

Motor Trend tested a '61 Impala 409 Super Sport, which offered a glimpse into how the cop cars with the 409 would run in 1962. The 11.25:1 compression, four-barrel carbureted engine producing 360 hp

Most fire departments use police package cars. The 1961 Chevrolets were available with five transmissions including a four-speed stick. (Bob Harrington)

The Los Angeles County Sheriff used the Biscayne in 1961. The police package included sintered brake shoes. (LASD)

was teamed with a four-speed Synchro-Mesh and a 3.36 ratio positraction rear axle. With the factory 8.00x14 tires, the 409 Super Sport hit 60 mph in 7.8 seconds and ran the quarter-mile in 15.3 seconds at 94.2 mph. As a comparison, the 1995 350-cid, LT-1 powered, 9C1 police package Caprice ran the quarter-mile in 16.3 seconds at 86.8 mph. The old big-block Chevy cop cars were fast.

Another mid-year 1961 release was the most meaningful and long-lived, high-performance retail package ever marketed by Chevrolet, the Super Sport (SS). In fact, the SS package lasted, on-again, off-again, as long as the V-8, rear-drive, four-door sedan itself. When the last Caprice 9C1 police car rolled off the Arlington, Texas, assembly line in 1996, Chevrolet also produced its last Impala SS. The police package and the Super Sport package shared components from the Super Sport's first year in mid-1961 to the last year for both in mid-1996.

In mid-1961, the SS package was a dealer-installed trim and performance package available on almost any Impala. Done to showcase the new 409-cid engine, the early SS package was reported to have required at least a 348-cid engine. The package included SS rear fender emblems, spinner hubcaps, a 7000 rpm steering column-mounted tachometer, narrow-band 8.00x14 whitewalls, a dash pad, package shocks and springs and heavy-duty brakes. This Super Sport package usually included power steering and power brakes with police, sintered metallic brake shoes.

In 1961, the Chevrolet Corvair-yes, Corvair-was available with the official police package. The Corvair was produced as a retail car from 1960 to 1969 but was available with a police package in only 1961 and 1962.

Chevrolet billed the Corvair as:

"America's most advanced thrift car—fills a unique role in police department needs. Big cities will like the Corvair's extra-easy maneuverability in traffic. Local sheriff's offices will like the way Corvair handles a hundred-odd jobs quickly and willingly. Small municipalities will find that Corvair's low price lets them add an extra car to the force. All will like the Corvair's overall economy."

The Corvair evoked a love-hate response. Some car purists called it the most significant automobile of the post-World War II era. Ralph Nader branded it 'Unsafe At Any Speed.' It was certainly one of the most unusual and unique high-volume vehicles ever produced by a major automaker.

The Corvair's most unconventional feature was the drivetrain layout. The Corvair used a rear-engine, air-cooled, horizontally-opposed (pancake) six-cylinder engine. It had a fully independent, Quadri-Flex suspension with front and rear coil springs, a unitized, Monostrut Body by Fisher, and a rear transaxle. The 108-inch wheelbase car weighed just 2,380 pounds.

The Unipack power team combined the aluminum engine and transaxle into one unit. The engine used steel cylinder sleeves but the block, heads and intake manifold were aluminum with cast cooling fins.

The Turbo-Air Six engine had gained five cubic inches from the 1960 introduction to now displace 145 cubic inches. This dual one-barrel carbureted 8.0:1 compression engine came in two power versions. The standard Turbo Air produced 80 hp, while the Super Turbo Air generated 98 hp. The Super Turbo Air used a special high-lift cam, heavy-duty valve springs, recalibrated twin one-barrel carbs and a larger, less restrictive exhaust system.

The Corvair used a rear-mounted three-speed Synchro-Mesh, four-speed Synchro-Mesh or Powerglide automatic (80 hp engine only). The final drive ratio was a choice of 3.27, 3.55 or 3.89.

The Corvair was profoundly not a successful police car. The early generation Corvairs oversteered badly under hard cornering. The early models also had a tendency to throw the main centrifugal blower belt. Since this was strictly an air-cooled engine, the loss of the blower belt nearly always resulted in fired bearings and a warped block and heads, with little warning to the driver.

The oil cooler failed to keep the oil cool if the driver did not keep the engine rpm up. Oil accounted for at least 40 percent of the engine cooling. Under cold weather conditions, the twin carburetors were prone to icing. The passenger compartment was heated and the windshield was defrosted by an exhaust-heated blower. This frequently produced excessive carbon monoxide fumes in the cabin.

The Corvair's poor mechanical reliability and engine malfunctions earned it a spot on the *Consumer Reports* list of "undesirable" models for every year it was produced as a retail car.

Ralph Nader's book claims about the stability, handling and rollover characteristics of the 1960-1963 Corvairs were eventually discredited by the Department of Transportation and the National Highway Traffic Safety Administration. By the time the book was published, the second generation 1965-1969 Corvairs were out.

These new Corvairs featured a Corvette-inspired rear suspension. This eliminated the problems associated with the Volkswagen-style swing-axle. With the new rear suspension, these Corvairs handled extremely well at all speeds. They proved this in Sports Car Club of America (SCCA) sanctioned competition on parking lots, airstrips and wide open road racing courses.

With a 108-inch wheelbase, the Corvair was placed in the same late-1960s SCCA autocross class as the small-block Camaro and Mustang. The four-barrel carbureted, 140 hp Corvairs routinely humiliated these much more powerful pony cars by taking class wins at the regional and national level. But they never caught on as police cars.

In 1960, the California Highway Patrol began a study of six police cars with wheelbases shorter than its 122-inch minimum. This involved a year-long field test to determine their adaptability to patrol work. This would have given the 119-inch Biscayne a shot at the na-

tion's most prestigious police contract. In 1961, after a full year in actual use, the CHP concluded:

"The smaller cars had less roadability, are more difficult to handle particularly at high speeds, are more tiring to drive and generally cannot live up to the extreme demands placed on a car which must operate at widely varying speeds on every type of terrain in all kinds of weather."

The Kansas City, Missouri, Police were among many urban departments to use the 1961 Chevy. Many urban squad cars used the two-barrel version of the 283-cid V-8. (Jim Post)

This conclusion ruled Chevrolet out. That was 1961 and probably right for the times. However, as the times changed, so would the cars. After all, the CHP's most famous police pursuit car, the Mustang 5.0 HO, had a mere 100.5-inch wheelbase and weighed just 3,035 pounds.

In 1961, Chevrolet did, however, capture the most prestigious of the non-state police contracts: the Los Angeles County Sheriffs Department, which is the nation's largest sheriffs department, and the third largest police department behind only New York City Police and Chicago Police. In 1961, the L.A. Sheriffs Department used the four-door Biscayne. Available documentation shows the Chevy squad was powered by the 348-cid/250-hp, four-barrel carbureted Turbo Thrust V-8 linked to a Turboglide automatic. The Alaska State Police, Iowa State Patrol, Kansas City, Missouri, Police and Indiana State Police also drove Chevrolets in 1961.

1961 Chevrolet Biscayne	
Engine	348 cid
Carb	4-bbl
HP	250 hp
Transmission	Turboglide
Axle	3.08
Wheelbase	119.0 in
Weight	3,980 lbs
0-60 mph	10.6 sec
0-100 mph	28.0 sec
Quarter-mile ET	17.2 sec
Quarter-mile Speed	79 mph
Top Speed	115 mph

Biscayne Police Engines for 1961			
Engine	Size & Carb	Compression	Horsepower
Hi-Thrift Six	235 cid, 1-bbl	8.25	135 @ 4000
Economy Turbo Fire V-8	283 cid, 2-bbl	8.5	170 @ 4200
Super Turbo Fire V-8	283 cid, 4-bbl	9.5	230 @ 4800
Turbo Thrust V-8	348 cid, 4-bbl	9.5	250 @ 4400
Super Turbo Thrust V-8	348 cid, 3x2-bbl	9.5	280 @ 4800
Turbo Thrust Special V-8	348 cid, 4-bbl	9.5	305 @ 5200
Turbo Thrust Special V-8	348 cid, 4-bbl	11.25	340 @ 5800
Super Turbo Thrust Special V-8	348 cid, 3x2-bbl	11.25	350 @ 6000

The Indiana State Police used Biscaynes in 1961. These were powered by the 348-cid V-8. The triple two-barrel version was the first carbureted bowtie police engine with "one horsepower per cubic inch of displacement." (Rick Hammer)

References for 1961

75 Years of Chevrolet, George Dammann, Motorbooks International

Standard Catalog of Chevrolet 1912-1990, Pat Chappell, Krause Publications

Illustrated Chevrolet Buyers Guide, John Gunnell, Motorbooks International

Trend-Setting 1961 Chevrolet Police Cars, Chevrolet Motor Division

Chevrolet Impala and SS, 1958-1971, R.M. Clarke, Motorbooks International

Chapter 8

1962: First 327 and 409 Engines

The state police in Indiana, Ohio and Wisconsin used the Biscayne in 1962. (Jerry Parker)

The 1962 model year gave cops two new engines for the full-size Chevrolet police car: the 327-cid small-block and the 409-cid big-block. This was also the first year for an entirely new kind of Chevy police car: the Chevy II.

On the full-size 1962 Chevrolets, the exterior sheet metal changed but the body and chassis was a carry-over from 1961. The unpopular Biscayne "Fleetmaster" was dropped. The retail cars were either Biscayne, Bel Air or Impala. Of these, the two-door and four-door Biscayne and the Biscayne station wagon are the only full-size Chevrolets mentioned in the official police literature.

The heavy-duty equipment designed specifically for police duty was now available as a Regular Production Option (RPO). RPO 400 included items of chassis equipment such as 15-inch wheels with 6.70x15 tires, sintered-metallic brake shoes, extra capacity coil springs, specially valved shocks, front sway bar and heavy-duty axle, front suspension joints and Synchro-Mesh transmissions and clutches.

For 1962, the 327-cid small-block replaced the 348-cid big-block as the medium power police engine. The 1962 327-cid V-8 was a bored and stroked version of the 283-cid engine that was introduced in 1957:

Engine	Bore	Stroke
283-cid V-8	3.875 in	3.00 in
327-cid V-8	4.00 in	3.25 in

The 327-cid engine was the first of the 4-inch bore small-blocks that would eventually include the Trans Am-inspired 302-cid and the legendary 350-cid powerplants. This was the first use of the 3.25-inch stroke. The 327-cid V-8 continued the reputation of Chevy small-blocks with hydraulic lifter versions up to 350 hp, solid lifter versions up to 365 hp and the famous 375 hp fuel-injected version.

The most powerful 327-cid engine put in a police car was 300 hp L74 used from 1962 through 1965. In reduced horsepower versions, the 327 was used in patrol cars through 1969. The 327 was the first of the "big-valve," small-block engines. The high performance versions had the 2.02-inch intake valves and 1.60-inch exhaust valves. These were the largest valves ever used on a small-block. Released in 1962, this intake and exhaust combination was big enough to work with the most powerful 1996 LT1 350-cid V-8.

The 327-cid police engine came in two versions. Both had 10.5:1 compression ratios, Carter four-barrel carbs, hydraulic lifters and dual exhaust. One was rated at 250 hp. The other had a larger four-barrel carb, special intake valves, larger intake ports, and a larger dual exhaust system. This version produced 300 hp. In 1962, the 283-cid V-8 was available only with a two-barrel carb while the 327-cid V-8 was equipped only with a four-barrel carb.

While only 142 409-cid engines were produced in 1961, this changed for 1962. With the 1961 engine production problems solved, Chevrolet reintroduced the 409. A total of 15,019 police and retail cars were powered by this big-block in 1962.

Cops got two new engines for 1962: the 327-cid small-block and the 409-cid big-block. A dual four-barrel carbureted 409-cid Biscayne ran a 14 second quarter-mile.

This perfect 1962 Bel Air was used by the Pennsylvania State Police. Six police engines from the 235-cid Six to the 409-cid V-8 were available. (Mike Novatnak)

By nearly all accounts, the 409-cid big-block was developed for NASCAR oval track racing. The 409-cid V-8 was a bored and stroked version of the 348-cid V-8 that was introduced in 1958. While both engines look identical from the outside, they are not made from the same block casting. The 409-cid engine is cast with a different water jacket core so the cylinders can be bored out to a larger diameter without making the jacket walls thinner. The 348-cid big-block was no longer available.

The 409-cid V-8 came in two strengths. Both versions had 11:1 compression, aluminum intake manifold, special pistons, high-lift camshaft, premium main and connecting rod bearings and solid lifters. The single four-barrel version now produced 380 hp. The dual four-barrel version with a special lightweight valve train cranked out 409 hp. This became the first Chevrolet police car engine to sport dual quad carbs. The 409 was the only police engine of any make or vintage to ever produce over 400 hp.

The aluminum intake manifold on the Chevrolet big-block has almost always meant large internal runners. The 348-cid W-block used a cast iron manifold. The otherwise identical 409-cid W-block used a painted aluminum manifold. The aluminum manifold had larger diameter internal runners.

The same concept holds true for the 396-, 402-, 427- and 454-cid engines. The lower horsepower engines got the cast iron manifold and the higher horsepower engines got the aluminum one. In the 1970 454-cid engine, for example, the 345 and 390 hp versions got the cast iron unit. These engines went into police cruisers. The 450 and 460 hp muscle car versions got the higher flow aluminum manifold.

In 1962, Chevrolet released a genuine police package for the 110-inch wheelbase Chevy II. The standard drivetrain included either a 153-cid four or a 194-cid Six. (Chevrolet)

Runners of both manifolds are as near equal length as possible, and are configured in smooth, sweeping bends. Uniform cross-sectional areas are maintained throughout runner length. The ratio of wall surface to cross-sectional area is kept to a minimum. Runners for the cast-iron manifold provide optimum torque and horsepower in the intermediate rpm ranges.

Simply stated, this means that in the engine mid-speed range, runner configuration is such that the induction system pulse initiated by the closing of an inlet valve reaches the inlet valve of the next cylinder to be fired at the approximate time of the valve opening. Thus, the charge of gasoline and air is "helped" into the combustion chamber. The aluminum manifold is similarly designed but sized to provide optimum charging at the high end of the engine speed range.

Chevrolet recommended this 11.0:1 compression, dual four-barrel carbureted 409 hp engine for "specialized pursuit duty." No kidding. A two-door Chevy with this drivetrain, four-speed Synchro-Mesh and 3.36 gears reached 60 mph in 6.3 seconds on the skinny 6.70x15 bias tires. It ran the quarter-mile in just 14.9 seconds. As a comparison, a four-door '62 Chevy fitted with the 283-cid, two-barrel

carbureted engine and two-speed Powerglide took 12.5 seconds to hit 60 mph and 20.3 seconds to clear the quarter-mile.

For 1962, the troublesome Turboglide was discontinued and two versions of the four-speed Synchro-Mesh were available. A wide-ratio unit could be mated to either the 327-cid V-8 or 409-cid V-8. A close-ratio four-speed was teamed only with the 409-cid V-8.

A wide variety of axle ratios were available in 1962. These included: 3.08, 3.36, 3.55, 3.70, 4.11 and 4.56. Positraction was available with nearly all of the rear gears. Major departments that used the full-size Chevrolet in 1962 included the state police in Indiana, Ohio, Pennsylvania and Wisconsin, and the Chicago Police.

A totally new police car was introduced in 1962: the Chevy II. The 110-inch wheelbase Chevy II retail car was developed in response to the increasingly popular Ford Falcon. In an unusual step, Chevrolet released the Chevy II with a formal police package in its first year as a retail car. Typically, the police version lags behind the retail version by one model year.

The Chevy II involved five different series based on both the powerplant and trim level. At the bottom end was the Chevy II "100" powered by either a four- or six-cylinder engine. These were consid-

The Corvair was introduced with a police package in 1961 and discontinued after 1962. The rear engine cars oversteered and overheated. (Chevrolet)

ered separate series. The 100 was the four-door sedan available with the Heavy-Duty Body Equipment Option, RPO 594, and Heavy-Duty Chassis Equipment Option, RPO 599. Other Chevy II models could be equipped with the police packages on special order.

The medium trim level Chevy II was the "300" available with either a four-cylinder or six-cylinder engine. The top trim level was the "Nova 400" powered only by the six-cylinder engine. As a historical note, the "200" was introduced when the Chevy II was released but was discontinued a short time later.

The standard equipment engine with the Chevy II police car was the Hi-Thrift 194-cid, one-barrel carbureted Six producing 120 hp. The Super-Thrift 153-cid, one-barrel carbureted four-cylinder rated at 90 hp was available, but only on special order. This was the first four-cylinder engine built by Chevrolet since the introduction of the six-cylinder in 1929.

A factory-offered, dealer-installed "kit" made either a 283-cid or 327-cid V-8 with up to 360 hp available in the retail Chevy II. While some of these cars may have also had the police RPOs, it is most improbable that any were ever actually used for police patrol.

The Chevy II featured single leaf, "Mono-Plate" rear springs and a coil spring front suspension. The transmission could be either the three-speed Synchro-Mesh or two-speed Powerglide.

The Corvair was again available with a police package. For 1962, the retail Corvairs were available with the Monza Spyder package powered by turbocharged 145-cid Six producing an honest 150 hp. This was not a police package engine.

Three 1962 police engines were available for the Corvair. These were all based on the 145-cid Six with twin one-barrel carbs. The standard transmission engine with an 8.0:1 compression produced 80 hp.

The Powerglide engine had a 9.0:1 compression and 84 hp. The top powerplant with 9.0:1 compression, special cam, heavy-duty valve springs and larger exhaust produced 102 hp. The Corvair was now available with a positraction axle.

Biscayne Police Engines for 1962			
Engine	**Size & Carb**	**Comp.**	**Horsepower**
Hi-Thrift Six	235 cid, 1-bbl	8.25	135 @ 4000
Turbo-Fire 283	283 cid, 2-bbl	8.5	170 @ 4200
Turbo-Fire 327	327 cid, 4-bbl	10.5	250 @ 4400
Turbo-Fire 327	327 cid, 4-bbl	10.5	300 @ 5000
Turbo-Fire 409	409 cid, 4-bbl	11.0	380 @ 5800
Turbo-Fire 409	409 cid, 2x4-bbl	11.0	409 @ 6000

References for 1962

Illustrated Chevrolet Buyers Guide, John Gunnell, Motorbooks International

Chevrolet Impala and SS, 1958-1971, R.M. Clarke, Motorbooks International

Standard Catalog of Chevrolet 1912-1990, Pat Chappell, Krause Publications

75 Years of Chevrolet, George Dammann, Motorbooks International

Chevrolet Police Cars for 1962, Chevrolet Motor Division

Chapter 9

1963: De-tuned 327 and 409 Engines

A 283-cid two-barrel V-8 powered 1963 Biscayne. New for 1963, Chevrolet released a de-tuned 327-cid four-barrel V-8 for urban patrol. (Jennifer Sturgeon)

For 1963, the police package codes were changed to RPO B01 and Z04. Big news was a de-tuned 409-cid engine that could be teamed with a Powerglide transmission. (Jennifer Sturgeon)

For 1963, Chevrolet had two basic lines of police cars: The full-size Biscayne two-door and four-door sedan and station wagon, and the compact Chevy II 100 four-door sedan. The Corvair sedan was no longer available in police trim, however the Corvair Greenbrier police van was introduced in 1963.

The full-size cars were now available with a brand new six-cylinder engine, a de-tuned 327-cid V-8 designed to run on regular gas, a de-tuned version of the 409-cid V-8 that could be coupled with the Powerglide, or a dual four-barrel version of the 409 that pumped out 425 crime-crushing horsepower.

A Montreal 1963 Biscayne wagon. Police package station wagons were frequently used as ambulances. (John Carroll)

The police six-cylinder engine was totally new for 1963. The new Turbo-Thrift Six was 100 pounds lighter and much more compact than the old Hi-Thrift Blue Flame Six, which had remained basically unchanged since its introduction in 1937. While the total cubic inch displacement was similar, the new Six had a much larger bore and a much shorter stroke than the old Six.

Chevrolet used exactly the same bore and stroke in this new Six as it used in the Chevy II four-cylinder engine. Put another way, the 230-cid Six had the bore of a 283-cid V-8 and the stroke of a 327-cid V-8. The Rochester one-barrel carb was carried over to the new Six, the compression ratio was similar and the peak horsepower for both engines was similar.

Engine	Bore	Stroke	Comp.	HP
'62 Hi-Thrift 235 cid Six	3.56 in	3.94 in	8.25	135 @ 4000
'63 Turbo-Thrift 230 cid Six	3.875 in	3.25 in	8.50	140 @ 4400

The modern short-stroke engine design with modified wedge chambers was perkier but the big gains were in economy. The new engine was more fuel efficient, which was a double-economy bonus since it was also so significantly lighter than the earlier Six. The 0-60 mph time for a full-size Biscayne with Powerglide was 17.0 seconds. Yes, that is slow but it is faster than the older Six even when fitted with a three-speed Synchro-Mesh.

The de-tuned 327-cid V-8 rated at 230 hp was a special engine. This was designed specifically for police use. The 250 hp and 300 hp versions of the 327-cid small-block used a 10.5:1 compression ratio. This required premium grade gasoline. Chevrolet backed the compression ratio off to 8.6:1 to allow the use of regular grade gas.

This special police engine used the same free-flowing heads as the 250 hp and 300 hp versions and the same four-barrel carb and dual exhaust as the 250 hp engine. The result was 230 hp, most of the performance of the higher compression engines, and a big saving in fuel costs. The 250 hp and 300 hp engines were carry-overs from 1962.

In comparison, the 283-cid, two-barrel carbureted engine picked up 25 hp from its 1962 version. The '63 version used a higher-lift cam.

The combustion chambers were smaller, which increased compression from 8.5:1 to 9.25:1. Special damper springs were added to control valve spring surge. This allowed the tweaked 283 to reach peak horsepower at a much higher 4800 rpm.

A Biscayne with this 283-cid/195-hp, two-barrel carbureted engine and a three-speed Synchro-Mesh hit 60 mph in 10.7 seconds. In comparison, a Biscayne with a 327-cid/300-hp, four-barrel carbureted V-8 and a two-speed Powerglide reached 60 mph in 9.0 seconds.

Big news for the 409-cid big-block was a de-tuned version that could be bolted to the newly-improved heavy-duty Powerglide automatic. Chevrolet saw the clear trend in law enforcement was toward the automatic and away from the stick shift. It was important to have its biggest engine teamed with an automatic.

Chevrolet backed off the compression ratio from 11.0:1 to 10.0:1. It used a regular lift camshaft and replaced the solid lifters with hydraulics. The de-tuned engine shared the four-barrel carb, aluminum intake and dual exhaust with the L31 400 hp version. The result was a L33 409-cid engine producing a lazy 340 hp at peak. The key, however, was the torque.

The L80 409-cid/425-hp dual four-barrel carbureted engine produced 425 pound-feet of torque at 4200 rpm. The L33 409-cid/340-hp "de-tuned" engine produced 420 pound-feet of torque at 3200 rpm. Even more, the de-tuned engine had a flat torque curve from 1200 rpm to 4400 rpm. This gave the police engine a lot of punch regardless of where in the power band the two-speed Powerglide happened to place the engine when the power was needed.

Car Life (March 1963) drove the Impala equipped with the 409-cid/340-hp engine, Powerglide automatic and 3.36 highway rear gears. The full-size Super Sport reached 60 mph in 6.6 seconds and ran the quarter-mile in 15.2 seconds.

By the 1963 model year, the big-block V-8 had gained widespread popularity as the way to achieve quicker acceleration and faster top speeds. The big-blocks were fairly low revving engines so they got along just fine with low maintenance hydraulic lifters. A single four-barrel carb was all these massive engines seemed to need to pull out stumps all day long. No fuel injection failures. No multiple carburetion imbalances. No revving to 6500 rpm. No excessive cam duration, which prevents a good idle. (Cops love to sit with engines idling.) No

38

This 1963 Biscayne was used by the San Carlos, California, Police as a K-9 car. Note the off-center Federal Beacon-Ray. (Darryl Lindsay)

extreme compression ratios that force the use of premium fuel and make cold weather starts impossible.

By 1963, the relatively docile, flat torque curve big-blocks were being used by all carmakers: Pontiac 421-cid, Dodge and Plymouth 383-cid, Oldsmobile 394-cid, Ford and Mercury 390-cid and Chrysler 413-cid. The Chevrolet 409 was one of the club with its 340 hp version.

The big-block version of the Powerglide had several heavy-duty components beyond those found in the small-block Powerglide. The internal gears were also different. The Powerglide bolted to the 409 used 1.82 gears while the transmission coupled to the small-block used 1.76 gears. The small-block Powerglide upshifted at 4500 rpm while the big-block Powerglide upshifted at 5000 rpm. This, of course, seems backwards.

The 1963 model year was also the year of the Z11 427-cid/430-hp Super Stock engine. Of course, the Z11 was never used as a police engine any more than the Dodge 426-cid/425-hp "hemi" engine ever was. Yet to this day, rumors of both still persist. That is just wishful thinking on the part of some nostalgic enthusiasts!

Another non-police engine from 1963 was, in fact, the prototype for the very real 396-cid, later 427-cid and later still 454-cid police engines. This was the 1963 Mark II NASCAR 427 "mystery" engine with the staggered valve, or "porcupine" valve train layout. The 396-cid big-block would appear in 1965.

The two top engines for 1963 were the 400 hp and 425 hp versions of the 409. The 400 hp version was a brash street engine; how-

This 1963 Biscayne was pushed beyond its limits in a pursuit. A 1962 KCMO Ford "accident investigator" car is in the background. (Jim Post)

39

ever, the 425 hp, dual four-barrel version was an honest, Super Stock-class drag racing engine.

With the release of the 340 hp, de-tuned version, Chevrolet implied that the dual four-barrel, 425 hp version of the 409 might not be the ideal police engine even for unbridled pursuit duty.

In fact, of the 340 hp version, Chevrolet wrote, "A husky, high-torque engine that's ideal for modern police use. Recommended for high-speed highway pursuit where blistering acceleration and outstanding performance are vital."

In the 1963 police literature, Chevrolet listed six different option packages after consulting with police departments across the nation to see what they wanted. This, of course, is where the demand for the regular fuel 327-cid engine came. The six "standard" ordering packages included powertrains from the 230-cid/140-hp engine to the 409-cid/340-hp V-8. With all the engine horsepower hype and bravado aside, most fleet managers were looking for economy and reliability first, and reasonable vehicle performance second. The demand for Super Stock or NASCAR levels of performance was extremely rare. And Chevrolet had engines for those handful of cops who needed that kind of performance.

For 1963, the police package codes were changed. The Police Package Body Equipment was now RPO B01 while the Police Package Chassis Equipment was now RPO Z04.

The 1963 Chevy II police car was a carry-over from its 1962 introduction with only a few exceptions. It appears the police package was limited to only the 100 four-door. The four-cylinder was no longer listed as an available engine for the police cars.

Major departments patrolling in 1963 Chevrolets included the Iowa State Patrol, Missouri State Highway Patrol and the Kansas Highway Patrol.

Biscayne Police Engines for 1963			
Engine	Size & Carb	Compression	HP
Turbo-Thrift 230 Six	230 cid, 1-bbl	8.5	140 @ 4400
Turbo-Fire 283 V-8	283 cid, 2-bbl	9.25	195 @ 4800
Special Turbo-Fire 327 V-8	327 cid, 4-bbl	8.6	230 @ 4400
Turbo-Fire 327 V-8	327 cid, 4-bbl	10.5	250 @ 4400
Turbo-Fire 327 V-8	327 cid, 4-bbl	10.5	300 @ 5000
Turbo-Fire 409 V-8	409 cid, 4-bbl	10.0	340 @ 5000
Turbo-Fire 409 V-8	409 cid, 4-bbl	11.0	400 @ 5800
Turbo-Fire 409 V-8	409 cid, 2x4-bbl	11.0	425 @ 6000

1963 Chevrolet Impala Two-door Hardtop		
Engine	409 cid, 4-bbl	327 cid, 4-bbl
Compression	10.0:1	10.5:1
Horsepower	340 @ 5000	250 @ 4400
Torque	420 @ 3200	350 @ 2800
Transmission	Two-speed Powerglide	Two-speed Powerglide
Rear Axle	3.36 ratio, positraction	3.08 ratio
Weight	3,877 lbs	3,829 lbs
Wheelbase	119 in	119 in
Tires	8.00x14, 4-ply	7.50x14, 2-ply
Fuel Economy	12 mpg	14 mpg
Performance		
0-60 mph	6.6 sec	10.4 sec
0-100 mph	19.4 sec	n/a
Quarter-Mile E.T.	15.2 sec	17.8 sec
Quarter-Mile Speed	90.0 mph	78.0 mph
Top Speed	124 mph	106 mph

References for 1963

1963 Chevrolet Police Cars, Chevrolet Motor Division

Illustrated Chevrolet Buyers Guide, John Gunnell, Motorbooks International

Chevrolet Impala and SS, 1958-1971, R.M. Clarke, Motorbooks International

75 Years of Chevrolet, George Dammann, Motorbooks International

Standard Catalog of Chevrolet 1912-1990, Pat Chappell, Krause Publications

"Chevy for 1963," Robert Ackerson, Standard Catalog of Chevrolet 1912-1990

Chapter 10

1964: Chevelle Mid-Size Police Car

This award-winning Vermilion County, Illinois, Sheriff Bel Air is one of the best Chevy squad cars on the police car show circuit. It is powered by a 283-cid V-8. (Jennifer Sturgeon)

The full-size Chevrolet was generally unchanged for 1964. The chassis equipment Z04 and body equipment B01 police packages were once again based on the Biscayne trim level in two-door, four-door and station wagon.

Again, Chevrolet pushed six different option packages as a way to make police car buying more sensible and more specific for the task:

"Designed for all around utility work where outstanding economy is the prime consideration" was the 140 hp Turbo-Thrift 230-cid Six package.

"Specify this package when urban cruising and pursuit are prime requirements. Big displacement V-8 delivers peak performance on regular gasoline" was the 230 hp Special Turbo Fire 327-cid V-8 package.

"Designed for high-speed highway pursuit. High torque engine delivers outstanding acceleration and performance" was the 340 hp Turbo-Fire 409-cid V-8 package.

The 400 hp and 425 hp versions of this 409-cid big-block were mentioned but definitely not emphasized. This would be the last year for either of these two high compression, big-block engines in police cars. As a performance reference, an Impala retail car equipped with the single four-barrel carb, 400 hp version of the 409 reached 60 mph in 7.5 seconds and ran the quarter-mile in a sizzling 15.3 seconds. Again, these high-torque engines were limited by relatively skinny tires.

The British car magazine, *Motor*, tested the Chevrolet Impala 283-cid engine, with two-barrel carb, with Powerglide in its August 1964 issue. The large V-8 engine, imposing overall size, low feedback steering, mere two-speed transmission and thirsty 15.3 mpg fuel economy was a bit of a culture shock. They could not even imagine a 409 big-block of any horsepower rating let alone the 425 hp dual four-barrel version. Their 283-cid test car hit 60 mph in 12.7 seconds, ran the quarter-mile in 19.2 seconds and had a top speed of 108.3 mph.

In 1964, Chevrolet introduced a totally new line of mid-size cars under the name Chevelle.

Nameplate	Overall Length	Wheelbase	Width
Biscayne	209.9 in	119.0 in	79.6 in
Chevelle	183.9 in	115.0 in	74.6 in
Chevy II	182.9 in	110.0 in	69.9 in

As a side note, the 1994 mid-size Chevelle had the same 115-inch wheelbase as the 1955 full-size One Fifty and was close to the 115.9-inch full-size 1996 Caprice.

The Chevelle was offered as both a retail car and with the police packages in a wide variety of drivetrain options. While the Chevelle quickly caught on with the enthusiasts, it was not at all popular with cops until the late-1970s. Police officers wanted long wheelbase cars, period. They went to mid-sized cars only when forced to do it. It was only the success of the Nova police car, developed in the mid-1970s by *Motor Trend* magazine and the Los Angeles County Sheriffs Department, that paved the way for the Chevelle under the Malibu name to become widely accepted as a police car in the late-1970s.

This Ankeny, Iowa, Police 1964 Biscayne is a straight and clean urban cruiser. Note the siren in front of the beacon. (John Evers)

The Chevelle was introduced to the retail market in two series. These were the Chevelle 300 in two-door and four-door sedans and four-door station wagons, and the Chevelle Malibu in four-door sedan, two-door hardtop, convertible and station wagon. The B01 and Z04 full-duty police packages were available for only the low-price 300 four-door sedan. The Chevelle shared its body platform with the Oldsmobile F-85, Pontiac Tempest and Buick Skylark.

With the release of the Chevelle, Chevrolet introduced yet a third basic frame and suspension in its police car lines. The full-size Biscayne used the cruciform frame with full coil suspension. The midsize Chevelle had the perimeter frame and coil suspension while the Chevy II was designed with the unitized body and coil front suspen-sion with single leaf rear suspension. The Chevelle's platform was officially called "torque box design perimeter frame."

The Chevelle police car was available in four powerplants: 194-cid/120-hp Six; 230-cid/155-hp Six; 283-cid/195-hp V-8 and 283-cid/220-hp V-8. The 194-cid Six was transferred from the previous year's Chevy II. The 230-cid Six was similar to the same engine used in the full-size Biscayne, except the Chevelle version produced 15 more horsepower. The Biscayne Six used an "economy-contoured" cam while the Chevelle Six used a "general performance" cam.

The two-barrel version of the 283-cid V-8 used at 195 hp was shared by all three 1964 Chevrolet police platforms: Biscayne, Chevelle and Chevy II. New and exclusive to the Chevelle among po-

The 1964 Chevrolets such as this Ankeny, Iowa, Police unit were available with engines from the 230-cid/140-hp Six to the 409-cid/425-hp V-8. (John Evers)

Police had their choice of three bowtie cruisers in 1964: the 119-inch Biscayne such as this Eureka Springs, Arkansas, Police unit, the 115-inch Chevelle and the 110-inch Chevy II. (Jim Post)

The 1964 model year was the last for the high compression versions of the 409-cid engines. The 400-hp, single four-barrel Biscayne ran the quarter-mile in 15 seconds. (Jim Post)

lice cars was the four-barrel version of the 283-cid V-8, which now produced 220 hp. This engine required premium fuel. This was quite comparable to the 327-cid Special Police V-8 in the Biscayne, which produced 230 hp on regular fuel.

The Chevelle police engines could be teamed with four transmissions: three-speed Synchro-Mesh, four-speed Synchro-Mesh, two-speed Powerglide automatic and three-speed Synchro-Mesh Overdrive. The four-speed was restricted to V-8 engines. The three-speed used with the sixes was a wide-ratio while the three-speed bolted to the V-8s had closer spaced gearing. RPO Z04 included 14-inch wheels and 7.50x14 oversize rayon cord tires instead of the 6.50x14 retail car tires.

The Chevy II was back in police trim for 1964 with a much wider selection of drivetrains. The 194-cid/120-hp Six was standard; however, the 153-cid/90-hp Super Thrift four was back in the lineup. The bigger news was the more powerful Chevy II engines including the 283-cid V-8.

New for 1964 was the 230-cid/155-hp version of the Turbo Thrift Six. Chevy II shared this engine with the Chevelle. Again, the 230-cid Six used in the mid-size and compact Chevys had more power than the version used in the full-size Chevy. Both engines had an 8.5:1 compression, one-barrel carb, hydraulic lifters and single exhaust. The difference was strictly the cam grind. The 140 hp version used in the

Biscayne had the "economy contoured" cam lobes. The 155 hp version used in the Chevelle and Chevy II used a "general performance" lift and duration.

The Chevy II was available with a three-speed Synchro-Mesh, four-speed Synchro-Mesh and two-speed Powerglide automatic depending on the engine. While 13-inch wheels and 6.00x13 tires were standard, 14-inch wheels and tires were optional.

In 1964, for the first time, the Chevy II was offered to cops with a V-8. This is the same 195 hp, two-barrel version of the 283-cid V-8 used by all three Chevrolet police cars. This was the first glimpse of the Nova police car that would revolutionize all police cars, not just the mid-size class, in the mid-1970s.

Little is heard of the Chevelle and Chevy II before the famous Los Angeles Sheriffs Department Nova, but these two Chevy police cars actually had been in service since the early-1960s. It took a national energy crisis to realize what good squad cars the Chevelle and Chevy II really were. This would be the last year for the Chevy II police car for a while. But it would be back.

Biscayne Police Engines for 1964			
Engine	Size & Carb	Comp.	Horsepower
Turbo-Thrift 230 Six	230 cid, 1-bbl	8.5	140 @ 4400
Turbo-Fire 283 V-8	283 cid, 2-bbl	9.25	195 @ 4800
Special Turbo-Fire 327 V-8	327 cid, 4-bbl	8.6	230 @ 4400
Turbo-Fire 327 V-8 (L30)	327 cid, 4-bbl	10.5	250 @ 4400
Turbo-Fire 327 V-8 (L74)	327 cid, 4-bbl	10.5	300 @ 5000
Turbo-Fire 409 V-8 (L33)	409 cid, 4-bbl	10.0	340 @ 5000
Turbo-Fire 409 V-8 (L31)	409 cid, 4-bbl	11.0	400 @ 5800
Turbo-Fire 409 V-8 (L80)	409 cid, 2x4-bbl	11.0	425 @ 6000

1964 Chevrolet Biscayne	
Engine	283 cid
Carb	2-bbl
Horsepower	195 hp
Transmission	Powerglide
Axle	3.36
Wheelbase	119 in
0-60 mph	12.7 sec
Quarter-Mile E.T.	19.2 sec
Top Speed	108.3 mph
Fuel Economy	15.3 mpg

Chevelle and Chevy II Police Engines for 1964				
Engine	Size & Carb	Comp.	HP	Car Line
Super-Thrift 153 Four	153 cid, 1-bbl	8.5	90 @ 4000	Chevy II only
Hi-Thrift 194 Six	194 cid, 1-bbl	8.5	120 @ 4400	Chevy II, Chevelle
Turbo-Thrift 230 Six	230 cid, 1-bbl	8.5	155 @ 4400	Chevy II, Chevelle
Turbo-Fire 283 V-8	283 cid, 2-bbl	9.25	195 @ 4800	Chevy II, Chevelle
Turbo-Fire 283 V-8	283 cid, 4-bbl	9.25	220 @ 4800	Chevelle only

References for 1964

1964 Chevrolet Police Cars, Chevrolet Motor Division

75 Years of Chevrolet, George Dammann, Motorbooks International

Chevrolet Impala and SS, 1958-1971, R.M. Clarke, Motorbooks International

Standard Catalog of Chevrolet 1912-1990, Pat Chappell, Krause Publications

Illustrated Chevrolet Buyers Guide, John Gunnell, Motorbooks International

Chapter 11

1965: 396 and Turbo Hydra-Matic

For 1965, Chevrolet dramatically restyled the Biscayne sedan. The sheet metal was changed from the square lines of 1964 to a much more rounded, fuselage shape. More importantly, these new body panels were mounted on a brand new chassis.

This was the year of the "wide stance" look and it started with a full perimeter "girder-guard" frame. The old Safety-Girder X-frame was replaced with full length box rails and four cross-members. At the point where the frame narrows to clear the front wheels, a special torque box was added. This torque box construction controlled flexing and prevented stress concentrations in this critical area.

From this model year on, cops strongly favored the Chevy full-frame type of police construction. The unibody concept pioneered on Dodge and Plymouths in 1957 was never fully accepted by law enforcement and was certainly never perceived as an advantage such as the Chrysler torsion bar front suspension. The full-frame, Body by Fisher would remain a strong selling point among cops for three decades. It was simply considered stronger and more durable.

For 1965, Chevrolet also increased the track of the Biscayne. The front tread increased by a full 2.2 inches while the rear tread was widened by an impressive 3.1 inches. This made the cars more laterally stable at pursuit speeds.

The front suspension was a new strut rod independent design. Along with control arms, the angled strut rods gave improved control over bumps and holes. The rear end got a new link-type suspension. This included new short suspension arms and a critical; lateral-control, panhard rod. This increased rear end roll stiffness without increasing the spring rate.

The Biscaynes still understeered but not as badly and once the suspension was set after entering a turn, the car could be steered with the gas pedal much easier. This was especially true of the engine with 300 hp or more.

For 1965, the Biscayne was the low-priced series among the full-size Chevrolets. The police packages were once again based on the Biscayne in two-door and four-door sedan and four-door station wagon. The more expensive trim levels were Bel Air, Impala and Super Sport.

The frame change, wider stance and slightly longer overall length resulted in a heavier vehicle, but not as much as might be expected. The '64 four-door checked in at 3,305 pounds while the same trim level '65 four-door weighed 3,380 pounds.

The 1965 model year started off with most of the same engine options as the 1964 model year, at least for the Biscaynes. One change was the lack of the 409-cid big-block either in 400 hp or 425 hp versions. These never were popular police engines and neither of them was available on '65 police cars. The most potent engine was the 340 hp version of the 409.

The only other change to the engine lineup at the beginning of the model year was to the Special Police 327-cid/230-hp engine. The compression was boosted from 8.6:1 to 8.75:1 without a change in horsepower. The police literature lists this engine as having a two-barrel carb but this is with near certainty in error. All other vintages of the 327-cid/230-hp V-8 used a four-barrel carb and the repair manuals make no mention of a two-barrel version.

The big news for engine options was the February 1965 mid-year releases. The W-block V-8 introduced in 1958 as a 348-cid "truck" engine and in 1961 as a 409 was phased out. The Mark IV production engine based on the 1963 Mark II "Daytona Mystery Engine" was introduced. This was now the famous 396-cid big-block complete with the "porcupine head" valve layout.

The canted-valve, "porcupine head" gets its name from the angle of the valve train. Fisher & Waar offer an excellent description of the canted-valve layout:

"For maximum volumetric efficiency current design theory holds that inlet and outlet ports must be as straight as possible, consistent with surrounding component design requirements, and have a minimum change in shape. Inlet and exhaust-port configuration, as well as inlet and exhaust-valve positioning, are worked out with extreme care to produce the optimum induction and exhaust-flow characteristics.

The police Biscayne was restyled for 1965 with a new full-perimeter frame and a wide-stance look. (Chevrolet)

In mid-1965, Chevrolet released a blockbuster police powertrain: the 396-cid big-block teamed with the three-speed Turbo-HydraMatic. (Chevrolet)

"Because of Chevrolet's independent ball-stud rocker-arm arrangement and individual inlet and exhaust porting in the heads, it was possible to cant the inlet valve toward the inlet port. The result is unrestricted inlet ports with fairly uniform cross-section to reduce the changes of direction that the fuel/air mixture must make to enter the combustion chamber. However, because of differences in the angles at which the inlet ports enter the cylinders, two cylinders on each side breathe considerably better than their mates.

"Although both the intake and the exhaust valves have been tipped toward their respective ports, the inlet valves have been favored in the carefully thought out design. Intake valves are set at an angle of 26 degrees to the cylinder bore axis and the exhaust valves are set at 17 degrees when viewed from the front or rear of the engine. Viewed from the side of the engine both valves tilt 5 degrees away from this same axis. The combustion chamber is an elongated cavity rotated 18 degrees from the longitudinal axis of the head.

"In taking advantage of the tilted exhaust valves, the exhaust ports have a large radius, producing a gradual direction change and an unrestricted uniform cross-section throughout their length.

"The merits of this canted-valve cylinder-head design stack up like building blocks. Offsetting exhaust valves toward outer cylinder walls minimizes exhaust port lengths to reduce heat loss into the coolant. Individual porting for each cylinder and the versatility of independent rocker-arm systems provides still another benefit. Keep in mind that inlet and exhaust valves within the same combustion chamber are tilted away from each other along the engine longitudinal axis, as well as the transverse axis. This causes the valve heads to move away from the adjacent cylinder walls as each valve opens, instead of paralleling them. Unshrouding the valves in this manner improves incoming and outgoing gas flow which increases the volume of mixture drawn into the cylinder for each engine cycle.

"The modified-wedge-type combustion chamber has a large quench area for cooling the mixture so that detonation is minimized and a centrally located spark plug, which results in uniform flame propagation across the top of the piston. The compactness of the chamber improves thermal efficiency by reducing the ratio of chamber surface to chamber volume.

"In this design there is relatively little piston surface exposed to the high temperatures of combustion; therefore there is less heat to be dissipated through the piston head to the skirts...and into the cylinder walls."

The Chevrolet big-block weighs about 680 pounds with all cast iron components. With aluminum heads, this "rat" engine weighs 610 pounds. The big-block with aluminum heads and an aluminum block weighs just 460 pounds. Recall that the cast iron-equipped small-block tips the scales at 550 pounds.

The first appearance of a "rat" engine with "porcupine" valves was the February 1963 Daytona 500 where Junior Johnson stunned the crowd with 166 mph speeds. His car was powered by the Chevrolet Mark II 427-cid "Mystery Engine." This remained a rare, NASCAR racing engine for two years. Then in February 1965, as a mid-year engine, Chevrolet released the Turbo-Jet 396 V-8 based on the porcupine head Mystery Engine.

Chevrolet engineers and enthusiasts refer to the big-blocks as "Mark" engines. Mark I was the wedge block 348- and 409-cid series of engines. Mark II was the 427-cid Mystery Engine first used at the 1963 Daytona NASCAR race. Mark III was a developmental engine that resulted in the 396-cid big-block but was never released. Mark IV is the 396-, 402- 427- and 454-cid Turbo-Jet series of engines that were produced from 1965 through 1976 for passenger cars. The Turbo-Jet 454 is still produced as a Chevrolet truck engine.

The big-block Chevrolet V-8s, starting with the canted-valve 396 in 1965, are among the most potent engines ever produced. These engines rival the exotic Chrysler Corporation 426-cid hemi engine for sheer power output and breathing. In fact, these canted-valve Chevy big-blocks are called semi-hemi engines.

One big difference exists between these two styles of engine. The complex and expensive Chrysler 426-cid hemi was never a police package engine. On the other hand, the equally potent 396-, 427- and 454-cid engines were all used in multiple thousands of ordinary Chevy police cars from mid-1965 through 1976.

The 396-cid big-block was available in three horsepower versions: 325 hp, 375 hp and 425 hp. The only one even rumored for police 1965 Biscaynes was the 325 hp engine. Most police package cars are produced in one or two special runs near the beginning of the model year. This is done to meet police fiscal budgets that typically end in December and start again in January. Frequently, the first cars produced in any one model year are police package cars. Almost no police production runs are made past the mid-year mark. For this reason, the mid-year engine releases had almost no effect on actual in-service police cars. While it is certainly possible for a '65 Biscayne police package car to have a 396-cid V-8, it is unlikely.

Also released mid-year were a more powerful small-block and a brand new Six. The small-block was a four-barrel version of the 283 pumping out 220 hp. This was an available police engine but, again, for a limited time. This four-barrel carbureted engine was not carried-over for the 1966 model year as a formal police engine.

The 250-cid, one-barrel carbureted Six was new for mid-year 1965. Producing 150 hp, this heavy-duty Six would power police cars for the next six years straight. It would be dropped from 1972 to 1976 but be back again in 1977. The new 250-cid Six was basically a stroked version of the old 230-cid Six:

Engine	230 cid	250 cid
Bore	3.875 in	3.875 in
Stroke	3.25 in	3.53 in

With the release of the 396-cid rat engine, Chevrolet started new engine technology. For the rest of the 1960s, the six-cylinder engine would be called Turbo-Thrift, the small-block V-8 would be named Turbo-Fire, and big-block V-8 would bear the title Turbo-Jet.

At least as important as the 396-cid engine, in mid-1965 Chevrolet released its brand new, and long overdue, three-speed Turbo Hydra-Matic transmission. All things considered, the two-speed Powerglide was not a very good transmission, in spite of being popular. It had a high rate of repair since its introduction.

The Powerglide was introduced in 1950 for the DeLuxe series only. By 1954, this two-speed automatic became available on the One Fifty models most used by cops. By 1965, historian John Gunnell noted, "surveys showed heavy transmission problems in 1965, which might be why the Turbo Hydra-Matic was phased-in late that year."

In contrast to the Powerglide, the Turbo Hydra-Matic was indeed a great transmission. Objective and unbiased auto enthusiasts regard the General Motors Turbo Hydra-Matic to be in nearly the same durability class as the Chrysler TorqueFlite. Chevy police cars were badly in need of a rugged three-speed automatic to keep pace with Plymouth

The 283-cid small-block was the most popular police engine for city police work. In mid-1965, a 155-hp, four-barrel version of this V-8 was released.

The 250-cid inline Six was new for 1965. This was a stroked version of the 230-cid Six. This 155-hp Six would power police cars through 1979. (Greg Reynolds)

The police package 1965 Chevelle was available only with a fuel-miser, 194-cid Six. This mid-size was used strictly for non-emergency work. (Chevrolet)

and Ford. Now they had one, even though the two-speed Powerglide continued to be available.

Also new for mid-1965 was the name Caprice. RPO Z18 was the Caprice Custom Sedan option to the Impala four-door sedan retail car. This is the first use of the name that would carry Chevrolet police cars from 1987 through 1996. The Z18 package included a heavier frame, suspension changes, black-accented grille and rear trim panel, special wheel covers and Caprice hood emblems. The '65 Caprice sedan equipped with the 325 hp version of the new 396-cid big-block and the new three-speed Turbo Hydra-Matic accelerated to 60 mph in 8.4 seconds and ran the quarter-mile in 16.5 seconds.

The larger and heavier full-size Chevys got bigger wheels for 1965. The small-block and convertible retail cars used 7.75x14 tires while the big-block and station wagon retail cars got 8.25x14 rubber. In contrast, the police cars continued to use 15-inch tires. This year the 7.75x15 rubber was mounted on one-half-inch wider, 15x5.5 inch wheels.

In late-1964, *Car & Driver* test drove a 409-cid/340-hp Chevrolet with a two-speed Powerglide:

"Driving the 409 SS is not the startling experience one might expect. The 420 pound-feet of torque are always in greater evidence than the 340 horsepower. Even within the rather limited scope of Chevrolet's venerable two-speed Powerglide unit, there were no low spots in the 409's performance and it accelerated smoothly from any speed. Our test car was equipped with the standard 3.31 rear axle, which is a lovely ratio for turnpikes and open road cruising, but won't break any records in the stoplight Grand Prix.

"Without punishing the transmission, and with two people in the car, the 409 SS ran an easy 16.4-second standing quarter-mile and might have been persuaded into the mid-

15 second zone by really trying. The whole trip was very subdued and there was very little impression of the big beast traveling over 90 mph at the end of the trap.

"Handling is not exactly what you might expect from a massive 1965 car, but it is there. The well-located suspension gives a soft, relatively roll-free ride with the standard dose of understeer. This latter trait is probably exaggerated in the 409 version, due to the powerplant's considerable margin in weight over the standard 327. Nonetheless, the automobile is perfectly mannerly and the understeer is both predictable and controllable.

"Once the car has been thrust into a fast corner and its customary attitude of understeer has been established, it can be pointed by throttle adjustments in very satisfactory fashion. The car is nose-heavy enough so that too much power will cause the rear end to slew off line in what might be mistaken as oversteer. Chevrolet does have an RPO handling kit available for the car that includes heavier springs and shock absorbers and this may correct the situation."

The chassis RPO *Car & Driver* referred to was, of course, the Z04 police package. In the same year, the British magazine *Autosport* tested a 283-cid-powered Impala with a Powerglide:

"Standing starts do not provoke wheelspin and from a standing to 60 mph takes just over 12 seconds... a maximum of 107 mph is reached on the longer straights."

Big changes took place to the Chevelle and Chevy II police cars. The Chevy II was *not* available in a police package for 1965. The choice of engines on the police Chevelle dropped from four in 1964 to just one in 1965: the 194-cid/120-hp Six.

After just one year as a police car, Chevrolet quickly discovered the Chevelle was being used for strictly detective and non-emergency use, period. Since this was taxi-class police work, Chevrolet wisely offered just the thriftiest six-cylinder engine. The two-barrel and four-barrel carbureted 283-cid V-8s and even the 230-cid engine were simply overkill for the dull duty performed by these Chevelles.

In 1965, the year of the greatest domestic automobile sales in history, and a moment that many experts view as the apogee of the car business, 1,068,614 Impalas (plus 94,364 Caprices, which are little more than a deluxe Impala) were sold—11 percent of all the cars unloaded in the United States that year! Its sales exceeded the combined output of all its rivals: Galaxie 500, Fury III, Coronet and Catalina, and established the Impala, for the entire period of the middle 1960s, as America's four-wheeled sweetheart.

Chevrolet Big-Block Police V-8 Engines				
cid	Bore	Stroke	Head Design	Police Era
348	4.125	3.250	wedge block	1958-1961
396	4.094	3.760	porcupine	1965-1969
402	4.126	3.760	porcupine	1972
409	4.312	3.500	wedge block	1962-1965
427	4.251	3.760	porcupine	1966-1969
454	4.251	4.000	porcupine	1970-1976

Biscayne Engines for 1965			
Engine	Size & Carb	Comp.	HP
Turbo-Thrift Six	230 cid, 1-bbl	8.5	140 @ 4400
Turbo-Fire 283 V-8	283 cid, 2-bbl	9.25	195 @ 4800
Turbo-Fire 327 V-8	327 cid, 2-bbl	8.75	230 @ 4400
Turbo-Fire 327 V-8 (L30)	327 cid, 4-bbl	10.5	250 @ 4400
Turbo-Fire 327 V-8 (L74)	327 cid, 4-bbl	10.5	300 @ 5000
Turbo-Fire 409 V-8 (L33)	409 cid, 4-bbl	10.0	340 @ 5000
Mid-Year (February) Releases			
Turbo-Thrift Six (L22)	250 cid, 1-bbl		155 @ 4200
Turbo-Fire 283 V-8 (L77)	283 cid, 4-bbl		220 @ 4800
Turbo-Jet 396 V-8 (L35)	396 cid, 4-bbl		325 @ 4800

References for 1965

75 Years of Chevrolet, George Dammann, Motorbooks International

Illustrated Chevrolet Buyers Guide, John Gunnell, Motorbooks International

1965 Chevrolet Police Cars, Chevrolet Motor Division

Chevrolet Impala and SS, 1958-1971, R.M. Clarke, Motorbooks International

Standard Catalog of Chevrolet 1912-1990, Pat Chappell, Krause Publications

Chapter 12

1966: 427-cid Big-Block

New for 1966, the porcupine-head, canted-valve 396-cid big-block was bored out to 427 cid. The 390-hp version was available to cops. (Greg Reynolds)

In 1966, Chevrolet expanded its full-size retail series to five cars: Biscayne, Bel Air, Impala, Super Sport and now Caprice. The Caprice had been a trim option in 1965.

The changes to the sheet metal on the full-size sedans were minor. The '65s have parking lamps in the grille in a narrow front bumper and two round, small taillight lenses per side for the Biscayne. The '66s have parking lamps in a wide front bumper and large, horizontal rear lenses.

The main Chevrolet police cars for 1966 were specifically built around the Biscayne and the upscale Bel Air. The Chevelle and Chevy II are not covered in the official police literature except for this note:

"The chassis, body and engine items listed on these two pages in six groupings represent police engine packages that include the items most wanted by law enforcement agencies. However, if preferred, any Chevrolet model (including those in Chevelle and Chevy II lines) may be ordered with whatever separate extra-cost Options are best suited to your department's requirements."

It was becoming harder to tell a Chevy police car from a retail car. In fact, as in past years, the Z04 police chassis and B01 police body packages seemed to be heavy-duty RPOs that could be ordered on literally any Chevy. It was these two packages that made a Chevy police car.

The six groupings referred to in the police literature were the six standard police combinations with the shortest delivery time. Other combinations were apparently available but would have either longer lead times, or be subject to a minimum order or both. The Chevrolet literature makes it clear, "Other engines and transmissions are available details from your Chevrolet dealer."

Police-Duty Power Team Selector		
Engine-all models	**Transmission**	**Axle Ratio**
390 hp Turbo-Jet 427 V-8	three-speed four-speed (2.52:1 Low) four-speed (2.20:1 Low)	3.31
	Turbo Hydra-Matic	3.07
325 hp Turbo-Jet 396 V-8	three-speed four-speed (2.52:1 Low) Powerglide Turbo Hydra-Matic	3.07
275 hp Turbo-Fire 327 V-8	three-speed four-speed (2.54:1 Low) Powerglide Overdrive	3.31 3.07 3.73
230 hp Turbo-Fire 327 V-8	three-speed four-speed (2.54:1 Low) Powerglide Overdrive	3.31 3.73
195 hp Turbo-Fire 283 V-8	three-speed Powerglide Overdrive	3.31 3.73
155 hp Turbo-Thrift six-cylinder	three-speed Powerglide Overdrive	3.31 3.73

The 427-cid/390-hp Chevrolet four-door sedan reached 60 mph in 7 seconds and ran the quarter-mile in 15 seconds. (Greg Reynolds)

This 1966 NYPD Biscayne was assigned to Staten Island. This was the first year for the huge McDermott raised arm emergency lights. (Ned Schwartz)

The 250-cid/155-hp Six was the new standard Six for 1966. This was introduced mid-year 1965. The 275 hp version of the 327-cid small-block was also new for 1966. This is midway between the 250 hp and 300 hp engines from '65. The 325 hp rated 396-cid rat engine was introduced in mid-1965. This was the big-block police engine that made the most sense. It did everything the 409-cid/340-hp V-8 could do, but better.

Only the big-blocks were available with the great Turbo Hydra-Matic three-speed transmission. The small-blocks had to make do with the two-speed Powerglide, which is yet another good excuse to pick the big-block.

Chevrolet wanted to make it clear the 396 was both new and special:

"One of Chevrolet's newest and most advanced V-8 designs. Develops 325 horsepower at 4800 rpm from 396 cubic inches. A strong cylinder block forms the foundation for this remarkable engine. Wide-base main bearing caps clamp the crankshaft against sturdy bearing bulkheads. Main and connecting rod bearings are extra durable. Cylin-

der heads are entirely new and include individually spaced inlet and exhaust ports, valves which tilt in fore-and-aft directions as well as from side to side and reduce the change of direction required by the incoming fuel-air charge. Other standard features: four-barrel carburetor, hydraulic valve lifters, permanently sealed fuel pump with an extra-large diaphragm, 2-1/2-inch single exhaust system with muffler and resonator, independent operating mechanism for each valve, new automatic choke, positive-shift starter."

As good an engine as the 396-cid V-8 was, it was instantly overshadowed by the mighty 427-cid big-block available in police cars for 1966.

"Chevrolet's largest displacement V-8 engine. Develops 390 horsepower at 5200 rpm from 427 cubic inches with four-barrel carburetor and hydraulic valve lifters. Basic design features are identical to the 396-cid V-8 hefty cylinder block, extra-rigid crankshaft clamping, strong main and connecting rod bearings. Inclined-valve cylinder heads with individual intake and exhaust ports provide extremely free breathing for outstanding efficiency. Additional features of this 390 hp engine: full dual exhaust system with precision-cast large free-flow alloy iron exhaust manifolds; 2-1/2-inch diameter exhaust pipes; and oval reverse-flow mufflers."

Engine	396 cid	427 cid
Bore	4.094 in	4.251 in
Stroke	3.760 in	3.760 in

The 427-cid big-block was available in a 390 hp "street" version and a 425 hp "special" version. The cops got the street version to chase the kid with the special version.

These full-size Chevys were quick. *Car & Driver* tested a 427-cid Caprice with three-speed Turbo Hydra-Matic against a 428-cid Ford Custom with the three-speed C6 Cruise-O-Matic. The big-block 390 hp Chevy reached 60 mph in 7.6 seconds compared to 8.1 seconds for the big-block 360 hp Ford. The 427-cid Chevy ran the quarter-mile

This 1966 Biscayne station wagon was used by the Montreal Police as an ambulance. These were extremely durable. (John Carroll)

A 1966 NYPD Biscayne on patrol in mid-town Manhattan. This is the only year in the 1960s the NYPD used Chevrolets. (Ned Schwartz)

in 15.7 seconds at 90 mph. This easily beat the 428-cid Ford's 16.5 second and 83 mph performance.

In other drivetrain news, the three-speed Synchro-Mesh was now fully synchronized in all forward gears. This allowed the officer to downshift into first while the squad car was still moving. For decades, first gear was not synchronized. The car had to be stopped before the transmission could be put in first gear. That was a real hassle and it resulted in a lot of chipped gears from frustration.

The four-speed Synchro-Mesh was available with the 327-cid and larger V-8s. This came in M20 wide-ratio and M21 close-ratio versions. The close-ratio four-speed was available only on the 427-cid/390-hp police engine. The three-speed Turbo Hydra-Matic was available with any big-block engine. The two-speed Powerglide was still available on the 250-cid Six right up to the Turbo-Jet 396.

The Australian car magazine, *Modern Motor*, tested a '66 Chevy with the 327-cid/230-hp four-barrel carbureted V-8. They were happy enough with the straight line performance from the Powerglide-equipped, four-door sedan. With 3.55 rear gears, the Chevy hit 60 mph in 10.0 seconds and 100 mph in 38.6 seconds. The sedan ran the quarter-mile in 18.2 seconds and had an absolute top speed of 102.8 mph.

Like all of the motoring public *Modern Motor* wanted an extra gear in the transmission, which is where the Turbo Hydra-Matic comes in. They were not happy with the 11-inch drum brakes and that was based on the low-power 230 hp sedan. It would be one more model year before front disc brakes were an option. Their biggest complaint was with the soft suspension that allowed too much roll and wheel spin even with a new torque link. The simple addition of the Z04 police suspension package would have solved the handling problem on this non-police, retail Impala.

Road Test magazine was on hand when the Los Angeles Police and Los Angeles County Sheriffs Departments tested squad cars for 1966. This was an era when both agencies forbid power steering because it reduced road feel at pursuit speeds. Likewise, power brakes were not allowed and this meant disc brakes were not allowed. The pedal pressure with disc brakes is so high that in nearly all cases disc brake cars got a vacuum-power assist.

Then as now, the L.A.-area cop tests involved a series of 90 mph panic stops followed by a 60 mph stop for score. The sintered-metal shod Biscayne passed easily. The squads were then run around the two-mile road racing course laid out on the L.A. County fairgrounds in Pomona. The police pursuit driving instructors check for body roll, suspension stability and throttle and brake response during this preliminary handling review.

The average lap speeds for these 1966 police package cars were:

Plymouth Belvedere	383-cid/330-hp	82.77 mph
Oldsmobile 88	425-cid/370-hp	82.17 mph
Dodge Coronet	383-cid/330-hp	81.47 mph
Chevrolet Biscayne	396-cid/325-hp	81.44 mph
Oldsmobile F-85	330-cid/320-hp	80.54 mph
Ford Custom	390-cid/315-hp	disqualified

Cars that passed the preliminary handling review were eligible to bid on the police contract. The low bid in 1966 for both the LAPD and LASD was the Belvedere. The Biscayne would capture the LASD contract the next year.

About the big-block Chevy, *Road Test* wrote:

"All observers commented on the excellent brakes (Morain metallic) which exhibited consistently minimum required pedal pressures and straight, smooth stopping power.

"Another comment from all was the improvement noted over previous Chevrolets submitted for testing. The front suspension has been improved greatly compared to former years. The car oversteers slightly and its back end swings out moderately but seems relatively easy to control. The Chevy does not roll in turns as in previous years and is acceptable as a patrol car.

"This change from earlier examples submitted is credited to Chevy engineers who have been pressed by the fleet sales department to come up with suspension packages which will pass the LA Police tests."

In addition to the Chicago Police, the Dallas Police, New York City Police, and Suffolk County, New York, Police all drove Chevrolet police cars.

Chevrolet Police Engines for 1966			
Engine	**Size & Carb**	**Comp.**	**HP**
Turbo-Thrift Six	250 cid 1-bbl	8.5	155 @ 4200
Turbo-Fire 283 V-8	283 cid 2-bbl	9.25	195 @ 4800
Turbo-Fire 327 V-8	327 cid 4-bbl	8.75	230 @ 4400
Turbo-Fire 327 V-8	327 cid 4-bbl	10.5	275 @ 4800
Turbo-Jet 396 V-8	396 cid 4-bbl	10.25	325 @ 4800
Turbo-Jet 427 V-8	427 cid 4-bbl	10.25	390 @ 5200

References for 1966

75 Years of Chevrolet, George Dammann, Motorbooks International

Illustrated Chevrolet Buyers Guide, John Gunnell, Motorbooks International

1966 Chevrolet Police Cars, Chevrolet Motor Division

Chevrolet Impala and SS, 1958-1971, R.M. Clarke, Motorbooks International

Standard Catalog of Chevrolet 1912-1990, Pat Chappell, Krause Publications

"Police Test the '66s," staff report, *Road Test*, May 1966

Chapter 13

1967: Front Disc Brakes

Front disc brakes were new for Chevrolet police cars in 1967. These had so much pedal pressure that vacuum-assisted power brakes were mandatory when discs were ordered. (Chevrolet)

The rear suspension and steering linkage on the 119-inch B-body was tweaked for 1967. This was the first year for the energy-absorbing steering column. (Chevrolet)

For 1967, the full-size Chevrolet was significantly restyled but retained the 119-inch wheelbase. The car line continued to be divided into five series: Biscayne, Bel Air, Impala, Super Sport, and Caprice. The high volume police packages were once again based on the Biscayne and Bel Air two-door and four-door sedans and four-door station wagon.

In 1967, Chevrolet introduced the Camaro as an answer to the Ford Mustang. The Camaro was not available with a police package and would not even be considered for police use until 1979. In 1979, the California Highway Patrol began its Special Purpose Vehicle Study. This involved four very different police cars in four highly specialized roles. One of these was the 1979 Camaro Z28. The Z28 proved a pony car would work for police use but was outbid by the Mustang, which became the darling of the CHP fleet in 1982.

The U.S. Border Patrol used Camaros and Firebirds in the mid-1980s as drug interdiction pursuit vehicles but these were retail cars. It was not until 1991 that Chevrolet released the B4C Special Service Package for the Camaro. The '91 Camaro B4C immediately took the police top gun status from the Mustang 5.0 HO.

In 1967, both the 302-cid and 350-cid V-8s were released. The 350-cid engine used the same bore as the 327-cid V-8 but the stroke was increased again to 3.480 inches. The 302-cid V-8 was intended specifically as a SCCA Trans-Am racing engine. The 302-cid engine used the same 4.001-inch bore as the 327 and 350 engines. However, it used the shorter 3.000-inch stroke of the 283-cid V-8 to stay inside the 5.0-liter Trans Am engine limit. All these engines had the same rod and main journal sizes, the same rod lengths and the same bore spacings.

The 1967 302-cid V-8 was a de-tuned (but only slightly) factory racing engine. SCCA Trans-Am racing rules required the race engine be based closely on the street engine. Chevrolet simply de-stroked the 327 but kept the awesome 2.02-inch intake and 1.60-inch exhaust valves. This made it "over-valved" for the street with 290 hp from a single four-barrel carb. However, in race trim, the engine was perfectly flowed to produce 450 hp from dual four-barrel Holley carbs on a cross ram manifold. This engine was never a Chevrolet police package engine.

In 1967, the 327-cid V-8 was stroked from 3.250 to 3.484 inches. The result was the 350-cid small-block that remained nearly un-changed through the 1996 model year. The 350 was not a police en-gine until 1969. For years, the 350 would be just another variation of the Chevy small-block. However, its ideal balance of horsepower and torque would allow it to outlast all other small-blocks including the larger 400-cid version.

The 350 would eventually be fitted with big valves, aggressive cam profiles, high compression heads and fuel injection. In 1993, an LT1 version of the 350 would power the B4C special service package Camaro. In 1994, for the first time, an LT1 engine would power the 9C1 police four-door sedan.

When released for 1967, Camaro engines up to and including the 396-cid/325-hp V-8 were available to compete against the 390-cid Mustang GTA. In December 1966, the famous Z28 package was of-fered. The engine was a de-stroked 327 now displacing 302 cubic inches. Designed specifically to meet SCCA Trans Am road racing rules, this 5.0-liter, huge-valve engine was under-rated at 290 hp.

Late in the 1967 model year, Chevrolet released the SS 350 and SS 396 packages for the retail Camaro. The 350-cid small-block V-8 produced 295 hp while the 396-cid big-block V-8 generated 375 hp. From the late-1960s until the early-1990s, Camaros were the cars that cops chased, not the cars that cops used.

Again, Chevrolet offered six main engine-chassis packages for po-lice use. And again, the automaker was clear that other choices existed:

"The range of Chevrolet's special police packages per-mit a broad selection of vehicles for varied law enforcement needs. Each of the six packages is based on a specific engine and chassis, including many heavy-duty items. However, if preferred, any Chevrolet model may be ordered with those separate, extra-cost options best suited to your department or agency requirements. Your Chevrolet dealer can provide you with complete information."

These six engine-based packages were identical to 1966 except for minor horsepower changes. The regular-fuel, 327-cid V-8 with four-barrel carb was now rated at 240 hp, up 10 hp from 1966. The top gun 427 was now down 5 hp to 385 hp although no one noticed.

The biggest news for 1967 was front disc brakes:

"Good brake performance with low maintenance is vital to the overall success of any police vehicle. Chevrolet has three sure-stopping brake versions for 1967 that meet the most demanding tests.

"Front wheel disc brakes provide maximum stopping power regardless of conditions. These brakes are fade-free, even under repeated high-speed emergency stops.

"Or you can specify Chevrolet's sintered-metallic brakes on your police cars. Unaffected by moisture, these brakes feature high resistance to heat and fading, positive stopping in heavy traffic or hilly terrain.

"Standard on all Chevrolet police vehicles are the famed Safety-Master brakes with bonded organic linings. Drums are 11 inches in diameter. The brakes are vented and drums have wide cooling flanges for rapid heat dissipation."

When the special-order, sintered-metallic brakes were ordered, power brakes were recommended. When the special-order, front disc brakes were ordered, power brakes were mandatory. The disc brake cars got special 15x6-inch wheels with cooling slots and 8.15x15 tires.

The rear suspension was also upgraded for 1967. The upper and lower control arm pivot points were relocated to reduce driveline movement and produce a more vertical path during moderate to hard acceleration. The upper control arms were shorter for 1967. All this kept the driveshaft in closer alignment with the differential.

The steering was also improved for 1967. The redesigned steer-ing linkage of the parallel relay Ball-Race system was placed to the rear for better control when braking and turning. This improved steer-ing geometry also improved tire wear. This was also the first year for an important safety feature: the energy-absorbing steering column.

In 1967, *Motor Trend* tested each of the Low Priced Three se-dans: Chevrolet Impala Super Sport, Ford Galaxie 500 and Plymouth Sport Fury. These were retail cars but quite close to the police package versions of these two-door sedans. In fact, the more-Spartan police models are a bit lighter, handle better, accelerate faster and stop short-er than the retail cars. However, this comparison is still meaningful for police car enthusiasts especially since all three had the "heavy-duty" police-type suspension.

All three makes were based on 119-inch wheelbases and all weighed around 4,300 pounds. All had high compression, big-block, four-barrel carbureted engines, three-speed automatics, numerically low rear gears and front disc brakes. *Motor Trend* thrashed all three of these sedans for hundreds of miles and the Chevrolet came out on top. *Motor Trend* noted:

"The sporty Impala registered the best overall accelera-tion times. It is certainly no slouch in the handling depart-ment either. We put it through some twisty mountain roads at a vigorous pace and never got ourselves crossed up or had to use part of the other half of the roadway. There's under-steer, of course, but not the roll-your-front-tires-under kind; just easily corrected steering, and always predictable.

"During braking from 60 mph, the front end does a notice-able dive, but still keeps traction on the rear wheels, allowing them to do their share of braking work. No pumping or other brake pedal manipulation is needed to bring the Super Sport to a quick halt, just steady pressure. The front wheels remain steerable and the car follows a straight line to rest.

"Our Super Sport went as well as it stopped, displaying excellent power reserve at all highway speeds, and without a lot of accompanying engine noise when the throttle was put in contact with the carpet. It also displayed quick accel-

The Indiana State Police used 396-cid-powered Biscaynes for turnpike patrol in 1967. Note the vented wheels used with front disc brakes. (Jerry Parker)

eration times throughout the range, and all this with a 2.73 rear end ratio.

"Versatile performer on the test track and quiet worker on short hops, Turbo Hydra-Matic is the best thing that's happened to Chevy transmissions in ages. The Super Sport's road-worthiness is a compromise between sporty-car cornering and luxury car cruising, with the emphasis on the latter."

Chevrolet did indeed make police fleet news in 1967. It captured the large and prestigious Los Angeles County Sheriffs Department contract. As in the past, this meant passing the rigorous LASD vehicle tests and then submitting the most competitive bid. The vehicle selected was the Chevrolet Biscayne four-door sedan powered by the 396-cid/325-hp V-8 with four-barrel carb. These squad cars all had the terrific Turbo Hydra-Matic three-speed transmission. The big-block Biscayne was also used by the Nebraska Safety Patrol and on turnpikes by the Indiana State Police.

Car Life magazine tested the 427-cid-powered '67 Impala Super Sport with a Turbo Hydra-Matic and 3.07 gears:

"The SS 427's most impressive feature, logically, is the 427 engine. At 385 bhp, the configuration is new this year. Coupled with a Turbo Hydra-Matic, and Positraction differential, the engine stands at the head of a formidable powertrain, Granted, it falls into the heavy blunt instrument class but forward progress starts immediately.

"During acceleration runs, the biggest problem was controlling rear wheel spin from a dead stop. The engine seemed willing to rev well past its published limits. There was an orange segment on the tachometer at 5200-5500 rpm; the automatic was shifted L-1, L-2, D within this range. Drivers were careful to avoid the red, which started at 5500, for two reasons: No one wanted to risk breaking the engine, and the bhp peak is at 5200, so it was fruitless to press much past that point."

The biggest-block Chevy hit 60 mph in 8.4 seconds and 100 mph in 22.3 seconds. It ran the quarter-mile in 15.75 seconds with a trap speed of 86.5 mph. The top speed of the 427-cid/385-hp sedan was 125 mph.

Low Priced Three Comparison			
	Chevrolet	**Ford**	**Plymouth**
Model	Impala SS	Galaxie 500	Sport Fury
Engine	396 cid	390 cid	383 cid
Carb	Rochester 4-bbl	Autolite 4-bbl	Carter 4-bbl
Horsepower	325	315	325
Torque	410 lb-ft	427 lb-ft	425 lb-ft
Compression	10.25:1	10.5:1	10.0:1
Transmission	3-speed auto	3-speed auto	3-speed auto
Type	Turbo Hydra-Matic	Cruise-O-Matic	TorqueFlite
Rear Gears	2.73:1	2.75:1	3.23:1
Tires	8.25x15	8.45x15	8.25x14
Brakes, f/r	disc/drum	disc/drum	disc/drum
Wheelbase	119 in	119 in	119 in
Curb Weight	4,340 lbs	4,243 lbs	4,319 lbs
0-60 mph	9.1 sec	9.2 sec	9.6 sec
1/4 mi ET	17.0 sec	17.4 sec	17.4 sec
1/4 mi Speed	83 mph	82 mph	81 mph
Braking 60-0 mph	183 ft	158.5 ft	189.5 ft

Chevrolet Police Engines for 1967			
Engines	Size & Carb	Comp.	HP
Turbo-Thrift 250 Six	250 cid, 1-bbl	8.5	155 @ 4200
Turbo-Fire 283 V-8	283 cid, 2-bbl	9.25	195 @ 4600
Turbo-Fire 327 V-8	327 cid, 4-bbl	8.75	240 @ 4400
Turbo-Fire 327 V-8	327 cid, 4-bbl	10.0	275 @ 4800
Turbo-Jet 396 V-8	396 cid, 4-bbl	10.25	325 @ 4800
Turbo-Jet 427 V-8	427 cid, 4-bbl	10.25	385 @ 5200

References for 1967

Chevrolet Impala and SS, 1958-1971, R.M. Clarke, Motorbooks
    International
75 Years of Chevrolet, George Dammann, Motorbooks International
Standard Catalog of Chevrolet 1912-1990, Pat Chappell, Krause
    Publications
1967 Chevrolet Police Cars, Chevrolet Motor Division
"3 of a Kind," Steve Kelly, *Motor Trend*, March 1967

The 427-cid big-block pumped out 385 hp in 1967. The Chevy squads with this engine ran a 15-second quarter-mile and had a top speed of 125 mph. (*Law and Order*)

Chapter 14

1968: The 307 and Large-Journal Small-Blocks

The number of separate models among the 1968 full-size, retail Chevrolets dropped from five to four: Biscayne, Bel Air, Impala and Caprice. The Super Sport series was downgraded to simply an option on any two-door Impala. The police cars remained based on the Biscayne and Bel Air. Unlike times in the past, no mention whatsoever is made in 1968 of any other Chevrolet models being available with police options. This does not mean a police-equipped Chevelle or Chevy II was impossible. It does, however, mean they probably did not exist.

The full-size '68 Chevrolet is easily distinguished from the similar '67 model by side marker lights now required by law. All cars made after January 1, 1968, also had to be equipped with shoulder harnesses for the driver and passenger. The '68 Chevy already had dual chamber master cylinders and an impact absorbing steering wheel column, also mandated by Federal law. The '68 Chevrolet is also different from the '67 version since the newer model has the hood raised in the rear near the cowling to "hide" the "Hide-A-Way" windshield wipers.

In 1968, the new base V-8 for the full-size Chevrolet was the Turbo-Fire 307. The 307 was either a stroked 283-cid small-block or a de-bored 327-cid small-block, depending on your perspective.

The 307 was intended to extend the life of the rugged 283-cid V-8. The 283 block was equipped with a 327 crank to obtain a longer stroke and more torque. With 200 hp, the 307-cid V-8 produced 5 hp more than the 1967 283-cid V-8.

The 307 was an on-again, off-again police engine in both the full-size Chevrolet and the intermediate Chevelle/Malibu. This was never developed into either a high economy engine or a high output engine. The 307 was dropped after the 1973 model year.

The 307 was made by stroking the 283-cid V-8 to the 327's length of 3.250 inches. The 307 and 283 engines share the same 3.875-inch bore.

Engine	283 cid	307 cid	327 cid
Bore	3.875 in	3.875 in	4.00 in
Stroke	3.00 in	3.25 in	3.25 in

After a 10-year police career, the 283-cid small-block was retired. However, the new 307-cid V-8 would never live up to the reputation for either performance or durability chalked up by the 283. While both the 283 and 327 had their wild past with "one horsepower per cubic inch of displacement," the 307-cid V-8 was always mild. Do not confuse the feeble 307 with the 305 of the 1980s and 1990s or with the Trans-Am-inspired 302, which was never a police engine.

The 307-cid block was made without nickel in the iron casting alloy. This meant it showed significant wear after just 60,000 miles. Engine builders claim this shorter-stroke, bigger-bore V-8 will run circles around an equally-equipped 305-cid V-8. That is probably true with some aftermarket engine work. However, for Original Equipment police car applications, the factory never produced a high performance, or even a four-barrel version of the 307.

A Suffolk County, New York, Police 1968 Biscayne K-9 unit powered by a 327-cid/275-hp V-8. The state police in Arizona and Washington also used Biscaynes in 1968. (Ned Schwartz)

The Nassau County, New York, Police used a mix of cars for "highway patrol" duties. The 1968 Biscayne is powered by the 396-cid/325-hp V-8. (Ned Schwartz)

Perhaps the worst aspect of the newest small-block V-8 was the only automatic teamed to the 305 was the two-speed Powerglide. This transmission was long overdue to be obsoleted.

From 1955 through 1967, the Chevrolet small-blocks of various sizes had the same small crankshaft journal diameters. The crankshaft rod journals were 2.000 inches and the crankshaft main journals were 2.300 inches. All this changed for 1968.

In 1968, Chevrolet made a major design change in the block, crank and connecting rods. To reduce the loads and forces on the bearings, the rod journals were increased to 2.100 inches and the main journals were increased to 2.450 inches. From this 1968 "large-journal" design came the reliability and durability of the Chevrolet small-block as we know it today. This change also allowed a new variety of bore and stroke combinations.

For 1968, the police 327-cid V-8 was indeed upgraded to the "large-journal" block. The new-for-1968, 307-cid V-8 was released with these new, larger bearing dimensions.

Popular Science tested the "Low Priced Four" four-door sedans in the January 1968 issue: Chevrolet Impala, Ford Galaxie 500, Plymouth Fury III and AMC Ambassador SST. These cars all had two-barrel carbureted small-block V-8s, automatic transmissions, similar rear gears and power disc brakes. The weight of the vehicles varied a lot but the wheelbase was nearly identical for all four cars.

These were all retail cars without heavy-duty suspensions or drivetrains, but the comparison is still helpful for police enthusiasts.

A large number of patrol cars in heavily-urban areas are equipped exactly like these test sedans.

Jan Norbye and Jim Dunne were not kind to the Chevrolet for one clear and significant reason: the two-speed Powerglide transmission. "Low range in the two-speed Powerglide is a poor compromise between torque requirements at 5 and 45 mph.... Chevrolet's one big fault centers on the two-speed Powerglide. It just hasn't got the versatility of the three-speed automatic transmission in the other cars."

The 283-cid V-8 was replaced with the 307-cid V-8 in 1968. The Chicago Police, however, used Biscaynes powered by the 250-cid Six. (Greg Reynolds)

The 250-cid Six in this Chicago Police 1968 Biscayne gave it a top speed of just 90 mph. This was also the year for the "large journal" small-block V-8. (Greg Reynolds)

Norbye and Dunne were right, of course. The Powerglide hid any of the strengths of the brand new 307-cid V-8. This was such a poor combination that the 307-cid V-8 was dropped from full-size sedan police service after this model year.

The other drivetrain changes for 1968 were minor. The regular fuel 327 with four-barrel carb picked up another 10 hp to achieve a 250 hp rating. This was earning a reputation among fleet managers and patrol officers alike as being a great police engine. It was both economical and powerful when it had to be. This was the smallest V-8 to be teamed with the Turbo Hydra-Matic.

The final driveline change was the dropping of the Overdrive transmission based on the three-speed Synchro-Mesh. This was simply not popular any longer, nor could it be fitted to the more powerful engines. The clear trend was away from stick shifts and toward automatics. Now that Chevrolet had a reliable automatic with three-speeds, the Overdrive three-speed manual was simply obsolete.

For 1968, Chevrolet changed the police package designation. The Z04 chassis options and B01 body options were now officially the "B07 police equipment option" or "B07 police car package." Standard police tires were 8.25x14 on drum brake cars and 8.15x15 on disc brake cars.

The Arizona Highway Patrol, Washington State Patrol, Chicago Police, Suffolk County, New York, Police and the Nassau County, New York, Police were among major departments who patrolled in 1968 Chevrolets.

1968 Chevrolet Four-door Sedans	
Powerplant	**Top Speed**
250 cid, 155 hp	90 mph
307 cid, 200 hp	105 mph
327 cid, 250 hp	108 mph
327 cid, 275 hp	109 mph
396 cid, 325 hp	112 mph
427 cid, 385 hp	121 mph

Chevrolet Police Engines for 1968			
Engines	**Size & Carb**	**Comp.**	**HP**
Turbo-Thrift 250 Six	250 cid, 1-bbl	8.5	155 @ 4200
Turbo-Fire 307 V-8	307 cid, 2-bbl	9.0	200 @ 4600
Turbo-Fire 327 V-8	327 cid, 4-bbl	8.75	250 @ 4800
Turbo-Fire 327 V-8	327 cid, 4-bbl	10.0	275 @ 4800
Turbo-Jet 396 V-8 (L-35)	396 cid, 4-bbl	10.25	325 @ 4800
Turbo-Jet 427 V-8 (L-36)	427 cid, 4-bbl	10.25	385 @ 5200

Four-door Sedan Comparison				
	Chevrolet	**Ford**	**Plymouth**	**American Motors**
Model	**Impala**	**Galaxie 500**	**Fury III**	**Ambassador SST**
Engine	307 cid, V-8	302 cid, V-8	318 cid, V-8	290 cid, V-8
Carb	2-bbl	2-bbl	2-bbl	2-bbl
HP	200	210	230	200
Torque	300 lb-ft	300 lb-ft	340 lb-ft	285 lb-ft
Compression	9.0	9.0	9.2	9.0
Transmission	2-spd auto	3-spd auto	3-spd auto	3-spd auto
Type	Powerglide	Cruise-O-Matic	TorqueFlite	Shift Command
Rear Gears	3.08	2.80	2.94	3.15
Tires	8.25x14	7.75x15	8.15x15	7.75x14
Brakes, f/r	power disc/drum	power disc/drum	power disc/drum	power disc/drum
Wheelbase	119 in	119 in	119 in	118 in
Curb weight	3,900 lbs	3,685 lbs	3,650 lb	3,220 lb
Brake from 60 mph	150.8 ft	181 ft	172.3 ft	149 ft
Accelerate to 60 mph	14.0 sec	13.2 sec	11.2 sec	12.1 sec
Emergency lane change	60 mph	60 mph	55 mph	60 mph
48 ft. serpentine	25 mph	22 mph	22 mph	20 mph
Fuel Economy	15.1 mpg	15.3 mpg	14.7 mpg	16.2 mpg

References for 1968

"These Family Sedans Pack Some Surprises," Norbye & Dunne, *Popular Science*, January 1968

1968 Chevrolet Police Cars, Chevrolet Motor Division

75 Years of Chevrolet, George Dammann, Motorbooks International

Chevrolet Impala and SS, 1958-1971, R.M. Clarke, Motorbooks International

Standard Catalog of Chevrolet 1912-1990, Pat Chappell, Krause Publications

Illustrated Chevrolet Buyers Guide, John Gunnell, Motorbooks International

Chapter 15

1969: First 350-cid "Mouse Motor" V-8

A great many changes took place with Chevrolet police engines for 1969. Chevrolet's most famous police engine was introduced this year. The Chevelle 300 was back in full police uniform packing a 396-cid V-8. Right smack in the middle of the muscle car craze, this was one of Chevrolet's most interesting years.

The big Chevrolets were totally redesigned for 1969. With the same 119-inch wheelbase they grew longer and heavier again. The full-size Chevy would continue to gain size and weight through 1976. The '69 full-size bowties are easy to spot by their integrated, massive, bumper-grilles. The B07 police package was available on the Biscayne and Bel Air.

With no fanfare whatsoever, the greatest police and retail engine of all time was released in 1969. This engine would power the famous Nova police car of the mid-1970s. It would be the primary Chevrolet police engine from 1977 through 1996. This small-block V-8 would be the engine used in The Ultimate Pursuit Car, the Camaro B4C.

In retail form, this small-block would power tens of thousands of SS Novas, Z28 and SS Camaros, SS Chevelles, SS Monte Carlos, SS Impalas and generations of Corvettes. This enhanced small-block would be in the drivetrain for pickup trucks, vans and station wagons. It would also be the definitive choice for custom street rods, and would be the most widely used marine and jet-boat engine.

This small-block V-8 would eventually be promoted from being a Chevrolet engine to being a General Motors "corporate" engine. In this role, it would power nearly every full-size and mid-size model of passenger car from Buick, Cadillac, Oldsmobile and Pontiac.

This optimized small-block would be produced in far greater numbers than any other V-8 from any other carmaker. In fact, this en-gine would exceed the engines that powered the Ford Model T and Volkswagen Beetle in all-time worldwide sales. Only the Ford 302 and the Chrysler Corporation 318 V-8s rival the sheer longevity of this most famous Chevrolet engine.

In its later-model, fuel-injected form, this small-block V-8, straight from the factory, would push long-wheelbase, full-size four-door police sedans to top speeds of more than 142 mph. At one time, this was possible only from the most powerful versions of big-block V-8s, and most big-block sedans were nowhere near that fast.

This small-block would become the most hot-rodded engine of all time. It would power sanctioned race cars on oval tracks, dirt tracks, drag strips and road racing courses. In its various horsepower ratings under the code "LT1", this engine would simply be legendary. This engine, of course, is the Turbo-Fire 350-cid V-8. It would be bored (and stroked) to displace 400 cubic inches but that version would not last. In its 350-cid form, this would become the most successful and reliable engine in the history of General Motors.

The 255 hp and 300 hp versions of the 350-cid V-8 quietly filled the spots left vacant by the previous year's 250 hp and 275 hp versions of the 327-cid V-8. The 350-cid engine was simply a stroked 327-cid small-block:

Engine	327 cid	350 cid
Bore	4.00 in	4.00 in
Stroke	3.25 in	3.48 in

A New York City Housing Police 1969 Biscayne. These squad cars were all powered by the 250-cid Six. (Jim Benjaminson)

A 1969 Biscayne station wagon with a 327-cid V-8. This was also the first year for the now-famous 350-cid small-block. (Ned Schwartz)

The new base V-8 for 1969 was the 327-cid engine now for the first time in full-size police cars in two-barrel form. This two-barrel version producing 235 hp replaced the '68 307 with two-barrel carb, which produced 200 hp. This was the only version of the 327 used in any police sedan for 1969. The 307-cid/200-hp engine was gone from full-size cars but was the base V-8 for the police '69 Chevelle.

An odd development for 1969 was a two-barrel version of the 396-cid big-block. In fact, the only 396-cid engine available in the full-size Biscayne and Bel Air was this 265 hp, two-barrel version. This was a response to Ford, which offered a wide variety of big-block two-barrel carbureted engines. This was supposed to offer both big-block power and two-barrel fuel mileage.

Jan Norbye and Jim Dunne of *Popular Science* thrashed four full-size retail sedans that are the basis for most police fleets. This time they selected big-block engines but all fed by two-barrel carburetors. All the sedans had power front disc brakes and all had heavy-duty, police-type suspensions. This time around the *Popular Science* test Chevy had a Turbo Hydra-Matic!

Norbye and Dunne recognized that the heavy weight of these sedans made for a great ride and high directional stability. They also realized that this sheer weight was the enemy of acceleration, caused handling problems, increased fuel consumption, increased tire wear and threw an extra load on the brakes. Cops began to realize this too during the fuel crisis of the early-1970s and the pioneering work of Los Angeles Sheriff "technical" reserve deputy and *Motor Trend* executive editor, John Christy.

Norbye and Dunne repeatedly emphasized the advantages of a heavy-duty suspension on these sedans. The heavy-duty suspension is often thought of as an offshoot of some towing package. This is partly true, but for every make of car these heavy-duty components were either specifically developed for export cars or for police use. The rear anti-sway bar, for example, was expressly developed for police use.

Popular Science praised the Chevrolet for excellent steering and handling. "The Impala was beautifully obedient up to its limit in the lane change test. Body roll proved moderate throughout this phase." In fact, Jan Norbye ended the evaluation by selecting the Chevrolet Impala as his overall choice over the other three full-size sedans. His recommendation carried a lot of influence back then. Said Norbye:

"I'll go for the Chevy. The straight-ratio steering suits me more than the variable-ratio in the Pontiac (which Dunne had selected). I think its handling response is more predictable. It's obvious that for '69, Chevrolet has put more money than usual in the Impala, probably in an effort to take the lead away from Ford in the areas of comfort, luxury and quiet. I think Chevy has done it."

One surprise that came out of this *Popular Science* review was the overall fuel economy. In the late-1960s, the thinking behind getting good mileage from heavy cars was to use big-block engines but to starve them with two-barrel carbs and team them with low (numerically) rear gear ratios such as 2.29 and 2.56. Yet these sedans only got 10 to 12 mpg. Police cars equipped this same exact way would average just 6 to 7 mpg in actual service.

The low rear gear hurt the mileage in city traffic and the two-barrel carb hurt the mileage when something less than emergency-response performance was needed. While this two-barrel, low gearing setup may have worked to improve mileage in some retail applications, this setup could not have produced worse mileage for police use.

By the mid-1970s, the Los Angeles County Sheriffs Department would revolutionize police fleet thinking. The LASD would prove it could get better overall fuel mileage from four-barrel carbureted, moderately geared sedans.

Constant stop and start police use forced the officers to give their cars full throttle just to get the car to move, let alone when they needed to move quickly, but not at full speed. With proper-gearing and four-barrel carbureted engines, the cops got the vehicle response they wanted with a much less aggressive throttle. Of course, this combination also gave better emergency-response performance, too.

This mighty Turbo-Jet 427 was available in two power levels for 1969. One was the 335 hp version to replace the previous year's 396-cid/325-hp engine. This de-tuned 427-cid big-block still had 10.25:1 compression but a much milder cam than the more potent 427. The second version was the 390 hp version, which was a minor tweak over the prior year's 385 hp engine.

Motor Trend checked out a 427-cid/390-hp Impala with the close-ratio four-speed Synchro-Mesh and 3.31 rear gears with positraction. As for sheer performance, *Motor Trend* said "it is practically a supercar." Even with a 4,200 pound curb weight, the big sedan reached 60 mph in 7.7 seconds. It also ran a 15.5 second quarter-mile at 90 mph. They expected that, but were pleasantly surprised with the handling and braking (which is important to cops).

"Going through tight corners is always road hugging business. Steering is neutral in normal corners, but aggressive driving brings on built-in understeer. Controlled oversteer occurs in sharp power drifts coming out of turns of less than 90 degrees.

"Chevrolet power front disc brakes and drum rear, which our car had, have been great ever since they were introduced. Stops were always straight and easy to control. Even after repeated use during high-speed acceleration runs up to 122 mph, there was no fade or burning with the Impala brakes."

The 1969 model year held big news on transmission availability. The three-speed Turbo Hydra-Matic was finally available on every police powerplant from the Turbo-Thrift Six to the Turbo-Jet 427 V-8. That's right. All police engines could be teamed to the great Turbo Hydra-Matic. This change was way overdue. The Powerglide still hung on, however. It, too, was available on engines ranging from the 250-cid Six through the 300 hp version of the 350-cid V-8.

One of today's most cherished muscle cars, the 396-powered '69 Chevelle, was available from Chevrolet to do some official stoplight Grand Prix ticket writing. The Chevelle had been absent from the formal lineup of Chevrolet police cars for a couple of years. Chevrolet billed the Chevelle as "The Concentrated Chevrolet." It was all Chevy police car, in "just the right size." This was again well before the mid-1970s trend to go to smaller police cars.

The Chevelle was available with the B07 police package only in the 116-inch wheelbase four-door sedan. The '69 Chevelle two-door with a 112-inch wheelbase was not available with police gear.

The Chevelle 300 Deluxe was available in powertrains ranging from the Turbo-Thrift 250-cid Six for detective work up to the Turbo-Jet 396-cid V-8 for the most aggressive freeway pursuit duties.

The full-size Biscayne and Bel Air got two-barrel carburetors and merely 9.0:1 compression on their 396-cid big-block engines. However, in the Chevelle, the 396 came with a Rochester spread-bore four-barrel carb and the full 10.25:1 compression. Instead of a 265 hp rating, the Chevelle's Turbo-Jet 396-cid V-8 pumped out an honest 325 hp.

One of the Chevelle police engines was the 307-cid small-block. In fact, this 200 hp Turbo-Fire was the base V-8 for the police Chevelle. This stroked 283 V-8 was removed from the big car line and was restricted to the Chevelle and Nova series. The Chevy II name had been dropped.

As a great addition, the three-speed Turbo Hydra-Matic was available in the Chevelle for every engine size. Of course, the two-speed Powerglide was also available up through the 350-cid V-8.

The Los Angeles Police Department was responsible for one big piece of police pursuit gear on all makes of 1969 police packages. The LAPD patrolled the narrow, twisty Pasadena Freeway among all the other "handling courses" in Southern California. They helped to develop a rear anti-sway bar or stabilizer bar. This greatly reduced understeer on big-engined, intermediate-sized police cruisers and literally made these cars handle like pony cars.

The rear sway bar was required for all LAPD contracts from 1969 on. Chevrolet made this a part of the B07 police package on the Chevelle when either the 350 or 396 engine was ordered. With the P65 special tires and power disc brakes, either one of these police Chevelles would be nearly impossible to outrun.

The 1969 model year was the height of the supercar, muscle car, econo-racer craze. All the major car magazines ran comparisons of the Chevelle SS 396 versus the competition. The other cars to have at the time included Plymouth GTX 440, Dodge Charger R/T 440, Ford Cobra 428 CJ, Pontiac GTO 400, Buick GS 400, Mercury Cyclone 428 CJ, Plymouth 426 Hemi or 383 Road Runner and Dodge Super Bee 440 Six Pack.

During the muscle car era, cops could cruise the streets in a 1969 396-cid Chevelle. Police package big-block Chevelles ran the quarter-mile in 14 seconds. (Chevrolet)

The Newark, New Jersey, Police used economical six-cylinder Biscaynes in 1969 for traffic enforcement. Note the fender-mounted siren. (Ned Schwartz)

These were the "muscle cars" of the late 1960s as opposed to the "super stock" cars of the early 1960s. These '69 big-block intermediates would run the quarter-mile in the 13 to 15 second brackets and have trap speeds from 90 to 105 mph. The top speeds varied a great deal depending on the rear gear ratio, of course. However, these muscle cars with rear gears near 3.55 ran from 125 to 140 mph. The '69 Chevelle with the 396-cid/325-hp V-8 was in this class. And the cops could have them.

Car and Driver tested a number of econo-racers including the 325 hp version of the 396 used in the police Chevelle. Versions of this engine up to 375 hp were available in retail Chevelles. Their test car had the Turbo Hydra-Matic, 3.55 positraction, power discs and heavy-duty suspension so it was almost exactly the machine the cops would have. It hit 60 mph in just 5.8 seconds and 100 mph in 15.2 seconds. The big-block Chevelle cleared the quarter-mile in 14.4 seconds at 97.4 mph.

The Nassau County, New York, Police used 1969 Biscaynes for "Highway Patrol" duties. These were powered by a two-barrel version of the 396-cid engine. This was thought to give the best balance between power and economy. (Ned Schwartz)

Car & Driver was impressed by the LAPD-inspired handling characteristics of the big-block Chevelle:

> "...it was unbeatable in handling, and good handling is a lovely thing to have around the house. The credit goes to the new heavy-duty suspension package that uses a rear sway bar to reduce understeer. We liked it a lot. The car corners flat and allows good directional control right up to the limit of adhesion. All this is complemented by Chevrolet's very accurate power steering..."

Motor Trend also tested a big-block Chevelle except their car had the L34 396-cid/350-hp engine instead of the police-spec Z25 325 hp big-block. This car also had 3.55 gears and a Turbo Hydra-Matic transmission.

Motor Trend emphasized the 396's "porcupine heads in which valves are angled toward their ports and intake and exhaust passages are individually ported."

The *Motor Trend* test Chevelle did not have a rear sway bar and they complained about understeer. That is what the rear sway bar solved. The *Motor Trend* 350 hp Chevelle was loaded with options and as a result had slower acceleration than the *Car & Driver* 325 hp Chevelle. The 350 hp version ran a 15.4 second quarter-mile at 92 mph. They concluded: "Runs fast, even with power options (like air conditioning)."

The police in Chicago, Newark, New Jersey, Nassau County, New York, and with New York City Housing used Chevrolet police cars in 1969.

Biscayne and Bel Air Police Engines for 1969			
Engine	**Size & Carb**	**Comp.**	**HP**
Turbo-Thrift 250 Six	250 cid, 1-bbl	8.5	155 @ 4200
Turbo-Fire 327 V-8	327 cid, 2-bbl	9.0	235 @ 4800
Turbo-Fire 350 V-8	350 cid, 4-bbl	9.0	255 @ 4800
Turbo-Fire 350 V-8	350 cid, 4-bbl	10.25	300 @ 4800
Turbo-Jet 396 V-8 (L-66)	396 cid, 2-bbl	9.0	265 @ 4800
Turbo-Jet 427 V-8 (LS-1)	427 cid, 4-bbl	10.25	335 @ 4800
Turbo-Jet 427 V-8 (L-36)	427 cid, 4-bbl	10.25	390 @ 5200

Chevelle Police Engines for 1969			
Engine	**Size & Carb**	**Comp.**	**HP**
Turbo-Thrift 250 Six	250 cid, 1-bbl	8.5	155 @ 4200
Turbo-Fire 307 V-8	307 cid, 2-bbl	9.0	200 @ 4600
Turbo-Fire 350 V-8	350 cid, 4-bbl	9.0	255 @ 4800
Turbo-Jet 396 V-8 (L-35)	396 cid, 4-bbl	10.25	325 @ 4800

Full-Size Car Comparison				
	Chevrolet	**Ford**	**Plymouth**	**Pontiac**
Model	**Impala**	**Galaxie**	**Fury III**	**Catalina**
Engine	396 cid	390 cid	383 cid	400 cid
Carb	2-bbl	2-bbl	2-bbl	2-bbl
HP	265 @ 4800	265 @ 4400	290 @ 4400	290 @ 4600
Torque	400 @ 2800	390 @ 2600	390 @ 2800	428 @ 2500
Compression	9.0	9.5	9.2	10.5
Transmission	3-spd auto	3-spd auto	3-spd auto	3-spd auto
Type	Turbo Hydra-Matic	Cruise-O-Matic	TorqueFlite	Turbo Hydra-Matic
Rear Gears	2.56	2.75	2.76	2.29
Tires	8.25x14	8.55x15	8.25x15	8.55x15
Brakes, f/r	power disc/drum	power disc/drum	power disc/drum	power disc/drum
Wheelbase	119 in	121 in	120 in	122 in
Curb Weight	4,218 lbs	4,206 lbs	4,172 lbs	4,267 lbs
Brake from 60 mph	195 ft	198 ft	175 ft	161 ft
Accelerate to 60 mph	11.3 sec	11.6 sec	11.0 sec	10.6 sec
Emergency lane change	58 mph	60 mph	58 mph	58 mph
48 ft. serpentine	30 mph	28 mph	25 mph	28 mph
Fuel Economy	11.4 mpg	10.2 mpg	12.1 mpg	11.7 mpg

References for 1969

Illustrated Chevrolet Buyers Guide, John Gunnell, Motorbooks International

"Analyzing Supercars," Bill Sanders, *Motor Trend*, January 1969

"Six Econo-Racers," staff report, *Car & Driver*, January 1969

"Supercars in Pursuit Clothing," A.R. Roalman, *Car Life*, November 1968

"Full Size Family Cars," Norbye & Dunne, *Popular Science*, February 1969

Chevrolet Introduces 1969, Chevrolet Motor Division

75 Years of Chevrolet, George Dammann, Motorbooks International

Standard Catalog of Chevrolet 1912-1990, Pat Chappell, Krause Publications

Chevrolet Impala and SS, 1958-1971, R.M. Clarke, Motorbooks International

Chapter 16

1970: First 454-cid Big-Block V-8

The 1970 model year was more a year of losses than of new features. The Turbo-Fire 327 V-8 was gone. The Turbo-Jet 396 V-8 was gone. The Turbo-Jet 427 V-8 was gone. The four-speed Synchro-Mesh was gone. The list of available axle ratios was shortened. The B07 police package for the Chevelle was gone, sort of.

In 1970, the full-size Chevrolet was remodeled slightly. The massive encircling bumper-grille from 1969 was replaced with a much more conventional, and lighter, separate bumper, grille and hood chrome strips.

The B07 police package for 1970 was based on the Biscayne and Bel Air and on the Brookwood and Townsman station wagons. For the first time, these police cars were four-door sedans only. The two-doors were hardtops restricted to the Impala and Caprice series. The wheelbase for the full-size Chevrolets remained at 119 inches.

A tiny footnote on the B07 police package said: "Other models may be specially ordered." This almost certainly meant the B07 police package could be added to the two-door Impala and Caprice for cops wanting a two-door model.

It is possible this obscure note was intended to leave the door open to police-equipped Chevelles and Novas. However, as in past years, if the official police literature did not specifically list a model, few if any police versions of the model existed. Even when police models such as the Chevelle and Chevy II were advertised, fewer than 1,000 units per year were sold in the 1960s.

The B07 police package did include one new piece of equipment for 1970: power front disc brakes. This was added as standard equipment with little hype. For the record, the California Highway Patrol had experimented with Airheart front and Budd rear disc brakes as early as 1964.

The two standard police engines for 1970 were the 250-cid Six and the 350-cid, two-barrel carbureted V-8. Importantly, both these engines ran on regular grade gasoline. This 350 was the largest standard V-8 ever put in the full-size Chevrolet. This two-barrel version was new to cop cars for 1970. The standard equipment transmission was the three-speed Synchro-Mesh but it was available only on these two engines. The four-speed Synchro-Mesh was not available on any police engine.

In a continuing odd twist with automatic transmissions, both the two-speed Powerglide and the three-speed Turbo Hydra-Matic were now optional on all police engines. If for some reason, a department wanted to bolt the two-speed Powerglide to a 390 hp Turbo-Jet big-block, Chevrolet would do it. The greatest majority of automatic transmissions selected by cops were, however, the Turbo Hydra-Matic.

The 350-cid V-8 was used in all kinds of police package cars including this Suffolk County, New York, Police wagon. The 350-cid was available in 250-hp and 300-hp versions. (Ned Schwartz)

By 1970, the 350-cid small-block caught on among cops. This Redding, California, Police Biscayne could run the quarter-mile in 16 seconds. (Darryl Lindsay)

The primary axle ratio for the two standard equipment engines was the 3.31 gear. The rear gear for the 350-cid/300-hp V-8, and both horsepower versions of the big-block was the 3.07 ratio. While positraction was an option for all ratios, other gear ratios do not appear to have been readily available.

The big news for 1970 was a brand new big-block: the Turbo-Jet 454-cid V-8. This was the largest police engine ever offered by Chevrolet. The 454 replaced the 427-cid V-8 outright. The 345 hp version of the 454-cid big-block replaced the 335 hp version of the 427. The 390 hp version of the 454, in turn, replaced the 390 hp version of the 427.

The big news for 1970 was the largest police engine ever made by Chevrolet: the 454-cid V-8. The canted-valve big-block came in 345-hp and 390-hp versions. (Chevrolet)

As a side note, the 396-cid big-block was gone from the police ranks. The 396 was still available in retail cars in 1970. This was the year the 396 actually displaced 402 cubic inches thanks to a larger bore, but it kept the name "396". This 402-cid V-8 would be a police engine in just one year, 1972.

The retail cars got a 400-cid small-block in 1970, however, this small-block was not a 1970 police package engine. While the displacement was similar, the 400-cid small-block wedge would never "replace" the 396-cid porcupine head big-block.

On the other hand, the 454-cid big-block was a worthy replacement for the 427-cid engine. The 427 was a bored out 396 with the same stroke. The 454 was a stroked 427 with the same bore.

Engine	396 cid	427 cid	454 cid
Bore	4.094 in	4.25 in	4.25 in
Stroke	3.76 in	3.76 in	4.00 in

In general, a shorter stroke tends to move the horsepower upwards in the rpm range. A longer stroke tends to produce the horsepower at lower engine speeds.

In 1968, Chevrolet was investigating a replacement for the 427-cid big-block. It ran a test comparing a 396-cid V-8 with a 392-cid prototype big-block to check out a concept it had for a 430-cid engine. In this test the 4.09-inch bore by 3.76-inch stroke 396 was the control engine. A 4.25-inch bore by 3.46-inch stroke 392 was the test engine.

The shorter stroke, bigger bore prototype engine had more horsepower, more torque and less friction at nearly all speeds. The problem was that this combination also produced an engine with dirtier emissions. From this test Chevy engineers knew to simply length-en the stroke of the 427 to get their next generation big-block. The result was the "Mr. Clean" 454.

The Chevrolet 454-cid V-8 was designed to take on the Ford 460, Pontiac 455 and Chrysler Corporation 440. By most accounts, the 454 was the best engine of the bunch simply due to its better valve train layout using the so-called porcupine head. The 454 was certainly available with the highest horsepower rating. In its 1970 450 hp retail version, the 454 easily outranked the famous Mopar 440-cid Six Pack (three two-barrel carbs) retail engine producing 390 hp. It even produced more power than the legendary Chrysler Corporation 426-cid hemi-head engine that used dual four-barrel carbs to reach 425 hp.

In the 1970 police cars, the 454-cid big-block was available in two versions. Both had four-barrel carbs, 10.25:1 compression and, of course, hydraulic lifters. The general performance cam version with single exhaust produced 345 hp. Dual exhaust was an option. The high performance cam version with dual exhaust produced 390 hp.

The British magazine, *Autocar*, tested the somewhat intimidating and imposing 454-cid Impala. This big bore brute was clearly not the kind of sedan the Brits were used to testing. However, they found its good points as it would apply to any American driver:

"The car we tested had a V-8 of nearly 7.5 litres, with a claimed gross power output of 345 bhp. On the road the car offers a remarkable combination of docility plus terrific response. Most overtaking in the Impala is done with just a whiff of throttle, but if there is ever the need to get by quickly a firm stab on the acceleratormakes the car fairly bound forward.

"Full throttle acceleration from rest sweeps the car to 100 mph in just over 33 seconds and the standing quarter-mile acceleration time of 16.8 seconds is outstandingly quick for such a big car. Above 100 mph the acceleration rapidly tails off, but the car will go on building up speed to an impressive enough maximum of 116 mph.

"The most outstanding improvement to American cars in recent years has been not so much how they go, but how well they stop, and the Impala has big disc brakes at the front and drums at the rear. Terrific servo action gives that excess sensitivity which used to be associated with American self-servo drum brakes in the past. A mere 20 pound touch on the pedal gives more than 0.5 g retardation, while on a wet road 35 pound load gave a maximum of 0.76 g with rear wheels locked and the whole car slewing badly. On a dry road a maximum of 0.96 g was obtained, accompanied by clouds of smoke from the tyres, which left heavy black lines.

"The big improvement has come in the reduced tendency to fade, and although there was a pungent smell of burnt linings there was only a moderate increase in pedal loads during our fade tests from 70 mph.

"Control is simplified by an exceedingly good high-geared power steering. Too often American cars have ultra-light power steering which is far too low-geared, so that what is saved in effort applied is lost in the amount of twirling needed. On the Impala it takes only three turns from lock to lock. The higher gearing takes out that feeling of vagueness and slop which has in the past been such a noted-characteristic of so many American cars.

"Cornering is good for the class of car, and although there is quite a lot of roll it is not troublesome, and the car can be hurried along a twisting secondary road at quite high speeds, providing there is plenty of width. Understeer is dis-guised to a large extent by the power steering as long as the roads are dry.

"The suspension has long travel and effective damping, so there is no sickening float on undulations, and the ride generally is taut and level. There is very good absorption of minor irregularities, though it does not cope so well with a really rough unmade track."

Their overall conclusion was:

"Power steering better than usual and brakes much more fade resistant. Faultless automatic transmission. Very quiet and smooth. Poor fuel consumption but plenty of performance."

With a retail 2.56 axle, the *Autocar* 454-cid Impala was actually quite under-geared. The top speed would have been higher and, of course, the acceleration would have been greater with a numerically higher rear gear. Evidence of this is a top speed of 118 mph at 3750 rpm. This was well below peak horsepower at 4400 rpm. This was easily a 15 second bracket, 130 mph top end sedan with the correct axle ratio.

Road Test magazine tested a 1970 Impala powered by the 350-cid/300-hp small-block bolted to the three-speed Turbo Hydra-Matic:

"We drove it on freeways with their high speeds and over rutted mountain roads where we seldom reached 20 miles an hour. While the Impala was most certainly built more for freeways and city streets, we found no fault with it on dirt roads aside from the undeniable fact that it is a big car. Even such a car as this, particularly with the heavy-duty "F40" suspension on the test car, will take you almost anywhere if you drop the Hydra-Matic down into a low range and take your cotton-picking time.

"Braking was particularly impressive for this large, 4,200-pound car with a stop from 60 mph in 138 feet. This is 30 to 40 feet shorter than the average Detroit barge, and is a product of the wide tires and the large brakes. Happily front disc brakes are standard equipment with 11-inch finned drums on rear. We did a bit of high-speed driving along a winding mountain road, landing on the brakes both hard and late as we took the turns. No sweat at all. They slowed the Impala down fast and true every time with no sign of fading."

The 300 hp Impala ran the quarter-mile in 16.15 seconds with a trap speed of 81 mph.

The 1970 model year was the last year for high compression engines from General Motors. Chrysler Corporation maintained its high compression engines for one additional year. After 1971, no one made a truly high performance, high compression police engine. The big-block engines themselves survived the emission control crunch. However, they were de-tuned with low compression ratios and mild cam grinds. The 1970 Turbo-Jet 454-cid V-8 with a 10.25:1 compression and 390 hp was the last of an era.

The 454-cid V-8 would carry the Chevrolet big-block banner from 1970 through "The Great Downsizing" after 1976. It would be the most powerful bowtie police engine at a time when even big-blocks were drained of their power. Cops would turn to the 454 just to give them the performance they used to have from a 396 or 327 in the high compression days. The 454 would always be remembered as the last Chevrolet police big-block.

However, as we review the history of Chevrolet police drivetrains, we must remember the 454 was a true high performance, high compression engine for just one year, the 1970 model year. On the other hand, the 427-cid big-block probably deserves the praise that most enthusiasts give to the 454.

When the 427 was introduced in 1966 it produced a full 390 hp from its 10.25:1 compression. It remained a pure and unbridled, bad-to-the-bones big-block through 1969 when it was discontinued. Nearly all of the 427-cid V-8s were the genuine stump-pullers that enthusiasts imagine when they think of a police big-block.

1970 Chevrolet Bel Air		
Engine	350-cid V-8	454-cid V-8
Carb	4-bbl	4-bbl
HP	300	345
Transmission	three-speed THM	three-speed THM
Axle	3.31 (retail)	2.56 (retail)
Wheelbase	119.0 in	119.0 in
Weight	4,205 lbs	4,400 lbs
0-60 mph	n/a	9.0 sec
0-100 mph	n/a	33.7 sec
Quarter-Mile ET	16.1 sec	16.8 sec
Quarter-Mile Speed	81 mph	79 mph
Top Speed	n/a	118 mph
Fuel Economy	n/a	10.3 mpg

Biscayne and Bel Air Engines for 1970			
Engine	Size & Carb	Comp.	HP
Turbo-Thrift 250 Six	250 cid, 1-bbl	8.5	155 @ 4200
Turbo-Fire 350 V-8	350 cid, 2-bbl	9.0	250 @ 4800
Turbo-Fire 350 V-8	350 cid, 4-bbl	10.25	300 @ 4800
Turbo-Jet 454 V-8 (LS-4)	454 cid, 4-bbl	10.25	345 @ 4600
Turbo-Jet 454 V-8 (LS-5)	454 cid, 4-bbl	10.25	390 @ 5000

Note: The LS-5 454 has dual exhaust and a high performance cam. The 250 and 350 with two-barrel carb use 3.31 rear gears. All other police engines used 3.07 rear gears.

References for 1970

The Chevrolet Seventies, Chevrolet Motor Division
Chevrolet Impala and SS, 1958-1971, R.M. Clarke, Motorbooks International
Illustrated Chevrolet Buyer's Guide, John Gunnell, Motorbooks International
75 Years of Chevrolet, George Dammann, Motorbooks International
Standard Catalog of Chevrolet 1912-1990, Pat Chappell, Krause Publications

These two 1970 Biscaynes show the heavy wear and tear typical of a big city police department. These are all six-cylinder cars. (Ned Schwartz)

Chapter 17

1971: 400-cid V-8 and Longer Wheelbases

The headline-making news from Chevrolet in 1971 was a release of the retail Vega. This Volkswagen Beetle and Ford Pinto fighter was never a police car. With a 97-inch wheelbase, the Vega was the smallest pure Chevrolet ever produced up to that point. This record was set again in 1976 with the 94.3-inch wheelbase Chevette.

In stark contrast to the 1971 trend toward small cars, the 1971 full-size Chevrolet actually got bigger. A lot bigger. For 1971, the wheelbase of the Biscayne, Bel Air, Impala and Caprice models was increased to 121.5 inches. The full-size Chevrolet had a 119-inch wheelbase for the previous 12 years. Also remodeled for 1971 were the other General Motors cars using the "B-body" platform: Buick Le-Sabre, Oldsmobile Delta Eighty-Eight and Pontiac Catalina.

Dimensions	1970	1971
Wheelbase	119.0 in	121.5 in
Length	216.0 in	216.8 in
Width	79.8 in	79.5 in
Height	55.5 in	54.1 in
Track, f/r	63.4/63.3 in	64.1/64.0 in
Weight	3,759 lbs	3,888 lbs
Tires, retail	E78-14	F78-15

The overall length of the full-size Chevrolet had grown on a more or less yearly basis. The 0.8-inch growth for 1971 was typical of the annual rate for the past five years. The Chevrolet literature read, "We have been building up to this much police car for years."

The 1971 Biscayne was 18 inches longer overall, 6 inches wider, had a 6.5-inch longer wheelbase and weighed 750 pounds more than the 1956 One Fifty. This unhealthy weight gain would continue until the 1977 model Chevrolet. As a side note, the police station wagon had grown from a 119-inch wheelbase in 1970 to a 125-inch wheelbase in 1971.

In 1970, Chevrolet pushed its small-block to the absolute limits of displacement. History would prove the automaker actually went too far with its 400-cid version of the small-block.

The 400 was made possible by removing some water passages and joining the cylinder walls together. This increased the strength of the thin wall castings, but it also caused an entirely new set of problems. "Siamesing" the cylinder walls allowed this new engine block to keep the same external dimensions and the same 4.400-inch bore spacings as all other small-blocks. Chevrolet was able to achieve a 4.126-inch bore with this radical small-block design. The stroke was a long, 3.750 inches. This "giant" 400-cid small-block was a retail car and truck engine from 1970 through 1980 and a police car engine from 1971 through 1976.

In 1971, Chevrolet increased the wheelbase of the Biscayne from 119 inches to 121.5 inches. This was as long as a Chevrolet police sedan would ever get. (Ned Schwartz)

For 1971, Chevrolet released the 400-cid "giant" small-block V-8 for use in police cars. The siamese-cylinder block is different from other Chevrolet V-8 blocks. (Chevrolet)

The 400-cid small-block uses a different block from the other Chevrolet small-blocks. First, the block has had the water passages removed from between the cylinders. Second, the main bearing journal diameters are larger. The pre-1968 small journal crank has 2.300-inch mains while the post-1968 large journal crank has 2.650-inch main journals.

The 400-cid small-block is far more than just a bored and stroked 350. It is an entirely different engine that frankly does not share the reliability and durability of the legendary, post-1968 small-blocks.

Heads from the 400-cid engines cracked at a higher rate than other Chevrolet small-blocks. This is because the 400-cid engine runs hotter as a result of both the "siamese" cylinders and the longest stroke of any bowtie small-block. Cracks usually occur on the exhaust seat in the combustion chamber of the head.

On the 400, six steam holes were drilled into each block deck. Corresponding holes were drilled into the cylinder heads to prevent steam pockets from forming in the cooling system. The 400 also cracks between the steam holes on the deck surface.

In 1971, the full-size Chevrolet sedan received a refined "Advanced Full Coil" suspension to go with its new wheelbase. This included full upper and lower front A-arms. Other new changes included flush-mounted door handles, thinner windshield pillars, a 10 percent bigger windshield, the new "Astro-Ventilation", open-type rocker panels, double-panel roof, an inside hood release, forward-mounted steering gear, wider, six-inch wheels on a larger bolt circle, and a windshield-hidden radio antenna. The '71 police station wagon got a new rear suspension using leaf springs instead of coil springs.

For 1971, all Chevrolet police engines from the Turbo-Thrift 250-cid Six to the mighty Turbo-Jet 454-cid V-8 had the compression ratio lowered to 8.5:1. The police literature contained this note explaining the lower compression engines:

In 1971, all Chevrolet police engines from the 250-cid Six to the 454-cid big-block V-8 had the compression ratio lowered to 8.5:1. This cost up to 50 hp. (Ned Schwartz)

"For 1971, all Chevrolet engines have been designed to operate efficiently on the new no-lead or low-lead gasolines. In addition to the lower exhaust emissions attainable with this engine/fuel combination, there are benefits in longer life for your spark plugs, exhaust system and other engine components. If these no-lead, low-lead gasolines are not available, any leaded regular grade gasoline with a research octane number of 91 or higher may be used."

For example, the 350-cid V-8 with four-barrel carb was reduced from the 1970 ratio of 10.25:1 to 8.5:1 for 1971. The result was a 30 hp drop to 270 hp. The top 1971 big-block was the 454-cid/365-hp V-8 with four-barrel carb. This produced 390 hp in 1970 when it had a 10.25:1 compression ratio.

This power loss was not strictly a drop in compression. Cam grinds and carb calibrations were also changed. Corporation-wide, General Motors was continuing its efforts to de-emphasize speed. Compression was lowered to allow lower octane gas to be used in compliance with federal standards. Overall, this drop from a 10.25:1 to a 8.5:1 ratio caused a 25 to 50 bhp reduction in small-blocks and big-blocks alike.

The combination of emission controls for all engines and escalating insurance premiums for muscle car engines forced the lower compression ratios industry wide. However, General Motors was the first to take action. Only a few Corvette and Camaro engines had a compression greater than 8.5:1 and these were just 9.0:1 engines.

In 1971 Chrysler Corporation still had four engines with 10.2:1 to 10.5:1 compression ratios. Ford had four engines with a compression ratio over 11.0:1 and three engines with a squish over 10.0:1 including a big-block with two-barrel carb and 10.5:1 compression.

Subtle differences exist between the police and retail drivetrains in the horsepower and especially in availability. For example, the 400-cid small-block was a retail engine in 1970 but not used in cop cars until 1971. The 400-cid/255-bhp V-8 with two-barrel carb was available in full-size retail cars in 1971 but not police cars.

The 400-cid engine with four-barrel carb was rated at 300 bhp in retail cars but had a 310 bhp rating in police form. Police fleet service is the only known use for this rare 310 bhp version of the 400-cid small-block. Most retail and enthusiast engine manuals overlook this horsepower variation.

The three-speed Synchro-Mesh was still standard equipment on the retail Chevrolets with 350-cid V-8s but was not available on a police package Chevrolet with a V-8. The two-speed Powerglide was listed as an option with the 350 with two-barrel carb on the retail cars but was likewise not available on the police cars.

In 1971, the entire auto industry changed the way it rated horsepower. The older system, called brake or gross horsepower, was measured without a transmission attached to the engine. The engine ran open exhaust and was free of power-robbing accessories. The brake horsepower technique did not even require the engine to run its own water pump let alone a generator, air pump or power steering pump.

In 1971, the Society of Automotive Engineers method for measuring net horsepower was adopted. Following SAE procedure J245, the engine was now required to run the test with all power accessories, muffled exhaust and the transmission and torque converter in place.

The combination of lower power from less compression and a different way to rate power was a shock to car enthusiasts everywhere. The big, bad 454 that used to carry a 390 brake horsepower rating now had a 285 net horsepower label. That can be read as more than a 100 hp loss unless you are careful and knowledgeable. Likewise, the 300 bhp version of the 350 with four-barrel carb was now packing just 175 net hp.

In 1971, the net hp rating averaged about 75 percent of the brake hp ratings, but this varied widely and wildly by engine. It did, however, put an end to "advertised" horsepower readings forever. In loose

The 1971 Biscayne station wagon used a 125-inch wheelbase. With lower compression and heavier bodies, it took a lot of engine to get these police cars to move. (Ned Schwartz)

terms, the 260 net hp from the LT1 350 in the 1994 to 1996 Caprice is about 345 bhp under the old system. This, of course, does not count the flat, peak torque curve made possible by electronic fuel injection and computer-controlled spark.

Chevrolet changed its engine marketing terminology in 1971. The term "Turbo-Fire" used to mean small-block V-8 while "Turbo-Jet" used to mean big-block V-8. For 1971, the 400 with two-barrel carb retail engine was called a Turbo-Fire. However, this small-block V-8 fitted with a four-barrel carb was called a Turbo-Jet. Turbo-Jet did not mean four-barrel now either. The 350 with four-barrel carb was still called a Turbo-Fire engine.

In the fall of 1970, Chevrolet was hit with one of the longest work stoppages in its history. Just as the production of the '71 models was about to begin, a 65-day strike cut the model year short. As a result, only 37,600 Biscayne four-door sedans and 20,000 Bel Air four-door sedans were produced as '71 models. This was exactly half of the 1970 production of these two cars. These were the two cars upon which the police package was based. This makes the police '71 Chevrolet much more rare than other years.

Chevrolet Police Small-Block V-8s					
Introduction	**1955**	**1957**	**1962**	**1969**	**1971**
Engine	265 cid	283 cid	327 cid	350 cid	400 cid
Bore	3.750 in	3.875 in	4.001 in	4.001 in	4.125 in
Stroke	3.000 in	3.000 in	3.250 in	3.480 in	3.750 in
Carb	4-bbl	4-bbl	4-bbl	4-bbl	4-bbl
HP	180 hp	220 hp	300 hp	300 hp	310 hp

1971 Chevrolet Biscayne		
Engine, Carb, HP	**Fuel Economy**	**Top Speed**
250-cid I-6, 1-bbl, 145 hp	15.5 mpg	91 mph
350-cid V-8, 2-bbl, 245 hp	13.1 mpg	105 mph
400-cid V-8, 2-bbl, 255 hp	11.7 mpg	106 mph
350-cid V-8, 4-bbl, 270 hp	12.3 mpg	109 mph
400-cid V-8, 4-bbl, 310 hp	11.6 mpg	113 mph
454-cid V-8, 4-bbl, 365 hp	10.6 mpg	115 mph

Biscayne and Bel Air Police Engines for 1971					
Engine	**Size & Carb**	**Brake HP**	**SAE net hp**	**Axle**	**Trans**
Turbo-Thrift 250 Six	250 cid, 1-bbl, 8.5:1, single	145 bhp @ 4400	110 nhp	3.08	3-speed or Powerglide
Turbo-Fire 350 V-8	350 cid, 2-bbl, 8.5:1, single	245 bhp @ 4800	165 nhp	3.42	Turbo Hydra-Matic
Turbo-Fire 350 V-8	350 cid, 4-bbl, 8.5:1 single	270 bhp @ 4800	175 nhp	3.42	Turbo Hydra-Matic
Turbo-Jet 400 V-8	400 cid, 4-bbl, 8.5:1 dual	310 bhp @ 4800	260 nhp	3.42	Turbo Hydra-Matic
Turbo-Jet 454 V-8 (LS-5)	454 cid, 4-bbl, 8.5:1, dual	365 bhp @ 4800	285 nhp	3.08	Turbo Hydra-Matic

References for 1971

75 Years of Chevrolet, George Dammann, Motorbooks International
1971 Police Cars, Chevrolet Motor Division
Illustrated Chevrolet Buyers Guide, John Gunnell, Motorbooks International

Standard Catalog of Chevrolet, Pat Chappell, Krause Publications
Chevrolet Impala and SS, 1958-1971, R.M. Clarke, Motorbooks International

The Ankeny, Iowa, Police fleet of 1971 Biscaynes. A 65-day strike at Chevrolet made the 1971 four-door sedan one of the rarest Chevrolet police cars. (John Evers)

Chapter 18

1972: 402-cid Big-Block V-8

The 1972, full-size Chevrolets were big, big cars. The curb weight tipped the scales at a hefty 4,045 pounds. This marked the first time the Biscayne four-door sedans reached the two-ton weight bracket.

The police package was available for the Biscayne, Bel Air and Impala and in their respective station wagons, Brookwood, Townsman and Kingswood. Again, the Biscayne and Bel Air were available only as a four-door sedan. The Impala was available as a four-door sedan, two-door hardtop coupe, four-door hardtop sedan and two-door custom coupe. This was the first model year that the Impala was specifically included as a police package car.

The '71 and '72 models were similar, but different enough to at least tell apart. The '71 had a classic egg-crate grille with large turn signal lenses on the front fender extension caps. This was quite similar to the '67 turn signals. For 1972, the grille was much more formal and the front fender extension caps contained only the side markers. The turn signals were now in the bumper.

Chevrolet made a number of drivetrain changes for 1972. First of all, the Turbo-Thrift 250 Six was gone. The full-size police cars were way too heavy to be powered by 110 nhp, one-barrel carbureted Six. This was still a retail engine but not available on any police package car, even the lighter police Chevelle.

Second, after too many years of hanging on, the two-speed Powerglide automatic transmission was gone. In its place was a "small-block" Turbo Hydra-Matic 350. This was used with the 307-, 350- and 400-cid police small-block engines. A larger, "big-block" Turbo Hydra-Matic 400 was used with the 402- and 454-cid police engines.

Also gone from the police lineup was the three-speed Synchro-Mesh manual transmission. This had served law enforcement well for decades. As of 1972, all full-size retail and police Chevrolets came with an automatic transmission and power steering as standard equipment.

The big news concerning police engines was the Turbo-Jet 402 V-8. This bored-out 396-cid big-block was new for police cars in 1972.

Engine	396 V-8	402 V-8	454 V-8
Bore	4.094 in	4.126 in	4.251 in
Stroke	3.760 in	3.760 in	4.000 in

In 1970, Chevrolet bored out the L78 396-cid big-block from 4.094 inches to 4.126 inches. The result was the 402 engine that Chevy continued to call a "396" at least for retail cars. In the police

The Jersey City and Newark, New Jersey, Police were among many urban departments to use the Biscayne in 1972. (Ned Schwartz)

The 1972 Biscayne was too heavy for the 250-cid Six. All 1972 Chevrolet police cars had at least a 350-cid V-8. (Ned Schwartz)

A 1972 Bel Air that was still in-service with the Frohna, Missouri, Police in 1996. Don't be fooled by the 400 engine emblems. This car has a 402-cid big-block.

The 402-cid canted-valve, porcupine-head big-block was only available in police cars in 1972. The single exhaust version produced 210 hp.

literature the automaker accurately labeled the new engine as a Turbo-Jet 402 V-8.

The new 402 was otherwise identical to the 396 with one exception. The new engine used a lower profile intake manifold. This gained needed hood clearance but reduced the engine performance throughout the entire operating range.

Even though the 402-cid rat engine was a 1970 retail engine, it was not until 1972 that it would be used in police package cars. In 1970 and 1971, the only big-block police engine was the 454. Again, the 400-cid engine was a small-block and the 402 was a big-block.

The '72 402-cid V-8 was available in two power levels. These were actually the same LS-3 four-barrel carbureted engine with an 8.5:1 compression. The 210 nhp engine had a single exhaust while the 240 nhp engine used dual exhaust. The 1972 model year was the only time the 402-cid engine was used in a police car. It was discontinued after 1972.

The 240 nhp version of the 402 was available only in sedans and coupes and was not available in station wagons. The 402-cid big-block itself was not available in any power level in the state of California. Neither was the 454-cid big-block in any form. The last Chevrolet big-block for the California cops was '71 LS-5 454, and that engine required dual exhaust to meet California emission standards.

For 1972, two versions of the Turbo-Jet 454 V-8 were available for police package cars. Both had 8.5:1 compression ratios and four-barrel carbs. Like the 402, the 230 nhp version had single exhaust and the 270 nhp version had dual exhaust. This 230 nhp version was available only in station wagons. Because of emission constraints, even the dual exhaust version of the 454 was down 15 nhp from 1971.

The '72 models had a few other subtle changes. These full-size police package cars now had a rear stabilizer bar as standard equipment. This was indeed an absolute requirement to get these nose-heavy, long wheelbase squad cars to handle well. Another change was a coolant recovery system. These engines ran so hot to keep emissions under control that a radiator overflow and return system was needed. This also allowed the officer to check the coolant level in the radiator when the engine was hot without removing the radiator cap.

A special word of caution is in order for police cars wearing the "400" engine emblems on the front fenders. This "400" emblem was used for squad cars powered by the 400-cid, two-barrel carbureted small-block. The "400" emblem was *also* used on squad cars powered by either version of the 402-cid, four-barrel carbureted big-block! Put another way, the two-barrel version of the "400" was the 400-cid small-block. The four-barrel version of the "400" was one of the 402-cid big-blocks. A squad car with "400" emblems and dual exhaust meant it had the 240 nhp 402. Other than that, there was no way from the exterior to tell a two-barrel carbureted 400 rated at 170 nhp from the four-barrel carbureted 402 rated at 210 nhp. Yet a big difference existed in both performance and vintage value between the small-block and the big-block.

Finally, the tire size was upgraded one size from F78x15 to G78x15. This change alone signals the kind of vehicle weight Chevrolet engineers knew they had to deal with. The big-block cars got H78x15 rubber.

For 1972, Chevrolet changed its police package coding. RPO B07 now referred to Police Chassis Equipment. RPO BY2 was now used to specify Police Body Equipment.

Also for 1972, the Chevelle was back in police trim again after a two-year leave. "Chevelle: fits more patrols, more parking spots and more city budgets." This was the first time the police package was referred to as Central Office Purchase Order (COPO) 9C1. The 9C1 package would eventually become the main police package designation for full-size cars. Smaller squad cars would use 9C3 packages. "Special service" packages that do not meet internal Chevrolet durability requirements for police packages, would use the code B4C.

The '72 Chevelle 9C1 package was restricted to the 116-inch wheelbase, four-door sedan. A minimum order of 10 vehicles was required. These cars came with beefed up frames, heavy-duty engine features, 3.31 ratio heavy-duty rear axle, heavy-duty front lower control arms, high-capacity cooling system, 61-amp generator, 80-amp battery and a calibrated police speedometer.

The 9C1 package also required a heavy-duty front and rear suspension with front and rear sway bars, power front disc and rear drum brakes and a heavy-duty front seat. A long list of Special Order options included 8.25x15 "police service" tires, heavy-duty front and rear rubberized mats, bucket seats, roof wiring, roof reinforcement and a remote trunk opener.

Chevrolet intended the Chevelle 9C1 to be powered by the Turbo-Fire 350 V-8. This low-compression, four-barrel carbureted, dual exhaust, small-block produced 175 nhp. In fact, this was the only police Chevelle engine available in California. Cops in the Other 49 could also equip the Chevelle with the dual exhaust Turbo-Jet 402 V-8 rated at 240 nhp. In an odd twist, if the COPO 9C1 equipment was not ordered, the Chevelle came standard with the Turbo-Fire 307 V-8. This was apparently geared toward light-duty detective-type police work as opposed to uniformed patrol.

In 1972, *Motor Trend* tested the full-size Chevrolet Caprice along with the Ford LTD. Both were powered by 400-cid engines. The Chevy used the two-barrel, 170 nhp version of the Turbo-Jet 400 V-8, which was a police package engine. Fitted with a Turbo Hydra-Matic 350 and 3.42 rear gears, the massive Chevrolet took 11.3 seconds to reach 60 mph. It ran the quarter-mile in 18.4 seconds at just 76 mph.

In addition to major police agencies in Missouri and New York, the 1972 full-size Chevrolet was used by the West Virginia State Police (Impala) and the Arizona Highway Patrol.

The 1972 Biscayne, such as this Floral Park, New York, unit, was used by urban and rural police departments alike. The state police in Arizona, Missouri, New York and West Virginia drove 1972 Chevrolets. (Ned Schwartz)

Chevelle Police Engines for 1972			
Engine	Size, Carb, Comp, Exhaust	SAE net hp	Trans
Turbo-Fire 307 V-8	307 cid, 2-bbl, 8.5, single	130 @ 4000	THM 350
Turbo-Fire 350 V-8	350 cid, 4-bbl, 8.5, dual	175 @ 4000	THM 350
Turbo-Jet 402 V-8 (LS-3)	402 cid, 4-bbl, 8.5, dual	240 @ 4400	THM 400

Full-Size 1972 Chevrolet Police Powerteams				
Engine	Size, Carb, Comp, Exhaust	SAE net hp	Trans	Axle
Turbo-Fire 350 V-8	350 cid, 2-bbl, 8.5, single	165 @ 4000	THM 350	3.42
Turbo-Jet 400 V-8	400 cid, 2-bbl, 8.5, single	170 @ 3400	THM 350	3.42
Turbo-Jet 402 V-8 (LS-3)	402 cid, 4-bbl, 8.5, single	210 @ 4400	THM 400	3.08
Turbo-Jet 402 V-8 (LS-3)	402 cid, 4-bbl, 8.5, dual	240 @ 4400	THM 400	3.08
Turbo-Jet 454 V-8 (LS-5)	454 cid, 4-bbl, 8.5, single	230 @ 4000	THM 400	3.08
Turbo-Jet 454 V-8 (LS-5)	454 cid, 4-bbl, 8.5, dual	270 @ 4000	THM 400	3.08

References for 1972

75 Years of Chevrolet, George Dammann, Motorbooks International

1972 Police Cars, Chevrolet Motor Division

Illustrated Chevrolet Buyers Guide, John Gunnell, Motorbooks International

Standard Catalog of Chevrolet, Pat Chappell, Krause Publications

Chapter 19

1973: Leaner Carbs, Milder Cams, EGR

For 1973, the name "Biscayne" was dropped. This had been used since 1958. The full-size '73 Chevrolet police cars were based on the Bel Air and the Impala. The B07 police chassis equipment and BY2 police body equipment packages were available on the four-door sedans, two-door coupe and the two-seat and three-seat station wagons in both trim levels.

Subtle improvements for 1973 included a transistorized voltage regulator, 5-mph bumpers, an exhaust gas recirculation system (EGR), stronger roofs and thicker side guard door beams. Larger, G78x15 tires were now standard.

The front and rear bumpers were now bumper systems. To meet the 5 mph federal impact standards the front bumper system was made

For 1973, the B07 and BY2 police packages were available on the Bel Air such as this Kearny, New Jersey, Police unit—and the Impala. The Biscayne nameplate was dropped. (Ned Schwartz)

This 1973 Elizabeth, New Jersey, Police unit is packing a 400-cid small-block. This two-barrel V-8 produced 150 hp. (Ned Schwartz)

up of an outer bumper, inner bumper, attaching brackets, transfer yokes and the "enersorber." This device absorbed impacts exactly like a shock absorber. The rear bumper system was less complicated and did not use the "enersorber."

The big change in police engines for 1973 was the loss of the 402-cid big-block. The overall power levels were down so much on 1973 engines that it took a 454-cid big-block to equal a 1972 402-cid big-block. In fact, the '72 402-cid, four-barrel carbureted, dual exhaust engine produced 240 nhp and the '73 454-cid, four-barrel carbureted, dual exhaust engine produced 245 nhp. This across-the-board drop in horsepower squeezed-out the smaller big-block. The next closest engine was the four-barrel carbureted 350-cid V-8 rated at 175 nhp.

With leaner carbs, milder cams and less aggressive timing curves, every 1973 police engine suffered the same fate. This was true even though the compression ratios all remained around 8.5:1. The 400 with two-barrel carb lost 20 nhp, the 350 with two-barrel carb lost 20 nhp, and the big, bad 454 with four-barrel carb and dual exhaust lost 25 nhp.

It would not be until the 1994 LT1 that a Chevrolet police sedan had an engine as powerful as the '72 LS-5. The '94 350 LT1 produced 260 nhp compared to the '72 454 LS-5 at 270 nhp and the '73 454 LS-5 at 245 nhp. Some police officers would spend their entire 20-year career with pursuit police engines that had a maximum net horsepower under 250 nhp.

The big news for the '73 Chevelle was the wider availability of mid-size models. In 1972, the 9C1 package was restricted to the 116-inch wheelbase, four-door sedan. In 1973, the police package was expanded to almost any Chevelle model. This included the 116-inch four-door sedan, 112-inch two-door coupe and the two-seat and three-seat station wagons. The police package came in both the Chevelle Deluxe and the Chevelle Malibu.

In 1973, the police Chevelle was powered by a 350-cid/175-nhp, four-barrel carbureted engine with dual exhaust, period. No optional engines. The 307-cid small-block and the 402-cid big-block from 1972 were gone. In fact, this 350-cid/175-nhp V-8 was the only carry-over from 1972.

The police Chevelle was perky for the era. At 3,435 pounds, the 175 nhp Chevelle had 5.1 hp for each 100 pounds of vehicle weight. The full-size Bel Air weighed 4,087 pounds. With the 245 nhp big-block, the Bel Air had 6.0 hp per 100 pounds, and was only a bit faster than the Chevelle. However, with the 350-cid/175-nhp engine, the Bel Air power to weight ratio dropped to just 4.3 hp per 100 pounds. The small-block-powered Chevelle was much faster than the small-block-powered Bel Air.

The Chevelle A-body sedans and coupes were extensively re-modeled for 1973. The sedan grew one inch wider and six inches longer overall while keeping the same 116-inch wheelbase. The length was now 207.9 inches. Part of this change was a totally new chassis:

"The new Chevelle perimeter frame, with increased torsion and beam strength, includes sturdier box section side rails of increased material thickness. Wider front and rear treads and wider wheels contribute to overall vehicle stability. Improved handling control and smoother, quieter ride result from significant suspension refinements. Front suspension camber coefficient changes provide improved tire-to-road surface contact during cornering with reduced squeal and longer tread wear. Repositioning of the control arm pivot shafts allows increased cushioning of high impact forces.

"A slightly higher positive camber setting for the front left wheel gives a more uniform and stable steering feel on high crown road surfaces while maintaining excellent turnpike cruise stability. Increased rear suspension damping results from new shock absorber positioning and control arm bushing refinements. Finally, the front and rear suspensions are 'fine tuned' to achieve the desired degree of controlled response to each driving maneuver. Front

With milder cams and leaner carbs, it took a 454-cid engine in 1973 to equal the horsepower from the 402-cid powerplant in 1972. The 350-cid police Chevelle was about as fast as the 454-cid Bel Air. (Ned Schwartz)

disc brakes, standard on all models, improve directional control during braking and give increased resistance to fade and the effect of water."

The Wyoming Highway Patrol was just one of the major police departments to drive Chevrolets in 1973.

Police Drivetrains for 1973				
Engine Size, Carb Compression, Exhaust	SAE net hp	Trans	Axles	Models
350 cid, 2-bbl, 8.5, single	145 @ 4000	THM 350	3.42, 3.08	All full-size
350 cid, 4-bbl, 8.5, dual	175 @ 4000	THM 350	3.42, 3.08	Full-size sedans, coupes
400 cid, 2-bbl, 8.5, single	150 @ 3200	THM 350	3.42, 3.08	All full-size
454 cid, 4-bbl, 8.25,single	215 @ 4000	THM 400	3.42	Full-size wagon only
454 cid, 4-bbl, 8.25, dual	245 @ 4000	THM 400	3.08	Full-size sedans, coupes
350 cid, 4-bbl, 8.5, dual	175 @ 4000	THM 350	3.42	All Chevelle

References for 1973

75 Years of Chevrolet, George Dammann, Motorbooks International

1973 Police Cars, Chevrolet Motor Division

Illustrated Chevrolet Buyers Guide, John Gunnell, Motorbooks International

Standard Catalog of Chevrolet, Pat Chappell, Krause Publications

Chapter 20

1974: Malibu Mid-Size Police Car

The Chicago Police fleet manager checks out the new paint scheme on the 1974 Bel Air. (Greg Reynolds)

For 1974, the B07 and BY2 police packages were available for the Bel Air and Impala four-door sedan, Impala two-door coupe and both trim levels of two-seat and three-seat full-size station wagon. In the Chevelle line, the 9C1 police package was available for the Malibu and Malibu Classic four-door sedan and two-door coupe. The two-seat and three-seat Chevelle station wagons were no longer available in police trim.

This Walhalla, North Dakota, Police 1974 Bel Air is powered by the 454-cid/235-hp big-block. It could pass anything but a gas station. (Jim Benjaminson)

The wheelbase on the full-size sedans and coupes remained at 121.5 inches. Likewise, the four-door Malibu was 116 inches and the two-door Malibu had a 112-inch wheelbase.

For 1974, the full-size Chevrolets boasted a new, heavier-gauge frame. This increased platform rigidity and improved the ride and noise isolation. The frame and rear suspension lower control arms also got a new corrosion-resistant coating. Disc brake sensors that produced an audible signal when the pads needed to be replaced were also new.

The front suspension got larger upper control arm bushings and ball joint seals. A magnet was added in 1974 to the power steering pump to collect metallic debris in the system. Also new for '74 was a front seat belt and ignition interlock system. This prevented the engine from being started unless the front belts were fastened. This irritating and trouble-prone interlock was frequently disconnected or overridden.

The police drivetrains for 1974 were a carry-over from 1973 with a few exceptions. The 350-cid, four-barrel carbureted, dual exhaust engine was gone completely. The 350 with four-barrel carb would be the primary powerplant from 1977 through 1988, but was not available for 1974.

The other missing engine was the single exhaust, and station wagon-only version of the 454-cid big-block. For 1974, the wagon used the same rat engine as the sedans and coupes but got a special 3.42 axle ratio. The 454-cid-powered sedans were only available with 3.08 rear gears.

A 1974 Bel Air used by the Santa Clara, California, Police. Because of emission laws, the only 1974 police engine certified for California was the 454-cid with dual exhausts. (Darryl Lindsay)

To get the LS4 454-cid V-8, the police department had to order the "High Speed Pursuit Package," which in turn required the B07 police chassis equipment package. The High Speed Pursuit Package included the 454-cid/235-nhp engine, more durable upper and lower control arm bushings, rear stabilizer bar, severe duty front and rear brakes and H78x15 nylon police high speed tires.

By 1974, the emissions standards established by the California Air Resources Board (CARB) were having a major affect on carmaker and engine availabilities. It was becoming so expensive to develop and to certify an engine and drivetrain package for just California that automakers did not even try on many engines.

On the full-size Chevrolet, for example, the L65 350-cid, two-barrel carbureted and the LF6 400-cid, two-barrel carbureted engines were simply not available in California. This meant that no drivetrain for the police Chevelle was available in 1974. The LT4 400-cid, four-barrel carbureted engine was certified for California but was only available on full-size station wagons. While the 3.42 rear gear was standard on these LT4-powered wagons, the wagons headed to California were required to have 3.08 rear gears.

With all of the emissions restrictions, Chevrolet had just one California-certified engine for its full-size police sedans and coupes in 1974. This was the LS4 454-cid, four-barrel carbureted V-8 with dual exhaust, a 3.08 axle and 235 nhp. This was a great engine for high-speed pursuit. However, this excluded Chevrolet from bidding on urban contracts that had put limits on the maximum engine size. All this explains why Chevrolet did so much work to develop the mid-size Nova police package.

In 1974, *Motor Trend* wrung out a Chevrolet Caprice Classic, Ford LTD Brougham and Plymouth Gran Fury sedan. These were the absolute top-of-the-line cars from the original Low Priced Three. These, of course, were not low-priced cars any longer, and had not been for a decade. The interiors of these cars were far more plush than any cop under the rank of inspector, chief or sheriff would ever see.

However, each used a police-based drivetrain, towing-grade suspension and power disc brakes.

These were all monstrous vehicles with 121- to 122-inch wheelbases, 220- to 223-inch overall lengths, and curb weights from 4,373 to 4,860 pounds. The Chevrolet was the longest sedan but actually the lightest. Even though this was in the middle of the gasoline embargo, and urban congestion was a household word, these full-size cars captured one-third of the new car market.

Of the Caprice's radial-tuned suspension, *Motor Trend* wrote:

"...a radial tire package that transforms a run-of-the-mill sedan into an excellent handling machine. Where a few full-size cars of the past had handling characteristics somewhat akin to driving a bathtub half-full of water, this year's lot is dramatically different. All offer radial tires either as standard or optional and the radial improvement must be experienced to be believed.

"The optional Goodyear HR78x15 radials on the Caprice are the first example of the so-called "GM Radial," a tire painstakingly designed by GM for use only on its cars that will be built by all its suppliers....Both dry and wet weather handling are superb and the traction in snow is said to be so good that the need to switch to snow tires has practically been eliminated.

"The Caprice's radial package also includes a rear stabilizer bar, thicker front bar, modified shock valving, a larger power-steering gear with better on-center handling and better road feel....It all adds up to greatly improved handling that's both stable and precise..."

In terms of performance, the Chevrolet was a winner. First, it had the shortest braking distance and the best control:

"...The Chevy gets the nod since its straight-as-an-arrow stops inspired a great deal of confidence. The other two stopped nicely but the Plymouth pedal felt mushy and the

In Southern California, the police car to beat in 1974 was the 401-cid-powered AMC Matador, such as this LAPD unit. While not reliable, these cars were whip-quick. (LAPD)

Ford had a tendency to slew sideways in a stand-on-it panic halt."

The Chevrolet sedan also had a good quarter-mile run. The 460-cid, four-barrel carbureted Ford was a few tenths quicker but the 454-cid, four-barrel carbureted Chevy had a faster trap speed and a faster 0-60 mph time.

For 1974, the Chevelle was back in police trim with a couple of changes. First, the L48 350-cid, four-barrel carbureted V-8 with dual exhaust and 175 nhp used in 1973 was not available. The new Chevelle engine was the LF6 400-cid, two-barrel carbureted V-8 with single exhaust producing just 150 nhp. The second change was that the Chevelle was simply not available in California in any form.

The '74 9C1 package Chevelle had a Turbo Hydra-Matic transmission and 3.42 rear gears. This package also included all of the heavy-duty suspension, cooling, electrical and brake features. The 9C1 package was once again available on both the 112-inch wheelbase two-door coupe and 116-inch four-door sedan in both Malibu and Malibu Classic trim levels.

From 1972 to 1974, the mid-size police car to beat was, beyond all question, the AMC Matador with a 401-cid, four-barrel carbureted V-8. The Matador was used by the Los Angeles Police Department from 1972 to 1974 and made famous in the TV series, "Adam 12." The Matador was also used by the Los Angeles County Sheriffs Department from 1973 to 1974, in addition to other police agencies around the country.

During an era of extremely sluggish police car performance, the Matador 401 was whip-quick. It was not a reliable nor durable police car; however, it handled well, had reasonably good brakes, and it was fast. For better or worse, by all accounts the Matador was a better mid-size police car than the Chevelle with a 400-cid, two-barrel carbureted V-8. The Nova 9C1 would save Chevrolet's reputation when the Matador was used as a benchmark during Nova testing. However, for the time being, the Matador was enjoying its 15 minutes of fame.

Motor Trend tested all the intermediate-sized '74 sedans. Some of these had police drivetrains, but others did not. Of the Chevelle, they noted:

"Chevelle with its stout rear sway bar and radials does the best job (of handling)."

On the performance-fuel economy tradeoff they noted:

"It's what's inside the engine that counts rather than sheer size and axle ratio."

The small-block, 400-cid, two-barrel carbureted V-8 with a 3.08 axle averaged 13.7 mpg. The Chevelle was second behind only the Cutlass with a 350-cid, four-barrel carbureted V-8 in this test of five intermediates.

In 1974, the Chevelle was available in the other 49 states with the B07 and BY2 police packages and the 400-cid/150-nhp, two-barrel carbureted police engine. The '74 Nova was not available with any police gear, period. However, the '74 Nova became the test platform for one of the most popular and highly engineered police cars to ever hit the streets, especially in Southern California.

The Nova police car got its notoriety from *Motor Trend* Executive Editor John Christy. Christy was also a Specialist Reserve Deputy with the Los Angeles County Sheriffs Department. Christy made technical changes to the LASD vehicle test procedures to make them more realistic, more accurate, more detailed and more relevant. This new test method paved the way for mid-size cars to replace full-size cars in many patrol areas.

The '74 Nova tested by the LASD was powered by a 350-cid/185-hp, four-barrel carbureted V-8 with a Turbo Hydra-Matic transmission and 3.08 rear gears. This engine was totally unique to the police Nova. The chassis was a mixture of standard and optional Nova SS and Camaro Z28 parts. The brakes were from the full-size Bel Air. The power steering had Z28 valving, which gave more road feel and response. The suspension had front and rear sway bars. The Nova used specially-developed, Firestone E70x14 pursuit tires.

The COPO 9C1 Nova, jointly developed by the Los Angeles County Sheriffs Department and *Motor Trend* magazine, is the most important police car Chevrolet ever made. The Nova 9C1 revolutionized the police use of mid-size patrol cars in exactly the same way as the special service package Ford Mustang got cops to rethink pursuit cars.

Full-Size Sedan Comparison			
	Chevrolet	**Ford**	**Plymouth**
Model	**Caprice Classic**	**LTD Brougham**	**Gran Fury Sedan**
Engine	454 cid, 4-bbl	460 cid, 4-bbl	400 cid, 4-bbl
Horsepower	235 nhp	200 nhp	205 nhp
Transmission	Turbo Hydra-Matic	Cruise-O-Matic	TorqueFlite
Rear Gear	2.73	3.00	3.23
Brakes	disc/drum	disc/drum	disc/drum
Tires	HR78x15	JR78x15	HR78x15
Wheelbase	121.5 in	121.0 in	122.0 in
Curb Weight	4,373 lbs	4,860 lbs	4,676 lbs
Performance			
0-60 mph	9.6 sec	10.8 sec	10.4 sec
Quarter-Mile E.T.	17.9 sec	17.6 sec	18.2 sec
Trap Speed	82 mph	80 mph	78 mph
60-0 mph Braking	133 feet	139 feet	139 feet

Police Drivetrains for 1974					
RPO	**Engine, Carb, Exhaust**	**SAE hp**	**Trans**	**Axles**	**Models**
L65	350 cid, 2-bbl, single	145 nhp	THM 350	3.42, 3.08	Full-size sedans, coupes
LF6	400 cid, 2-bbl, single	150 nhp	THM 350	3.42, 3.08	Full-size sedans, coupes
LT4	400 cid, 4-bbl, single	180 nhp	THM 350	3.42, 3.08	Full-size wagons only
LS4	454 cid, 4-bbl, dual	235 nhp	THM 400	3.08 only	Full-size sedans, coupes
LS4	454 cid, 4-bbl, dual	235 nhp	THM 400	3.42 only	Full-size wagons only
LF6	400 cid, 2-bbl, single	150 nhp	THM 350	3.42 only	All Chevelle

Mid-Size Sedan Comparison				
	AMC	**Chevrolet**	**Ford**	**Dodge**
Model	**Matador**	**Chevelle**	**Torino**	**Coronet**
Engine	410 cid, 4-bbl	400 cid, 2-bbl	460 cid, 4-bbl	360 cid, 4-bbl
Horsepower	255 nhp	150 nhp	220 nhp	200 nhp
Transmission	Torque Command	Turbo Hydra-Matic	Cruise-O-Matic	TorqueFlite
Rear Gear	3.54	3.08	3.25	2.71
Brakes	disc/drum	disc/drum	disc/drum	disc/drum
Tires	FR78x14	GR78x15	HR78x14	HR78x14
Wheelbase	114 in	116 in	114 in	118 in
Curb Weight	4,055 lbs	4,250 lbs	4,615 lbs	3,850 lbs
Performance				
0-60 mph	8.5 sec	11.4 sec	8.3 sec	9.5 sec
1/4-mile E.T.	15.96 sec	18.02 sec	16.4 sec	16.6 sec
1/4-mile Speed	87.4 mph	76.5 mph	85.1 mph	84.7 mph
60-0 mph Braking	160 ft	161 ft	152 ft	125 ft

References for 1974

"Return of the Intermediates," Jim Brokaw, *Motor Trend*, August 1974

"The Intermediates," staff report, *Motor Trend*, January 1974

"New '74 Sedans," John Fuchs, *Motor Trend*, November 1973

1974 Chevrolet Police Vehicles, Chevrolet Motor Division

Chapter 21

1975: Nova, Motor Trend, *Los Angeles Sheriff*

The 1975 Bel Air station wagon driven by the Milwaukee fire battalion chief. This was the first year for steel-belted radials. (Greg Reynolds)

For 1975, the Bel Air and Impala got a new look. They now resembled the '74 Caprice Classic and the Cadillac. Once again, the Bel Air and Impala shared the same bodies and roof lines as the Caprice but used a different front end design. For 1975, the wheelbases, lengths and widths were unchanged from 1974.

For 1975 the B07 and BY2 police packages were once again based on the Bel Air four-door sedan, the Impala four-door sedan and two-door sport coupe, and the two-seat and three-seat station wagon in both trim levels. This would be the last year for the Bel Air nameplate introduced in 1953.

The full-size Chevrolets received a number of subtle improvements. These included heavier-duty front lower control arm bushings, thicker steel in the frame side members, ducting of the outside air to the air cleaner instead of the hot, under-hood air, tandem power brake booster and a High Energy Ignition.

This was also the year of the catalytic converter. All models got a single catalytic converter to control exhaust emissions. This required no-lead gasoline. As a result, 1975 was the year that fuel filler neck openings were reduced in size to prevent the use of leaded gas.

In 1974, the standard equipment tire was the G78x15 bias belted tire. Steel belted HR78x15 radials were a RPO in 1974. The "high speed pursuit" package that included the 454-cid V-8 required H78x15 nylon bias police-grade tires.

For 1975, the standard tire size was upgraded to HR78x15 steel belted radials. The "high speed pursuit" package included the H78x15 nylon police high-speed tires. The 454-cid V-8 engine never came with radial tires in any of its service years. COPO tires included H78x15 nylon bias belted tires and HR78x15 and HR70x15 fabric belted radials.

This was also the first year of steel-belted radials. These were built to GM's specifications. Chevrolet still called for police spec bias-belted tires when the High Speed Pursuit Package and the 454 were ordered. This package also included a metal manifold heat shield to insulate the exhaust manifold from other under-hood components. The operating temperatures on these early emission-controlled engines were extremely hot. The 454 used dual exhaust, however, all the gases passed through a single catalytic converter.

The police drivetrains for 1975 were greatly expanded compared to 1974. New engines included the 250-cid Six (again) and one new California version of the small-block. Some axle ratio restrictions were put into effect. The LF6 400-cid, two-barrel carbureted V-8 producing 150 nhp was gone for 1975. In its place for California cars only was the LM1 350-cid, four-barrel carbureted V-8 producing 155 nhp. Chevrolet was quite clear that the LM1 was "available only for sale and/or registration in California" when powering a Bel Air, Impala or Chevelle. This was the only engine for the police Nova. When used in the Nova, the LM1 350-cid, four-barrel carbureted V-8 was available in all 50 states.

On the full-size Chevrolet and the intermediate-size Chevelle, this LM1 engine used a true single exhaust system with a single catalytic converter. On the compact-size Nova, this engine still used a single catalytic converter but had dual tailpipes.

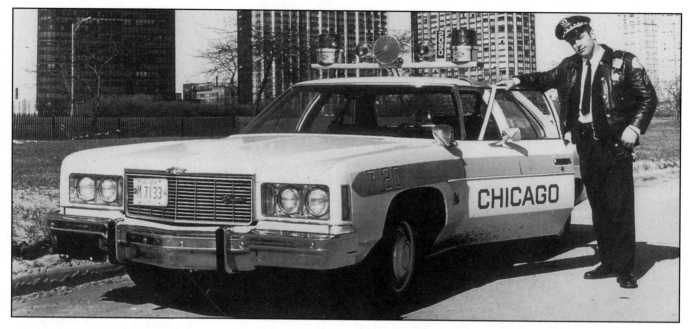

The police package in 1975 was based on the Bel Air—such as this Chicago Police unit—and the Impala. This was the last year for the Bel Air nameplate. (Lee Hamilton)

The 250-cid, one-barrel carbureted, inline Six was back in the police engine lineup for the Chevelle only. This detective-class engine produced just 105 nhp. With the Turbo Hydra-Matic transmission and standard equipment 2.73 rear gears, this combination set a new standard for low performance. The maximum engine available for the Chevelle was the four-barrel carbureted 400-cid V-8 producing 175 nhp.

In 1974, the full-size sedans and coupes came standard with a 3.42 axle ratio on all the small-block powertrains. A 3.08 axle was available but optional. This changed for 1975. In the full-size cars with 350-cid engines, the 3.08 gear was standard and no other axle ratio was available. This was an unsuccessful attempt to improve fuel economy. All it really did was degrade engine responsiveness and lower overall vehicle performance.

This situation was worse yet on the full-size cars with the 400-cid small-block. Instead of a 3.42 or 3.08 axle ratio such as the '74 cars used, the '75 models were restricted to only a 2.73 gear. These cars were much slower than the '74 models with 5 nhp more and better gearing.

The police Chevelle had similar gearing restrictions. The '74 models all came with 400-cid, two-barrel carbureted small-blocks and 3.42 rear gears. The '75 400 now had a four-barrel carb but 2.73 or 3.08 rear gears. The other Chevelle small-blocks required 2.73 gears, period.

Certain engines were not available in California for 1975. This included the 350-cid/145-nhp, two-barrel carbureted V-8 and the 454-cid/215-nhp, four-barrel carbureted V-8. Cops in California had their choice of only the 350-cid/155-nhp engine with four-barrel carb or the 400-cid/175-nhp engine with four-barrel carb in the full-size Chevrolets. These same two engines, plus the 250-cid/105-nhp Six were available on the police Chevelle. All California-bound engines required the "California Emission Equipment" package, which choked off about 10 net horsepower in addition to published readings (except the LM1).

The 1975 model year was the low point for the 454-cid cop engine. The compression was reduced to an all-time Chevrolet low of 8.15:1. The dual exhaust was choked through a single catalytic converter. The '75 four-barrel carbureted big-block produced a mere 215 SAE net horsepower. This was hardly a "rat engine."

Just four years prior, in 1971, this same basic engine produced 285 SAE net horsepower. The 350 pound-feet of torque from the '75 engine was a weakling compared to the 1971 465 pound-foot version. And these engines all had a compression ratio between 8.15:1 and 8.5:1. Of course, none of these vintages were even in the same league as the 1970 454-cid brute with 10.25:1 compression and 300 SAE nhp.

For 1975, the Chevelle received the same minor improvements as the full-size Chevrolet. The front suspension caster was tweaked for improved tracking, and the shocks got different valving for a better ride. GM-spec 78-series, steel belted radials were now standard; however, HR70x15, 70-series fabric belted radials were optional. The COPO 9C1 Chevelle police package was available for both the 116-inch wheelbase, four-door sedan and the 112-inch wheelbase, two-door coupe in both Malibu and Malibu Classic trim levels.

What would be the biggest police car news from Chevrolet in years was the 1975 Nova with the COPO 9C1 police package. Few police cars in history have had the impact of the '75 Nova 9C1. The Nova would be the car-of-choice for large urban police and sheriffs departments all over the country.

With this Nova, Chevrolet became a major force in the police market. The Nova 9C1 instantly unseated the AMC Matador and successfully blocked first the Dart/Valiant and then Aspen/Volare. Chrysler Corporation was shut out of this end of the police market by a compact Chevy designed specifically for police work. The durable, engineered Nova 9C1 literally opened the door at police departments for other Chevrolet models to compete. When the '77 downsized full-size Chevy arrived, Chevrolet was set to literally take the police market away from Chrysler.

Until the Nova 9C1, Chevrolet had been tied with Ford for second choice behind Plymouth. The Nova changed all that. It established Chevrolet as a source for highly developed squad cars specifically engineered for police duty.

The most influential police car ever made by Chevrolet was the 1975 police package Nova. Chevrolet, *Motor Trend* and the Los Angeles County Sheriff completely revolutionized the way cops thought about compact cars. (Chevrolet)

In its first year of specialized police service, the carefully developed and highly engineered Nova 9C1 came just one way: The Nova used the LM1 350-cid, four-barrel carbureted V-8 with the M40 Turbo Hydra-Matic 350 and a 3.08 rear axle ratio. No other engines, transmissions or axle ratios were available.

The 350-cid/155-nhp V-8 was specifically developed for maximum horsepower and maximum torque under the constraints of the California emissions laws. This was the first four-barrel version of the 350 since 1973. It was down 25 nhp from that era but all engines were down in power.

Actually, the LM1 was heavily tweaked. Rather than simply adding a California Emissions Package to an already existing engine, Chevrolet built the LM1 with the Emissions Package as a starting point. Carb jetting, ignition timing, valve sizes, and cam profiles were selected to make the most from this engine and still be perfectly compliant with the emissions laws.

The police Nova was a police package car in the truest sense. Each piece in the drivetrain was selected with the same care as the components in the LM1 engine. The built-up Nova was loaded with fluid coolers, and fitted with heavy-duty chassis components. Chevrolet used heaviest-duty Nova SS and Camaro Z28 suspension components and the brakes from the full-size Bel Air and Impala. The '75 Nova got a brand new body and styling. In fact, it was the most remodeled of any '75 Chevrolet model, and the first significant Nova body change in eight years. The total glass area was increased. The windshield, for example, was 15 percent larger. The wheelbase, however, remained at 111 inches.

The retail Nova was available as a four-door sedan and a two-door coupe. The police package, however, was based strictly on the six-passenger, four-door sedan.

The Nova got all the emissions and safety upgrades for 1975 as did the other Chevrolet models including a catalytic converter, double roof panels, High Energy Ignition, larger diameter exhaust, outside ducted air intake and threaded fuel tank cap with smaller diameter filler hole. The Nova also got a new steering gear location now forward of the front wheel centerline.

The COPO 9C1 police package included the special "California V-8" and heavy-duty suspension, brakes and cooling. The retail tire was either an E78x14 bias-ply tire or an ER78x14 steel belted radial. However, the police package tire for the Nova was an E70x14 "wide oval" bias belted tire mounted on a special 14x7 heavy-duty wheel.

The Los Angeles County Sheriffs Department thrashed a number of 1975 police package cars; however, they disqualified even more of them before the vehicles were even unloaded from the travel trailer. The Ford Torino, Ford LTD, Mercury Montego and Mercury Marquis all equipped with 460-cid engines were refused. These cars either exceeded the maximum allowable engine size or the maximum allowable wheelbase dimensions or both. The Pontiac LeMans with its 400-cid V-8 had engineering delays that prevented it from being tested in time.

The result was a four-way showdown between the Plymouth Fury 360, Dodge Coronet 360, AMC Matador 401 and the Chevrolet Nova 350.

The Nova 9C1 turned in a competitive overall performance compared to the two larger and more powerful street veterans. And it did so with a numerically lower rear axle and bias-belted tires compared to much larger pursuit radials. To pass the first hurdle, the Nova 9C1 was given an acceptable rating around the Pomona EVOC track at the L.A. County Fairgrounds.

The 1975 Nova 9C1, such as this St. Louis Police unit, was powered by a 350-cid/155-hp V-8 with dual exhaust and 3.08 gears. This was the ultimate urban police car. (St. Louis Police)

The 1975 Nova had a 111-inch wheelbase. The police package included a Camaro suspension and Bel Air brakes. (St. Louis Police)

The Nova 9C1 produced an average 0-60 mph and 60-95 mph acceleration but out-braked and out-evasively handled the bigger sedans. The Nova had a controlled fluid temperature heat rise and scored well in the areas of officer ergonomics and communication equipment installation. The real Nova 9C1 victory came during the 72-mile gas mileage test under combinations of urban and rural surface streets and freeway driving. It bested the Matador in-service car by more than 2 mpg.

The LASD recommended that one-third of its enormous 1975 fleet of police cars be made up of the Nova. This would give the LASD an opportunity to both validate its new vehicle test procedure and to give the Nova a formal, large-scale, in-service, field test. With the LASD, it would be continuous Chevrolet from then on: First, the Nova, then the Malibu, then the Impala.

This 1975 LASD vehicle test was a stunning victory for Chevrolet in general and Nova in particular.

1975 LASD Test Results			
	Chevrolet	**Plymouth**	**AMC**
Model	**Nova 9C1**	**Fury A38**	**Matador**
Engine	350 cid, 4-bbl	360 cid, 4-bbl	410 cid, 4-bbl
HP	155 nhp	190 nhp	255 nhp
Transmission	Turbo Hydra-Matic	TorqueFlite	Torque Command
Rear Gear	3.08	3.21	3.15
Wheelbase	111 in	117.5 in	118 in
Tires	E70x14	GR70x15	GR70x15
Test Weight	3,760 lbs	4,330 lbs	4,235 lbs
Performance			
Test Track	Acceptable	Acceptable	Acceptable
0-60 mph	9.0 sec	8.5 sec	8.5 sec
60-95 mph	14.8 sec	16.0 sec	11.1 sec
Brake Power	1.1 g	.92 g	.98 g
Lane Changes	.80 g	.75 g	.71 g
Skid Pad	.82 g	.71 g	.75 g
Ergonomics	68.3 points	63.9 points	61.4 points
Ave. Fluid Temp.	232 deg F	231 deg F	242 deg F
Technician Score	86.6 points	49.1 points	74.5 points
Mechanics Score	64.5 points	72.8 points	70.8 points
Fuel Economy	15.6 mpg	11.8 mpg	13.4 mpg
Quarter-Mile Speed	83.5 mph	81.5 mph	87.0 mph

Bel Air and Impala Police Engines for 1975				
RPO	**Engine, Carb, Exhaust**	**SAE net hp**	**Transmission**	**Axle**
L65	350 cid, 2-bbl, single	145 nhp	THM 350	3.08
LM1	350 cid, 4-bbl, single	155 nhp	THM 350	3.08
LT4	400 cid, 4-bbl, single	175 nhp	THM 350	2.73
LS4	454 cid, 4-bbl, dual	215 nhp	THM 400	3.08

Chevelle and Nova Police Engines for 1975					
RPO	**Engine, Carb, Exhaust**	**SAE net HP**	**Transmission**	**Axles**	**Models**
L22	250 cid, 1-bbl, single	105 nhp	THM 350	2.73, 3.08	Chevelle only
L65	350 cid, 2-bbl, single	145 nhp	THM 350	2.73 only	Chevelle only
LM1	350 cid, 4-bbl, single	155 nhp	THM 350	2.73 only	Chevelle only
LT4	400 cid, 4-bbl, single	175 nhp	THM 350	2.73, 3.08	Chevelle only
LM1	350 cid, 4-bbl, dual	155 nhp	THM 350	3.08 only	Nova only

References for 1975

Vehicle Testing and Evaluation Program, Los Angeles County Sheriff, 1974-1975

1975 Chevrolet Police Vehicles, Chevrolet Motor Division

75 Years of Chevrolet, George Dammann, Motorbooks International

Standard Catalog of Chevrolet, Pat Chappell, Krause Publications

Chapter 22

1976: Last Long Wheelbase, Big-Block Sedan

After the overwhelming success of the high-performance, fuel-efficient, six-passenger, police-tough Nova in 1975, it is easy to imagine what vehicle was on the cover of the 1976 Chevrolet Police Vehicles catalog: the COPO Nova 9C1. In fact, the compact Nova was now listed first in the official police literature, followed by the intermediate Chevelle, then the full-size Chevrolet.

The Chevrolet literature brought the logic of the Los Angeles County Sheriffs Department tests to the attention of police fleet administrators. On the back cover:

"Today's police administrators are aware that there's a lot more to consider in selecting a police vehicle than just purchase price. For that reason, many law enforcement agencies are weighing the total cost of owning and operating a vehicle during its period of service.

"This procedure, called Life Cycle Cost/Performance Evaluation includes the following criteria: initial cost, fuel economy, parts replacement cost, resale value, general patrol capability, human factors such as driver comfort, mechanical evaluation including downtime and serviceability, heat tests and the adaptability of communications equipment.

"When it comes time to evaluate your department's needs and the vehicles available, you may want to consider a Life Cycle Cost/Performance Evaluation. And when you do, we think you'll find Chevy Nova is a practical new alternative to the traditional police vehicle."

The irony of this advice to consider an alternative to the traditional police vehicle was the back cover containing this advice also contained a full page photo of the full-size Impala. However, the facts were clear. The Nova 9C1 was forging an entirely new segment of the police car market. It was right for the times.

The Impala, however, was still getting beaten up by the Dodge Monaco and Coronet and Plymouth Gran Fury and Fury. The Impala was simply not yet right for the times. That would change in 1977. But for the time being, the Nova 9C1 was the darling of the nation's police fleet. Chevrolet knew this and played it up.

Chevrolet emphasized that the St. Louis, Missouri, police had 189 of the Novas, the Los Angeles County Sheriffs Department had 75 more units and the Madison, Wisconsin, police had 32 police Novas. This made it clear that the Nova 9C1 was a good fit in big, medium and small urban police departments. Actually, the St. Louis Police would become one of the most fleet progressive agencies in the country. They jumped on the police-engineered Nova, and were among the first departments in the nation to make widespread use of front-wheel drive Celebrities and then Luminas.

The Nova 9C1 lineup was expanded to include both the four-door sedan and the new-for-1976 two-door coupe. Both these cars had the same 111-inch wheelbase.

The Nova 9C1 was nearly a complete carry-over for 1976. Chevrolet Fleet, the Los Angeles County Sheriffs Department and *Motor Trend* magazine had developed the perfect compact police cruiser over the past two years. No one expected much to change. In fact, the

The 1976 Nova 9C1 was the clear winner of the Los Angeles County Sheriff police car tests. The Nova out-accelerated, out-braked and out-cornered all of the competition. (LASD)

With the input of Chevrolet and *Motor Trend*, the Los Angeles County Sheriff developed the Nova 9C1 into the ideal car for the times. This 1976 Nova deserves its place in the LASD Museum. (LASD)

only real improvement for 1976 was a special rear seat on the four-door sedans. This gave improved knee and entry/exit room.

The LM1 "California V-8" was the only engine offered in the Nova 9C1. This was basically unchanged for 1976, however, it was listed at 165 nhp. Again for 1976, the LM1 350-cid, four-barrel carbureted V-8 was restricted for sale and/or registration to the state of California, except when powering the Nova 9C1. The police Nova sent to all 50 states used this "California V-8."

The GM-specification steel-belted tires, which were standard equipment for all Chevrolet retail and some police cars in 1975, caused some confusion among cops. For 1976, Chevrolet made it clear:

"GM-specification steel belted radial tires and bias belted tires are available options for police chassis-equipped vehicles although not recommended for high speed use. Contact your local Chevrolet dealer, zone or regional sales personnel for ordering of all tires."

Steel belted radials were all the rage for retail cars and for police cars used for detective work. However, police cars used for high speed emergency responses needed to use fabric belted radials or bias belted tires. After the death of a state trooper due to a steel belt separation, it would be years before steel belted radials gained high speed ratings and police confidence. Chevrolet joined all automakers in urging the use of fabric (Kevlar) belted radials until the steel belted radials were speed rated for operations up to 130 mph.

For 1976, the Nova 9C1 came with FR70x14 fabric belted radials. This was one size larger than in 1974 and a radial instead of the 1974 bias belted tire. This was a great match.

The Chevelle 9C1 was also a carry-over for 1976. The engine sizes and horsepower, and the geographic restrictions were almost exactly the same. Such as in the Nova 9C1, the LM1 350-cid, four-barrel carbureted V-8 was now rated at 165 nhp. This engine and the 400-cid/175-nhp four-barrel carbureted V-8 were the only Chevelle police

The 1976 Nova 9C1 came only one way: 350-cid/165-hp V-8, three-speed Turbo Hydra-Matic transmission and 3.08 gears. It reached 60 mph in 9.6 seconds and got 14.6 actual mpg. (LASD)

engines available in California. The 250-cid Six, 350-cid, two-barrel carbureted V-8 and the 400-cid, four-barrel carbureted V-8 were available for use in the other 49 states.

The 9C1 police package was available on the 116-inch wheelbase, four-door sedan and the 112-inch wheelbase, two-door coupe in both Malibu and Malibu Classic trim levels. The police Chevelle came standard with H78x15 nylon bias belted police special tires and HR70x15 fabric belted police radials were optional.

The 1976 Impalas, such as this Missouri State Highway Patrol unit, are the last of the long wheelbase Chevrolets. After 1976, the wheelbase would remain at 116 inches. (MSHP)

The news for the full-size Chevrolet was the dropping of the Bel Air nameplate. The 9C1 police package was now based on the Impala and on the Impala S "fleet model" four-door sedans. The Impala S fleet model was RPO YH8. The Impala two-door sport coupe was no longer available in a police package. For the first time in years, neither was a full-size station wagon available in cop gear.

In its last year as a real full-size sedan, the big Chevrolet retained its 121.5-inch wheelbase. The '76 Impala did, however, get new front end styling and a brand new grille. The '76 Impala now had the same front end appearance as the unique '75 Caprice.

The 1976 model year was as significant for Chevrolet as 1978 would be for Ford, Dodge and Plymouth. This was the last year for the 400-cid "giant" small-block V-8. This was the last year for the 454-cid big-block V-8. After 1976, the largest Chevrolet police engine would be the 350-cid V-8.

The 454-cid big-block was perked up a bit for its last year. It was back "up" to 8.25:1 compression and 225 hp. However, unlike the 3.08 rear gear used in the 1975 Bel Air, the 1976 454-powered Impala received 2.73 rear gears.

The 1976 model year was the last for the 121.5-inch wheelbase full-size Chevrolet. In 1977, the wheelbase was reduced to 116 inches where it would stay until the demise of the full-size Chevrolet after 1996. The only full-size 1976 Chevrolet to get the police package was the Impala and only in a four-door. For the first time, the full-size police package sales code was 9C1.

The last model year for a big-block engine of any displacement in any model of Chevrolet police car was 1976. This was the 454-cid, four-barrel carbureted V-8. Dodge and Plymouth kept their 440-cid big-block through the 1978 model year. Ford also retained its 460-cid big-block for use in police cars through 1978.

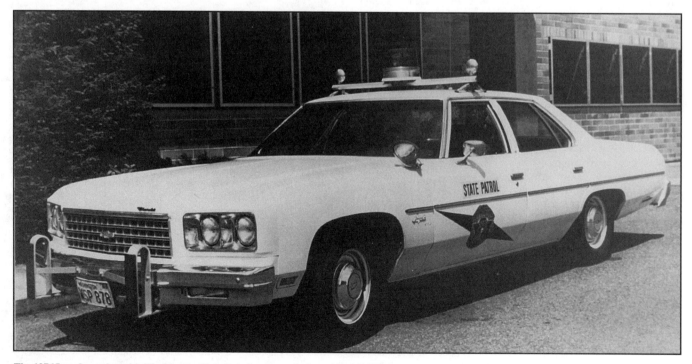

The 1976 Impala, such as this Washington State Patrol unit, are the last of the big-block and "giant" small-block Chevrolets. After 1976, the largest police engine would be the 350 cid. (WSP)

This early exit by Chevrolet certainly gave Chrysler, and to a much lesser degree Ford, an edge in the police fleet market. However, the advantage from Chevrolet not having a big-block was much more an illusion than reality. By 1976, the porcupine-head, 454 was barely wheezing along with just 225 nhp. In reality, it would not be missed.

Rather than throwing in the towel first, Chevrolet was actually responding to the police vehicle trends first. Chevrolet had a huge jump on Chrysler and Ford in coming out with a small-block-powered four-door sedan that gave police performance, had acceptable emissions and good fuel economy.

All police carmakers knew the "King Kong," big-block engines were going to be history. Vehicle performance is simply a matter of the power to weight ratio. Chevrolet greatly downsized its full-size four-door sedans to keep about the same overall performance when using the small-block engines.

Model	1976	1977
	Impala four-door	Impala four-door
Wheelbase	121.5 in	116.0 in
Weight	4,222 lbs	3,564 lbs
Max. Engine	454 cid, 4-bbl	350 cid, 4-bbl
SAE Net HP	225 nhp	170 nhp
Net Torque	360 lb-ft	270 lb-ft
Pounds per HP	18.8	20.9
Pounds per Torque	11.7	13.2

Dodge and Plymouth downsized their cars slightly for 1978 while keeping the 440-cid/225-nhp engine. This gave them total dominance in the area of police pursuit performance. However, this was the beginning of the end of the Chrysler Corporation dominance. It would lose the 400-cid and 440-cid big-blocks after 1978.

Chrysler Corporation would also lose its 360-cid small-block after 1981. When that happened, Chevrolet took over. From its stronghold in Southern California, Chevrolet moved East and North with its full-size four-door police sedans. It would take exactly 10 years from the demise of the Chevy big-block to a position of bowtie dominance in the police market.

The 1976 police Impala was used by the Missouri State Highway Patrol, South Dakota Highway Patrol, Washington State Patrol, Chicago Police, Wyoming Highway Patrol and Honolulu Police while the 1976 Nova was used by the San Francisco Police and Los Angeles County Sheriffs Department among many others.

The 1976 model year began the across-the-models use of the term "9C1" to define the police package. This replaced the separate B07 police chassis equipment and BY2 police body equipment packages from 1975. Also gone was a separate High Speed Pursuit Package built around the 454-cid engine. The one 9C1 police package covered all of the heavy-duty equipment needed for this kind of service. The 9C1 tires were the H78x15 bias belted police-spec tires, however, HR78x15 and HR70x15 fabric belted radials were available.

The engine sizes and restrictions for the full-size Impala were the same as for 1975. The LM1 350-cid, four-barrel carbureted V-8 and the LT4 400-cid, four-barrel carbureted V-8 were the only California-authorized engines. At the beginning of the model year the LM1 350 was available for California-bound police cars only. However by mid-model year, a Federal version of this 350 with four-barrel carb was available. Chevrolet had really big plans for this particular small-block. Other engines for use in the other 49 states included the 350 with two-barrel carb, 400 with four-barrel carb and the 454 with four-barrel carb.

The Los Angeles County Sheriffs Department performed its annual tests on 1976 model year vehicles. Many of the Fords and Mercurys except the Montego 400-cid V-8 were disqualified for specification problems. The Dodge Coronet 400-cid V-8 was disqualified because of unacceptable handling and braking. American Motors, once the owner of the Southern California police market—which is still a mystery to most automotive enthusiasts—did not submit any 1976 vehicles for testing.

The Nova 9C1 was the clear and heads-up winner. It had the fastest 0-60 mph and 60-95 mph times and the quickest quarter-mile trap speeds. It generated an incredible 1.2 g of braking force, and equaled or bested all the other cars on the evasive maneuvers course and the skid pad. The Nova 9C1 had the best actual gas mileage by far and was competitive in all the other measured and subjective categories.

When the results were weighted and totaled, the Nova 9C1 was the best overall performing squad car by a big margin over the best from Dodge, Plymouth, Pontiac, Mercury and Ford.

The LASD was so happy with the Nova 9C1 that it ran the car as its exclusive black-and-white patrol car in 1976, 1977 and 1978. This was as long as the Nova came with a 9C1 police package.

Bel Air and Impala Police Engines for 1976				
RPO	Engine, Carb, Exhaust	SAE Net HP	Transmission	Axle
L65	350 cid, 2-bbl, single	145 nhp	THM 350	3.08
LM1	350 cid, 4-bbl, single	165 nhp	THM 350	3.08
LT4	400 cid, 4-bbl, single	175 nhp	THM 350	2.73
LS4	454 cid, 4-bbl, dual	225 nhp	THM 400	2.73

Chevelle and Nova Police Engines for 1976					
RPO	Engine, Carb, Exhaust	SAE Net HP	Transmission	Axle	Models
L22	250 cid, 1-bbl, single	105 nhp	THM 350	3.08	Chevelle only
L65	350 cid, 2-bbl, single	145 nhp	THM 350	2.73	Chevelle only
LM1	350 cid, 4-bbl, single	165 nhp	THM 350	2.73	Chevelle only
LT4	400 cid, 4-bbl, single	175 nhp	THM 350	3.08	Chevelle only
LM1	350 cid, 4-bbl, dual	165 nhp	THM 350	3.08	Nova only

Power Drop in 454-cid, 4-bbl Dual Exhaust Police Engines			
Year	Ratio	Horsepower	Torque
1970	10.25:1	390 brake hp	500 lb-ft
1971	8.5:1	365 brake, 285 net	465 lb-ft
1972	8.5:1	270 SAE net hp	390 lb-ft
1973	8.25:1	245 SAE net hp	375 lb-ft
1974	8:25:1	235 SAE net hp	360 lb-ft
1975	8.15:1	215 SAE net hp	350 lb-ft
1976	8.25:1	225 SAE net hp	360 lb-ft
1977	Discontinued for Police Cars		

References for 1976

Vehicle Testing and Evaluation Program, Los Angeles County
  Sheriff, 1975-1976
1976 Chevrolet Police Vehicles, Chevrolet Motor Division
75 Years of Chevrolet, George Dammann, Motorbooks International
Standard Catalog of Chevrolet, Pat Chappell, Krause Publications

1976 Los Angeles Sheriff Vehicle Tests						
	Chevrolet	**Dodge**	**Plymouth**	**Pontiac**	**Mercury**	**Ford**
Model	Nova 9C1	Dart A38	Fury A38	LeMans	Montego	Torino
Engine	350 cid, 4-bbl	360 cid, 4-bbl	360 cid, 4-bbl	400 cid, 4-bbl	400 cid, 2-bbl	400 cid, 2-bbl
HP	165 nhp	175 nhp	175 nhp	185 nhp	144 nhp	144 nhp
Axle	3.08	3.21	3.21	3.08	3.25	3.25
Weight	3,720 lbs	3,725 lbs	4,150 lbs	4,305 lbs	4,555 lbs	4,650 lbs
Wheelbase	111 in	111 in	117.5 in	116 in	118 in	118 in
0-60 mph	9.5 sec	10.6 sec	11.0 sec	12.1 sec	10.8 sec	11.2 sec
1/4 Speed	82.9 mph	78.9 mph	79.1 mph	73.0 mph	80.0 mph	78.6 mph
Skid Pad	.80g	.77g	.78g	.74g	.77g	.73g
Brake Power	1.2g	1.0g	1.1g	.87g	.97g	1.0g
Fuel Mileage	14.6 mpg	12.8 mpg	11.3 mpg	11.9 mpg	12.7 mpg	12.5 mpg
Weighted Score	66.67 pts	60.86 pts	62.47 pts	58.99 pts	60.49 pts	disqual.

Chapter 23

1977: Downsized B-Body Impala

The 1977 Impala, like this ex-Chicago Transit Authority unit, had a 5.5 inch shorter wheelbase and weighed 637 pounds less than the 1976 Impala.

The 1977 Impala 9C1 with a 350-cid/170-hp V-8 had a 0-60 mph time of 9.7 seconds and a top speed of 117 mph.

In 1977, Chevrolet fielded three 9C1 police package sedans: Impala, Chevelle and Nova. The emphasis in 1977 for all law enforcement vehicles was the better performance and, at the same time, better fuel economy that was available from the intermediate-size squad cars. For example, the Dodge Aspen and Plymouth Volare with engines from the 225-cid, one-barrel carbureted Six to the 360-cid, four-barrel car-

bureted V-8 were new for 1977. Mercury introduced its compact Comet and intermediate Cougar with police packages. Pontiac hyped its 3.8-liter V-6-powered LeMans.

The full-size Chevrolets were dramatically changed for 1977. In fact, the changes from 1976 to 1977 were far greater than the more recent and obvious changes as the 1990 square car became round for

1991. The downsized, full-size Chevrolet Impala was 5.5 inches shorter in wheelbase, 10.6 inches shorter overall and 4 inches narrower but 2.5 inches taller than the 1976 car. The 1977 models were an average of 700 pounds lighter than comparable 1976 models.

For 1977, the 400-cid "giant" small-block and the 454-cid big-block were both gone. The 1977 L65 350-cid, two-barrel carbureted V-8 was replaced by the LG3 305-cid, two-barrel carbureted V-8. The smaller V-8 however kept the same 145 nhp rating. Since the full-size car was no longer full-size, the L22 250-cid, one-barrel Six was now a base engine for the Impala.

The mid-1970s were a bit disappointing for Chevrolet police fleet sales. In December 1977, *Car and Driver* magazine did a review of the squad cars driven by the state police and highway patrol in all 50 states. The 1976 and 1977 model years were in use at the time the article was written. The '78s had not yet been built. Of the '77 models, none were Chevrolets. Plymouth led the pack with thirty, Dodge had eight, Ford was used by seven states and Pontiac patrolled five states.

The reason for the lack of bowtie cruisers was clear. The maximum engine size from Chevrolet was 350 cubic inches. Even though the downsized small-block Chevy ran as well as the longer, big-block Chevy, image is everything. The Mopars had 400-cid and 440-cid big-blocks, the Fords had 460-cid big-blocks and the Pontiacs had 403-cid big-blocks.

With the loss of the big-block, Chevrolet was essentially out of the police car business in 1977 and 1978. It was not until the 1979 model year that Chevrolet was on equal footing again. The biggest Mopar engine then was the 360-cid small-block. All Ford had then was the 351-cid Windsor.

The police car market is 60,000 vehicles per year. From the late-1980s to mid-1990s, Chevrolet had just more than half of the business selling 36,000 police cars per year. At any one time, there are about 160,000 police cars in-service. In stark contrast, in 1977, Chevrolet sold just 2,500 9C1 Impalas. Sales of less than 1,000 units barely justify a police program.

Chevrolet tried to put the best possible spin on its downsized, small-block-powered Impala. The new car was truly the way things were going to be for police cars; however, it was a little early for cops to accept this reality. Actually, this gave Chevrolet a two year jump on everyone else to get the maximum performance from a non-big-block cruiser.

The 1977 model year was the beginning preparation for 1982 and 1983 when Chevrolet would wrestle the Los Angeles Police and Los Angeles Sheriffs Department business away from Chrysler Corporation for good. However, Chevrolet Fleet knew they had a tough sales job on their hands as long as other police cars were still available with big-blocks. Here is how they introduced the radically-different 1977 full-size Chevrolet:

"The '77 Impala is a new generation Chevrolet that makes more efficient use of space and materials than previous Impalas. This gives the room and comfort of a full-size interior, but with less exterior bulk. It also permits reduced curb weight which eases the demands on power and fuel. Impala's comfort, impressive driving characteristics and new efficiency make it an ideal choice for highway patrol or as a partner to an established vehicle such as our Nova for a dual-team concept. EPA mileage estimates: 22 mpg highway, 17 mpg city, with new standard Six, auto transmission and 2.73 axle."

- New aerodynamic styling
- New highly maneuverable 116-inch wheelbase chassis with tighter turning circle (38.8 feet curb-to-curb) than 1976 Impala
- More front and rear head room and more rear leg room than 1976 Impala
- More usable trunk space than 1976 Impala
- New single-loop front seat and shoulder belt system
- Molded full foam seat construction
- New interior trim fabrics and colors
- New instrument panel
- Turbo Hydra-Matic transmission
- Power steering
- Speedometer face includes metric numerals
- New built-in diagnostic terminal for engine electrical system
- Delco Freedom battery never needs water

The California Highway Patrol tested a small number of 1977 Impalas for Enforcement Class duties. It was hard for the small-block Impala to compete against the big-block Dodge. (Darryl Lindsay)

- High Energy Ignition system
- Power front disc/rear drum brake system with disc brake
  audible wear sensors
- Carburetor outside air induction and early fuel
  evaporation systems standard on all engines.

In 1977, the Impala 9C1 was available with either the LM1 350-cid, four-barrel carbureted V-8 or the L22 250-cid, one-barrel carbureted Six. Both were teamed with the Turbo Hydra-Matic transmission and 3.08 rear gears. Both engines had a true single exhaust. The Impala 9C1 was available as either a four-door sedan or two-door coupe. Both models shared the B-platform with a 116-inch wheelbase.

The 110 nhp inline Six was reintroduced to the Impala for 1977. Full-size Chevrolet police cars were powered by six-cylinder engines up through 1971. By 1972 these cars became just too big and heavy for the Six. Now that the 1977 full-size Chevy was lean and trim, the six-cylinder engine became a workable, economical powerplant again.

The 1977 Impala 9C1 package included a special high-effort power steering using a revised spool valve, and a longer pitman arm that effectively made a quicker steering ratio. The suspension was an upgrade from the famous F41 sports suspension. The police suspension starts as the F41, which includes stiffer coil springs, front and rear, stiffer rear suspension bushings, stiffer body mounts, front and rear sway bars, and stiffer shock absorbers. The frame side rails are beefed up. Compared to the F41 suspension, the police package has a one-inch rear sway bar versus the F41's .86 inch bar. To work with the stiffer rear suspension, the rear shocks have been re-valved to be stiffer. The 9C1 package also includes metal-impregnated front brake pads, larger rear brake drums and a revised front-to-rear brake proportioning.

For the July 1978 issue, *Car and Driver* test drove the leaner 1977 Impala 9C1 powered by the LM1 350-cid, four-barrel carbureted V-8. The 116-inch wheelbase squad car had the three-speed Turbo Hydra-Matic and a positraction 3.08 rear end. The 0-60 mph time was 9.7 seconds with a top speed of 117 mph. These stats would remain basically unchanged for the next dozen years.

This level of police car performance is bleak; however, consider the times. A 1977 L82-powered Corvette with a 350-cid/210-nhp V-8, Turbo Hydra-Matic transmission and 3.55 rear gears took a full 8.8 seconds to hit 60 mph and had a quarter-mile speed of 82 mph. Ironically, the LM1-powered police Nova 9C1 outperformed the Corvette with an 8.6 second 0-60 mph time and an 85 mph quarter-mile speed. The point is, however, all the cars were slow in the late-1970s, both sports cars and police cars alike.

In 1975, Chevrolet released the 262-cid V-8. This tiny small-block had a 3.671-inch bore, a 3.100-inch stroke and a compression ratio of 8.5:1. This two-barrel carbureted, 110 nhp engine was never a police package engine. It was discontinued after the 1976 model year.

The replacement for the 262-cid V-8, which was released in 1976, was the famous 305-cid V-8. This had a unique bore of 3.736 inches but shared the same 3.480-inch long stroke crank as the 350-cid V-8. This engine was designed to provide an ideal balance between horsepower and torque and the emission standards of the time. This was a police package engine from 1977 through 1993.

In 1985, the highest performance 305-cid retail engines were equipped with Tuned Port Injection (TPI). Most police and retail 305-cid V-8s continued to use Throttle Body Injections (TBI). The 305-cid V-8 would be replaced in 1994 by the 4.3-liter (265-cid) V-8. This engine reminded many enthusiasts of the original Chevy small-block from 1955.

The Chevelle 9C1 was available in the 116-inch wheelbase, four-door sedan or the 112-inch wheelbase, two-door coupe. This meant the downsized Impala and the intermediate four-door Chevelle had exactly the same wheelbase. The Chevelle would be powered by the L22 250-cid, one-barrel carbureted Six, the LG3 305-cid, two-barrel carbureted V-8 or the LM1 350-cid, four-barrel carbureted V-8. The LG3 305 V-8 was not available in the Impala. A police department wanting this intermediate-power engine for economy reasons in a bigger car had to buy the Chevelle.

The 1977 Chevelle Malibu and Malibu Classic got new grilles, new taillights and new interior trim but were otherwise carry-overs from 1976.

The 116-inch wheelbase Chevelle 9C1 was so similar to the 116-inch wheelbase Impala 9C1 that the Chevelle would not be offered in 1978. It would, however, be back as a Malibu in 1979, replacing the Nova 9C1.

The police Nova 9C1 was available as either a four-door sedan or two-door coupe. For the first time the LG3 305-cid, two-barrel carbureted V-8 was available in addition to the legendary LM1 350-cid, four-barrel carbureted V-8. All police Novas came with the Turbo Hydra-Matic transmission. The 305-cid/145-nhp V-8 got 2.56 rear gears while the 350-cid/170-nhp V-8 used 3.08 rear gears. Both cars had single exhaust even though they had dual tailpipes.

Chevrolet was extremely proud of the successes of the police Nova. The factory literature emphasized:

"The Los Angeles Sheriffs Department ordered 222 specially-equipped '76 Novas after an exhaustive testing, evaluation and comparison program. Nova's potential for police application is recognized by the use of a specially-equipped Nova by the Law Enforcement Assistance Administration in its design concept program for a police car of the future."

The 1977 Nova 9C1 was the clear car-of-choice for urban police departments. In 1977, the Nova became available with a two-barrel version of the 350 cid. (*Motor Trend*)

A 1977 Nova 9C1 at a National Nostalgic Nova show. The Nova 9C1 reached 60 mph in 8.6 seconds winning the LASD tests. (Dave Dotson)

The Boston Police used the 1977 Nova 9C1 as did the St. Louis Police, the Jacksonville, Florida, Sheriff and the Los Angeles County Sheriff. (John Antonelli)

This prototype car deserves a quick mention. In 1977, the Law Enforcement Assistance Administration (LEAA) and Aerospace Corporation jointly developed a "car of the future." This was a 1977 Chevy Nova with a V-8 engine that performed on four cylinders during normal patrol but could kick in all eight cylinders whenever necessary.

Field tests on this squad were conducted in Dallas and New Orleans. It featured advanced engine system gauges, centralized emergency equipment controls and four-wheel anti-lock brakes. Overall, the mobile "test lab" was not popular among cops. However, certain features used on the LEAA prototype Nova were well received and eventually found their way into police packages.

In 1977, the Los Angeles County Sheriffs Department conducted its annual tests of police vehicles. Out of a field of eight police cars from Dodge, Plymouth, AMC and Pontiac, the Chevrolet Nova was the clear winner over the second place Pontiac LeMans. The Nova 9C1 had both the best overall vehicle performance and the lowest in-service operating costs.

Full Size Chevrolet Comparison		
	1976	**1977**
Wheelbase	121.5 inch	116 inch
Weight	4,222 lbs	3,564 lbs
Engine	400 cid, 4-bbl	350 cid, 4-bbl
HP	175 nhp (LT4)	170 nhp (LM1)
0-60 mph	10.7 sec	10.8 sec

Chevrolet Police Engines for 1977				
RPO	**Engine, Carb, Exhaust**	**SAE Net HP**	**Trans**	**Axle**
L22	250 cid, L6, 1-bbl, single	110	THM	3.08
LM1	350 cid, V-8, 4-bbl, single	170	THM	3.08
LG3	305 cid, V-8, 2-bbl, single	145	THM	2.56

1977 Chevrolet Impala 9C1	
Engine	LM1 350 cid
Compression	8.5:1
Carb	4-bbl Rochester Quadra Jet
Power, SAE Net	170 @ 3800
Torque	270 @ 2400
Transmission	Three-speed Turbo Hydra-Matic
Trans Gears	2.52, 1.52, 1.00
Axle Ratio	3.08:1
Wheelbase	116 inch
Suspension, front	Coil springs, sway bar
Suspension, rear	Coil springs, sway bar
Brakes, front	11.9 inch vented disc, power
Brakes, rear	11.0x2.0 finned iron drum, power
Wheels	15x7
Tires	Goodyear Police Special, HR70-15
0 to 60 mph	9.6 sec
Top Speed	117 mph

1977 Los Angeles County Sheriff's Department Vehicle Tests								
	AMC	Chevy	Dodge	Dodge	Plymouth	Plymouth	Pontiac	Pontiac
Model	Matador	Nova	Aspen	Monaco	Fury	Volare	Catalina	LeMans
Engine (cid) Carb	360, 2-bbl	350, 4-bbl	360, 4-bbl	360, 4-bbl	360, 4-bbl	360, 4-bbl	403, 4-bbl	403, 4-bbl
HP, SAE net	129	165	160	160	160	160	185	185
Axle Ratio	3.15	3.08	3.21	3.21	3.21	3.21	2.41	2.41
Wheelbase (in)	118	111	112.7	117.4	117.4	112.7	115.9	116
Weight (lbs)	4,090	3,690	3,875	4,250	4,250	3,985	3,900	4,130
0 to 60 mph	10.9	8.6	12.3	11.8	11.8	11.6	10.3	10.8
1/4 mile Trap Speed	79	85	77	77.9	77.6	77.5	81.9	79
Lateral G-force	.68g	.81g	.75g	.74g	.70g	.70g	.75g	.75g
Braking G-force	.75g	.75g	.87g	.88g	.76g	.88g	.89g	.88g
Fuel Economy, Actual	13.36	14.57	11.73	10.93	11.82	12.22	13.74	13.87
TOTAL SCORE	61.2	67.4	59	58.5	58.4	57.8	59.7	62.4
Life Cycle Costs, 70,000 miles service	$4,235	$3,884	$4,824	$5,177	$4,787	$4,630	$4,118	$4,080

References for 1977

"A Civilian Bear-Spotter's Guide," David Abrahamson, *Car & Driver*, December 1977

"Chevrolet Impala 9C1," Rich Ceppos, *Car & Driver*, July 1978

"1977 Chevrolet Marked the Beginning of a Revolution," Robert C. Ackerson, *Standard Catalog of Chevrolet*, Krause Publications

1977 Chevrolet Police Vehicles, Chevrolet Motor Division

"Police Cars for 1977," staff report, *American City and County*, October 1976

1977 Vehicle Testing and Evaluation Program, Los Angeles County Sheriffs Department

Chapter 24

1978: Nova Dominates in Last Year

In 1978, Chevrolet police cars included the Nova 9C1 and the Impala 9C1. Both were available as a four-door sedan and two-door hardtop. The '78 Chevelle was not available with the police package.

In the late-1970s, the Nova, not the Impala, was the darling of Chevrolet's police fleet. The Nova had an ideal police package and was unmatched by anything the competition had to offer. The Nova revolution started in Southern California and spread across the entire county. The Nova 9C1 was the definitive police car for large city police and urban sheriffs departments.

The Impala 9C1, on the other hand, had nothing special or unique to offer. It got good mileage for a full-size car. However, all of the competition had full-size, small V-8-powered cars that got good mileage, too. The Impala lacked the larger 400-, 440- and 460-cid engines offered by Pontiac, Dodge, Plymouth, Ford and Mercury. This made it unpopular with state police and rural sheriffs departments.

The Nova 9C1 clearly carried the Chevrolet banner in the bleak years when the competition had big-block police engines and Chevy did not. The Nova was listed first in the text describing the '78 vehicles in the police literature. It was "Nova and Impala," not "Impala and Nova" as it had been in the past. The Nova 9C1 was on the cover of the police car flyer. The Nova 9C1 features were listed at the top of

A slick-top 1978 Impala being used by the Los Altos, California, Police. This was the first year the 305-cid V-8 was available in the full-size bowtie police car. (Darryl Lindsay)

A 1978 Los Altos, California, police Impala. In tests conducted by the Michigan State Police, the 350-cid Impala did very well against the big-block cars from Ford, Dodge, Plymouth and Pontiac. (Darryl Lindsay)

A slick-top 1978 Menlo Park, California, Police Nova. These 350-cid, four-barrel-powered cars got the best actual fuel economy of any police car at 14.1 mpg. (Darryl Lindsay)

In 1978, the Nova 9C1 used in California, such as this Visalia, California, Police unit, used the 350-cid/160-hp four-barrel V-8. (Darryl Lindsay)

each page, followed by the Impala 9C1. The Impala was actually represented as being "a partner to a vehicle such as the Nova, functioning in a dual-team concept."

The Chevy literature urged police fleet managers to conduct a Life Cycle Cost/Performance Evaluation. Chevrolet knew in such an evaluation the Nova 9C1 would come out ahead of all other police cars: compact, intermediate or full-size.

"NOVA. Almost exactly what a contemporary police vehicle should be. Not a lightweight but light enough to permit high performance with a moderate-displacement V-8. Excellent space utilization that combines a tall, comfortable interior with a compact exterior that can maneuver easily in tight quarters. And a strong, simple but proven design. Qualities like these borne out by extensive testing and evaluation programs conducted by various departments

101

throughout the U.S. help explain Nova's growing acceptance for police fleets. In fact, in May 1977, 246 1977 Nova police vehicles were delivered to the Jacksonville (Fla.) Sheriffs Office...the largest compact police vehicle delivery in Chevrolet history. Now, that's acceptance!"

A new, and possibly confusing, optional engine was available in the '78 Nova. Keep in mind the mid- and late-1970s engines had a wide variety of emission controls. One set of smog gear was used with Federal engines. These were the standard engines with the normal emission controls used by nearly everyone.

Another set of smog controls came on engines headed to California. Police cars in California were required to meet California emission standards until 1982. After that time, emergency vehicles were required only to meet the less restrictive Federal emission standards. Yet another set of emissions equipment came on engines in the other 49 states for patrol jurisdictions designated as "High Altitude" by the Environmental Protection Agency.

These emission controls robbed a bunch of horsepower. The California emissions package, for example, reduced the output of most V-8s by 10 nhp and most sixes by 20 nhp, depending on the engine. For this reason, use great care when reviewing a horsepower rating, and be double-sure before calling any published rating incorrect.

For example, the police car tests performed by the Los Angeles County Sheriffs Department involved engines with California emission packages, obviously. Tests that started in 1978 by the Michigan State Police involved engines with Federal emission packages. It doesn't matter now because the LASD and the MSP now test exactly the same vehicles. However, it mattered a great deal in the late 1970s

and early 1980s when much less powerful engines were used in LASD test vehicles.

With all this in mind, the new Nova 9C1 engine was the Special Equipment Order (SEO) IB4 350-cid, four-barrel carbureted V-8. This produced 170 nhp and was only available with Federal emission controls. The now-famous LM1 350-cid, four-barrel carbureted V-8 producing 160 nhp was available for both High Altitude and California markets.

To keep this confusing, the same LM1 designation was used for Federal, California and High Altitude engines for the Impala powerplants. The Federal LM1 produced 170 nhp and the California and High Altitude LM1 engines produced 160 nhp. All this is to say that the Federal 350-cid engine used in the police Nova was *not* the popular LM1. It was the IB4.

After downsizing the full-size B-body cars for 1977, the mid-size A-body Chevelle Malibu was downsized for 1978. At this time, a new 200-cid V-6 became standard on the Malibu.

The wheelbase was dropped from 116 to 108 inches. These 1978 Malibus were 12 to 22 inches shorter and 500 to 800 pounds lighter than the 1977 Chevelles. To further distinguish the old from the new, the name Chevelle was dropped. The Malibu was not available in a police package for 1978, but it was for 1979.

The '78 Impala was mostly a carry-over from the big restyling in 1977. The grille and taillights were styled differently and the big squad also got a larger power brake booster. Since the Chevelle was no longer in the police lineup, the Impala was now available with the LG3 305-cid, two-barrel carbureted V-8.

No 1978 police car was faster around a tight road course than the Nova 9C1. In its last year as a police package, the Nova 9C1 easily won the Los Angeles County Sheriff's tests. (LASD)

The only other change in the Impala was an overall reduction in gear ratios in an attempt to improve fuel economy. The axle ratio used with the 250 Six was dropped from 3.08 (1977) to 2.73 (1978). The axle ratio used with the 305 V-8 in the 116-inch 1977 Chevelle was dropped from 2.56 to 2.41 for use in the 305 V-8-powered 116-inch 1978 Impala. The 3.08 rear gears used with the LM1 350 V-8 were unchanged.

A 3.08 "performance axle" for Federal engines only was listed in the fleet literature for the 250 Six and 305 V-8. This performance axle was not available at the beginning of the model year and was pending emissions certification. That never happened. Some of the later-issue fleet literature has this Impala performance axle option crossed off. The police Nova with the 305 V-8 and California emissions package also used a numerically lower 2.41 rear gear instead of the previous year's 3.08 ratio.

In 1978, the Michigan State Police began testing police package cars. This test protocol was different from the Los Angeles County Sheriffs Department. The MSP emphasis was on absolute top speed, 0-100 mph times and lap times around the Michigan International Speedway road racing course.

The MSP reviewed ergonomics and communication gear access in a subjective way pioneered by the LASD. The LASD used actual fuel consumption on a carefully selected 99-mile test loop. The patrol car mileage was exactly 60 percent of the mileage during the test loop. The MSP, however, used the published EPA "city" mileage figures for its analysis.

The LASD process is a pass-fail test. The lowest bid among the passing or qualifying squad cars is awarded contracts from the LASD.

Under the MSP test procedure, the cars are ranked by how well they did in each test area. One percent of the lowest bid price is used as an adjustment figure. The car with the highest weighted average performance under the vehicle tests is given a dollars and cents advantage. The MSP buys the squad car with the lowest performance-adjusted price.

The leaner, meaner Impala did much better in this objective MSP testing than anyone expected from the small-block powered squad car. During these tests, Chevy's vision of the future, when small-blocks would rule, was proven correct.

The Impala was the lightest police car at 3,996 pounds. This gave it an advantage in braking, fuel economy and acceleration. It had about the same power to weight ratio as the 400-cid big-block Monaco. When all the testing was done, the 350-cid Impala had the second fastest road course times, second fastest 0-100 mph times, third fastest top speed, the second shortest braking distances and was tied for the best fuel economy.

The 400-cid LTD II and 350-cid LeSabre were disqualified for acceleration times being too slow. The 440-cid Fury was awarded the contract based on the most performance for the price formula. The Impala, which was ignored by cops in 1977 because it lacked a big-block, turned heads in 1978 when its actual performance was measured. Its actual performance was far better than its perceived performance.

The Los Angeles County Sheriffs Department vehicle tests have a completely different emphasis than the tests conducted by the Michigan State Police. The LASD tests are more urban and fleet maintenance oriented while the MSP is more rural and performance oriented. Not surprisingly, the full-size, 116- to 118-inch wheelbase cars did not fare as well as the compact, 111- to 113-inch wheelbase cars in Los Angeles. But Chevrolet had that base solidly covered by the Nova 9C1.

The Nova 9C1 had the fastest 0-60 mph times, the highest quarter-mile trap speeds, the second best brakes, the best suspension, and the best fuel mileage. When the score was tallied, the Nova 9C1 was the clear winner over the second Dodge Aspen.

This was the last year for the police package Nova. In 1979, the baton would be passed to the downsized Malibu. While the Malibu 9C1 was less-heralded than the tradition-breaking Nova 9C1, the Malibu 9C1 was used in even larger numbers.

The Nova 9C1 revolutionized the way cops thought about compact police cars. The Nova 9C1 was probably Chevrolet's most significant police car.

Chevrolet Police Engines for 1978 (Federal Specs)				
RPO	Engine, Carb	SAE Net HP	Trans	Axle
L22	250 cid, L6, 1-bbl	110 nhp	THM	2.73
LG3	305 cid, V-8, 2-bbl	145 nhp	THM	2.41
LM1	350 cid, V-8, 4-bbl	170 nhp	THM	3.08

1978 Michigan State Police Patrol Vehicle Test Results						
	Buick	**Chevrolet**	**Dodge**	**Ford**	**Plymouth**	**Pontiac**
Model	**LeSabre**	**Impala**	**Monaco**	**LTD II**	**Fury**	**Catalina**
Engine (cid) Carb	350, 4-bbl	350, 4-bbl	400, 4-bbl	400, 2-bbl	440, 4-bbl	400, 4-bbl
HP, SAE	155 nhp	170 nhp	190 nhp	166 nhp	255 nhp	180 nhp
Axle Ratio	2.73	3.08	3.21	3	2.71	3.08
Weight (lbs)	4,077	3,996	4,369	4,611	4,413	4,057
Wheelbase (in)	115.9	116	117.4	118	117.4	115.9
Road Course Lap Time	96.6 sec	92.7 sec	93.6 sec	93.5 sec	91.1 sec	93.7 sec
0-100 mph	46.4 sec	33.7 sec	34.4 sec	41.0 sec	24.8 sec	34.6 sec
Top Speed, mph	110	115	117	115	133	110
Braking, ft/sec2	21.1	24.3	22.6	19.2	23.3	25.1
Ergonomics, pts	312	311	286	282	286	312
Communications pts	58	62	93	68	93	53
Fuel, EPA City	15	15	13	13	10	14
Adjusted Bid Price	disqual	$5,679	$5,582	disqual	$5,397	$5,663

1978 Los Angeles County Sheriffs Dept. Vehicle Tests						
	Chevrolet	Chevrolet	Dodge	Ford	Mercury	Plymouth
Model	**Impala**	**Nova**	**Aspen**	**LTD II**	**Cougar**	**Volare**
Engine (cid) Carb	350, 4-bbl	350, 4-bbl	360, 4-bbl	400, 2-bbl	400, 2-bbl	360, 4-bbl
HP (CA)	160 nhp	160 nhp	160 nhp	168 nhp	168 nhp	160 nhp
Axle Ratio	3.08	3.08	2.71	2.75	2.75	2.71
Weight (lbs)	4,020	3,650	3,890	4,560	4,560	3,880
Wheelbase	116	111	112.7	118	118	112.7
0-60 mph, sec	10.7	9	10.7	12.3	11.2	10.6
Quarter-Mile Trap Speed	78	83	78	74.5	76	79
Braking Power	.860g	.905g	.843g	.925g	.785g	.800g
Skid Pad, 200 ft. dia.	.763g	.825g	.800g	.700g	.725g	.800g
Fuel Economy, actual	14	14.1	13.9	12	12.3	13.5
TOTAL SCORE	63.2	68.9	67	64.3	63.5	66.1

References for 1978

Engineered Police Vehicles for 1978 From Chevrolet, Chevrolet Motor Division

1978 Patrol Vehicle Specs, Evaluation and Purchasing Program, Michigan State Police

1978 Vehicle Testing and Evaluation Program, Los Angeles County Sheriffs Dept.

75 Years of Chevrolet, George Dammann, Motorbooks International

Standard Catalog of Chevrolet, Pat Chappell, Krause Publications

Military Police 1957 One Fifty. (Chuck Schroedel)

Clinton County, Indiana, Sheriff 1960 Bel Air.

Iowa Highway Patrol 1961 Biscayne. (Robert Parks)

Front view of a California Highway Patrol 1979 Camaro.

San Francisco, California, Police 1987 Caprice. (Bill Hattersley)

Los Angeles County Sheriff 1990 Caprice. (Bill Hattersley)

Nevada Highway Patrol 1992 Camaro.

Chicago Police 1966 Bel Air. (Greg Reynolds)

Iowa State Patrol 1988 Caprice. (Robert Parks)

California State University Police 1986 Celebrity. (John Yeaw)

Los Angeles County Sheriff 1976 Nova.

Delaware State Police 1989 Caprice. (John Yeaw)

Nevada Highway Patrol 1990 Caprice. (John Yeaw)

Dallas, Texas, Police 1991 Caprice. (Terry Feine)

Seattle, Washington, Police 1992 Caprice. (Bill Hattersley)

Royal Canadian Mounted Police 1993 Caprice. (Bill Hattersley)

Front view of Randolph County, Illinois, Sheriff 1995 Caprice. (Jennifer Sturgeon)

Chapter 25

1979: CHP Special Purpose Vehicle Study

The big news for 1979 was the downsized Malibu 9C1 four-door sedan and two-door coupe. These replaced the incredible Nova 9C1. The '78 Nova had a 111-inch wheelbase. In comparison, the '79 Malibu had a 108.1-inch wheelbase. Even still, the '79 Malibu had greater interior room and a larger trunk than the '78 Nova.

The "new-sized" Malibu had a full-perimeter frame and a four-wheel coil spring suspension. The Malibu 9C1 was available in the L26 200-cid, two-barrel carbureted V-6 producing 94 nhp, the LG4 305-cid, four-barrel carbureted V-8 producing 160 nhp and the LM1 350-cid, four-barrel carbureted V-8 producing 170 nhp.

The California and altitude emissions packages reduced the V-8 horsepower by 5 nhp. The V-6 was only available with Federal emission controls. All Malibu 9C1 squads, regardless of engine or emissions package, used 2.73 rear gears, a three-speed automatic, and single exhaust.

Car and Driver reviewed the new Malibu 9C1 police car in its February 1979 issue:

"The 9C1 happens to be one of the best American sedans extant—if not the best. There's 113 mph of pursuit speed available, even with a speed-sapping light bar on the roof. And if the roof is 'clean,' the 9C1 is probably good for almost 120 mph. But that's not all. This Malibu can zigzag through the twisty bits like O.J. wiggling through a crowded airport. Double-nickel defiers never had it so bad."

Car and Driver explained that the famous F41 sport suspension package was the foundation upon which the 9C1 police package is built. From the F41, Chevrolet added a larger diameter rear sway bar to bring the steady state handling closer to neutral.

They found harder front control arm bushings and stiffer front sway bar grommets quickened the transient steering response. Stiffer body mounts with the 9C1 police package than the F41 sport package also added to the quicker steering response. The F41 and 9C1 packages share springs, shocks and steering gears.

Car and Driver was also impressed with the Malibu's police brakes, which included semi-metallic brake linings, a larger capacity brake booster and revised front to rear proportioning.

"The result of all this special attention is that a 9C1 can do just about everything better than its F41 brother. The 9C1's extra measure of road sense makes snaking through your favorite esses even more fun than it is in the F41. And that's saying a lot."

While any retail customer could order the 9C1 police suspension package, only the cops could order the 350-cid/170-hp four-barrel carbureted V-8. The civilian Malibu were limited to the 305-cid/160 hp four-barrel carbureted V-8.

Police Product News also reviewed the new police Malibu. While the Malibu was smaller than the legendary Nova, *PPN* felt the Malibu was the better handling car. It pitted the Malibu 9C1 against the police Volare A38, and also felt the Malibu handled better than the Volare.

"In handling ability, we felt there was a marked difference in the two cars. Both cars came equipped with all the heavy-duty suspension systems made especially for police

A 305-cid-powered 1979 Malibu under test with the California Highway Patrol. The CHP liked the handling, fuel economy and braking on the Malibu 9C1. (Darryl Lindsay)

This 1979 Impala was used by the Lorain County, Ohio, Sheriff. With no automaker offering a big-block V-8, the 350-cid Impalas gained in popularity. (Darryl Lindsay)

packages. And of course the Malibu came with General Motors' famous positraction.

"The Malibu's handling is excellent and the steering is lively and responsive. Body roll is very minimal through sharp, high speed corners. In power turns the rear end held like glue. The Malibu's overall cornering ability was tight and flat, with good control and feedback to the steering wheel."

The 1979 Impala was a near-total carry-over from 1978. The 116-inch wheelbase four-door sedan and two-door coupe were powered by the L22 250-cid, one-barrel carbureted inline Six, the LG3 305-cid, two-barrel carbureted V-8 or LM1 350-cid, four-barrel carbureted V-8. This was the last year for the inline Six.

The rear gears were 2.41 for the 305 V-8 and 3.08 for the 350 V-8 for all emissions packages. The Six used 2.56 gears for Federal engines and 2.73 gears with California engines. As a side note, retail Impalas powered by the LM1 350 came with rear gears as low as 2.41.

In 1979, the Chevrolet Impala with its LM1 350 V-8 was on much more equal footing with all other makes of police car. All the big-blocks and large displacement small-blocks were gone, period. The largest engine from Ford was the 351-cid Windsor V-8. The largest engine from Dodge and Plymouth was the 360-cid V-8. Pontiac and Buick were no longer players.

At 195 nhp, the Mopar 360 V-8 had a 25 horsepower advantage over the Chevy 350 V-8. However, the 116-inch wheelbase Impala weighed 125 pounds less than the 118.5-inch wheelbase St. Regis and Newport.

In 1979, the Mopars outran the bowtie and the bowtie whipped the blue ovals. Chevy fans would have just one more year of this kind of performance. In 1981, when the Mopar 360 V-8 gave way to the Mopar 318 V-8, it would be the Era of Chevrolet through 1996.

In the late-1970s, General Motors was involved in a controversial lawsuit. The owner of a retail Oldsmobile discovered that his engine was a Chevrolet-marque 350 instead of an Oldsmobile-marque 350. For 1979, the police literature first published a disclaimer that clarified this issue:

"A word about engines: The Chevrolets in this catalog are equipped with GM-built engines produced by various divisions. Please see your dealer for details."

Popular Science reviewed the 1979 Chevrolet Caprice 350 V-8 in comparison to the Ford LTD 351 V-8 and the Chrysler Newport 360 V-8. The Caprice rated higher than the LTD and Newport in fuel economy, handling, quietness and ease of entry and exit.

"Chevrolet's Caprice Classic rates superior marks in just about every category.... The Chevy was not only the fastest in each test, it also felt more controllable. Its predictable handling reactions were designed to improve on the low skill level of the average driver. In fairness, it should be pointed out that the Caprice had the highly recommended optional F41 (police) sports suspension....EPA ratings of the 350-cid Caprice show it as the most efficient of the three by as much as two mpg.

"Much has been written about the numerous good points of the smaller Caprice since its introduction two years ago. It is the most satisfying full-size sedan you'll drive this year, benefiting from two years of honing....Among the Caprice's outstanding features are sure handling, quiet ride, high reliability of power systems, and the elegant simplicity of its instrument panel....The Caprice still narrowly remains the pick of the pack....Chevrolet Caprice is still King of the full-size cars."

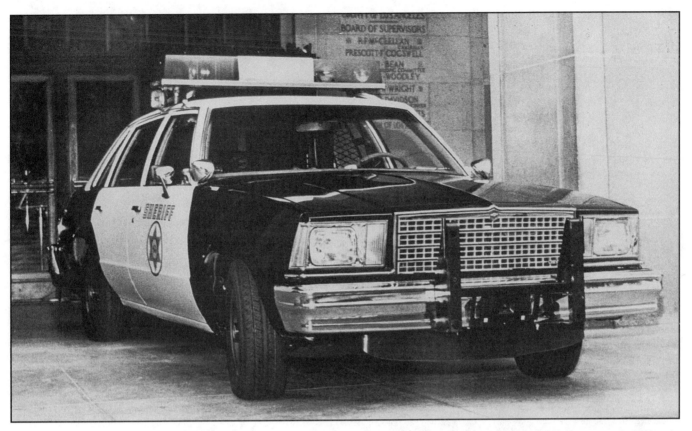

The big news for 1979 was the 108-inch wheelbase Malibu 9C1. Used by the Los Angeles County Sheriff, the 350-cid Malibu had a top speed of 113 mph. (LASD)

The Los Angeles County Sheriffs Department was among many departments, large and small, to use the 1979 Malibu 9C1 powered by the LM1 350 V-8. It came in third of the four mid-size cars tested by the LASD in terms of actual performance. However, these are pass-fail tests to determine the eligibility to bid. Chevrolet turned in the lowest bid of the qualifying squad cars. The Malibu 9C1 was the patrol car in 1979 for the LASD.

The Michigan State Police tested five full-size police cars in 1979: Chevy Impala, Chrysler Newport, Dodge St. Regis, Ford LTD and Ford LTD II. The more powerful St. Regis turned in the best performance while the Impala was right in the middle of the pack. The two Fords were disqualified for failing to meet top speed and acceleration requirements.

Once again, however, when it came to the most performance for the fleet dollar, Chevrolet won. The Impala's vehicle performance was high enough to give the big Chevrolet the lowest "adjusted" bid. The Impala 9C1 was the Michigan State Police patrol car for 1979. It was also used by the state police in Indiana, Maine, Washington, and North Carolina.

In 1979, Chevrolet tried a mini-small-block again. Known as the 4.4-liter V-8, this 267-cid small-block used the 3.480-inch stroke of the 350-cid engine. To achieve 267 cubic inches, this engine used a 3.500-inch bore. This is the smallest bore ever used on a Chevrolet small-block. The bore of the '55 265-cid V-8, for example, was 3.750 inches.

This "square" 267-cid, two-barrel carbureted engine had good emission results but just 125 nhp. Along with the 1975 454-cid V-8, this was the only Chevrolet V-8 engine to use a compression ratio as low as 8.2:1. This was used as an Impala 9C6 and Malibu 9C6 *taxi* engine in 1981 but never as an official police package engine. This 267-cid V-8 was discontinued after 1981.

The 1979 model year Impala was the last to use an inline six-cylinder engine. Chevy police cars had been powered by overhead valve inline sixes since long before the 1935 Blue Flame "stovebolt" Six. In 1980, the 250-cid, one-barrel carbureted inline six-cylinder was replaced by the 229-cid, two-barrel carbureted V-6. Both produced the same horsepower at 115 nhp, however, the smaller 229-cid V-6 produced slightly less torque.

The 200-cid, two-barrel carbureted V-6 used in the Malibu would also give way to the 229-cid, two-barrel carbureted V-6 in 1980. This would mean a 21 nhp increase in output. The 305-cid, two-barrel carbureted V-8 used in the Impala would also be dropped for 1980 in favor of the four-barrel version currently used in the 1979 Malibu.

The period immediately after the demise of the big-block was an especially rough one for state troopers and highway patrolmen. For 50 years, these officers had nearly the most powerful cars on the road. Now, they had mid-size and full-size four-door sedans with a small-block V-8 choked off with emissions gear. In the late-1970s and mid-1980s, the fastest police four-door sedans produced top speeds well under 120 mph.

The California Highway Patrol was the first to be affected by this loss of power. They lost their 440-cid V-8 after 1978. The CHP 1979 Dodge St. Regis used a 360-cid V-8. The 1979 St. Regis was bigger than the 1978 Fury, so the 1979 Dodge was even slower than the engine sizes show. Top speed dropped from 133 mph to 123 mph.

The news for the CHP in 1980 was worse yet. The only Mopar engine approved by the California Clean Air Resources Board (CARB) was the 318-cid V-8. Top speed with the 318-powered, 118.5-inch wheelbase St. Regis was just 115 mph. The CHP saw this coming and had a plan.

The North Carolina State Patrol used the 1979 Impala as did the state police in Maine, Washington and Michigan. (Greg Reynolds)

The Indiana State Police used the 1979 350-cid Impala. These 170-hp cruisers had a top speed of 113 mph and got 16 mpg. (Jerry Parker)

The big news for 1979 was the Special Purpose Vehicle Study conducted by the California Highway Patrol. This study was a direct result of the loss of the big-block V-8 and the downsizing from 122-inch wheelbase cars to 116- and 117-inch wheelbase cars.

One of the alternatives on how to deal with the changing police cars was a mixture of vehicles with different designs within one fleet. Some of the vehicles would be smaller four-door sedans with multi-purpose abilities. Others would be special purpose vehicles such as sport coupes and station wagons that would be intended for specific police tasks.

Because the mixed fleet concept was a radical departure from the existing CHP procedures, the CHP decided to thoroughly investigate the proposal. In late-1978, using 1979 model vehicles, the Special Purpose Vehicle Study began.

CHP executive management wanted to include vehicle designs that would probably be available after 1985, which appeared to be a stability point in the pattern of vehicle change. By using 1978 manufacturer forecasts, the department identified three 1979 vehicles that were presumed comparable to post-1985 designs. Based on this, the following models were selected for testing:

Sport Coupe-1979 Chevrolet Z28 Camaro, 350-cid V-8
Compact Sedan-1979 Chevrolet Malibu, 305-cid V-8
Compact Sedan-1979 Ford Fairmont, 302-cid V-8
Station Wagon-1979 Plymouth Volare, 318-cid V-8

In an effort to simulate mixed fleet management conditions, three of each of the 1979 models were assigned to four test areas throughout the state. This resulted in a total of 12 test vehicles in each area. The balance of each local fleet consisted of the basic police sedan.

Each test area was selected because it represented a sampling of statewide operating conditions. Roadway design, topography, climate and traffic patterns were incorporated into the selection process. It was hoped that potential problems arising from a specific model's inability to perform in a particular region could be documented. The four test areas included Redding, Bakersfield, West Los Angeles and El Centro.

Redding Area

This area is located in rural northern California. A variety of roadway designs are present. Two lane country roads, frequently traveled mountainous highways (i.e. SR 299), and Interstate 5 are located in the Redding Area. Its topography includes both long mountain grades and the northern Sacramento valley. The climate changes seasonally from severe cold and snow in winter to extreme 100 degree plus heat in summer.

Bakersfield Area

This area is located in the central portion of the state and is the high speed link between northern and southern California. Two major freeways traverse this area and both handle a large volume of north-south traffic. One of these freeways is SR 99, which carries most of the north-south San Joaquin valley traffic and the other is Interstate 5. I-5 is a highly traveled freeway with numerous speeding violations. Aside from freeways, Bakersfield Area also has a variety of suburban and rural roadways. Climate ranges from rainfall in winter to severe heat in summer. High wind, dust storms and thick fog are not uncommon occurrences during the year.

El Centro Area

Located just north of the California-Mexico Border, this area is generally a flat region. There are some suburban communities, however, most of the El Centro Area is farming or open desert. As a result, high winds, dust storms, occasional flooding, and extreme heat can occur. A variety of designs are present. Most of these roadways are in good physical condition, which often leads to numerous high speed violations.

West Los Angeles

Located in the more densely populated Los Angeles metropolitan area, much of the area is older freeway with little or no shoulder. Extremely heavy traffic volumes are frequently present and especially during commute hours. This command enjoys moderate climate conditions, with corresponding seasonal changes in wind, precipitation, and temperature.

1979 Chevrolet Camaro Z28

The Camaro Z28 used by the CHP was a showroom stock, retail version without the benefit of a police performance package or a higher performance "Corvette-type" engine. It was identical to every other Camaro Z28 that rolled out of the Van Nuys assembly plant with just three exceptions.

In an effort to increase top speeds, the CHP got an exemption from the California Clean Air Resources Board (CARB) to change axle ratios. In 1979, the retail Camaro Z28 came with either 3.42 or 3.73 rear gears. The CHP changed the axle ratio to 3.08. As a reference, the police package Malibu used 2.73 gears while the police 350-cid Impala used 3.08 gears.

The brakes were also upgraded. The Camaro Z28 was fitted with the Nova police package brakes. Recall that these came from the full-size Bel Air back in 1975. The Nova brakes included front discs with sintered metallic linings and finned rear drums.

The third exception was the tires. Retail Camaro Z28s came with steel belted radials. At the time, these were not recommended for sustained high speed driving. The CHP got involved in one 50 mile long, 100 mph pursuit every day. The factory OEM radials were replaced with Firestone fabric-belted tires designed for police use.

The CHP Camaro was a real Z28 complete with front air dam, rear spoiler, bucket seats and console shifter. The colorful Z28 decals were removed. The aluminum wheels were painted black.

The Camaro Z28 was powered by a 350-cid/160-hp V-8 with a four-barrel carb and two-bolt main bearings. This was similar to the LM1 350-cid V-8 used in the police package Malibu. With California emissions, the LM1 police 350-cid V-8 used in the Malibu and Impala produced 165 hp. The differences between the police 165 hp LM1 and the retail 160 hp 350-cid V-8 used in the retail Camaros are uncertain. The Camaro engine had every last bit of California-required smog gear. The small-block V-8 was bolted to a three-speed Turbo Hydra-Matic transmission equipped with a first gear blockout.

The CHP had problems installing nearly all of the police gear required for a traffic enforcement vehicle. The one-half-inch diameter hole in the A-pillar caused concern the roof support strength would be compromised. Chevrolet advised the roof supports were already stronger than required by federal safety standards.

The conventional radio antenna could not be installed on the Camaro due to the rear fender and trunk design. A base-loaded whip antenna was finally mounted in the center of the roof. No room existed in the engine compartment for the siren and public address speaker. It had to be mounted on the front pusher bar. Fifteen years later, this would be the preferred location of a siren.

The pusher bumper was a real challenge. The pusher bars were specially built to work with the Camaro's front end. The polyurethane front end of the Camaro extends two feet past the frame. The added weight of a thick gauge metal push bumper on the front end could have caused a handling problem, caused some structural damage or accelerated front wheel bearing wear. CHP's Motor Transport Section tested several push bumper designs made of several kinds of metal. They finally decided upon a steel construction. None of the earlier concerns became a problem.

One of the dozen 1979 Camaros tested by the California Highway Patrol during its Special Purpose Vehicle Study. The Camaro was the first pony pursuit car, not the Mustang. (Darryl Lindsay)

The 1979 CHP Camaro was a genuine Z28 complete with front chin and rear deck spoilers. The rear gears were changed to 3.08 to gain a 124 mph top end. (Jim Post)

The 1979 CHP Camaro was powered by a 350-cid V-8. All Camaros got police Nova front brakes. Some Camaros got custom-made pusher bars. (Darryl Lindsay)

In an attempt to reach as high a top speed as possible, the Camaros were all "slick-top," meaning no roof-mounted lightbar. Even an aerodynamic lightbar can rob 10 mph from the top end of an otherwise 130 mph car. A-pillar mounted spotlights rob 1.5 mph each. However, both red (left) and white (right) spotlights were required by California law for these traffic enforcement vehicles.

For emergency lights, the CHP mounted two six-inch rear warning lights on the driver's side rear package tray. These red and amber lights faced out the sloping rear window.

The trunk of the CHP Camaro needed to carry an assortment of emergency equipment: radio transmitter unit, flares, first aid kit, fire extinguisher, spare tire and so on. Chevrolet resolved some of the problem by fitting each of the 12 Camaros with a "space-saver" tire. This allowed the rest of the equipment to fit. However, it caused one problem in the event of a flat tire. The flat tire would not fit in the trunk because all the space was taken up except the space needed for a space-saver tire. The innovative CHP traffic officers simply put the flat tire on the seat in the rear passenger compartment. Even that was a tight and awkward fit.

By far the most problems involved the installation of the shotgun. In most CHP cruisers, the shotgun is locked in a vertical position against the front dash. The interior design and sloping roof line prevented this mounting location. The center console mounted gear shifter prevented placing the Remington 870 horizontally either in front of, or between, the rear seats.

The CHP attempted to mount the shotgun on the inside of the trunk lid, but this did not allow fast enough access to the weapon. They then experimented with shotguns fitted with folding stocks. With the stock folded, the shotgun was short enough to mount vertically to the dash; however, the mounting lock would not accept the shotgun. They tried pistol grip-only shotguns but the CHP officers were less proficient with these guns.

The CHP, with permission from the Bureau of Alcohol, Tobacco and Firearms, shortened the barrel by six inches but this caused the shot pattern to open up too much. Finally, and again with permission from the ATF, the CHP shortened the barrel by two inches. With a slight modification to the locking mechanism, everything now fit.

1979 Chevrolet Malibu 305-cid V-8

The Malibu used by the CHP was fitted with the 9C1 police package. This 108.1-inch wheelbase, four-door mid-size sedan was anticipated to be the "large sedan of 1985 and beyond." The CHP Malibu was equipped with the LG3 305-cid V-8 producing 125 hp with California emissions gear. The only change the CHP made to the Malibu was to replace the OEM wheels with those constructed of thicker gauge steel.

The CHP kept detailed maintenance, downtime and fuel mileage records for all test vehicles. CHP traffic officers logged between 44,000 and 88,000 miles on each of the test Camaros and Malibus during the 18-month evaluation. The Camaros averaged 51.6 hours of downtime per month and 11.8 mpg. The Malibus averaged 34.0 hours of downtime per month and 12.3 mpg.

The heat of El Centro, the continuous high speeds around Bakersfield, and the mountain grades around Redding, took a heavy toll. Of the 12 Z28 test cars, nine had to have the engine replaced. Five of the engines were overhauled, because of piston or main bearing failure, at least once before getting a new block. Only the three Z28s driven in the urban Los Angeles traffic did not need new engines.

A Redding Z28 lost a rod bearing at just 3,600 miles and the number 6 piston at 16,000 miles. The two other Redding Z28s each lost their number 6 pistons at between 8,000 and 9,000 miles. One El Centro Z28 also dumped a piston after 8,000 miles.

The CHP Motor Transport mechanics were not at all happy with the Camaro. Rumors spread around Los Angeles and Detroit of factory sabotaged engines. A "get-the-cops" attitude at the Van Nuys assembly plant may have led to these early engine failures. If so, it backfired. The CHP eventually bought Mustangs and Camaros are now made in Ste-Therese, Quebec, Canada.

Of these nine ill-fated Camaros, none of them got more than 26,000 miles without a major failure. All the CHP test Camaros came with two-bolt main blocks. One of the Redding cars actually went through two engines until Chevrolet began using the bulletproof four-bolt main engines as replacements. That solved the problem.

Overall, the CHP officers noted the usual drawbacks about using a pony car in a police role. The doors were much longer than the four-door sedan doors they were used to opening. The center console made it difficult to exit via the passenger side. Prisoner carrying space simply did not exist.

From a performance view, however, the CHP officers could not have been happier with their Camaro Z28s. The bowtie pony cars hit 60 mph in 9.8 seconds, 100 mph in 27.6 seconds. It ran the quarter-mile in 16.8 seconds at 81.6 mph and had a top speed of 123.6 mph. With semi-metallic front pads, the braking was smooth, straight and short with no brake fade, lockups or wheel hop. The Z28 suspension allowed little body roll, and negligible front end dive or rear end squat. The road feel was good and the steering response was reported as fast.

The four-door Malibu was much easier than the Camaro to compare directly to the four-door St. Regis used in 1979 as the CHP Enforcement-Class vehicle. The lighter but much less powerful Malibu had a lower top speed than the St. Regis, and a slower acceleration to 100 mph. The Malibu was described as having excellent brakes and favorable handling qualities. The Malibu got better gas mileage than the St. Regis. Major repair on the Malibus during the 18 month study was minimal.

The CHP considered the Special Purpose Vehicle Study a total success. This was a tremendous learning experience. The CHP was able to find answers to questions about operating a mixed fleet, and questions about downsized and special purpose vehicles as they relate to officer safety and convenience, prisoner transportation, equipment installation and overall vehicle performance.

The study findings can be summarized as follows:

The CHP can successfully operate a mixed fleet of enforcement vehicles. Downsized vehicles are capable of performing most enforcement duties. Downsized vehicles do not necessarily impair officer safety except when inadequate performance is present. Downsized four-door sedans do not significantly affect prisoner transportation. However, the two-door configuration of sport coupes may necessitate some modification to routine prisoner transportation practices. The installation of the necessary police equipment can require extensive experimentation for two-door coupes. This problem is minimal in a vehicle with a four-door design. Initially, there is the possibility of officer concern over reduced vehicle per-

formance, but this should diminish as each officer becomes more familiar with the downsized vehicles.

Here is what the CHP said about the special purpose Camaro and the downsized Malibu:

Sport Coupe-Chevrolet Z28 Camaro

"This vehicle type possesses performance capabilities indicative of the traditional enforcement vehicle. Design characteristics may force modifications of enforcement equipment and installation procedures. Seating design, especially in the rear, may necessitate a change in the department's prisoner transportation seating policy. The low ground clearance of sport coupes may cause some strains to field officers while entering and exiting the vehicle; however, officers should be able to adapt with very little problem. The different exterior configuration of a sport coupe may increase the public's voluntary compliance with traffic laws. This is due to their inability to easily recognize the silhouette of a sport coupe as a police car. A sport coupe may be good for officer morale. Cargo capacity is limited; however, load readjustment and additional space saving equipment can help to overcome this problem. A sport coupe can be an effective enforcement vehicle, especially in those locations where high performance is needed. The use of a sport coupe can be a valuable asset to a public relations program."

Compact Sedan-Chevrolet Malibu

"The basic sedan design, although smaller in size, is still acceptable for enforcement work. Interior design is more important than before because the interior space has been reduced. Larger officers may find a particular interior design incompatible due to dashboard configuration or the placement of the steering column and seat. Reduced performance in downsized sedans is sufficient for most enforcement work. However, there are conditions such as steep mountain grades and areas noted for many high speed violations which would require more performance than is available in these sedans."

The CHP 440-cid 1978 Monaco was great, the CHP 360-cid 1979 St. Regis was tolerable, the CHP 318-cid 1980 St. Regis was not acceptable, and the CHP 318-cid 1981 Diplomat was the fastest four-door police sedan available, but not fast enough. The 18 month 1979 Specialty Vehicle study was just being completed as top speed problems got statewide attention. Stung by low top speed cars for too long, the CHP wanted a good old-fashioned pursuit car.

Armed with the 18 month study involving the Camaro Z28 and tired of slow cars, the CHP set up some pursuit car specs:

0-60 mph   10 sec maximum
Top Speed   120 mph minimum

The Camaro Z28 bid $11,445 against the Mustang GL bid of $6,868. The Ford that chased Porsches for a living was born.

The CHP 1979 Chevrolet Camaro brought us the more famous CHP 1982 Ford Mustang. The police Mustangs bridged the performance gap until 1991. In that year, the Chevrolet Caprice 9C1 broke the 130 mph barrier. This was the first full-size, police four-door sedan to reach those speeds since the big-blocks of 1978. In 1994, the 5.7-liter LT1-powered Caprice reached 141 mph. By 1995, the 4.6-liter SOHC V-8-powered Crown Victorias were up to 132 mph.

The special service package Mustangs, and, after 1990, the special service package Camaros have done their job. The computer-controlled, fuel-injected small-block-powered four-door sedans now have big-block performance.

1979 CHP Special Purpose Vehicle Study					
	Chevrolet	**Chevrolet**	**Ford**	**Plymouth**	**Dodge**
Model	**Camaro**	**Malibu**	**Fairmont**	**Volare SW**	**St. Regis***
Engine	350 cid	305 cid	302 cid	318 cid	360 cid
Carb	4-bbl	4-bbl	2-bbl	4-bbl	4-bbl
HP (CA)	160 hp	125 hp	133 hp	155 hp	195 hp
Transmission	3-spd THM	3-spd THM	3-spd auto	3-spd auto	3-spd auto
Axle	3.08	2.73	2.73	2.41	3.23
Wheelbase	108.0 in	108.1 in	105.5 in	112.7 in	118.5 in
Curb Weight	3,522 lbs	3,222 lbs	2,961 lbs	3,533 lbs	3,746 lbs
0-60 mph	9.8 sec	12.2 sec	12.0 sec	14.6 sec	11.3 sec
0-100 mph	27.6 sec	44.2 sec	44.0 sec	50.2 sec	34.4 sec
1/4 mi Speed	81.6 mph	73.5 mph	77.2 mph	72.7 mph	77.1 mph
Top Speed	123.6 mph	107.8 mph	106.8 mph	109.5 mph	117.5 mph
Gas Mileage	11.8 mpg	12.3 mpg	13.3 mpg	12.8 mpg	10.2 mpg
Repairs**	$48.36/K	$31.65/K	$24.54/K	$20.58/K	$25.80/K
Downtime	51.6 hr/mo	34.0 hr/mo	20.2 hr/mo	32.3 hr/mo	30.2 hr/mo
*The Dodge St. Regis was the CHP E-class vehicle for 1979					
** Maintenance dollars per 1,000 miles					

1979 Michigan State Police Vehicle Tests					
	Chevy	**Chrysler**	**Dodge**	**Ford**	**Ford**
Model	**Impala**	**Newport**	**St. Regis**	**LTD**	**LTD II**
Engine & Carb	350 cid, 4-bbl	360 cid 4-bbl	360 cid 4-bbl	351 cid 2-bbl	351 cid, 2-bbl
SAE HP	170 nhp	195 nhp	195 nhp	142 nhp	151 nhp
Axle Ratio	3.08	3.21	3.21	3.08	2.47
Weight, 2 on board	4,398 lbs	4,520 lbs	4,530 lbs	4,332 lbs	4,882 lbs
Wheelbase (in)	116	118.5	118.5	114.4	117.9
Road Course Time	93.46 sec	91.36 sec	91.65 sec	95.14 sec	97.88 sec
0-100 mph	35.3 sec	31.5 sec	30.2 sec	63.3 sec	66.7 sec
Top Speed, mph	112.5	121.3	122.9	105.4	111.1
Braking, ft/sec2	23.8	21.8	21.4	18.6	20.1
Ergonomics, pts	311	321	322	301	266
Communications, pts	130	98	98	108	125
EPA City Economy	16	12	12	14	13
Results, overall	third	second	first	disqual	disqual

References for 1979

1979 Chevrolet Police Vehicles, Chevrolet Motor Division

1979 Patrol Vehicle Specs, Evaluation and Purchasing Program, Michigan State Police

1979 Vehicle Testing and Evaluation Program, Los Angeles County Sheriffs Department

"Smaller, Full-Size Cars," Jim Dunne and Ed Jacobs, *Popular Science*, January 1979

75 Years of Chevrolet, George Dammann, Motorbooks International

"Chevrolet Malibu 9C1", Rich Ceppos, *Car and Driver*, February 1979

"Police Packs '79", Bob Lay, *Police Product News*, September 1978

Special Purpose Vehicle Study, California Highway Patrol, September 1982

Chapter 26

1980: First V-6-Powered, Restyled Impala

For 1980, the B-body Impala received its first re-styling since its major downsizing in 1977. The 1980 Impala was more aerodynamic than the previous year. The hood was lower and the rear deck was higher. The grille was much different with the bowtie now prominently placed in the center. The 1980 Impala was also 100 pounds lighter than 1979, thanks to an increased use of aluminum and thinner pieces of higher strength steel. The six-cylinder powered Impalas received aluminum intake manifolds.

All Impalas received one-piece, side guard door beams. The gas tanks were also increased from 21 gallons to 25 gallons. The restyled rear sheet metal resulted in a trunk that was one cubic foot larger.

The remodeled Impala used a side-lift frame jack that lifted by the full perimeter frame, not the bumper. The Impala 9C1 was available as a four-door sedan and a two-door coupe.

The 1980 police powertrain lineup included the new LC3 3.8-liter (229-cid), two-barrel carbureted V-6 in addition to the LG4 305-cid, four-barrel carbureted V-8 and the LM1 350-cid, four-barrel carbureted V-8. Due to emission qualifications, neither the LC3 V-6 nor the LM1 V-8 were available in California.

While Ford had come out with a four-speed automatic overdrive transmission, both the Impala and the Malibu used the three-speed Turbo Hydra-Matic. However, the Turbo Hydra-Matic was upgraded with a lockup torque converter clutch. This clutch locked the flywheel to the driveshaft. A mechanical lockup replaced the fluid coupling. The fluid coupling represented about a four percent loss of efficiency. Lockup torque converters gave Chevrolets better fuel economy in 1980 without going to a four-speed automatic overdrive transmission. The lockup torque converter unlocked as the transmission downshifted under heavy throttle.

The 1980 Impala with a 229-cid V-6 was EPA rated at 18 mpg city and 26 mpg highway. This was the highest ratings ever for a full-size Chevrolet. In mid-1980, Chevrolet released a "special economy equipment package" for the Impala. Based on the 229-cid V-6, this made the Impala the first full-size, gasoline-powered car to reach 20 mpg city. Either way, with a 25 gallon tank, the V-6-powered Impala had a 500 mile cruising range.

The 3.8-liter (229-cid) two-barrel carbureted engine was the first V-6 used in the full-size Chevrolet but it would not be the last. Also for 1980, the full-size Impala was available with a four-barrel version of the 305 V-8. This LG4 engine was the only engine in either car line to be certified for California.

The 1980 Impala was 100 pounds lighter than the 1979 models thanks to an increased use of aluminum. For the first time, a 3.8-liter V-6 powered the police Impala. (Chevrolet)

For 1980, the Impala, such as this NYPD Photo unit, received a lockup torque converter. (Greg Reynolds)

A Visalia, California, Police 1980 Malibu. The 305-cid Malibu also won the bid with the Los Angeles County Sheriff. (Darryl Lindsay)

For 1980, the Malibu 9C1 was available in both a four-door sedan and a two-door coupe. With few exceptions, the Malibu 9C1 was a carry-over from 1979. Again, Chevrolet pushed the Life Cycle Cost concept.

"Increasingly important to Public Safety departments is the cost of keeping a police vehicle in service, mile after mile, month after month. Initial purchase price is no longer the only or best indicator of product value. The process of recognizing and considering most important factors is known as Life Cycle Cost/Performance Evaluation.

"These factors include initial cost, plus fuel economy, parts replacement, resale value, police capability, human environment factors, as well as mechanical evaluations such as potential downtime and serviceability of both car and equipment. This process of Life Cycle Cost/Performance Evaluation is now used by Law Enforcement agencies in many parts of the country."

In 1980, Michigan State Police expanded their testing to include both full-size cars with wheelbases from 114.4 to 118.5 inches, and for the first time mid-size cars with wheelbases from 105.5 to 112.7 inches. The full-size cars were expected to have an engine size large enough to meet the acceleration and other performance requirements. This usually meant the largest engine possible.

The mid-size cars were, however, limited to specific small displacement V-8s. The Malibu was specified to have the 305 V-8 for bidding purposes. However, as a service to other police departments nationwide, the MSP was willing to test the Malibu with the 350 V-8. The performance requirements and minimum qualifying standards for the full-size and mid-size cars were different, of course.

The Malibu 305 V-8 did well against the Aspen 318 V-8, Fairmont 225 V-8 and Volare 318 V-8. It had a competitive top speed at 113 mph, and the fastest quarter-mile time at 19.2 seconds. It had middle-of-the-pack braking distances and fuel economy. However, the Malibu clearly won the most heavily weighted MSP test: lap times around the MIS road racing course. It was 2.4 seconds faster than the closest competitor.

In terms of outright performance, the Malibu was the clear overall winner during the influential MSP tests. However, its performance was not high enough to offset all of its higher bid price. Under the

MSP protocol, the Volare 318 V-8 was found to have the most bang for the buck. In this regard, the Malibu 9C1 was not able to carry the baton passed to it by the Nova 9C1.

In a direct, info-only comparison between the more powerful Malibu 350 V-8 and the Aspen 360 V-8, the Malibu had a slight performance advantage. The Aspen 360 V-8 had a 20 nhp advantage that gave it an edge in top speed, and 0-90 mph times. The Malibu 350 V-8, however, had the best braking distances and better fuel economy. More importantly, the Malibu 350 V-8 had the quickest road course times.

Under the MSP protocol, a full 50 percent of the total score is made up from the road course time and the EPA city fuel economy figures. While the bid results were not published for these mid-size cars with larger engines, the Malibu 350 V-8 was the overall winner in terms of performance.

The 1980 MSP tests for the full-size cars were disappointing for the bowtie crowd. The Impala 350 V-8 was disqualified from bidding for failing to meet the MSP acceleration standards. The MSP required their full-size cars to reach 100 mph in 43 seconds. The Buick LeSabre 350 V-8 was likewise disqualified.

The MSP sets their acceleration requirements based on the previous year's performance. They take the average of the previous year's acceleration times for the qualifying cars then subtract 10 percent. This forces continued improvement in order to qualify year to year.

The Impala 350 V-8 was still behind the power curve established by the Mopar and Ford big-blocks from 1978 and the higher output Mopar 360 V-8 from 1979. The statistical average caught up with the Impala in 1980.

The Impala was able to achieve the MSP top speed requirement of 110 mph but only by .4 mph. The Impala had a competitive road course time, the second best brakes and the second best fuel economy.

The Impala 350 V-8 actually lost fair and square to the Plymouth Gran Fury 360 V-8. That is okay. By this exact same MSP test protocol, the Impala and Caprice would win fair and square for 10 years in a row starting in 1987.

The outcome for Chevy fans was much better during the Los Angeles County Sheriffs Department vehicle tests held later in the year. The Malibu 305 V-8 took on the Fairmont 255 V-8, LTD 351 V-8 and

The 1980 Malibu, such as this LaHabra, California, Police unit, was available with the 3.8-liter V-6, 305-cid V-8 or 350-cid V-8. (John Bellah)

the Gran Fury 318 V-8. The Malibu 9C1 did not turn in the best performance in any one category but placed well in each test phase. Chevrolet then clinched the LASD contract by submitting the lowest bid of all the qualified squad cars. The LASD, and numerous other municipalities such as St. Louis, Missouri, Police all used the Malibu with one engine or another in 1980.

Popular Science reviewed five full-size "family cars," which also included many platforms used by cops:

Buick LeSabre	231 cid, 4-bbl V-6 turbo
Chevrolet Caprice	305 cid, 4-bbl V-8
Ford LTD	351 cid, 2-bbl V-8
Plymouth Gran Fury	318 cid, 2-bbl V-8
Pontiac Bonneville	350 cid, fi, V-8 diesel

"As did its GM sisters in this test, the Caprice received some significant aerodynamic changes to its sheet metal for 1980. Under the skin, though, the GM cars all have still basically the same chassis introduced in 1977....Aided by a lockup torque converter, the Caprice delivered the best gasoline-powered fuel economy at 55 mph, and the second-best in the other (35, 45) speed categories."

In 1980, the New York City Police fleet managers actually tested the Citation as a police car. The First Precinct seriously deployed a small fleet of Citation squad cars in preparation for widespread use of this tiny car by NYC-PD cops. These were *not* police package cars! The headlines of the October 28, 1980, *New York Post* read "No prisoners please-the car's too small."

"Question: How do you fit a big police officer into a small car? Answer: Snugly!

"Officers big and small are fast learning to cope with smaller new police cars. The Plymouth Horizon, Ford Fairmont and Chevy Citation are among the new smaller-and more fuel efficient-cars replacing previous roomier models. All of them have been test-driven by the Motor Transport Division and found to be 'safe and serviceable,' according to a police spokesman.

"Six-foot-two 265-pound Police Officer Matthew Johnson of Manhattan's Ericsson Place stationhouse is one of many officers filling out a two-page questionnaire to evaluate the car's performance. And how do the officers like the smaller models? Well, the Plymouth Horizon has been catching most of the complaints, with the others rank-

In 1980, the NYPD actually tested the Citation for uniformed patrol. The Freeport, New York, Police took the search for economy one step further with this 1980 Chevette. (Ned Schwartz)

ing just a drop better, we're told. The most frequent complaint is of officers having trouble getting a prisoner into the back seat unless he's cooperative."

For the record, the Chevrolet Citation had a 104.9-inch wheelbase. That is 3.2 inches shorter than the already downsized Malibu. The retail Citation was powered by a 151-cid inline, four-cylinder rated at 90 hp. While these tiny cars got 25 mpg, they also had top speeds under 85 mph and 0-60 mph catch times of about an hour. Fortunately, the NYC-PD Citation never went beyond the field testing stage. Within just two months, all of these matchbox cars were withdrawn from service.

Chevrolet Police Engines for 1980

Code	Engine	SAE HP	Models
LC3	229 cid, 2-bbl V-6	115 nhp	Impala, Malibu
LG4	305 cid, 4-bbl V-8	155 nhp	Impala, Malibu
LM1	350 cid, 4-bbl V-8	165 nhp	Impala, Malibu
Impala axle ratio 2.73 (V-6), 3.08 (V-8)			
Malibu axle ratio 2.41 (V-6), 2.73 (V-8			

1980 Michigan State Police Patrol Vehicle Tests
114.4- to 118.5-inch Wheelbase

	Buick	Chevrolet	Dodge	Ford	Plymouth
Model	LeSabre	Impala	St. Regis	LTD-S	Gran Fury
Engine Carb	350 cid, 4-bbl	350 cid, 4-bbl	360 cid, 4-bbl	351 cid, v/v	360 cid, 4-bbl
SAE HP	155 nhp	165 nhp	185 nhp	172 nhp	185 nhp
Axle Ratio	2.73	3.08	2.94	2.73	2.94
Weight (lbs)	4,146	3,934	4,100	4,030	4,053
Wheelbase (in)	115.9	116	118.5	114.3	118.5
Road Course Time, sec	96.2	92.8	91.8	92.2	90.8
0-100 mph, sec	49.4	46.2	36.7	37.3	35.5
Top Speed (mph)	113.1	110.4	122.7	120.5	124.6
1/4 mi. Time	19.5	19.1	18.4	18.5	18.2
1/4 mi. Speed	74.3	73.3	77.5	77.8	76.8
Braking from 60 mph	168	169	171.1	171.4	182.5
EPA City Mileage	15	14	11	14	11
Adjusted Bids	disqual	disqual	$6,518	$7,105	$6,392

1980 Michigan State Police Patrol Vehicle Tests
105.5- to 112.7-inch Wheelbase

	Chevrolet	Dodge	Ford	Plymouth	Chevrolet	Dodge
Model	Malibu	Aspen	Fairmont	Volare	Malibu	Aspen
Engine Carb	305 cid, 4-bbl	318 cid, 4-bbl	255 cid, 2-bbl	318 cid, 4-bbl	350 cid, 4-bbl	360 cid, 4-bbl
SAE HP	155 nhp	155 nhp	119 nhp	155 nhp	165 nhp	185 nhp
Axle Ratio	2.73	2.94	2.26	2.94	2.73	2.94
Weight (lbs)	3,484	3,673	3,109	3,673	3,501	3,734
Wheelbase (in)	108.1	112.7	105.5	112.7	108.1	112.7
Road Course Time	93.3	96.2	95.7	96.2	92.2	92.7
0-90 mph, sec	33.4	32.3	49.1	29.4	31.9	25.7
Top Speed	113.4	117.3	111.6	120	110.8	122.2
1/4 mi. Time	19.2	19.6	20.7	19.3	19	18
1/4 mi. Speed	73.5	73.3	68.5	74.8	74.3	77.5
Braking from 60 mph	164.1	177.3	158.1	167.8	156.1	161.7
EPA City Mileage	17	16	18	16	14	13
Adjusted bids	$6,109	$6,110	disqual	$5,788	info only	info only

References for 1980

1980 Chevrolet Police Vehicles, Chevrolet Motor Division
1980 Vehicle Testing and Evaluation Program, Los Angeles County Sheriffs Department

1980 Patrol Vehicle Specs, Evaluation and Purchasing Program, Michigan State Police
"Full-Size Cars," Jim Dunne and Ed Jacobs, Popular Science, April 1980

Chapter 27

1981: Malibu 9C1, the Police Car of the Year

In 1981, the Impala and Malibu were mostly carry-overs from 1980. The powerplants were still the 229-cid/115-hp V-6, 305-cid/155-hp V-8 and the 350-cid/165-hp V-8. All three engines were available in both squad cars with one exception. The 229-cid V-6 was not certified for use in California. In California, the 231-cid V-6 developed by Buick was again used in both the police Impala and police Malibu.

The Malibu received a slightly restyled grille for 1981. The Impala got a plastic master cylinder reservoir and front disc brakes with less drag. Both cars were upgraded with a new Computer Command Control that adjusted the air to fuel mixture and spark timing.

In 1981, the retail cars equipped with 5.0-liter V-8s came with the new four-speed automatic overdrive transmission. This four-speed transmission was not available in any police car in 1981 and would not be available until 1983.

The lean and mean Impala performed well during the 1981 Michigan State Police vehicle tests. The 350-cid Impala took on the 351-cid Ford LTD, 318-cid Dodge St. Regis and Plymouth Gran Fury and a 252-cid Buick LeSabre. The LeSabre was disqualified for failing to reach a minimum top speed of 105 mph.

The Impala was the fastest full-size, four-door sedan to reach 100 mph. The Impala had the most braking power and was given the highest ergonomics rating. Most importantly, the Impala was clearly the fastest police car around the MIS road racing course. Unfortunately,

the 318-cid-powered Plymouth Gran Fury bid low enough to offset the better performance from the Impala.

For 1981, the Impala had the same power advantage over the Mopar squads as the Mopars had had over the Impala since 1977. The powerful 360-cid/185-hp small-block used in the St. Regis and Gran Fury was gone. These 118.5-inch wheelbase cars were now powered by the 318-cid/165-hp small-block. This was the same engine-chassis combination that the *Los Angeles Times* called a "dog" when the cars were used by the California Highway Patrol.

The 1981 Chevrolet performance was quite a comeback compared to 1980 when the Impala was disqualified for failing to reach 100 mph fast enough. The Impala now reached 100 mph six seconds faster and, in fact, was the fastest police sedan tested by the MSP. Its quarter-mile time even broke into the 18 second bracket. The improved Impala was now quick enough to compete with the 360-cid-powered Mopars had they been available.

The real star in the 1981 Chevrolet police fleet, both from a performance standpoint and a contract-winning standpoint, was the Malibu 9C1. Powered by the 350-cid/165-hp four-barrel carbureted V-8, the Malibu won the Michigan State Police contract for mid-size cars. Powered by the 305-cid/155-hp four-barrel carbureted V-8, the Malibu won the Los Angeles County Sheriffs Department contract outright. The outcome of the LASD tests influence cops west of the Rockies while the MSP tests influence cops east of the Rockies. The two most important

An Arkansas State Police 1981 Impala powered by a 350-cid/175-hp V-8. These cars ran an 18 second quarter-mile. The top speed was 114 mph. (Greg Reynolds)

This 1981 Impala is in-service with the Union County, Tennessee, Sheriff. Engines ranged from a 3.8-liter V-6 to a 350-cid, four-barrel V-8. (Dave Dotson)

police departments in the country, when it comes to police cars, both pointed to the Malibu as the best police car of 1981.

In Michigan, the Malibu 350 V-8 beat the best mid-size cars from Dodge, Chrysler and Ford. It reached 100 mph in just over 40 seconds. It ran the quarter-mile in the low 18 second range, which was quite fast for sedans from the early 1980s. The top speed and braking distances were average for mid-size patrol cars. The big victory was during testing on the MIS road racing course. The Malibu 9C1 was far faster than any mid-size squad car. It was also faster than any full-size squad car.

In Los Angeles, the Malibu easily whipped the Dodge St. Regis. It was almost four seconds quicker around the road racing course at the Pomona Fairgrounds. All four test drivers, two from LAPD and two from LASD, commented that the Malibu handled well with the exception of a slight tendency to understeer in turns. The overall handling of the St. Regis was noted as "acceptable." Down the same drag strip used for the National Hot Rod Association's Winternationals, the 305-cid Malibu was 1.4 seconds ahead of the 318-cid St. Regis. Under the LASD gas mileage test method, a 72.1-mile drive under actual patrol conditions, the Malibu even had a higher fuel rating.

The Los Angeles County Sheriffs Department was completely satisfied with the Nova and Malibu police cars. According to LASD Fleet Operation Section memos:

> "...since our first acquisition of the Nova in 1976, the sedan fleet downtime has been reduced from almost 29 percent to the current (1981) level of between 6 and 7 percent including wrecks. While there are a number of other factors influencing that reduction, e.g., closer monitoring of the preventive maintenance schedule, etc., at least a part of the credit can be attributed to the reliability of the vehicle itself."

Sales of the retail Impala sagged in 1981 as the nation focused on front-drive subcompacts with high fuel mileage. Lower sales caused

speculation the full-size car would be dropped. These rumors would persist throughout the 1980s.

1981 Chevrolet Police Engines					
RPO	Type	Size	Carb	HP	Axle Ratio
LC3	V-6	3.8L/229 cid	2-bbl	110	2.73 (Impala), 2.41 (Malibu)
LG4	V-8	5.0L/305 cid	4-bbl	150	3.08 (Impala), 2.73 (Malibu)
LM1	V-8	5.7L/350 cid	4-bbl	175	3.08 (Impala), 2.73 (Malibu)

Los Angeles County Sheriffs Department 1981 Vehicle Test Summary		
	Chevrolet	**Dodge**
Model	Malibu 9C1	St. Regis A38
Engine, Carb	305 cid, 4-bbl	318 cid, 4-bbl
Transmission	Turbo Hydra-Matic	TorqueFlite
Axle	2.73	2.94
Tires	P205/70R14	P225/70R15
Pomona Fairgrounds		
Road Course Time	1:37.05 min	1:40.78 min
0-60 mph	10.9 sec	13.2 sec
1/4 mi. ET	18.0 sec	19.4 sec
1/4 mi. Speed	77.3 mph	71.1 mph
Top Speed	96 mph	90 mph
Fuel Efficiency	16.1 mpg	14.5 mpg

The Malibu 9C1 was the car to beat in 1981. The 350-cid version won the Michigan State Police mid-size tests. The 305-cid version won the Los Angeles County Sheriff's tests outright. (Darryl Lindsay)

The 1981 Malibu, such as this Quebec-area unit, ran an 18 second quarter-mile and still got an actual 16.1 mpg. (Neil Painchaud)

1981 Michigan State Police Patrol Vehicle Test Results (Full-Size Cars)					
	Chevrolet	**Buick**	**Dodge**	**Ford**	**Plymouth**
Model	**Impala**	**LeSabre**	**St. Regis**	**LTD**	**Gran Fury**
Engine & Carb	350 cid, 4-bbl	252 cid, 4-bbl	318 cid, 4-bbl	351 cid, 2-vv	318 cid, 4-bbl
HP, SAE	165 hp	125 hp	165 hp	165 hp	165 hp
Axle Ratio	3.08	3.23	2.94	2.73	2.94
Weight, test (lbs)	3,927	3,834	4,086	4,060	4,090
Wheelbase (in)	116.0	116.6	118.5	114.3	118.5
Road Course Lap Time	1:30.72	1:38.48	1:33.93	1:32.40	1:33.60
0-100 mph	39.98	n/a	45.72	42.16	42.22
Top Speed, mph	113.8	97.1	114.7	116.4	115.1
1/4 mi. E.T.	18.95	21.88	19.63	19.35	19.40
1/4 mi. Speed	75.00	66.25	74.50	74.75	75.25
Braking, ft/sec2	26.93	23.87	23.67	23.35	25.15
Ergonomics, pts	193.9	186.9	193.6	189.2	193.8
Fuel, EPA City	14.7	18.5	15.5	15.3	15.5
Adjusted Bid Price	$7,560	disqual	$7,733	$8,318	$7,516

1981 Michigan State Police Patrol Vehicle Test Results (Mid-Size Cars)						
	Chevrolet	**Chrysler**	**Chrysler**	**Dodge**	**Ford**	**Ford**
Model	**Malibu**	**LeBaron**	**LeBaron**	**Diplomat**	**Fairmont**	**Fairmont**
Engine & Carb	350 cid, 4-bbl	318 cid, 4-bbl	225 cid, 1-bbl	318 cid, 4-bbl	255 cid, 2-bbl	200 cid, 1-bbl
HP, SAE	165	165	85	165	115	88
Axle Ratio	2.73	2.94	2.94	2.94	2.73	2.73
Weight, Test	3,579 lbs	3,856 lbs	3,694 lbs	3,851 lbs	3,156 lbs	2,944 lbs
Wheelbase (in)	108.1	112.7	112.7	112.7	105.5	105.5
Road Course Lap Time	1:30.37	1:32.54	n/a	1:31.98	1:33.50	n/a
0-100 mph	40.27	45.24	n/a	42.71	65.79	n/a
Top Speed, mph	111.9	114.7	92.5	116.3	106.4	92.3
1/4 mi. E.T.	18.15	18.90	22.80	19.38	19.68	21.78
1/4 mi. Speed	74.75	73.50	61.75	75.50	71.00	63.50
Braking, ft/sec2	25.71	26.02	n/a	24.63	25.02	n/a
Ergonomics, pts	187.6	192.3	192.3	192.3	163.1	163.1
Fuel, EPA City	14.7	15.5	17.9	15.5	18.1	19.8
Adjusted Bid Price	$7,531	$7,691	disqual	$7,623	disqual	disqual

References for 1981

1981 Chevrolet Police Vehicles, Chevrolet Motor Division
1981 Vehicle Testing and Evaluation Program, Los Angeles County
    Sheriffs Department
1981 Patrol Vehicle Specs, Evaluation and Purchasing Program,
    Michigan State Police

A 1981 Chevette used by the New Orleans Police for parking enforcement. This was not a police package car. (Greg Reynolds)

Chapter 28

1982: CHP Adopts the Impala 9C1

This 1982 Malibu 9C1 guarded the streets of St. Louis. Its 229-cid V-6 produced 110 hp. (SLPD)

New for 1982, the Malibu Classic was restyled with quad headlights. The new Malibu grille was so similar to the Impala that speculation was again fueled the full-size car would be dropped. The full-size Impala was basically a carry-over from 1981.

In 1982, the Malibu Classic was available with either the 229-cid/110-hp V-6 or the 305-cid/145-hp V-8. The 350 V-8 was not available in the police Malibu Classic at all. The 229-cid V-6 was again replaced by the 231-cid V-6 for California cop cars. The Impala was available with either the 229-cid V-6 or the 350-cid/150-hp V-8. The 305-cid V-8 was not available in the police Impala. The same restrictions on the 229-cid V-6 apply to the Impala for California.

Ford was in its third year of having a four-speed automatic transmission in its police cars. While Chevrolet released a four-speed automatic for its 5.0-liter-powered retail cars in 1981, the 1982 police cars still used the three-speed Turbo Hydra-Matic 350. As a side note, Dodge and Plymouth police cars would not receive an overdrive automatic transmission before they were discontinued after 1989.

In 1982, the Michigan State Police tested a number of four-, six- and eight-cylinder patrol cars with wheelbases ranging from the 116.0-inch Impala to the 99.9-inch Aries K. Engine sizes varied from the Ford 351-cid V-8 to the Malibu 229-cid V-6 to the Aries K 135-cid four.

The 1982 Impala, such as this Aurora, Colorado, Police unit, ran a 19 second quarter-mile with top speeds of just 108 mph. This was bleak performance for a police car. (Greg Reynolds)

This North Platte, Nebraska, Police 1982 Malibu is powered by a 305-cid V-8. It had a 0-60 mph time of 10.8 seconds. (Monty McCord)

The 1982 model year police car tests were important. These results would predict police car performance for the next five years. For the rest of the 1980s, the Impala, and later Caprice, would be powered by a 350-cid, four-barrel carbureted V-8. Same for the LTD, and later Crown Victoria. The big Ford would have a 351-cid V-8 with a two-barrel variable venturi carb. Same for both Mopar squads. Through the 1989 model year, the Diplomat and Gran Fury would use the 318-cid, four-barrel carbureted V-8.

The changes to all police cars after 1982 would be minor. The Impala would get a four-speed overdrive transmission in 1983 and a fuel-injected 350 in 1989. The Mopars would change from Carter to Rochester carbs and from close-ratio to wide-ratio transmissions. Except for sleeker sheet metal in 1987, the Ford remained basically unchanged for the rest of the 1980s.

For 1982, the MSP combined the full-size and mid-size classes into one group. They simply required that their patrol car have a wheelbase of at least 105.5 inches. In this year of bleak vehicle performance, the MSP removed their 105 to 110 mph top speed requirement. The prospective squad car had to reach 100 mph in 48.5 seconds. Of the V-8-powered cars, the 255-cid Fairmont and the 305-cid Malibu failed to meet this standard. None of the four- and six-cylinder cars even came close.

All of the V-8-powered squads ran the quarter-mile in the 19 second bracket. The highest top speed of any vehicle tested was 116 mph. The big Impala reached only 107.8 mph. The Malibu hit 110.1 mph. Not a good year for the bowtie.

The 1982 MSP patrol vehicle tests were won fair and square by the Dodge Diplomat and Plymouth Gran Fury. Either the Diplomat or

A Yonkers, New York, Police 1982 Impala with a 3.8-liter V-6. The 305-cid V-8 was not available. (Ned Schwartz)

Due to emissions laws, the V-6 engine used by Malibu Police cars in California was the Buick-made 231-cid version. (Dave Dotson)

the Gran Fury would continue to win every year until 1987. In that year, the Caprice took over for the next 10 years straight.

In 1982, the Los Angeles County Sheriffs Department tested three mid-size and two full-size police cars. The LASD bid process is different than the Michigan State Police. Under the LASD method, the cars are required to perform well enough to qualify. The lowest bidder of the qualifying cars wins the contract. Under the MSP method, the performance of the cars is tested, the bids are received and a percentage of the bid is adjusted based on the performance.

The LASD tested the mid-size Malibu 350 V-8, Fairmont 255 V-8 and Gran Fury 318 V-8. The Malibu was the fastest of the group to 60 mph, and was the quickest down the quarter-mile. Most importantly, the Malibu turned in the best lap times around the Pomona Fairgrounds road course. In spite of this excellent performance, when the bids were opened, it was the Plymouth Gran Fury that was awarded the LASD contract.

Of the full-size cars, the Impala 350 V-8 outperformed the LTD 351 V-8. The Impala had quicker acceleration times and was much faster around the road course. The LTD, however, had a 2.5 mpg advantage over the Impala when it came to the 72-mile fuel economy test loop. Even though the Impala had a lockup torque converter, the

three-speed Turbo Hydra-Matic 350 simply could not compete with Ford's four-speed automatic overdrive C6.

The 1982 Impala was, however, selected by one of the nation's most prestigious police departments: the California Highway Patrol. This was the first time in nearly 30 years that the CHP patrolled in a Chevrolet. The last time the CHP used bowtie squad cars, the largest available engine was the stovebolt Six.

This also marked only the third time since 1956 that a police car other than a Chrysler product was used by the CHP. The Impala would turn out to be more of a competitor to the Dodge Diplomat in the 1980s than the Biscayne was to the Dodge Polara in the 1970s.

1982 Chevrolet Police Engines					
RPO	Type	Size	Carb	HP	Axle
LC3	V-6	229 cid/3.8L	2-bbl	110	2.73 (Impala), 2.41 (Malibu)
LG4	V-8	305 cid/5.0L	4-bbl	145	2.73 (Malibu only)
LM1	V-8	350 cid/5.7L	4-bbl	150	3.08 (Impala only)

Los Angeles County Sheriffs Department 1982 Police Car Tests					
	Ford	Plymouth	Chevrolet	Ford	Chevrolet
Model	Fairmont	Gran Fury	Malibu	LTD	Impala
Engine	255 cid V-8	318 cid V-8	305 cid V-8	351 cid V-8	350 cid V-8
Carb	2-bbl	4-bbl	4-bbl	2VV	4-bbl
Transmission	C6	727	350	C6 (OD)	350
Axle	2.73	2.94	2.73	2.73	3.08
0-60 mph	11.6 sec	11.3 sec	10.8 sec	10.9 sec	10.0 sec
1/4 mi. ET	18.4 sec	18.3 sec	18.1 sec	18.0 sec	17.6 sec
1/4 mi. Speed	76.4 mph	78.0 mph	77.8 mph	79.6 mph	79.0 mph
Road Course	96.2 sec	96.2 sec	95.4 sec	95.4 sec	93.8 sec
Gas Mileage	19.0 mpg	15.7 mpg	18.5 mpg	17.2 mpg	14.7 mpg

1982 Michigan State Police Patrol Vehicle Test Results (V-8 Cars)						
	Ford	**Chevrolet**	**Dodge**	**Ford**	**Plymouth**	**Chevrolet**
Model	**LTD**	**Impala**	**Diplomat**	**Fairmont**	**Gran Fury**	**Malibu**
Engine Carb	351 cid 2VV	350 cid 4-bbl	318 cid 4-bbl	255 cid 2-bbl	318 cid 4-bbl	305 cid 4-bbl
HP, SAE	165	150	165	115	165	145
Axle Ratio	2.73	3.08	2.94	2.73	2.94	2.73
Weight, test	4,086	3,996	3,875	3,200	3,863	3,672
Wheelbase (in)	114.3	116.0	112.7	105.5	112.7	108.1
Road Course Lap Time, sec	91.99	92.04	92.57	94.16	92.63	92.61
0-100 mph, sec	42.54	45.79	39.95	57.04	39.36	49.73
Top Speed, mph	115.8	107.8	115.4	107.0	116.3	110.0
1/4 mi. ET, sec	19.15	19.40	19.20	19.88	19.08	19.53
1/4 mi Speed, sec	75.5	73.0	75.3	72.0	76.5	72.5
Braking, ft/sec2	22.6	24.0	23.7	23.2	24.3	24.6
Ergonomics, pts	229.4	210.9	191.4	180.3	191.4	201.9
Fuel, EPA City	13.9	14.3	13.8	18.6	13.8	16.6

1982 Michigan State Police Patrol Vehicle Test Results (Four- & Six-Cylinder Cars)					
	Ford	**Plymouth**	**Chevrolet**	**Ford**	**Dodge**
Model	**Fairmont**	**Gran Fury**	**Malibu**	**Fairmont**	**Aries K**
Engine Carb	200 cid, 1-bbl	225 cid, 1-bbl	229 cid, 2-bbl	140 cid, 2-bbl	135 cid, 2-bbl
HP, SAE	87	90	110	92	84
Axle Ratio	2.73	2.94	2.41	3.08	2.78
Weight, test (lbs)	3,038	3,706	3,376	2,926	2,444
Wheelbase (in)	105.5	112.7	108.1	105.5	99.9
0-60 mph, sec	18.72	20.36	17.99	17.26	17.58
Top Speed, mph	97.3	96.2	100.6	103.4	97.4
1/4 mi. ET, sec	22.00	22.53	21.85	21.85	21.55
1/4 mi Speed, mph	64.8	62.3	65.3	67.5	66.3
Fuel, EPA City	19.7	17.9	20.8	20.5	25.0

References for 1982

1982 Chevrolet Police Vehicles, Chevrolet Motor Division

1982 Vehicle Testing and Evaluation Program, Los Angeles County Sheriffs Department

1982 Patrol Vehicle Specs, Evaluation and Purchasing Program, Michigan State Police

Chapter 29

1983: Four-Speed Overdrive Automatic

In 1983, after two years in retail use, the Impala with the 350-cid V-8, was finally teamed with a four-speed overdrive automatic, the 700R4. Oddly enough, the 1983 Chevrolet police vehicle catalog says nothing about this upgrade. However, the 1983 Michigan State Police vehicle test summary clearly lists the "700R4" transmission and specifically lists this as having both a lockup torque converter and an overdrive.

The 1983 Malibu equipped with the 305-cid V-8 retained the old three-speed Turbo Hydra-Matic 350 transmission. The 1983 Impala fitted with the 229-cid V-6 also kept its three-speed Turbo Hydra-Matic 250 transmission.

The Turbo Hydra-Matic 700R4 used a 0.67 overdrive ratio for the fourth gear. This was the same as having a three-speed transmission with a 2.06 rear axle ratio. The other ratios in the 700R4 were 2.74 (first), 1.57 (second) and 1.00 (third).

Compared to the 318-cid, four-barrel carbureted Diplomat, 318-cid, four-barrel carbureted Gran Fury and 351-cid, 2VV (variable ven-

The St. Louis Police became famous for using mid-size and then front drive police cars before anyone else. This 1983 Malibu was used for uniformed patrol. (SLPD)

The 1983 Impala 9C1, such as this Alhambra, California, fire unit, came with a four-speed automatic transmission. The fourth gear was a .67 ratio overdrive. (C. Madderom)

A Guadalupe, California, Police 1983 Impala in classic black-and-white trim. The 350-cid, four-barrel versions had a 115 mph top speed. (John Yeaw)

turi) Crown Victoria, the 350-cid Impala now had the best EPA City and best EPA Highway fuel ratings. This was a major victory for the way things were with full-size sedans in the early-1980s. For example, in 1983, the MSP gave the fuel economy rating as much weight in the overall scoring as the lap times around the road racing course. These two phases made up exactly half of the total score.

Other than the upgrade to the four-speed overdrive automatic, the 1983 Chevrolet police fleet was mostly a carry-over from 1982. The Malibu 9C1 was available with either the 229-cid/110-hp V-6 or the 305-cid/145-hp V-8. The axle ratio on the V-6-powered Malibu was bumped up from 2.41 to 2.73 for a bit better acceleration. The Impala 9C1 was available with either the 229-cid/110-hp V-6 or the 350-cid V-8, which was now increased to 155 hp.

In 1983, the Impala and Malibu were available only as four-door sedans. This was the final year for the rear-wheel drive, six-passenger

Malibu. It would be replaced in both the retail and police market by the front-wheel drive Celebrity, introduced to the public in mid-1982.

In 1983, overall police vehicle performance edged up slightly. Among the four full-size sedans from Chevrolet, Ford, Dodge and Plymouth, the average quarter-mile time dropped from the low 19s to the high 18s. The top speed increased from a 1982 average of 114 mph to a 1983 average of 118 mph.

The biggest improvement came from the Impala. Among the four primary sedans, the Impala had the slowest quarter-mile elapsed time in 1982 at 19.40 seconds. In 1983, the Impala was the fastest four-door sedan with an 18.55 second elapsed time. Top speed was increased from a feeble 107.8 mph to a more competitive 115 mph.

The full-size Impala had been available with either a 250-cid in-line Six or a 229-cid V-6 since its downsizing in 1977. Many officers felt the 110 hp V-6 engine was simply too small for the 116-inch

The 1983 Malibu, such as this Pismo Beach, California, Police unit, was available with either a 3.8-liter/110-hp V-6 or a 5.0-liter/145-hp V-8. (John Yeaw)

The Pennsylvania State Police used this 1983 Malibu powered by a 305-cid V-8. This was the last year for a Malibu Police package. (Greg Reynolds)

wheelbase, 3,700-pound Impala. In 1983, the Michigan State Police confirmed their fears. The MSP tested 12 police and special service package cars ranging from the 5.0-liter Mustang to the 2.6-liter Reliant K. Only two cars had a slower quarter-mile than the 229-cid V-6-powered Impala: the 225-cid slant Six Diplomat and the 200-cid inline Six Fairmont.

In terms of sheer performance, the 305-cid Malibu and the 351-cid LTD Crown Victoria were the sedans to beat in 1983. The LTD had the fastest lap times and best ergonomics while the Malibu had the second fastest lap times, second strongest brakes, competitive 0-100 mph time and the best fuel economy. However, when the bid price was adjusted based on performance, the LTD was too expensive. With merely third place vehicle performance but an extremely low initial

price, the 318-cid Gran Fury won the bid. The Mopar squads would continue to offer the most bang for the buck until the 1987 Caprice.

A long list of major police departments used Chevrolet police cars in 1983. These included the Indiana State Police, Pennsylvania State Police, Los Angeles Police, Oregon State Police, Florida Marine Patrol, Broward County, Florida, Sheriff and Cook County, Illinois, Sheriff.

1983 Chevrolet Police Engines					
RPO	Type	Size	Carb	HP	Axle
LC3	V-6	229 cid/3.8L	2-bbl	110	2.73 Impala & Malibu
LG4	V-8	305 cid/5.0L	4-bbl	145	2.73 Malibu only
LM1	V-8	350 cid/5.7L	4-bbl	155	3.08 Impala only

1983 Michigan State Police Patrol Vehicle Test Results (Four- & Six-Cylinder Cars)					
	Chevrolet	**Dodge**	**Ford**	**Ford**	**Plymouth**
Model	**Impala**	**Diplomat**	**Fairmont**	**Fairmont**	**Reliant K**
Engine Carb	229 cid, 2-bbl	225 cid, 1-bbl	200 cid, 1-bbl	140 cid, 2-bbl	156 cid, 2-bbl
HP, SAE	110	90	92	90	93
Axle Ratio	2.73	2.94	2.73	3.08	3.02
Weight, test (lbs)	3,713	3,688	2,872	2,979	2,659
Wheelbase (in)	116.0	112.7	105.5	105.5	100.1
Road Course Lap Time	n/a	n/a	n/a	97.68	94.58
0-60 mph	17.4	18.8	17.7	18.4	15.5
Top Speed, mph	104.3	96.5	97.7	95.8	102.8
1/4 mi. ET	21.50	22.03	21.93	21.8	19.7
1/4 mi. Speed	67.0	63.5	66.3	65.0	68.0
Braking, ft/sec2	n/a	n/a	n/a	24.2	24.0
Fuel, EPA City	18.6	18.7	18.6	20.9	23.6

1983 Michigan State Police Patrol Vehicle Test Results (V-8-Powered Cars)							
	Chevrolet	Dodge	Ford	Chevrolet	Plymouth	Ford	Ford
Model	Impala	Diplomat	LTD-CV	Malibu	Gran Fury	LTD-CV	Mustang
Engine Carb	350 cid, 4-bbl	318 cid, 4-bbl	351 cid, 2VV	305 cid, 4-bbl	318 cid, 4-bbl	302 cid, cfi	302 cid, 4-bbl
HP, SAE	155	165	165	145	165	130	175
Axle Ratio	3.08	2.94	2.73	2.73	2.94	3.08	3.08
Weight, test (lbs)	3,993	3,887	4,059	3,516	3,881	3,892	2,970
Wheelbase (in)	116.0	112.7	114.3	108.1	112.7	114.3	100.4
Road Course Lap Times	92.21	93.54	90.59	92.13	92.64	n/a	88.31
0-100 mph	42.51	40.46	39.81	40.73	39.68	69.01	22.71
Top Speed, mph	115.0	118.8	117.9	116.3	120.0	104.4	132.0
1/4 mi. ET	18.55	19.30	18.83	18.78	19.10	19.93	16.68
1/4 mi. Speed	73.5	75.5	75.3	75.0	76.5	71.3	86.3
Braking, ft/sec2	23.2	24.3	24.0	24.5	24.9	n/a	25.0
Ergonomics, pts	188.4	196.3	202.9	185.1	196.3	202.9	n/a
Fuel, EPA City	14.8	14.0	14.0	17.8	14.0	16.6	17.0
Adjusted Bid	no bid	$8,259	$8,534	$8,069	$7,918	disqual	n/a

References for 1983

1983 Chevrolet Police, Taxi and Emergency Vehicles, Chevrolet Motor Division

1983 Patrol Vehicle Specs, Evaluation and Purchasing Program, Michigan State Police

75 Years of Chevrolet, George Dammann, Motorbooks International

Chapter 30

1984: Year of the Celebrity

The 1984 model year was celebrated as General Motors' 75th Anniversary. Almost to commemorate this, the Celebrity was released with a formal police package, replacing the Malibu.

> "The 1984 Celebrity Police: Advanced-Front-Wheel-Drive Performance. Introducing the specially modified front-wheel-drive Celebrity Police. An advanced-technology car designed to be roomy and quiet, yet displaying impressive steering control and braking on both wet and dry pavement. Its nimble performance, combined with state-of-the-art efficiency engineering, makes Celebrity Police an ideal choice for today's demanding police pursuit and patrol work."

While the Celebrity wore the 9C1 police badge, the "Special Celebrity Police" was considered by Chevrolet to be a special service package, not a full police package. The durability requirements for the full police package are higher. The Special Celebrity Police contained the following equipment that made it different from the regular production Celebrity: Reinforced cradle; special engine features; front and rear semi-metallic brake linings; vented, higher gauge wheels, 14x6-inch, five-bolt; specific body mounts; special police suspension includes front and rear stabilizer bars, special springs and shocks; higher cooling capacity radiator, temperature-controlled fan on models without air conditioning; low restriction exhaust; specific brake master cylinder; heavy-duty battery equivalent to 54-amp-hr, 500 CCA; A/C wide-open throttle cutoff switch, specific steering gear; SEO 7K2 85-amp Delcotron generator or SEO 7K5 108-amp Delcotron generator; SEO 7Z2 special police speedometer with 2 mph increments, 120 mph maximum.

Includes voltmeter, water temperature gauge, and trip odometer or SEO 7Z9 special police speedometer with 2 mph increments, 120 mph maximum or SEO 8A1 production speedometer (for undercover work); SEO 5SS police service tires, SEO 9A3 speedometer gear change must be ordered; SEO 6C1 heavy service front bench without armrest or SEO 6C4 heavy service 45/45 seat.

The front-wheel drive, V-6-powered Celebrity was introduced to the retail market in mid-1982. It was intended as a combination of small car economy with big car ride and room. The 104.9-inch wheelbase Celebrity had as much interior room as the 108.1-inch wheelbase Malibu. The Celebrity weighed 500 pounds less and was a foot shorter in overall length.

The Celebrity shared the same wheelbase as the Citation but was a foot longer overall. The pronounced wedge shape of the Celebrity with its low nose and high rear deck came from extensive wind tunnel testing.

The Celebrity was Chevrolet's first front-wheel drive police car but second into the police market. Chrysler was the first to offer a front-wheel drive police car with its Aries K and Reliant K in 1982. Ford did not field a front-wheel drive squad car until the 1990 Taurus.

The retail Celebrity was available with the 2.5-liter inline four or one of two 2.8-liter V-6 engines. The base 2.8-liter V-6 had an 8.5:1 compression and 112 hp. This was teamed with a three-speed transaxle. The High Output 2.8-liter V-6 used in the Eurosport had an 8.9:1 compression and 130 hp. The Eurosport received the four-speed transaxle. Both 2.8-liter V-6 engines used a two-barrel carb. The Special Celebrity Police used the 112 hp drivetrain.

Chevrolet's first front-wheel drive special service package car was the 1984 Celebrity 9C1, such as this unit used by the U.S. Marshals. The Celebrity had a 104.9-inch wheelbase. (Jim Post)

This 1984 California Highway Patrol Celebrity is powered by a 2.8-liter/112-hp two-barrel-carbureted V-6. It had a top speed of 111 mph. (Greg Reynolds)

The California Highway Patrol used the 1984 Celebrity to enforce commercial carrier laws. (Greg Reynolds)

The Celebrity 9C1 and the Celebrity Eurosport did however share the same specially-tuned F41 sports suspension. Both versions used 75-series radials on 14x6-inch steel sport wheels, and both versions shared heavy-duty front and rear sway bars.

The Impala was a straight carry-over for 1984. The available powertrains were the 229-cid V-6 with a three-speed automatic and 2.73 rear gears or the 350-cid V-8 with the four-speed overdrive automatic and 3.08 gears.

The 350 Impala ran well during the Michigan State Police patrol vehicle tests. Of the qualifying full-size cars, it had the fastest quarter-mile elapsed time, the strongest brakes and was tied for the best fuel economy. The Impala was now running the quarter-mile in the 17 second bracket.

During the critical Michigan International Speedway road course testing, the Impala posted the fastest lap times of any qualifying sedan. The Mopar squads, however, could not be beat. The Gran Fury

combined the highest top speed, the fastest 0-100 mph time and a low initial bid to capture the MSP contract for 1984.

In its rookie year as a police car, the Celebrity 9C1 split the MSP tests with the veteran Reliant K. The Plymouth had a faster road course time and better fuel economy. However, the Chevy had the faster 0-100 mph time, higher top speed and more durable brakes. The compact Special Celebrity Police reached nearly 111 mph.

1984 Chevrolet Police Engines						
RPO	Engine	Carb	HP	Trans.	Axle	Vehicle
LE2	173 cid/2.8L	2-bbl	112	3-spd 125C	3.06	Celebrity
LE3	229 cid/3.8L	2-bbl	110	3-spd 250C	2.73	Impala
LM1	350 cid/5.7L	4-bbl	155	4-spd 700R4	3.08	Impala

Los Angeles County Sheriffs Department 1984 Police Car Test Results					
	Chevrolet	**Chevrolet**	**Ford**	**Ford**	**Plymouth**
Model	**Celebrity**	**Impala**	**Crown Vic**	**LTD**	**Gran Fury**
Engine & Carb	2.8L V-6, 2-bbl	5.7L V-8, 4-bbl	5.8L V-8, 2VV	5.0L V-8, efi	5.2L V-8, 4-bbl
Axle	3.06	3.08	2.73	3.08	2.94
Weight (lbs)	3,055	3,942	4,096	3,429	3,888
Wheelbase (in)	104.9	116.0	114.3	105.6	112.7
Road Course, sec	97.8	95.1	94.9	92.3	96.2
0-60 mph, sec	12.3	10.0	10.9	9.2	12.3
1/4 mi. ET, sec	18.8	17.5	18.0	17.1	19.0
1/4 mi. Speed, mph	74.5	78.7	78.6	82.6	73.9
Gas Mileage	20 mpg	15.5 mpg	16.4 mpg	17.0 mpg	16.1 mpg

This sharp 1984 Impala 9C1 is powered by a 350-cid/155-hp V-8. The quarter-mile times were now down to 17 seconds. (Jim Post)

The Iowa State Patrol was among an increasing number of city, county and state police departments to drive bowtie squad cars in 1984. (Robert Parks)

1984 Michigan State Police Patrol Vehicle Test Results (Mid-Size and Pursuit Cars)						
	Chevrolet	Ford	Plymouth	Ford	Ford	Dodge
Model	Celebrity	LTD	Reliant K	Mustang	Mustang	Aires K
Engine & Carb	173 cid, 2-bbl	302 cid, cfi	156 cid, 2-bbl	302 cid, cfi	302 cid, 4-bbl	135 cid, 2-bbl
HP, SAE	112	165	101	165	205	96
Axle Ratio	3.06	3.08	3.22	3.27	3.27	3.02
Weight, test (lbs)	3,056	3,429	2,674	3,129	3,015	2,617
Wheelbase (in)	104.9	105.6	100.3	100.5	100.5	100.3
Road Course Lap Time, sec	93.15	n/a	92.88	86.81	n/a	n/a
0-100 mph, sec	61.54	29.89	n/a	25.99	20.77	n/a
Top Speed, mph	110.7	122.6	105.3	118.3	129.6	101.9
1/4 mi. ET, sec	19.95	17.76	19.51	16.88	15.90	21.5
1/4 mi. Speed, mph	71.8	79.5	71.0	83.5	89.0	71.0
Braking, ft/sec2	24.3	24.4	23.6	24.6	n/a	n/a
Fuel, EPA City	21.1	18.0	23.2	18.0	15.9	25.6

1984 Michigan State Police Patrol Vehicle Test Results (Full-Size Cars)						
	Chevrolet	Dodge	Ford	Plymouth	Plymouth	Ford	Chevrolet
Model	Impala	Diplomat	Crown Vic	Gran Fury	Gran Fury	Crown Vic	Impala
Engine & Carb	350 cid, 4-bbl	318 cid, 4-bbl	351 cid, 2VV	318 cid, 4-bbl	318 cid, 2-bbl	302 cid, cfi	229 cid, 2-bbl
HP, SAE	155	165	180	165	130	140	110
Axle Ratio	3.08	2.94	2.73	2.94	2.94	3.55	2.73
Weight, test (lbs)	3,920	3,879	4,084	3,888	3,853	3,961	3,752
Wheelbase (in)	116.0	112.7	114.3	112.7	112.7	114.3	116.0
Road Course Lap Time	89.97	90.40	90.07	90.01	n/a	88.41	n/a
0-100 mph, sec	37.18	34.57	40.36	34.43	60.75	n/a	n/a
Top Speed, mph	116.4	118.8	118.1	121.4	106.2	100.5	101.0
1/4 mi. ET, sec	17.80	18.23	19.25	18.20	19.5	19.8	21.9
1/4 mi. Speed, mph	76.0	76.8	76.5	77.5	71.8	69.8	64.8
Braking, ft/sec2	26.4	23.4	26.3	25.6	n/a	n/a	n/a
Ergonomics, pts	173.9	199.4	213.0	199.4	199.4	213.0	173.9
Fuel, EPA City	14.6	14.6	14.0	14.6	16.5	16.5	19.0

References for 1984

1984 Chevrolet Police, Taxi and Emergency Vehicles, Chevrolet Motor Division

1984 Vehicle Testing and Evaluation Program, Los Angeles County Sheriffs Department

1984 Patrol Vehicle Specs, Evaluation and Purchasing Program, Michigan State Police

Standard Catalog of Chevrolet, 1912-1990, Pat Chappell, Krause Publications

Chapter 31

1985: Fuel-Injected Impala & Celebrity

For 1985, both the Impala 9C1 and the Celebrity 9C1 were available with fuel-injected engines. These were the first injected police engines since the 283-cid small-block in 1958.

The fuel-injected Eurosport engine was a welcome addition for the Celebrity 9C1. Its 130 hp made the Celebrity a reasonably acceptable patrol car. This engine used multi-port fuel injection. Multi-port injection is different than throttle body injection. With multi-port, or multi-point as Chrysler called it, a stream of gasoline was injected into the cylinder, or the ports near the cylinder. Instead of a central injection point, the multi-port injection had six locations on a V-6 for the injection.

The author used an injected 1985 Celebrity for county-wide patrol and agrees completely with the Los Angeles County Sheriffs Department comments on the Celebrity:

"Engine response good to about 65 mph, then flattens out."

Apart from its small size, the injected Celebrity had excellent bottom end performance and handling. However, it just did not have enough top end acceleration and top speed to be an acceptable rural and dual lane traffic enforcement vehicle.

Numerous times during traffic enforcement, I had to radio ahead to other county or town marshal units in the direction the violator was heading. They stopped them on my authority then a few minutes later I showed up to issue the citation.

The worst example was a Taurus SHO just out for a Sunday cruise in rural Indiana. I clocked him moving at 100 mph flat, crossed the median and gave chase. He didn't speed up nor slow down and the Celebrity 9C1 simply could not close the gap. I was never going to catch him. He never did see my tiny red and blue Kojak light and he certainly did not recognize the Celebrity as a traffic enforcement vehicle when I drove into the median.

Fifteen miles ahead, I had a SOHC Crown Victoria pick him out of the traffic entering the city. The confused driver had been driving at the legal limit long before he met the marshal's Ford. Minutes later I came wheezing and smoking up to the stop. The Celebrity promptly stalled from the exertion of a 15-mile wide-open-throttle exercise. The SHO driver showed the appropriate humor for the Celebrity 9C1, which was way out of its league in traffic enforcement, by asking to get off with a warning. Nice try!

The fuel-injected Impala engine was the 4.3-liter (262-cid) V-6. It had a 9.3:1 compression and used a single exhaust. Throttle Body Injection (TBI) meant that the fuel was injected from a central throttle body. This is a casting that very much looked like a carburetor. Ford called its system Central Fuel Injection. A stream of gasoline was injected from a central location. The air and fuel mixed in the throttle body and intake manifold on the way to the cylinders.

The 262-cid V-6 was a bored out 229-cid V-6:

Engine	229 cid/3.8L	262 cid/4.3L
Bore	3.74	4.00
Stroke	3.48	3.48
Compression	8.6:1	9.3:1
Net HP	110	130

Hardcore Chevy small-block enthusiasts will immediately recognize the 262-cid V-6 as having exactly the same bore and stroke as the legendary 350-cid V-8. "It's a 350 with the back two cylinders chopped off," remarked B.L. Pritchett, sheriff of Benton County, Indiana. Of course, the 229-cid V-6 had exactly the same bore and stroke as the 305-cid V-8.

Chevrolet called the 4.3-liter engine "a standard V-6 that acts like a V-8." This 262 injected V-6 produced 130 hp. In comparison,

The Maryland State Police used the Impala 9C1 in 1985. These were all powered by the 350-cid/155-hp V-8. (Greg Reynolds)

In 1985, for the first time since 1958, a Chevrolet police car such as this Sycamore, Illinois, Police unit, was powered by a fuel-injected engine. The 4.3-liter EFI V-6 produced 130 hp. (Dave Dotson)

A close-up of the Nepean, Ontario, Canada, Police 1985 Impala. 1986 Impalas are on either side.

the retail 305-cid, four-barrel carbureted V-8 produced 155 hp. The 262-cid V-6 was a big step up from the 229-cid V-6. The author's department used a 4.3-liter V-6-powered Impala for rural sheriffs patrol. We put more than 140,000 miles on the squad car with no complaints.

The intent of the 262-cid V-6 was to have a better performing V-6 than the 229-cid engine while still achieving the same fuel economy. The 262-cid (4.3-liter) V-6 had an EPA city rating of 18.3 mpg with an EPA highway estimate of 27 mpg. With 20 hp less, the 1984 229-cid V-6 was rated at 19.0 mpg city, and 26 highway.

The 1984 V-6-powered Impala came with a three-speed automatic. This was the last year. For 1985 both the 262-cid V-6 and 350-cid V-8 police engines were teamed with the 700R4 four-speed automatic overdrive. Impalas and then Caprices would use four-speed automatics as the only transmission from 1985 through 1996.

The Impala received a totally new interior with a new instrument panel in 1985. This was the most extensive interior remodeling since the major redesign for 1977. This was the last year for the Impala

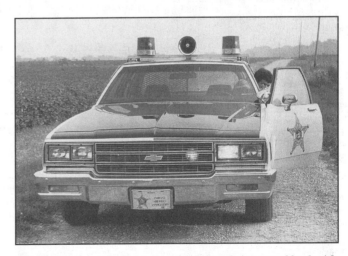

This Benton County, Indiana, Sheriff 1985 Impala is powered by the 4.3-liter V-6. It was indeed "a V-6 that acts like a V-8."

nameplate, which first appeared in 1958 retail cars. The Impala was the primary Chevrolet police car from 1976 through 1985. The 1976 Impala replaced the Bel Air nameplate. The 1986 platform for the full-size police car would be the Caprice. The 1985 Impala continued its tradition of having a different grille than the Caprice.

The 1985 Michigan State Police patrol car tests held one nasty surprise for the Impala powered by the brand new 4.3-liter V-6:

"...the Chevrolet Impala equipped with the 4.3-liter (262-cid) V-6 engine developed a transmission shifting problem very early in the testing. As a result of the problem which could not be readily repaired, no test data was produced for that vehicle."

This Impala happened to be equipped with the four-speed automatic overdrive 700R4. The 700R4 in the V-8-powered Impala performed flawlessly. The 1985 Los Angeles County Sheriffs Department Police car tests were an absolute disaster for both Chevrolet police cars. From the LASD report we read:

Chevrolet Impala

"The first vehicle tested this year was the Chevrolet Impala. During the Preliminary Handling Phase of testing the rear load bearing wheel began to bounce severely in the turns. Through the left turn the right rear wheel cleared the pavement by an estimated ten to fifteen inches. Through right turns the left rear wheel exhibited the same condition.

"Chevrolet representatives were at a loss to explain the reason for this unusual behavior on a normally reliably ve-hicle. Overnight the entire rear axle assembly was replaced and the steel belted tires were replaced with fabric belted tires. The Impala was re-tested but the condition persisted. As a result, further testing of this vehicle was terminated."

Chevrolet Celebrity

"Testing of the Celebrity proceeded smoothly with the results as indicated on the following pages. The fuel inject-ed, high output V-6 engine seemed to make a significant and positive difference in handling and acceleration.

"One area of concern was detected in the Heat Testing Phase of testing. Although tested in an ambient environment of 58 degrees Fahrenheit, the Celebrity developed an underhood temperature of 236.8 degrees. At that point the vehicle began to smoke as if on fire, and the hood was opened momentarily. The temperature dropped dramatically then began to rise again when the hood was closed. In addition, the transmission temperature rose to a maximum of 267.5 degrees Fahrenheit.

"At idle, the radiator temperature of the vehicle rose to a maximum of 236 degrees Fahrenheit before the fan commenced operation. The temperature cooled to approximately 206 degrees before the fan shut off and the temperature climbed to 236 degrees again, at which time the cycle repeated."

1985 Chevrolet Police Drivetrains						
RPO	**Type**	**Size**	**Carb**	**HP**	**Trans**	**Axle**
LB4	V-6	4.3L/262 cid	EFI	130	4-spd auto	3.08 Impala only
LM1	V-8	5.7L/350 cid	4-bbl	155	4-spd auto	3.08 Impala only
LE2	V-6	2.8L/173 cid	2-bbl	112	3-spd auto	3.06 Celebrity only
LB6	V-6	2.8L/173 cid	MFI	130	3-spd auto	3.18 Celebrity only
Note: EFI means Electronic Fuel Injection, aka Throttle Body Injection (TBI)						
Note: MFI means Multi-Port Fuel Injection, aka Port Fuel Injection (PFI)						

1985 Michigan State Police Patrol Vehicle Test Results (compact and pursuit cars)							
	Chevrolet	**Chevrolet**	**Dodge**	**Plymouth**	**Ford**	**Ford**	**Ford**
Model	**Celebrity**	**Celebrity**	**Aries K**	**Reliant K**	**LTD**	**Mustang**	**Mustang**
Engine & Carb	173 cid, 2-bbl	173 cid, pfi	135 cid, 2-bbl	156 cid, 2-bbl	302 cid, cfi	302 cid, cfi	302 cid, 4-bbl
HP, SAE	112	130	96	101	165	180	210
Axle Ratio	3.06	3.18	3.02	3.22	3.08	3.27	3.27
Weight, test (lbs)	3,047	3,076	2,652	2,706	3,414	3,108	3,101
Wheelbase (in)	104.9	104.9	100.3	100.3	105.6	100.5	100.5
Road Course Lap Time	n/a	92.78	n/a	94.11	89.07	86.36	85.59
0-100 mph	55.31	42.26	n/a	n/a	30.74	26.07	21.72
Top Speed mph	116.1	115.3	97.0	100.2	120.6	122.8	135.5
1/4 mi. ET	19.7	18.7	21.03	19.98	17.98	17.13	16.08
1/4 mi. Speed	71.5	75.0	67.75	69.0	79.0	83.00	87.0
Braking, ft/sec2	n/a	25.56	n/a	25.81	26.47	25.05	25.66
Fuel, EPA City	20.1	19.5	24.2	20.4	16.1	16.1	16.4

1985 Michigan State Police Patrol Vehicle Test Results (full-size cars)						
	Chevrolet	**Dodge**	**Ford**	**Plymouth**	**Ford**	**Plymouth**
Model	**Impala**	**Diplomat**	**Crown Vic**	**Gran Fury**	**Crown Vic**	**Gran Fury**
Engine & Carb	350 cid, 4-bbl	318 cid, 4-bbl	351 cid, 2VV	318 cid, 4-bbl	302 cid, cfi	318 cid, 2-bbl
HP, SAE	155	175	180	175	140	140
Axle Ratio	3.08	2.94	2.73	2.94	3.55	2.24
Weight, test (lbs)	3,906	3,998	4,095	3,902	4,182	3,771
Wheelbase (in)	116.0	112.7	114.3	112.7	114.3	112.7
Road Course Lap Time	90.82	90.83	89.67	90.69	n/a	n/a
0-100 mph	42.24	40.15	39.78	42.00	59.14	53.27
Top Speed, mph	114.3	117.6	116.9	119.4	104.4	116.1
1/4 mi. ET	18.85	19.10	18.80	19.23	19.53	20.05
1/4 mi. Speed	74.8	74.5	75.5	73.8	71.00	71.8
Braking, ft/sec2	25.92	27.11	26.34	26.6	n/a	n/a
Ergonomics, pts	206.0	199.4	202.6	198.4	202.6	198.4
Fuel, EPA City	13.3	12.6	12.6	12.6	15.6	16.1

Los Angeles County Sheriffs Department 1985 Police Patrol Vehicle Tests							
	Chevrolet	**Chevrolet**	**Ford**	**Ford**	**Plymouth**	**Ford**	**Ford**
Model	**Impala**	**Celebrity**	**LTD**	**Crown Vic**	**Gran Fury**	**Mustang**	**Mustang**
Engine & Carb	350 cid, 4-bbl	173 cid, MFI	302 cid, CFI	351 cid, 2VV	318 cid, 4-bbl	302 cid, CFI	302 cid, 4-bbl
HP	155	130	165	180	175	180	210
Transmission	4-spd	3-spd	4-spd	4-spd	3-spd	auto	stick
Axle	3.08	3.18	3.08	2.73	2.94	3.27	3.27
Road Course	96.8	93.8	93.2	93.9	94.1	89.6	88.1
0-60 mph	DNF	11.0	9.7	11.4	10.8	8.2	7.2
1/4 mi. ET	DNF	18.1	17.4	18.3	18.2	16.4	15.6
1/4 mi. Speed	DNF	77.0	81.1	76.7	77.2	87.8	91.2
Actual Mileage	DNF	21.1	16.8	14.4	13.8	17.1	20.7

References for 1985

1985 Chevrolet Police, Taxi & Emergency Vehicles, Chevrolet Motor Division

1985 Vehicle Testing and Evaluation Program, Los Angeles County Sheriffs Department

1985 Patrol Vehicle Specs, Evaluation and Purchasing Program, Michigan State Police

Standard Catalog of Chevrolet, 1912-1990, Pat Chappell, Krause Publications

Chapter 32

1986: First Caprice Police Car

This Idaho State Police 1986 Caprice was powered by the 350-cid V-8. This was the first year for a police Caprice. (Bill Hattersley)

The news for 1986 was the name of the full-size Chevrolet police car, Caprice. The Impala nameplate, introduced on 1958 retail cars, was the basis for the police package for 10 years from 1976 through 1985. In turn, the Caprice would be the basis of the police package in the 11-year span from 1986 through 1996. The name Caprice first appeared on 1965 top-of-the-line retail cars.

For 1986, the Caprice was restyled with a new grille and bumper filler panel, flush-mounted crest, and new rounded bezels for headlamps and marker lamps. Both coupes and sedans had restyled taillamps. Except for the one-piece headlight bezel in 1987, the 1986 styling would carry the Caprice until the massive redesign for 1991.

A 1986 Celebrity in-service with the Montgomery County, Maryland, Police. These cars had a top speed of 114 mph. (Greg Reynolds)

The styling of the 1986 Caprice, such as this Chicago Police unit, is unique. This was the year of the "new" style grille with the "old" style quad headlights. (Greg Reynolds)

Apart from the sheet steel, the 1986 Caprice was mostly a carry-over from the 1985 Impala.

In 1986, the Chevrolet Caprice and Pontiac Parisienne were the last traditional rear-drive, full-size "family sedans" left in the General Motors lineup. Because of this, rumors persisted that the famous B-body platform would be discontinued. However, the Caprice, Caprice Classic, Impala SS, Buick Roadmaster and Cadillac DeVille would have enough police and retail combined demand to last for another decade.

For 1986, the Celebrity was restyled for the first time since 1982. The Celebrity got a new grille but retained the quad headlights with separate bezels. Except for the new grille, the 1986 Celebrity was mostly a carry-over from 1985.

As in 1985, the Celebrity 9C1 was powered by a 2.8-liter (173-cid) V-6 engine. Again, as in 1985, the V-6 was available with either a two-barrel carb and a 112 hp rating or multi-port fuel injection and 125 hp. The only transaxle for the police package car was the three-

The 1986 Celebrity, such as this Glendale, Arizona, Police unit, used the 2.8-liter V-6. The Celebrity came with either a 112-hp fuel-injected engine or a 130-hp two-barrel-carbureted engine. (Jim Post)

speed 125C. The two-barrel carbureted engine used a 3.08 rear gear while the injected engine was teamed with a 3.18 final drive ratio.

The 1986 Caprice also shared the same powertrain as the 1985 Impala. The 4.3-liter (262-cid) TBI V-6 had a 140 hp rating and the 5.7-liter (350-cid) four-barrel carbureted V-8 produced 155 hp. Both versions used the 700R4 four-speed automatic and 3.08 rear gears.

For the first time ever, the 1986 Chevrolet police literature contained vehicle performance data. Acceleration and top speed results from GM's Milford Proving Ground were published for both the Caprice and Celebrity. Oddly enough, the Chevrolet data showed the Celebrity with a two-barrel carb to be faster than the fuel-injected Celebrity. Even more strange, the Milford data had both Celebritys with a top speed greater than the 5.7-liter Caprice. This was all in complete contrast to the Michigan State Police tests on 1986 model year police cars.

At the Michigan State Police patrol vehicle tests, the Caprice was competitive. It had the quickest quarter-mile time and the best fuel mileage of the qualifying sedans. Around the road racing course, all four of the police sedans were separated by just one-third of a second. The Dodge Diplomat eventually was awarded the MSP contract in one of the closest four-way races in years. This, however, would be the last year for a Dodge or Plymouth to capture the MSP. And no Ford ever won at MSP under their performance-based test procedure. From 1987 through 1996, the Chevrolet Caprice proved to have the most performance for the buck.

The Celebrity 9C1 continued to turn police heads at the MSP runoffs. In a showdown among front-drive compacts, the injected Celebrity had the fastest 0-100 mph time, the highest top speed, the strongest brakes and the quickest road course times. The real surprise came when the V-6-powered Celebrity was compared directly to the V-8-powered full-size traditional cruisers. The 2.8-liter Celebrity had a road course time just .03 second behind the 5.7-liter Caprice. Of the 13 full-size, mid-size and pursuit cars tested in 1986, the Celebrity had the second best brakes.

The average quarter-mile time for the four full-size V-8 cruisers was 18.5 seconds. The injected Celebrity reached the traps in just 18.3 seconds, and it hit 100 mph a half second ahead of the 351-cid Ford. Both the injected and carbureted Celebritys had a top speed of nearly 114 mph.

The 1986 Celebrity went out with a bang. This was the last year Chevrolet offered it with a police package. The Reliant K and Aries K would only be offered for one more year. Cops simply were not ready for front-drive, V-6-powered mid-size cars. These models sold fewer than 1,000 units per year. This did not justify the development of special police components.

After the 1987 Reliant K and Aries K, Chrysler would abandon the front-drive market for at least a decade. Ford would wait four years to introduce a police package for its 1990 Taurus, even though it was introduced to the retail market in 1986. It would not be until 1992 that Chevrolet equipped the Lumina with a special service package. When the 3.8-liter Taurus lapped the road racing course as fast as the 5.7-liter Caprice in 1991 it would not be the first time. The 2.8-liter Celebrity did it first in 1986.

1986 Chevrolet Police Drivetrains						
RPO	Type	Size	Carb	HP	Trans	Axle
LB4	V-6	4.3L/ 262cid	EFI	140	4-spd auto	3.08 Impala only
LM1	V-8	5.7L/ 350cid	4-bbl	155	4-spd auto	3.08 Impala only
LE2	V-6	2.8L/ 173cid	2-bbl	112	3-spd auto	3.06 Celebrity only
LB6	V-6	2.8L/ 173cid	MFI	130	3-spd auto	3.18 Celebrity only
Note: EFI means Electronic Fuel Injection, aka Throttle Body Injection (TBI)						
Note: MFI means Multi-Port Fuel Injection, aka Port Fuel Injection (PFI)						

1986 Michigan State Police Patrol Vehicle Test Results (Mid-Size Cars)						
	Ford	Ford	Dodge	Plymouth	Chevrolet	Chevrolet
Model	Mustang	Mustang	Aries K	Reliant K	Celebrity	Celebrity
Engine	302 cid pfi	302 cid pfi	135 cid tbi	153 cid tbi	173 cid pfi	173 cid 2-bbl
HP, SAE	200	200	97	100	125	112
Axle Ratio	3.27	3.08	3.02	3.22	3.18	3.06
Weight, test	3,238	3,216	2,615	2,692	3,075	3,034
Wheelbase (in)	100.5	100.5	100.3	100.3	104.9	104.9
Road Course Lap Time	84.22	85.49	n/a	91.79	89.76	n/a
0-100 mph	20.55	19.81	n/a	n/a	38.06	48.86
Top Speed, mph	126.1	137.2	101.0	103.0	113.8	113.6
1/4 mi. ET	15.8	15.5	20.7	19.7	18.3	19.5
1/4 mi. Speed	88.5	90.5	69.0	70.5	76.0	73.7
Braking, ft/sec2	24.31	26.43	n/a	26.42	26.43	26.43
Ergonomics, pts	147.9	147.9	n/a	165.0	164.0	164.0
Fuel, EPA City	17.5	17.3	23.3	19.6	18.1	16.8

1986 Michigan State Police Patrol Vehicle Test Results (Full-Size Cars)							
	Dodge	**Ford**	**Plymouth**	**Chevrolet**	**Plymouth**	**Ford**	**Chevrolet**
Model	**Diplomat**	**Crown Vic**	**Gran Fury**	**Caprice**	**Gran Fury**	**Crown Vic**	**Caprice**
Engine Carb	318 cid 4-bbl	351 cid 2VV	318 cid 4-bbl	350 cid 4-bbl	318 cid 2-bbl	302 cid pfi	262 cid tbi
HP, SAE	175	180	175	155	140	150	140
Axle Ratio	2.94	2.73	2.94	3.08	2.94	3.08	3.08
Weight, test (lbs)	3,897	4,092	3,929	3,956	3,871	3,934	3,792
Wheelbase (in)	112.7	114.3	112.7	116.0	112.7	114.3	116.0
Road Course Lap Time, sec	89.46	89.37	89.43	89.73	n/a	n/a	n/a
0-100 mph	36.07	38.49	36.58	37.96	43.11	46.57	55.40
Top Speed, mph	121.5	115.1	119.4	117.0	110.1	106.1	107.8
1/4 mi. ET	18.53	18.53	18.70	18.25	18.88	18.80	19.53
1/4 mi. Speed	76.5	76.5	76.3	76.0	73.8	72.3	70.3
Braking, ft/sec2	25.95	24.68	26.71	24.20	n/a	n/a	n/a
Ergonomics, pts	189.2	195.5	189.2	186.1	189.2	195.5	186.1
Fuel, EPA City	12.2	12.6	12.2	13.4	14.8	17.7	17.6

References for 1986

1986 Caprice and Celebrity 9C1, Chevrolet Motor Division

1986 Patrol Vehicle Specs, Evaluation and Purchasing Program,
Michigan State Police

Standard Catalog of Chevrolet, 1912-1990, Pat Chappell, Krause
Publications

Chevrolet Spotter's Guide, 1920-1992, Tad Burness, Motorbooks
International

Chapter 33

1987: Caprice Captures Michigan State Police

In 1987, a full 11 years after the drastic downsizing of 1977, the Caprice finally reaped the benefits. Chevrolet engineers and technicians had spent 11 long years tweaking the 350-cid V-8 for the most overall performance in the B-body platform. The suspension was steadily improved. The sheet metal got sleeker and sleeker.

The carb, intake, cam, heads, ignition and exhaust were all tuned to the gear ratios in the four-speed overdrive automatic and 3.08 rear axle. For 1987, the compression was bumped almost a half point and, for the first time, roller lifters were used. The result was a full 25 hp increase to an impressive 180 hp. This was as powerful as the engine in any police sedan. The engine was also higher-revving. The peak power was bumped from 3600 rpm to 4000 rpm. That was a good sign engineers were finally figuring out how to improve engine performance in spite of emission controls and economy goals.

All of the drivetrain components were a careful balance of performance, economy and durability. In 1987, 11 years of effort came together during the annual Michigan State Police patrol vehicle tests.

Dodge, Plymouth, Ford and Chevrolet all rolled out their best engineered police package four-door sedans. The Mopar squads were powered by the 318-cid, four-barrel carbureted V-8 with a three-speed TorqueFlite. The blue oval cruiser used the 351-cid, variable venturi V-8 teamed with the four-speed Cruise-O-Matic. The bowtie black-and-white had the 350-cid, four-barrel carbureted V-8 and the four-speed Turbo Hydra-Matic transmission. All of the patrol cars were rated between 175 and 180 hp. Less than 200 pounds separated the heaviest car from the lightest.

When all the tire smoke cleared, and the prices were factored by the sheer performance, the 1987 Caprice was the top cop car. The Mopars captured the MSP contracts in the early- and mid-1980s by having middle of the pack performance and the lowest prices. Chevrolet captured the MSP contracts using the same bid adjustment procedure by having the highest vehicle performance and middle of the pack prices.

The Caprice would remain the top cop car based on the MSP test methods for the next 10 years. This performance would influence police car purchases in at least 49 states. (Tests in California are conducted by the Los Angeles County Sheriffs Department and the California Highway Patrol.) The Caprice would not be outrun at any police run-off for a decade. It would retire from police service after 1996 still at the top of its game.

During the 1987 MSP tests, the Caprice had the fastest road course time, the quickest 0-100 mph time, the highest top speed, the best human engineering, and even the best fuel economy. The Caprice won five of the six MSP test categories. The two Mopars had the better brakes but the Caprice still stopped from 60 mph in just 150 feet.

Starting in 1987, the Caprice began to deliver the kind of performance that clearly separated it from other full-size police cars. The Caprice ran the quarter-mile in the high 17 second range. All the other qualifying sedans ran the quarter-mile in the high 18 to mid 19 second range. The Caprice hit 100 mph in 34.6 seconds. The other three makes hit 100 mph in 38.6 to 40.5 seconds. It really was the Caprice in one performance class and then everyone else in another performance class.

In 1987, the 350-cid Caprice 9C1 won the Michigan State Police patrol vehicle tests. The Caprice continued to capture the contract under the MSP test method for the next 10 years. (Dave Dotson)

The California Highway Patrol selected the Caprice for 1987. The 350-cid/180-hp V-8 pushed the bowtie sedan to 118 mph. (Greg Reynolds)

In 1987, the Caprice was available with the same two basic engines as in 1986. These included the 4.3-liter (262-cid) V-6 at 140 hp and the 5.7-liter (350-cid) V-8 now rated at an impressive 180 hp. The 350-cid small-block would steadily increase in power until it achieved 260 hp in LT1 trim.

Apart from vehicle performance, the 1987 Caprice is best known as the first year for two-in-one "composite" headlights. The two headlights per side were now covered by a single, wide lens. This covered both the high beam lamp and the low beam lamp and dramatically changed the look of the front end.

The 2.8-liter Celebrity was not available with a police package in 1987. Chevrolet would be out of the front-wheel drive police car business until the 1992 Lumina with the B4C special service package and again in 1993 with both the B4C special service package and the heavier-duty 9C3 police package. The Lumina would be powered by the 3.1-liter V-6.

The Indiana State Police continued its loyal use of the full-size Chevrolet in 1987. This was the first year for the one-piece headlight bezel. (Jerry Parker)

An Albany, California, Police 1987 Caprice. A boost in compression and the use of roller lifters pushed the horsepower of the 350-cid V-8 from 155 hp to 180 hp. (John Yeaw)

All 1987 Caprices, such as this Vancouver Police unit, had four-speed automatics and 3.08 gears. The 4.3-liter V-6 used EFI while the 350-cid V-8 used a four-barrel carb. (Bill Hattersley)

As a point of interest, the Michigan State Police and the Los Angeles County Sheriffs Department are not the only ones to test police cars. They are, however, the only ones to widely publish the annual results to all interested parties. The California Highway Patrol also conducts Enforcement-class vehicle tests each year. While the CHP does not distribute the results, they do make known their minimum performance standards.

To qualify to bid on the CHP Class "E" cars in 1987, the police car had to hit 60 mph in 13 seconds and 100 mph within 43 seconds. The patrol car had to have a top speed of at least 110 mph and be able to accelerate to 110 mph within two miles. The prospective CHP car also had to be able to run at wide-open-throttle for a minimum of 25 miles without damage to the drivetrain. They ran the cars at 80 mph for five miles and at 100 mph for five miles and then checked oil and fluid temperatures. The engine oil and transmission fluid could not exceed 275 degrees Fahrenheit while the power steering fluid could not exceed 300 degrees Fahrenheit.

We do not know the exact performance turned in by each of the police cars tested by the CHP. The results from the MSP tests give us a strong indication. We do know that at the end of the 1987 qualifying and bid procedure the CHP selected the Chevrolet Caprice as its Enforcement-class Special Service Vehicle.

The 1987 Caprice was one of the few police cars to ever interrupt the nearly continuous use of Chrysler products by the CHP. Since 1956, the use of a different make of Enforcement-class car than a Mopar had only happened four times: 1967 Oldsmobile Delmont 88, 1970 Mercury Monterey, 1982 Chevrolet Impala and 1984 Ford Crown Victoria. The Caprice took the bid in 1987 and Dodge got it back for its last year in 1988. Chevrolet was awarded the influential CHP contract in 1989. Ford had it from 1990 to 1993. In 1994 the bid went to the LT1 Caprice where it remained through 1996.

1987 Chevrolet Police Drivetrains						
RPO	Type	Size	Carb	HP	Trans	Axle
LB4	V-6	4.3L/262 cid	EFI	140	4-spd AOD	3.08
LM1	V-8	5.7L/350 cid	4-bbl	180	4-spd AOD	3.08

1987 Michigan State Police Patrol Vehicle Test Results (Full-Size)							
	Dodge	**Ford**	**Plymouth**	**Chevrolet**	**Chevrolet**	**Plymouth**	**Ford**
Model	**Diplomat**	**Crown Vic**	**Gran Fury**	**Caprice**	**Caprice**	**Gran Fury**	**Crown Vic**
Engine Carb	318 cid 4-bbl	351 cid VV	318 cid 4-bbl	351 cid 4-bbl	262 cid tbi	318 cid 2-bbl	302 cid pfi
HP, SAE	175	180	175	180	140	140	160
Axle Ratio	2.94	2.73	2.94	3.08	3.08	2.24	3.08
Weight, test (lbs)	3,885	4,079	3,924	3,948	3,803	3,895	4,051
Wheelbase (in)	112.7	114.3	112.7	116.0	116.0	112.7	114.3
Road Course Lap Time	89.95	88.59	89.77	88.22	n/a	n/a	n/a
0-100 mph	40.53	39.30	38.64	34.62	59.22	52.44	43.47
Top Speed, mph	116.9	115.2	117.5	118.0	106.0	113.3	109.2
1/4 mi. ET	19.35	18.93	19.18	17.85	19.90	20.63	18.55
1/4 mi. Speed	73.5	76.3	75.0	77.8	71.0	71.8	74.0
Braking, ft/sec2	27.2	25.7	27.4	26.12	n/a	n/a	n/a
Ergonomics, pts	199.9	193.2	199.9	215.3	215.3	199.9	193.2
Fuel, EPA City	12.7	12.9	12.7	13.9	18.3	14.8	17.5
Ranking	disqual	third	second	first	disqual	disqual	disqual

References for 1987

1987 Patrol Vehicle Specs, Evaluation and Purchasing Program, Michigan State Police

1987 Caprice Police Package, Chevrolet Motor Division

Standard Catalog of Chevrolet, 1912-1990, Pat Chappell, Krause Publications

Chevrolet Spotter's Guide, 1920-1992, Tad Burness, Motorbooks International

Chapter 34

1988: Last Carbureted Caprice

In mid-1987, just as the 1988 models were about to be introduced, the National Association of Fleet Administrators held their annual Law Enforcement Seminar. Police fleet managers expressed great concern that there was no new generation of four-door, V-8-powered, rear-drive sedans on the drawing boards. They were also quite unhappy at the overall lack of vehicle performance.

At the time, none of the large-engine full-size police cars had anti-lock brakes, four-wheel discs or fuel injection. Other passenger cars and sports cars had pulled out of the performance slump from the late-1970s to mid-1980s, but the police car had not. In fact, the police car was in the same 19-second quarter-mile bracket and had the same 118 mph top speed as police cars dating back to the early-1980s.

The police car was frequently the fastest car on the road. This was especially true during the mid-1970s and early-1980s. However, many retail cars had now clearly surpassed the performance available from any police sedan. Of course, the 1988 Porsches and Corvettes had 14 second quarter-mile ETs and top speeds over 150 mph. However, the 1988 Camaros, Mustangs and Firebirds ran 15 second ETs and topped out over 140 mph. No police sedan was a match for these cars.

The police fleet managers wanted fuel-injection on the Chevy 350, Ford 351 and especially Mopar 318. And they also saw the wide-spread use of front-drive cars and wanted assurances the V-8-powered, rear-drive sedan would be around for a while.

Dodge said the 318-cid V-8 was not going to get fuel-injection and the Diplomat was only promised through 1989. That turned out to be its last model year. Ford would not discuss the injected 351-cid V-8. The 302-cid V-8 was already injected. Ford promised the Crown Victoria only through 1989. It wanted cops to use the Taurus, which would be released with a police package in 1990. As it turned out, the Crown Victoria outlasted all police cars at the time including the Diplomat, Gran Fury, Mustang, Taurus and Caprice.

Of the three carmakers, Chevrolet was the most promising. In 1987, it told the fleet managers the Caprice would continue until 1991 at which point it would be restyled. That happened. It also said the full-size Caprice would continue through the mid-1990s. That happened. It is not clear if the fleet managers were told the 350-cid V-8 would get fuel-injection in 1989, just one model year away, but that, too, happened. And in 1991, the Caprice got rear discs and anti-lock brakes. After the mid-1980s when Chrysler stopped making improvements to rear-drive cars, Chevrolet clearly took the leadership position in making police cars.

The 1988 Caprice, such as this NYPD Emergency Services unit, was the last bowtie sedan to use a four-barrel carb on the 350-cid V-8. (Ned Schwartz)

A 1988 South Carolina State Police Caprice. By this year, the Caprice was the car-of-choice for most state police and highway patrols. (Dave Dotson)

The Minnesota State Police used the Caprice in 1988 as did the Michigan State Police and the Los Angeles Police. Note the industrial strength pusher bar. (Jim Post)

The 1988 Caprice, such as this Delaware State Police unit, ran an 18 second quarter-mile and had a 116 mph top end. (Greg Reynolds)

The 4.3-liter V-6 powered Caprice, such as this Baltimore Police squad car, ran a 19 second quarter-mile and had a top speed of 109 mph. (Ned Schwartz)

In terms of the drivetrain, the 1988 Caprice was a carry-over. The two engines were the 262-cid/140-hp V-6 and the 350-cid/180-hp V-8. Police cars sold to the Canadian market were not available with the 4.3-liter V-6. Instead, the Canadian cops got their choice of the 305-cid/170-hp V-8 or the 350-cid V-8. In 1989, the 305 would be available in the full-size Chevrolet for the first time since 1981.

Of great significance, 1988 was the last year for a Rochester four-barrel QuadraJet carburetor on the police 350-cid V-8. Mopar fans may remember that in 1985, Chrysler dropped the Carter four-barrel ThermoQuad in favor of the Rochester QuadraJet for its 318-cid, four-barrel carbureted Diplomat and Gran Fury engines. In an odd twist, the 1989 Mopar police cars would use the General Motors' QuadraJet while the 1989 Caprice 350-cid V-8 would drop the QuadraJet in favor of throttle body fuel injection.

During the 1988 Michigan State Police tests, the Caprice held off a surprisingly serious challenge from the Crown Victoria. The Diplomat and Gran Fury were not a threat.

The 180 hp Caprice and the 180 hp Crown Victoria turned in exactly the same lap times around the Michigan International Speedway 1.63-mile road racing course. Since they tied on the most heavily weighted (30 percent) phase of the MSP tests, this now put great significance on the less significant test areas.

The Caprice captured the 0-100 mph phase, which was weighted at 20 percent. However, the Crown Victoria grabbed the top speed honors by 1 mph to earn that 20 percent of the score. As an exception to the rule, in 1988 the Crown Victoria outbraked the Caprice to claim that 10 percent weighting. The Caprice countered with the best fuel economy, also weighted at 10 percent. The Caprice was given a better ergonomics rating than the Crown Victoria.

The differences between the individual vehicle performance and the average vehicle performance in each test phase were calculated. The Caprice was the clear winner by a margin much larger than winning two phases and tying one phase would indicate.

The Los Angeles Police had long ago written the Diplomat and Gran Fury out of their specs. They insisted that both LAPD black-and-white and LAPD plain colored four-door full-size police sedans have at least a 114-inch wheelbase (such as the Crown Victoria) and at least a 350-cid engine (such as the Caprice). The 112.7-inch wheelbase, 318-cid-powered Mopars were simply not eligible to bid. The LAPD's use of the Impala then Caprice started in 1982.

Likewise, the Los Angeles County Sheriffs Department shunned the Diplomat and Gran Fury due to their problematic L-shaped front torsion bars. The LASD's use of the Impala, then Caprice, started in 1985 and continued through 1995.

1988 Chevrolet Police Drivetrains						
RPO	Type	Size	Carb	HP	Trans	Axle
LB4	V-6	4.3L/262 cid	EFI	140	4-spd AOD	3.08
LM1	V-8	5.7L/350 cid	4-bbl	180	4-spd AOD	3.08

1988 Michigan State Police Patrol Vehicle Test Results							
	Dodge	**Ford**	**Plymouth**	**Chevrolet**	**Chevrolet**	**Plymouth**	**Ford**
Model	**Diplomat**	**Crown Vic**	**Gran Fury**	**Caprice**	**Caprice**	**Gran Fury**	**Crown Vic**
Engine Carb	318 cid 4-bbl	351 cid VV	318 cid 4-bbl	350 cid 4-bbl	262 cid tbi	318 cid 2-bbl	302 cid efi
HP, SAE	175	180	175	180	140	140	160
Axle Ratio	2.94	2.73	2.94	3.08	3.08	2.24	3.08
Weight, test (lbs)	3,930	3,965	3,910	3,982	3,827	3,873	3,982
Wheelbase (in)	112.7	114.3	112.7	116.0	116.0	112.7	114.3
Road Course Lap Time	89.27	88.60	89.43	88.60	n/a	n/a	n/a
0-100 mph	38.76	37.67	40.13	34.91	52.44	57.84	40.62
Top Speed, mph	117	117	117	116	109	110	108
1/4 mi. ET	18.59	18.84	19.01	18.03	19.90	20.18	18.35
1/4 mi. Speed	75.4	76.4	74.8	77.6	70.3	71.8	75.3
Braking, ft/sec2	24.92	26.79	23.74	25.55	n/a	n/a	n/a
Ergonomics, pts	228.3	208.8	227.1	226.9	226.9	227.1	208.8
Fuel, EPA City	12.7	12.4	12.7	13.5	19.0	14.6	17.3
Ranking	third	second	fourth	first	disqual	disqual	disqual

References for 1988

1988 Caprice Police Package, Chevrolet Motor Division

1988 Vehicle Testing and Evaluation Program, Los Angeles County Sheriffs Department

1988 Patrol Vehicle Specs, Evaluation and Purchasing Program, Michigan State Police

"Police Say Aging Cruisers Lack Zip to Zap New Hot Cars," Geoff Sundstrom, *Automotive News,* August 17, 1987

Chapter 35

1989: Fuel-Injected 350-cid Caprice

Set in beautiful Brown County, Indiana, an Indiana State Police 1989 Caprice. These were all powered by the fuel-injected 350-cid V-8. (Rick Hammer)

The 1989 Caprice was selected by the Virginia State Police (shown) and nearly every other major department from the Michigan State Police to California Highway Patrol. (Greg Reynolds)

The 1989 model year was a blockbuster for the Caprice. It was the police-car-of-choice for the California Highway Patrol and the Michigan State Police and nearly every department in between. With an announced mid-year demise of the Diplomat and Gran Fury, the vast majority of police departments followed the lead of the CHP and MSP.

The Caprice was not simply the default choice. In the year that Chrysler bowed out of the police car business, the Caprice was more changed than any year since 1977. The timing for the vastly superior Caprice was perfect. Police departments who had bought Mopar squad cars for generations were forced into the police car market for the first time.

It was a simple choice: either the Chevrolet Caprice or the Ford Crown Victoria. For all practical purposes, there were no other choices. At this time of decision, now was the time for Chevrolet to shine. And it did.

New for 1989, Chevrolet re-introduced the 305-cid V-8 in the Caprice. This was last available in the Caprice in 1981. Then, it was a 150 hp, four-barrel carbureted engine. Now, it was a 170 hp, throttle body fuel-injected engine. The 305-cid V-8 was one of the optional Camaro engines. The retail Camaro was available with the 170 hp, throttle body fuel-injected 350-cid V-8 and a 220 hp, port fuel-injected 305-cid V-8.

New for 1989, the 350-cid Caprice, such as this Wisconsin State Patrol unit, got throttle-body fuel injection. This bumped the horsepower from 180 to 190 and flattened the torque curve. (Greg Reynolds)

Chevrolet needed a 305-cid V-8 in the full-size Caprice to compete against the 302-cid V-8 in the full-size Crown Victoria for those departments wanting a small V-8. At 170 hp, the Chevy engine had a 10 hp advantage over the Ford. The 305-cid Caprice had a quicker road course time and a higher top speed. The 302-cid Crown Victoria had faster 100 mph and quarter-mile times and got better gas mileage. Overall, these two police cars were closely matched.

The real star in the 1989 engine lineup was the brand new LO5 throttle body fuel-injected 350-cid V-8. The horsepower increased from 180 to 190 thanks to both the fuel injection and a compression increase from 8.6:1 to 9.3:1. The peak torque remained the same at 285 pound-feet; however, the peak occurred 400 rpm lower at 2400 rpm for the injected engine. This is the so-called flattened torque curve.

The peak horsepower increased to 190 but so did the peak rpm. The four-barrel peak of 4000 rpm was raised to 4400 rpm for the injected version. This improvement in the rpm range lead directly to a huge change in rear gearing. The 350-cid Impala and Caprice had used 3.07 or 3.08 rear gears since the introduction of the 350 in 1969. New for 1989 were 3.42 ratio rear gears.

Of course, the 1989 had more rapid acceleration due to the flatter torque curve and a numerically higher gear ratio. Compared to the 18.0 second quarter-mile in 1988, in 1989 the Michigan State Police recorded a 17.6 second quarter-mile. Even more impressively, the 0-100 mph times fell from 34.9 seconds to 29.3 seconds. Since the quarter-mile speeds for both cars were around 78 mph, this means the injected Caprice pulled a lot harder than the carbureted Caprice toward the top speed. The carbureted Caprice took 1.25 miles to reach 110 mph. The injected Caprice hit 110 mph in just .95 mile.

The increased horsepower, flatter torque curve and better rear gears resulted in much quicker MIS road racing course lap times for the injected Caprice. It was 2.4 seconds quicker than the 1988 four-barrel carbureted Caprice. Recall that the Caprice and Crown Victoria had equal lap times in 1988. The Crown Victoria made no improvements for 1989 and was simply blown into the weeds by the injected Caprice. Around a 1.65-mile road course, a 2.4 second advantage works out to a 13 car-length lead for the Caprice over the Crown Victoria.

In spite of numerically higher rear gears, the injected Caprice actually had a 6 mph higher top speed, thanks to the wider power range. No police sedan had hit 122 mph since 1980. Also, in spite of the higher gear ratio, the injected Caprice carried a much better EPA City fuel rating. The gas mileage estimate improved from 13.5 to 14.3 mpg.

A Pennsylvania State Police 1989 Caprice. These cars ran a 16 to 17 second quarter-mile. (Greg Reynolds)

Throttle-body fuel injection pushed the top speed of the 1989 Caprice, such as this Missouri State Highway Patrol unit, to 122 mph. (Dave Dotson)

The Caprice captured four of the six Michigan State Police test phases including road course time, 0-100 mph acceleration, top speed and fuel economy. The lame-duck Diplomat had the best brakes and interior ergonomics. Between the 350-cid Caprice and the 351-cid Crown Victoria, the Caprice was clearly the better choice for cops looking at something other than a Mopar for the first time.

The 1989 Los Angeles County Sheriffs Department testing omitted the Dodge Diplomat and Gran Fury. The LASD tests take place in November of each year. The Mopar police car production ceased in mid-1989. The tests did however, include the 350-cid-powered Caprice and the Crown Victoria with both 302-cid and 351-cid powerplants.

The LASD noted the improved performance of the test vehicles:

"In 1981, the performance standards for this phase of testing (acceleration) were lowered to accommodate the decline in overall vehicle performance. Over the past few years, however, performance has improved to the point standards have been raised to their pre-1981 levels."

For the first time in ages, the full-size police Chevrolet ran the quarter-mile in the 16 second bracket. The two Fords were still in the 18 second bracket.

Around the Pomona Fairgrounds driver training road course, the Caprice was clearly the fastest sedan. LASD and LAPD test drivers said, "Overall handling very good, minimum body lean, good engine response, good braking." Of the 302-cid Crown Victoria they wrote, "Neutral to slight oversteer, moderate body roll and bouncing, good braking, no locking or pulling." Of the 351-cid Crown Victoria they were not so kind: "Bouncy in turns, neutral to understeer, excessive body lean, fair braking."

The demand was high for a powerful V-8 engine in a full-size rear-drive sedan even in the retail market. In the late-1980s, there were few full-size, rear-drive cars left. Retail customers wanted the 180 and 190

New for the 1989 Caprice, such as this Iowa State Patrol cruiser, was a fuel-injected 305-cid V-8. This was designed to compete against Ford's fuel-injected 302-cid engine. (Darryl Lindsay)

hp V-8s to tow trailers or simply for quicker acceleration. Some customers persuaded their local Chevrolet dealer to sell them the 350-cid police engine. The customers were thrilled but Chevrolet was not amused. This threw off its Corporate Average Fuel Economy (CAFE) ratings. For 1989, Chevrolet made its position clear in the police catalog:

"It is General Motors policy that the Chevrolet Caprice Police Package equipped with the 5.7-liter engine be sold only for usage by U.S., state, or local government primarily for police, law enforcement, or fire-fighting purposes."

1989 Caprice Powertrains

RPO	Type	Size	Induction	HP	Trans	Axle
LB4	V-6	4.3L/ 262cid	throttle body	140	4-spd AOD	3.08
LO3	V-8	5.0L/ 305cid	throttle body	170	4-spd AOD	3.08
LO5	V-8	5.7L/ 350cid	throttle body	190	4-spd AOD	3.42

1989 Los Angeles County Sheriffs Dept. Police Cars Tests

Model	Chevrolet	Ford	Ford
	Caprice	Crown Vic	Crown Vic
Engine	350 cid	351 cid	302 cid
Induction	throttle body	variable venturi	port injection
HP	190	180	160
Axle	3.42	2.73	3.08
0-60 mph, sec	8.93	10.57	11.11
Lap Times, sec	91.30	92.50	93.80
1/4 mi. ET	16.98	18.07	18.18
1/4 mi. Speed	82.3	79.7	76.6
Driver Rating*	8.4	7.2	7.4
Max. Oil Temp.	216 deg	231 deg	248 deg
Actual Mileage	14.6	15.1	13.8

* The driver rating is a subjective evaluation of the vehicle handling during the preliminary handling evaluation based on four drivers; rating scale is 1 to 10 with 10 being best.

1989 Michigan State Police Patrol Vehicle Test Results (pursuit-class)

	Dodge	Ford	Plymouth	Chevrolet
Model	Diplomat	Crown Vic	Gran Fury	Caprice
Engine, Carb	318 cid, 4-bbl	351 cid, VV	318 cid, 4-bbl	350 cid, tbi
HP, SAE	175	180	175	190
Axle Ratio	2.94	2.73	2.94	3.42
Weight, test	3,894 lbs	4,091 lbs	3,885 lbs	3,965 lbs
Wheelbase (in)	112.7	114.3	112.7	116.0
Road Course Lap Time	88.66	88.24	88.63	86.20
0-100 mph	38.95	36.55	38.02	29.35
Top Speed, mph	119.1	119.1	120.2	122.0
1/4 mi. ET	18.79	18.86	18.63	17.62
1/4 mi. Speed	75.5	77.1	76.2	79.8
Braking	26.32	26.09	26.01	26.03
Ergonomics	190.2	168.5	190.2	189.6
EPA City Fuel	12.7	13.1	12.7	14.3
Ranking	fourth	second	third	first

1989 Michigan State Police Patrol Vehicle Test Results (urban patrol-class)

	Chevrolet	Chevrolet	Ford	Plymouth	Dodge
Model	Caprice	Caprice	Crown Vic	Gran Fury	Diplomat
Engine & Carb	262 cid, tbi	305 cid, tbi	302 cid, pfi	318 cid, 2-bbl	318 cid, 2-bbl
HP, SAE	140	170	160	140	140
Axle Ratio	3.08	3.08	3.08	2.24	2.24
Weight, test (lbs)	3,872	3,960	4,132	3,895	3,876
Wheelbase (in)	116.0	116.0	114.3	112.7	112.7
Road Course Lap Time	92.51	88.83	89.49	n/a	n/a
0-100 mph	58.16	42.88	42.14	58.13	55.58
Top Speed, mph	109.0	114.1	110.0	111.2	113.6
1/4 mi. ET	20.50	19.01	18.77	n/a	20.23
1/4 mi. Speed	69.5	73.4	74.3	n/a	71.6
Fuel, EPA City	19.0	17.2	17.4	14.2	14.2

References for 1989

1989 Caprice Police Package, Chevrolet Motor Division

1989 Vehicle Testing and Evaluation Program, Los Angeles County Sheriffs Department

1989 Patrol Vehicle Specs, Evaluation and Purchasing Program, Michigan State Police

Chapter 36

1990: Door-Mounted Seat Belt Blues

The 1990 Caprice, such as this Lafayette, Indiana, Police cruiser, was the last of the squared-off body styles.

In 1990, the door-mounted shoulder harness stirred a safety controversy. This was the first and last year of this design. (Dave Dotson)

The 1990 model year was the last for the square-jawed, boxy Caprice. Little did cops know what Chevrolet stylists had in mind for 1991!

In terms of a powertrain, the Caprice was mostly a carry-over from 1989. The compression ratio on the 350-cid V-8 was boosted from 9.3:1 to 9.8:1. This did not increase the horsepower, which re-

mained at 190. It did, however, increase the torque by five pounds to 290 pound-feet.

The four-speed automatic overdrive was upgraded from the original 700R4, circa 1983, to the electronic-controlled 4L60 for the 262-cid V-6 and the 350-cid V-8. The 305-cid V-8 retained the older 2004R.

In 1990, the Virginia State Police was among the majority of states to use the 350-cid-powered Caprice. These police cars had a top speed of 122 mph. (Dave Dotson)

The Seattle, Washington, police used the Caprice 9C1 in 1990. Note the door-mounted shoulder harness and the fender-mounted emergency lights. (Bill Hattersley)

The 1990 model year was a shortened one for the Caprice. In the spring of 1990, the totally restyled 1991 Caprice was unveiled. Nearly everyone saw the 1991 Caprice for the first time as a police car not as a retail car.

In 1990, Chevrolet was rumored to have a 454-cid police V-8 as a mid-year release in the Caprice. This was supposed to be in response to state police departments in Wyoming and Montana. Discontinued in police cars, the 454-cid V-8 producing 290 hp remained a Chevrolet truck engine through at least 1996. Unfortunately, this rumor turned out to be only wishful thinking. It was, however, given credibility because Chevrolet Fleet did indeed have a 454-cid-powered 1990 Caprice. According to specialty vehicles manager, Bob Hapiak, this was strictly a one-of-a-kind development car. The 1990 police Caprice was never available with the 454-cid V-8.

In 1990, Chevrolet introduced the retail Lumina as a replacement for the Celebrity and a direct competitor to the Ford Taurus. The Lumina would be upgraded with a Special Service package for light-duty police work in 1992. The Lumina was based on the same GM10 platform used for the Buick Regal, Oldsmobile Cutlass and Pontiac Grand Prix. It would be powered by a 3.1-liter V-6.

At the critical Michigan State Police tests, the 1990 350-cid Caprice ran almost exactly as it did during its dynamite 1989 performance. The Caprice once again turned in a road course time more than two seconds ahead of the 351-cid Crown Victoria. The 0-100 mph time in the 29 second bracket and the top speed of 122 mph was like 1989. The Caprice outbraked the Crown Victoria and scored the most points for interior ergonomics. The Chevy 350-cid throttle body fuel-injected V-8 was rated by the EPA methodology to have a better city gas mileage rating than the Ford 351-cid variable venturi V-8.

That made it six victories in six MSP test phases. This was the first time, since 1978 when the MSP began testing, that one test car won all six phases. However, this would happen with the Caprice again in 1991 and again in 1996. During the 1996 vehicle tests, the last appearance of the Caprice, the LT1 Caprice beat the SOHC Crown Victoria in all six test phases to go out a true winner.

The 305-cid Caprice and the 302-cid Crown Victoria were much closer matched, and again they split the tests for small V-8, urban patrol cars. The 160 hp Crown Victoria had a better road course time, acceleration to 100 mph and fuel economy. The 170 hp Caprice had a higher top speed, stronger brakes and better ergonomics.

The King County, Washington, Police drove these 1990 Caprices. The 350-cid-powered Caprice was upgraded to the 4L60 electronic-controlled four-speed transmission. (Bill Hattersley)

In 1990, Ford released a police package for the front-drive, V-6 Taurus, which was introduced as a retail car in 1986. The Taurus was designed as a full-blown, heavy-duty police car. Weighing just 3,323 pounds, the 3.8-liter/140-hp mid-size sedan was fast. Among four-door sedans, the Taurus was second to only the 350-cid Caprice around the MIS road racing course. It was the second quickest to 100 mph.

The Taurus had a 114 mph top speed, which placed it behind the 350-cid Caprice and 351-cid Crown Victoria but ahead of all the other sedans. The brakes were average for a police sedan, but the 3.8-liter V-6 Ford engine was rated second to only the 4.3-liter V-6 Chevrolet engine in terms of EPA city fuel economy.

The 106.0-inch wheelbase Taurus, however, was rated dead last in terms of ergonomics. Even the cramped, 100.5-inch wheelbase police Mustang had a better interior space rating than the Taurus. The lack of interior room and persistent transaxle problems would lead to the demise of the Taurus police car after 1995.

In late-1990, Chevrolet faced the first of two of its most serious police controversies ever. Both were safety issues. The first was the door-mounted seat belt on the 1990 Caprice. The second was anti-lock brakes on the 1991 Caprice.

Door-mounted "passive front seat belt systems" were new to the 1990 Caprice, but had been used by General Motors on other models since 1987. The system on the 1989 Caprice was called a body-mounted, active system. A retractor was mounted to the "B" pillar near the floor. This was a three-point system with a single sliding buckle and a cinching-type latch. The system had an inertia locking mechanism with a swinging pendulum that locked during .5g of deceleration.

The system on the 1990 Caprice was called a door-mounted, passive system. The system used two retractors: one for the shoulder belt and one for the lap belt. When the single latch was buckled, a lap and shoulder belt were formed. The 1990 system used desensitizing solenoids on the retractors, an open-door sensor and a vehicle-speed sensor. With the seat belt latched and the vehicle in motion, the locking mechanism would lock to restrain the door from opening. At forces up to 5.0gs, the seat belt helped to keep the door closed. The system included pendulums that sensed forward, reverse and lateral accelerations and locked at .5g.

Door-mounted, three-point seat belts serve two purposes: one, hold the driver in the seat; two, restrain the door from opening in the event of an accident. The problem is if the front door opens during a crash, the driver would lose the effectiveness from the seat belt. In a one-car, officer-involved fatal accident in Maine, exactly that happened.

The National Highway Transportation Safety Agency (NHTSA) got involved in August 1990. The NHTSA concluded:

"GM vehicles equipped with the three-point system have consistently passed compliance tests for the automatic protection provisions of FMVSS-208, Occupant Crash Protection.... No type of safety belt, including automatic belts in the subject vehicles (1990 Caprice) or manual belts, can guarantee user injuries or ejections will be avoided under all vehicle crash conditions, including high speed impacts or rollovers...(In the Maine case, the door lock mechanism was ripped apart on impact.) GM vehicles have no more problems than other manufacturer's automatic safety belt systems and there was not statistical difference in door hinge and latch performance between GM vehicles and other manufacturers' products."

NHTSA regulations for 1990 models required either this type of a passive restraint or air bags. NHTSA ruled the 1990 Chevrolet system safe. The fatality in Maine was literally a one in a million circumstance. By 1991, Chevrolet installed air bags on the police Caprice and replaced the door-mounted belts with body-mounted belts similar to the ones used on the 1989 Caprice.

1990 Caprice Powertrains						
RPO	Type	Size	Induction	HP	Trans	Axle
LB4	V-6	4.3L/ 262cid	throttle body	140	4-spd AOD	3.08
LO3	V-8	5.0L/ 305cid	throttle body	170	4-spd AOD	3.08
LO5	V-8	5.7L/ 350cid	throttle body	190	4-spd AOD	3.42

1990 Michigan State Police Patrol Vehicle Test Results						
	Chevrolet	Ford	Chevrolet	Ford	Chevrolet	Ford
Model	Caprice	Crown Vic	Caprice	Crown Vic	Caprice	Taurus
Engine	350 cid, tbi	351 cid, VV	305 cid, tbi	302 cid, pfi	262 cid, tbi	232 cid, pfi
HP, SAE	190	180	170	160	140	140
Axle Ratio	3.42	2.73	3.08	3.08	3.08	3.37
Weight, test (lbs)	3,893	4,152	3,958	3,899	3,812	3,323
Wheelbase (in)	116.0	114.3	116.0	114.3	116.0	106.0
Road Course Lap Time	86.75	88.58	89.74	88.77	90.65	87.31
0-100 mph	29.71	34.02	42.60	38.67	53.09	34.00
Top Speed, mph	122.1	121.0	113.0	107.3	110.2	114.0
Braking, ft/sec2	24.23	22.96	24.23	22.96	24.23	23.30
Ergonomics pts	209.9	206.1	209.9	206.1	209.9	117.45
Fuel, EPA City	14.0	13.1	16.4	17.4	19.0	18.5

References for 1990

1990 Chevrolet Police Package, Chevrolet Motor Division
1990 Patrol Vehicle Specs, Evaluation and Purchasing Program,
    Michigan State Police

"Seat Belts: Are They Safe?" Tom Yates, *Law and Order*, March
    1991

Chapter 37

1991: New Caprice; First Camaro

Hudson. Whale. Jelly Bean. Shamu. Bathtub. Turtle. These are just a few of the derogatory nicknames given by cops to the restyled 1991 Caprice. The 1991 Caprice was the first significant sheet metal change since 1977.

Oddly enough, Chevrolet took a greater risk in downsizing its full-size sedan for 1977 than it did in making the same sedan simply sleeker and more aerodynamic for 1991. In 1977, the overall performance was much less than the 1976 model year due to the loss of the big-block. Not so for 1991. The 1991 Caprice had much more performance than the 1990 Chevy. The slick top 1991 Caprice hit a top speed of 130 mph for the first time in perhaps 20 years.

The 1991 Caprice was the butt of dozens of styling jokes. However, these soon gave way to profound respect for the sheer abilities of the "new" Caprice. This was the first year for the Anti-lock Braking System and a driver's side air bag on the Caprice. In spite of appearances, the 1991 Caprice would become the most significant Chevrolet police car since the mid-1970s Nova.

The engineering concept approval for the 1991 Caprice was given in February 1987. The new Caprice was unveiled at the 1990 Chicago Auto Show, in the heart of the largest full-size sedan retail market in the United States. A true 1990-1/2 but marketed as a 1991 model, the new Caprice hit the street in March 1990, after being on the drawing board less than three years. The 1991 Caprice was assembled in Willow Run, Michigan, and Arlington, Texas. By 1991, 60 percent of the police cars sold were Chevrolet.

The 1991 Caprice featured "aero-styling" and an aggressively sloped 62.5 degree windshield. This steep windshield plus the gradu-ally sloping backlight gave the Caprice, with a drag coefficient of .327, the best aerodynamics of any full-size Chevrolet.

The 1990 Caprice and 1991 Caprice appear to be as different as any two police cars can be. Not so. While the sheet metal was drastically changed, and the interior slightly changed, these were the only changes. Except for the Anti-lock Braking System, the chassis and powertrain were a straight carry-over from 1990, including rear drum brakes. Compared to the 1990 Caprice, the 1991 Caprice had the same wheelbase, and front and rear tread. The 1991 Caprice was a little longer, wider and taller, and had quite a bit more front shoulder room. Overall, however, the 1990 and 1991 cars are much more similar than the 1957 and 1958, the 1964 and 1965, the 1970 and 1971 and especially the 1976 and 1977.

The 1991 powertrain was comprised of the 350-cid throttle body fuel-injected V-8, which was bumped 5 hp to a 195 hp rating for 1991. However, the vehicle weight also grew by 240 pounds for 1991. For the first time since 1976, the full-size Chevrolet tipped the scales at over two tons.

For 1991, Chevrolet dropped the 4.3-liter V-6 from the Caprice police lineup. From 1991 through 1996, the full-size Chevrolet would be powered by three sizes of V-8s but they would all be V-8s. Once again, Chevrolet emphasized that the Caprice police package with the 5.7-liter 350-cid V-8 be sold only for law enforcement and fire-fighting use. The 5.7-liter V-8 engine was selected by 94 percent of police agencies. The only other drivetrain change was the 5.0-liter (305-cid) V-8 got 2.56 economy rear gears in 1991 compared to the 3.08 ratio used in 1990 Caprices.

The 1991 Caprice, such as this Benton County, Indiana, Sheriff unit, was dramatically restyled. The "aero" styling inspired jokes, but allowed the Caprice to reach a top speed of 130 mph. (Butch Pritchett)

The 1991 Caprice, such as this Missouri State Highway Patrol cruiser, is easy to tell from the 1992 Caprice. Regardless of wheel covers, the 1991 Caprice has black "B" and "C" pillars. (MSHP)

The 1991 Caprice, such as this Harris County, Texas, Sheriff vehicle, became infamous for its plastic wheel covers. Called "frisbees," these popped off so frequently that Chevrolet replaced them with full wheel stainless covers at no charge. (Terry Feine)

For 1991, the standard wheel cover was made from plastic. The gray "non-metallic" wheel cover soon became known as the frisbee. These wheel covers simply would *not* stay on the wheels. City cops lost them on the first pothole. County cops lost them on the first washboard gravel road. State cops lost them the first time they cut through a median. Lost hubcaps became such a problem that Chevrolet offered to replace the plastic wheel covers with optional PO3 stainless steel wheel covers at no charge.

New for 1991, the Caprice station wagon was available with a special service package. The wagon had the same 115.9-inch wheelbase as the four-door sedan. Unlike the sedan, the wagon was available only with the 305-cid/170-hp V-8.

During the annual Michigan State Police patrol vehicle tests, the 1991 Caprice was clocked as having a similar 0-100 mph time as the 1990 model. However, the 1991 model was two seconds slower around the MIS 1.64-mile road racing course. Braking on the 1991 Caprice in spite of the Anti-lock Braking System was also similar to the 1990 Caprice. The big difference was, of course, top speed. The sleek and round 1991 Caprice was 8 mph faster than the boxy and square 1990 Caprice.

The slightly higher 1991 engine output was offset by the heavier vehicle weight. The rear axle ratios were unchanged. The 1991 Caprice reached 130 mph simply due to the profound sheet metal changes. The Caprice would remain in the 130 mph bracket until the LT1 engine joined the force in 1994. In that year, the full-size Caprice would reach the 140 mph bracket.

Ford fans could laugh about the ugly appearance of the 1991 Caprice, and they did, but the laughter was stopped with the click of a stopwatch. The Ford Crown Victoria was a carry-over for 1991 in its last year before a remodeling even more revolutionary than the 1991

The 1991 Caprice, such as this Indiana State Police cruiser, came standard with anti-lock brakes for the first time. It took a while for cops to get used to ABS.

Caprice. The 1991 Caprice had changes to its suspension and sheet metal but retained the drivetrain. The 1992-1/2 Crown Victoria would be totally new including a first-ever overhead cam police V-8.

The 1991 Michigan State Police tests were a total runaway for Chevrolet. Compared to the 5.8-liter Crown Victoria, the 5.7-liter Caprice had the quickest road racing course lap time, the fastest 0-100 mph acceleration, the highest top speed, the strongest brakes, the most ergonomic interior and the best fuel economy. For the second year in a row, and for only the second time in the history of MSP testing, one police sedan won all six test phases: the Chevrolet Caprice.

Once again, the 5.0-liter Caprice and the 5.0-liter Crown Victoria split the MSP tests. The Crown Victoria took the heavily weighted road course and top speed tests to edge out the small-engined Caprice.

The Los Angeles County Sheriffs Department tests take place annually in mid-model year. By December 1990, the square Crown Victoria was not available. In fact, Ford would be out of the full-size police car business for 14 months until the release of the remodeled 1992-1/2 Crown Victoria. As a result, the LASD did not test a full-size Ford for the first time in decades. The 1991 LASD tests turned out to be an odd combination of Caprice versus Taurus and Camaro automatic versus Mustang stick.

About the 5.7-liter Caprice, the LASD and LAPD test drivers said:

"This vehicle had a heavy feel to it but was very predictable. I felt it was easy to control. Very good overall. Moderate body roll noted in turns. No loss of traction. Very good

engine response. Four-speed overdrive transmission shifting smoothly."

Of the 5.7-liter Camaro, the LASD and LAPD police instructors said:

"Fast vehicle, handles good, predictable in turns, minimal body lean, good acceleration. Overall handling excellent. Excellent engine response. Very good cornering ability. Brakes stopped well. Steering is so quick and suspension is so stiff that control at speed is difficult until you get use to it."

The 1991 Caprice was involved in one major and two minor controversies. The first minor problem was extremely short front disc pad life. The 1991 model used the same platform as the 1990 model. However, the 1991 had 57 percent of its weight on the front wheels making it much nose-heavier than the 1990 Caprice. Some of the 1991 Caprices went through front pads in as few as 5,000 miles. Chevrolet engineers later changed brake pad compounds and proportioned more of the braking power to the rear. This resolved the police complaints.

The second minor problem involved the new driver's side air bag, aka Supplemental Inflatable Restraint (SIR). This turned out to be simply a training issue. Cops wanted to know when the air bag was designed to inflate (14 mph impact), how to prevent the air bag deployment in rescue operations (disconnect the negative terminal from the battery), what to do about driver training cars used in EVOC courses, rescue operations or vehicle ramming training (disconnect air bag at base of steering column), and what makes the air bag inflate

In 1991, for the second year in a row, the Caprice won all six test phases conducted by the Michigan State Police. This would only happen three times and it was the Caprice every time. (Mike Kennedy)

(sodium azide reacts to produce nitrogen gas). Chevrolet fleet officials answered all these questions and more in an air bag video sent to all police departments.

The third area of concern proved to be a big problem for Chevrolet. The 1991 Caprice was fitted with the ABS II Anti-lock Braking System. For most cops, this was their first time in an ABS-equipped vehicle. Late in the 1991 model year, the lack of familiarity with anti-lock brakes turned into complaints that the Caprice anti-lock braking system either actually caused accidents, or at least did not stop the car in a way that would have normally prevented an accident.

The issue gained nationwide attention in May 1991 when a Beech Wood (Indianapolis) Police lieutenant died after he lost control of his Caprice during a high speed chase. The problem was further exasperated by the fact that the smooth ride and sound-proofed cabin might fool the driver into thinking he was going *slower* than he actually was. Anti-lock brakes do not change the laws of physics. A certain amount of energy must be dissipated by the brakes. Energy increases by the square of the velocity. It takes exactly twice the energy dissipation to stop a car going 85 mph as it does one going 60 mph.

Chevrolet stuck to its guns that this was a training issue not a design problem. It produced an extensive training video that explained the ABS, and showed what it would and would not do. This was sent to all police departments that bought a Caprice or that requested the

tape. Many departments organized special training sessions on the ABS with an emphasis not to pump the brakes. Most of all the officers had to be taught that the modulating brake pedal was not a sign of a problem. They had to be taught that pumping the brakes actually disengaged the ABS.

In the final analysis, Chevrolet was proven to be correct. There never was any problem with the Caprice anti-lock braking system. As cops got ABS-familiarity training, the complaints simply disappeared. With one exception, the ABS-equipped Caprice was repeatedly proven to be the best stopping four-door sedan during Michigan State Police testing. The Caprice would be fitted with rear disc brakes in 1994. This would set an all-time MSP testing record for stopping distances. In fact, in 1996, after an abusive series of 90 mph panic stops, the 4,249-pound Caprice actually stopped shorter than the 3,480-pound Camaro. The Camaro had previously set stopping distance records every year during MSP testing.

In 1991, Chevrolet made the Camaro RS available with the "B4C Special Service Package." The Camaro B4C was available with either a LB9 305-cid/230-hp V-8 bolted to a five-speed stick and 3.42 rear gears, or a L98 350-cid/245-hp V-8 teamed with a four-speed overdrive automatic and 3.23 rear gears.

Both the 305 and 350 Camaro engines used Tuned Port Injection (TPI). This is significantly different than throttle body injection (tbi).

In 1991, the Camaro RS was released with the B4C special service package. The 5.7-liter Camaro promptly set a Michigan State Police road racing track record. (Bob Ring)

A 1991 Nebraska State Patrol Camaro. With its 150 mph top speed, the Camaro quickly became the pursuit car of choice. (Dave Dotson)

The New York State Police used the 1991 Camaro B4C as a special traffic enforcement vehicle, as did the Indiana State Police and the California Highway Patrol. (Neal Kemp)

With a tuned port system, velocity matched and balanced runners deliver air to the cylinders. This is similar to the multi-point fuel injection.

The Camaro RS in 1991 used front MacPherson struts and a Salisbury (solid) live rear axle with a four-wheel coil spring suspension. In 1993, the Camaro would be upgraded to the Short-Long Arm, twin wishbone front suspension. The Camaro has always been rear-wheel drive.

The 1991 model year was the first time a Camaro had been marketed for police use. The Border Patrol used Camaros and Firebirds in the late-1980s for drug interdiction and illegal immigration enforcement. However, these were retail cars and did not have the special service package.

In addition to the powertrain, the B4C special service package included dual exhaust with dual converters, performance (not 1LE) suspension, 16x8-inch alloy wheels, P245/50R16 Z-rated radials, four-wheel disc brakes, limited slip rear axle, engine oil cooler, heavy-duty battery, 105 amp alternator, 145 mph speedometer, and air conditioning. As with the 1991 Caprice, the Camaro B4C was introduced in January 1990 as a 1991 model.

In 1982, the police Mustang gave traffic officers a profoundly more powerful squad car than the 350-cid Caprice, 318-cid Diplomat and 351-cid Crown Victoria. In 1991, the police Camaro gave traffic officers a profoundly more powerful pursuit car than the Mustang.

The Camaro had a clear performance advantage over the Mustang for the same price. The 101-inch wheelbase Camaro was the same overall size as the 100.5-inch Mustang. However, Mustang driving position was much more comfortable than the Camaro when it came to a 10-hour patrol shift, getting in and out of the car every 10 minutes, and stiffness of suspension.

Because both Chevrolet and Ford now had special purpose pursuit cars, for 1991 the MSP set up a special service package category.

This is similar to what it did for mid-size patrol cars in 1980 and 1981. Exactly the same weighting was applied to each test phase for the pursuit cars as was used for the four-door sedans. The road course times were awarded 30 percent of the total score. Top speed and 0-100 mph acceleration were each worth 20 percent of the total. The other three test phases were given a 10 percent weight.

The 5.0-liter HO Mustang LX had been the darling of the police fleet from California to Florida to New York since 1982. In 1991, the first year of the 5.7-liter Camaro RS, the era of the Mustang was officially over.

The Mustang had been a 135 mph top speed, low 16 second bracket quarter-mile pursuit car since the mid-1980s. In its first appearance at the MSP runoffs, the Camaro turned in an honest 150 mph top speed and a sizzling 15.0 second quarter-mile blast.

The Camaro's 150 mph top end was significant for other reasons than smokin' the Mustang. The highest, officially clocked top speed of any police package vehicle ever recorded had been 147 mph. This, too, was recorded at Chrysler's Chelsea Proving Ground. The vehicle was the 1969 Dodge Polara with the 440-cid, four-barrel carbureted "Magnum" V-8.

While not quite in the same four-door sedan class as the 1969 Polara, the 1991 Camaro was an official police car and was officially timed at 150 mph. It is doubtful a four-door police package sedan will ever exceed 147 mph. However, in terms of all time performance, the 1991 Camaro had set a new police vehicle record. And later-model special service package Camaros would break that new record.

Compared to the 5.0-liter Mustang with the four-speed automatic, the 5.7-liter Camaro with the four-speed automatic had the quickest road course time, the fastest 0-100 mph acceleration, the highest top speed and easily the strongest brakes. Brakes had always been a problem for the police Mustang. The police Camaro had four-wheel discs.

The 1991 Camaro, such as this Garland, Texas, Police unit, was available with two different drivetrains: a 5.0-liter V-8 with five-speed stick or a 5.7-liter V-8 with four-speed automatic. (Terry Feine)

The police Mustang had rear drums. The 1991 Mustang actually failed to meet the MSP braking standard of 22 feet per second squared.

The Mustang was rated as ergonomically superior to the Camaro, which is another great truth. The Mustang also had a higher EPA City fuel rating then the Camaro. When all the numbers were crunched, the Camaro had clearly won the 1991 MSP pursuit vehicle tests. The Camaro would win against the Mustang again in 1992 and in 1993. The special service package Mustang would be discontinued after the 1993 model year.

Honorable mention goes to the 1991 Ford Taurus. The front-drive mid-size was 15 hp stronger than the 1990 model. To the absolute amazement of all the cops at the MSP tests, the 3.8-liter Taurus had the fastest road course time of any police four-door sedan. It was a second faster than the 5.7-liter Caprice, two seconds faster than the 5.7-liter Camaro, two seconds faster than the 5.8-liter Crown Victoria and three-and-a-half seconds faster than the 5.0-liter Caprice and 5.0-liter Crown Victoria.

Among four-door sedans, the 155 hp Taurus had the second quickest 0-100 mph times and the second highest top speed behind only the 5.7-liter Caprice. The 3.8-liter Taurus beat the sister 5.8-liter Crown Victoria in four of the six performance areas including all three of the heavily-weighted test phases.

1991 Chevrolet Police Powertrains						
RPO	Engine	Induction	HP	Trans	Axle	Model
LO3	5.0L/ 305cid	throttle body	170	4-spd auto	2.56*	Caprice
LO5	5.7L/ 350cid	throttle body	195	4-spd auto	3.42	Caprice
LB9	5.0L/ 305cid	tuned port	230	5-spd stick	3.42	Camaro
L98/ B2L	5.7L/ 350cid	tuned port	245	4-spd auto	3.23	Camaro
*Caprice station wagon uses the LO3 engine but is equipped with 2.73 rear gears.						

1991 Michigan State Police Patrol Vehicle Test Results				
	Chevrolet	Ford	Chevrolet	Ford
Model	Camaro	Mustang	Camaro	Mustang
Engine	350 cid, pfi	302 cid, pfi	305 cid, pfi	302 cid, pfi
HP, SAE	245	225	230	225
Axle Ratio	3.23	2.73	3.42	3.08
Transmission	4-spd auto	4-spd auto	5-spd stick	5-spd stick
Test Weight (lbs)	3,463	3,251	3,393	3,185
Wheelbase (in)	101.0	100.5	101.0	100.5
Road Course Lap Time	81.08	83.80	82.45	83.06
0-100 mph	17.31	22.80	19.98	18.84
Top Speed, mph	150.0	136.1	149.1	135.5
1/4 mi. ET	15.05	16.54	15.84	15.33
1/4 mi. Speed	93.4	87.2	88.6	91.8
Braking, ft/sec2	26.63	21.68	25.17	n/a
Ergonomics, pts	146.0	167.3	146.0	167.3
Fuel, EPA City	16.4	16.8	16.5	16.9

1991 Michigan State Police Patrol Vehicle Test Results						
	Chevrolet	Ford	Chevrolet	Ford	Ford	Chevrolet
Model	Caprice	Crown Vic	Caprice	Crown Vic	Taurus	Wagon
Engine	350 cid, tbi	351 cid, VV	305 cid, tbi	302 cid, pfi	232cid, pfi	305 cid, tbi
HP, SAE	195	180	170	160	155	170
Axle Ratio	3.42	2.73	2.56	3.08	3.37	2.73
Weight, test	4,134	4,136	4,138	4,080	3,307	4,477
Wheelbase (in)	115.9	114.3	115.9	114.3	106.0	115.9
Road Course Lap Time	88.07	89.20	90.66	90.56	87.05	92.11
0-100 mph	29.24	34.54	41.84	40.98	29.62	42.23
Top Speed, mph	130.0	121.3	124.1	107.6	129.4	109.0
1/4 mi. ET	17.51	18.47	19.00	18.56	17.58	19.06
1/4 mi. Speed	79.6	78.1	74.3	74.7	79.7	71.09
Braking, ft/sec2	24.88	23.86	n/a	n/a	23.54	25.09
Ergonomics, pts	204.2	191.8	204.2	191.8	162.2	191.6
Fuel, EPA City	13.9	13.1	17.1	17.4	18.0	16.2

1991 Los Angeles County Sheriffs Department Tests				
	Chevrolet	Ford	Chevrolet	Ford
Model	Caprice	Taurus	Camaro	Mustang
Engine	5.7L, tbi	3.8L, pfi	5.7L, tpi	5.0L, pfi
Transmission	4-spd auto	4-spd auto	4-spd auto	5-spd stick
Axle	3.42	3.37	3.23	3.08
Wheelbase (in)	115.9	106.0	101.0	100.5
Road Course, sec	102.2	100.5	93.7	94.8
Braking, ft	145.7	159.1	134.1	156.8
0-60 mph, sec	9.4	9.9	7.0	7.7
1/4 mi. ET	17.28	17.64	15.56	16.12
1/4 mi. Speed, mph	81.3	80.3	91.9	91.4
Gas Mileage (mpg)	16.6	19.3	17.6	21.7
Water Temp.	175.7	169.9	194.2	200.5
Note: Minimum 0-60 mph performance is 11 seconds; minimum quarter-mile speed is 75 mph.				

Square vs. Round Caprices		
	1990	**1991**
Wheelbase (in)	115.9*	115.9
Overall Length (in)	212.2	214.1
Overall Width (in)	75.4	77.0
Overall Height (in)	56.4	56.7
Front Tread	61.7	61.8
Rear Tread	60.7	60.7
Head Room (f)	39.5	39.3
Shoulder Room (f)	60.9	63.4
Hip Room (f)	55.0	57.0
Leg Room (f)	42.2	42.2
Trunk Capacity	20.9	20.4
Fuel Capacity	25.0	23.0
*Prior to 1991, Chevrolet rounded this to 116.0 inches		

References for 1991

1991 Police Patrol Vehicle Evaluation Program, Michigan State Police

1991 Vehicle Testing and Evaluation Program, Los Angeles County Sheriffs Department

1991 Caprice Police Package, Chevrolet Motor Division

1991 Caprice Special Service Station Wagon, Chevrolet Motor Division

1991 Camaro Special Service Package, Chevrolet Motor Division

Chapter 38

1992: Lumina Special Service Sedan

New for 1992, Chevrolet released a special service package for the front-wheel drive Lumina. The Lumina B4C, such as this Baylor, Texas, Police unit, was powered by a 3.1-liter V-6. (Terry Feine)

For 1992, Chevrolet released a special service package for the front-wheel drive Lumina. Chevrolet's last front-drive police car was the 1986 Celebrity. The 107.5-inch wheelbase Lumina was powered by a 3.1-liter (191-cid) multi-port fuel-injected V-6. The 140 hp engine was teamed with a four-speed AOD transaxle with a 3.33 final drive. The P205/70 non-rated retail car tires were replaced with P215/65 H-rated radials. This was the only powertrain available.

The B4C special service package included heavy-duty seats. These would be replaced next year by Recaro bucket seats. The Lumina B4C also used the F41 "special sport" suspension with heavier-duty everything. The B4C package included a larger capacity radiator, an auxiliary engine oil cooler and an auxiliary transaxle oil cooler.

The police Lumina came with different wheels almost every year. For 1992, the lighter duty, special service package included retail steel wheels and full wheel covers. The certified speedometer went to 115 mph, which is also the speed to which the Lumina was computer-control speed limited.

The Lumina B4C was released with a special service package to compete against the more powerful Taurus equipped with the heavier-duty police package. The Lumina was well enough accepted by police to be released in both a B4C special service package and 9C3 police package for 1993.

The Lumina B4C used a retail 3.1-liter V-6 engine and the Euro's F41 "sport" suspension. Basically, the 1992 special service package Lumina is a Euro 3.1 with extra oil coolers and without the alloy wheels.

Chevy Fleet took heat from the Heat for not using the 3.4-liter, 200 hp Twin Dual Cam Z34 engine in the police Lumina. Their response was simple. This was the first year for the special service package and they were cautious about reliability, durability and maintenance expense of a DOHC engine used for police work. After all, Ford does not use the SHO engine in its Taurus police package car for the same reason. The Lumina B4C was an urban, light patrol vehicle. For heavy-duty traffic enforcement, get a 5.7-liter Caprice or better yet, a 5.7-liter Camaro.

With few exceptions, the 1992 police Caprice was a carry-over from the phenomenal 1991 model year. The 5.0-liter (305-cid) powered Caprice was now available with both 2.56 economy rear gears and 3.08 standard performance gearing.

The big news was a 10 hp increase in the 5.7-liter engine. The L05 350 was now rated at 205 hp. Again, this engine was restricted to police use and was not readily available for retail cars.

The 10 hp increase came from a less-restrictive exhaust. The diameters of the Y-pipe, collector and exhaust pipes were all increased. Chevrolet also designed a new, low restriction catalytic converter. Even though the muffler and resonator were unchanged from 1991, the exhaust back pressure dropped from 21 inches of mercury to just 15 inches.

Chevrolet also added a fresh air intake for the 1992 Caprice. Cooler air is more dense and allows more spark advance before detonation occurs. The end result of the exhaust and induction changes

The 1992 Lumina, such as this British Columbia Sheriff unit, had a top speed of 111 mph. The B4C package included auxiliary engine oil and transaxle oil coolers. (Bill Hattersley)

The 350-cid V-8 used in this Monroe County, Michigan, Sheriff 1992 Caprice got more horsepower thanks to a less restrictive intake and exhaust. It had a top speed of 133 mph. (Dave Dotson)

was more peak horsepower and the peak horsepower available under a wider variety of conditions.

The extra 10 hp is just what the 1992 Caprice needed to overcome the 250 pound weight gain from 1990. The 1992 Caprice was back in the 16 second quarter-mile bracket along with the Mustang automatic. The 1992 Chevy reached 100 mph more than three seconds quicker than the 1991 version. It was a second-and-a-half quicker around the MIS road racing course than the 1991 model.

In 1991, the 5.7-liter Caprice was required to use P235/70 V-rated tires. This is because the H-rating is 130 mph and the slick top 5.7-liter Caprice was now past that barrier. Of course, V-rated tires are more expensive both initially and come replacement time. For 1992, police departments could order smaller, P225/70 H-rated radials with the 5.7-liter engine. However, the VZ2 130 mph speed limiter had to be ordered if H-rated tires were used.

The 1991 and 1992 Caprices can be difficult to tell apart. Here are some hints. On the 1991, the "B" and "C" pillars are black, while the 1992 and newer models are body color. The gray plastic hubcaps are also a clue that the Caprice is a 1991. In 1992, the 9C1 police package included full stainless steel wheel covers, which solved the frisbee

problem. A black 1991 Caprice 9C1 with optional or replacement stainless wheel covers cannot be distinguished from a black 1992 Caprice 9C1 without referring to the VIN.

Chevrolet was truly nervous about the new Crown Victoria. On paper, the Ford had the edge. Its overhead cam 4.6-liter V-8 engine was rated 5 hp stronger than the 5.7 overhead valve bowtie powerplant. The Crown Victoria now had sleeker sheet metal with a .34 coefficient of drag similar to the .329 Cd for the Caprice. The Crown Victoria also weighed 100 pounds less than the Caprice. The new Ford also had four-wheel disc brakes with optional ABS and traction control. The big Ford even had 3.27 rear gears to go with the high-revving "modular" V-8 instead of the 2.73 gears used for ages with the 351-cid V-8.

The Michigan State Police conducted its acceleration and top speed tests first. The 5.7-liter Caprice clicked off a 0-100 mph time of 25 seconds and a top speed of 133 mph. With great expectation (Ford fans) and great apprehension (Chevy fans), the SOHC Crown Victoria took to the 4.7-mile oval at Chrysler's Chelsea Proving Ground next. It hit 100 mph in 28 seconds and had a top speed of merely 124 mph. Ford Fleet officials managed to convince Michigan State Police offi-

The 1992 Caprice, such as this NYPD precinct car, was available with the 305-cid V-8 and 2.56 "economy" gears. This combination produced a 128 mph top speed and 17.4 mpg. (Neal Kemp)

cials to allow a re-test under the theory the Crown Victoria was not shifting into fourth gear. The re-test, with a confirmed shift into fourth gear, gave the same results.

In fairness to Ford, the Crown Victoria that ran the 1992 Michigan State Police vehicle tests was the only police package Crown Victoria in existence at the time. It was literally a one-of-a-kind prototype. The engine's spark control calibration and electronic transmission calibration and shift points were all drastically different from the retail car. The MSP tests took place in September 1991. The Crown Victoria police car would not be released until March 1992.

Torque wins races, not horsepower. The 5.7-liter Chevy small-block had a 300 pound-foot to 270 pound-foot advantage over the 4.6-liter Ford SOHC V-8. Chevrolet fans breathed a sigh of relief. The Caprice had faced its stiffest challenge in years and was well on its way to winning the 1992 MSP tests. However, one incredibly ironic loss still awaited the bowtie crowd.

For 1992, the Caprice got larger rear wheel cylinders and a larger diameter vacuum assist. This should have improved braking performance. After Chevrolet spent all of 1991 defending its brakes and educating cops about Anti-lock Braking Systems, the 1992 Caprice turned in one of the worst stopping distances ever recorded for a full-size Chevrolet.

At the same time, the four-wheel disc Crown Victoria turned in one of the best braking distances ever recorded for any Ford police car. Fords have never been known for their superior brakes. With insult now added to injury, Chevrolet platform engineers assured everyone that rear discs and improved pads would soon be available. The Caprice received rear discs in 1994.

At the Michigan International Speedway road racing course, the 5.7-liter Caprice walked away with the best lap times for a sedan. The 5.7-liter Caprice ended up capturing four heavily weighted test phases to win the MSP contract for 1992.

Making a guest appearance at the 1992 MSP vehicle tests was the prototype Caprice with the Corvette LT1 280 hp V-8. This was a sequentially injected, tuned port 350-cid small-block using the first true dual exhaust on any Caprice since the early-1970s. The prototype used the four-speed AOD transmission and 3.08 gears. The LT1 Caprice had a 0-100 mph time in 21 seconds, a top speed of 143.5 mph, and a road course lap time two seconds faster than the 1992 LO5 Caprice. The LT1 was promised for the Camaro B4C in 1993 and the Caprice in 1994. And that is exactly what happened.

The disappointing performance from the brand new Crown Victoria was partially offset by the 3.8-liter Taurus running roughshod over the brand new 3.1-liter Lumina. All of the performance and ergonomic kudos went to the Taurus. The Lumina simply produced the best gas mileage. For the next three model years, the Lumina 9C3 would never be a match for the Taurus 55A. The police version of the Taurus was discontinued after 1995.

The 1992 Camaro B4C used 1LE four-piston twin caliper non-ABS brakes developed for the Corvette. During Michigan State Police testing, the Camaro set top speed and road course records. Even this 5.0-liter Camaro broke the 150 mph barrier.

The Wisconsin State Patrol used the 1992 Camaro B4C for special traffic enforcement. The Los Angeles County Sheriff EVOC instructors gave the Camaro B4C high praise for acceleration, braking and handling. (Darryl Lindsay)

The 1992 pursuit car tests were a blowout in favor of the Camaro B4C again. Both the Camaro and the Mustang were basically unchanged from 1991. As a result, their performance was also unchanged. The 5.7-liter Camaro reached a top speed of 152 mph and set a new MIS road course lap time record. The Camaro would be restyled for 1993 and receive a lot more power, ABS brakes and a better front suspension. The 1993 model year would be the last for the police Mustang.

For 1992, the Camaro B4C special service package included the four-piston, twin caliper 1LE front discs originally designed for the Corvette. This included 12-inch diameter disc rotors. The 1992 Camaro was not available with ABS. That was slated for 1993.

The 1992 Los Angeles County Sheriffs Department tests were basically an echo of the Michigan State Police tests with one big difference. In the four months between the two tests, the Chevy platform engineers *fixed* the braking problem. The ABS disc/drum Caprice stopped within six inches of the ABS disc/disc Crown Victoria during the final 60 mph panic stop. In other police package testing at the Pomona Fairgrounds, the Taurus outran the Lumina and the Camaro blew the doors off the Mustang.

The first phase of the LASD vehicle tests is a preliminary handling and test-driver's subjective evaluation. Police driving instructors from LASD and LAPD, drive each car around the 1.9-mile road course at the LA County Fairgrounds in Pomona. Here is what they said about the 1992 Chevrolets:

5.7L Caprice

Good handling, fast car, very low brake pedal on last 3 to 4 laps. Slight understeer to neutral steer handling characteristics, ABS worked well, good acceleration which could cause the vehicle to go into an oversteer condition if applied early when exiting a turn, vehicle was very predictable. Good acceleration, predictable handling, brakes very low at finish.

3.1L Lumina

Good car overall, underpowered. Overall good handling front-wheel drive vehicle, slight predictable oversteer, good firm brakes.

5.7L Camaro

Very fast, excellent handling. Good handling vehicle, good brakes, predictable oversteer, excellent acceleration. Good, firm braking.

The ABS was still new, even to police Emergency Vehicle Operation Course (EVOC) instructors. It would be yet another year for cops to learn how to drive aggressively with ABS. The key would turn out to be braking in a manner to avoid activating the ABS. The ABS works incredibly well, but when it is activated, it generates a lot of heat. Just as ABS does not allow the vehicle to violate the laws of motion, neither does it allow the brakes to violate the laws of thermodynamics. The braking system can handle only so much heat. Even after the advent of "carbon" pads from Performance Friction in the mid-1990s, cops were urged not to routinely activate the ABS during a pursuit.

1992 Chevrolet Police Powertrains					
RPO	Engine	HP	Trans	Axle	Model
LO3	5.0L/305 cid	170	4-spd AOD	2.56, 3.08	Caprice
LO5	5.7L/350 cid	205	4-spd AOD	3.42	Caprice
LHO	3.1L/191 cid	140	4-spd AOD	3.33	Lumina
LB9	5.0L/305 cid	230	5-spd man	3.42	Camaro
B2L	5.7L/350 cid	245	4-spd AOD	3.23	Camaro

1992 Michigan State Police Patrol Vehicle Test Results				
	Chevrolet	Ford	Chevrolet	Ford
Model	Camaro	Mustang	Camaro	Mustang
Engine	5.7L, pfi	5.0L, pfi	5.0L, pfi	5.0L, pfi
HP, SAE	245	225	230	225
Transmission	4-spd auto	4-spd auto	5-spd stick	5-spd stick
Axle Ratio	3.23	2.73	3.42	3.08
Weight, test (lbs)	3,458	3,221	3,390	3,183
Road Course Lap Time	80.56	82.54	81.56	82.69
0-100 mph	17.29	21.92	18.40	18.99
Top Speed, mph	152.0	136.1	150.0	136.0
1/4 mi. ET	15.10	16.25	15.49	15.41
1/4 mi. Top Speed	93.4	88.2	91.8	91.6
Braking, ft/sec2	26.74	22.45	26.32	n/a
Ergonomics, pts	178.0	169.2	178.0	169.2
Fuel, EPA City	16.8	17.6	16.5	16.7

1992 Michigan State Police Patrol Vehicle Test Results						
	Chevrolet	Ford	Chevrolet	Chevrolet	Chevrolet	Ford
Model	Caprice	Crown Vic	Caprice	Caprice	Lumina	Taurus
Engine	5.7L, tbi	4.6L, pfi	5.0L, tbi	5.0L, tbi	3.1L, pfi	3.8L, pfi
HP, SAE	205	210	170	170	140	155
Axle Ratio	3.42	3.27	3.08	2.56	3.33	3.37
Weight, test (lbs)	4,144	4,032	4,121	4,121	3,263	3,339
Wheelbase (in)	115.9	114.4	115.9	115.9	107.5	106.0
Road Course Lap Time	86.40	87.63	89.23	n/a	91.78	87.11
0-100 mph	25.87	28.58	35.53	36.40	41.87	30.29
Top Speed mph	133.0	124.1	114.0	128.1	111.0	128.0
1/4 mi. ET	16.89	17.48	18.44	18.43	18.67	17.66
1/4 mi. Speed	82.9	81.3	75.4	76.7	74.1	78.8
Braking, ft/sec2	21.38	26.41	n/a	n/a	23.10	24.62
Ergs., pts	212.1	189.4	212.1	212.1	169.4	196.8
Fuel, EPA City	14.0	18.5	17.4	17.4	18.6	17.1

1992 Los Angeles County Sheriffs Department Tests						
	Chevrolet	Ford	Chevrolet	Ford	Chevrolet	Ford
Model	Caprice	Crown Vic	Lumina	Taurus	Camaro	Mustang
Engine	350 cid	281 cid	191 cid	232 cid	350 cid	302 cid
HP	205	210	140	155	245	225
Axle	3.42	3.27	3.33	3.37	3.23	3.08
0-60 mph	9.06	9.51	11.32	9.61	6.70	7.56
1/4 mi. ET	17.01	17.45	18.34	17.47	15.27	16.21
1/4 mi. Speed	83.7	84.6	75.3	79.2	93.3	90.1
Road Course	100.0	100.4	106.4	100.1	94.6	95.1
Fuel Mileage	13.7	17.3	18.5	17.9	15.4	16.5
60-0 mph (ft)	178.9	178.4	179.4	159.0	163.8	160.4
Engine Temp.	252.6	236.5	254.4	257.8	205.6	242.1

References for 1992

1992 Vehicle Testing and Evaluation Program, Los Angeles County Sheriffs Department

1992 Police Patrol Vehicle Evaluation and Purchasing Program, Michigan State Police

1992 Caprice Police Package, 1992 Lumina Special Service Sedan, 1992 Camaro Special Service Package, Chevrolet Motor Division

Chapter 39

1993: LT1-Powered Camaro

During the 1992 mid-year release of the restyled Crown Victoria, Ford Fleet officials poked some good-natured fun at the styling of the 1991-92 Caprice. Ford officials urged the use of the Crown Victoria "to beautify America."

In 1993, Chevrolet corrected the styling mistake in its Caprice by opening the rear wheel wells. As such, it is extremely easy to identify 1991-92 vintage Caprices from the 1993-96 versions.

For the purist, the 1993 full stainless wheel cover has a gold bowtie in the center. The 1991-92 full stainless wheel cover has the word CAPRICE in the center of a blacked-out circle.

The powertrain for the 1993 Caprice was a carry-over from 1992. The 350-cid V-8 with 3.42 gears and the 305-cid engine with either 2.56 or 3.08 gears were the only choices. The police 5.7-liter/350-cid V-8 was once again restricted to police and fire use, but for the last time. In 1994 these would appear, in LT1 trim, in the Impala SS and Buick Roadmaster, performance names that cover two generations of enthusiasts.

The real changes came in the brakes. The front pads have more useable lining giving them 30 percent better wear. The rear brakes now use a compound for better wear under abusive conditions. The master cylinder piston area is larger. The ABS release logic has been improved for better performance while braking under washboard road conditions.

In 1992, the Lumina was released with a B4C Special Service package. After a year of reasonable fleet acceptance, in 1993 Chevrolet released two versions of the front-drive mid-size. One was the B4C Special Service Package. The other was the heavier-duty 9C3 Police Package.

Both were powered by the 3.1-liter/140-hp multi-port fuel-injected V-6 teamed with a four-speed automatic overdrive transaxle us-ing 3.33 final drive gears. Both used the Euro F41 "sport" suspension, larger radiator, auxiliary engine oil and transaxle oil coolers. Both have 115 mph speedometers, and heavy-duty alternators and batteries.

For 1993, both the police and the special service Luminas used the 15x6 aluminum wheels. These Euro-spec wheels are actually more durable than the pressed steel retail wheels. The B4C special service tire was the P205/70 non-speed rated radial. Optional on the B4C and standard with the 9C3 police package was the P215/65 H-rated Eagle GT+4. The only other difference between these two Luminas was the front seats. The special service package used 60/40 front seats while the police package used Recaro front bucket seats. These, too, were optional on the Lumina B4C.

In 1993, Chevrolet released the LT1 350-cid small-block V-8 for police work. It appeared first in the fourth generation Camaro special service package. In 1994 it would be available in the Caprice. Traffic enforcement would never be the same.

The big news for 1993 was the mid-year launch of the totally new Camaro. On behalf of the Benton County (Indiana) Sheriffs Office and *Law Enforcement Technology* magazine, the author went to Warren, Michigan, in late January 1993. I picked up from the GM Tech Center what I was told was the first production version of the B4C special service package Camaro. The B4C Camaros that ran at the September 1992 MSP vehicle tests were pre-production cars.

The fourth generation Camaro is powered by the LT1 350-cid V-8. The LT1 is not as much an engine code as it is a statement of advanced technology in pushrod small-block engines. The LT1 uses tuned port fuel injection to achieve 275 hp. This is 25 hp less than the

A Nassau County, New York, Police 1993 Caprice. This "Highway Patrol" unit used the 5.7-liter V-8 for 16 second quarter-mile times and a top speed of 132 mph. (Ned Schwartz)

For 1993, Chevrolet opened the rear wheelwells on the Caprice, greatly improving its appearance. This NYPD "radio motor patrol" used the 5.0-liter V-8 engine. (Neal Kemp)

Corvette's LT1 due to a slightly more restrictive intake and single muffler and catalytic converter. This is the most power the Camaro has had since 1971.

The 275 hp LT1 holds a 30 hp advantage over the B2L 350 used in 1992. The mid-level 305-cid police engine is no longer available in the Camaro. This would be the last year for this 5.0-liter V-8 in the police Caprice.

The 1993 Camaro B4C came with either the 4L60 four-speed overdrive automatic or the Borg-Warner T56 six-speed manual. The Borg-Warner T56 is also used in the Dodge Viper. The Corvette used a six-speed ZF transmission. Both versions of the Camaro B4C use 3.23 rear gears.

The Camaro's F-body platform is totally new. The front MacPherson struts have been replaced by a Short-Long Arm (SLA) twin A-arm front suspension. The benefits are greater wheel travel, less dive during braking, less bump steer and less wandering on uneven pavement even with 50-series tires.

Saginaw-powered rack and pinion steering was used for the first time on any Camaro. This replaced the recirculating ball steering for better on-center feel, steering response and road feedback.

New for 1993, the Camaro B4C came standard with ABS in addition to its four-wheel discs. The Camaro no longer used the 1LE dual front disc brakes. The single piston surface area on the 1993 Camaro was actually larger than the twin piston brakes developed for the Corvette. Additional safety equipment on the 1993 Camaro included dual side air bags.

In addition to the better suspension and improved brakes, the entire body of the 1993 Camaro was new. The semi-monocoque body blended reinforced steel with plastic panels for a 20 percent increase in structural rigidity compared to a single sheet welded steel unibody. The roof, doors and hatch were made from sheet molding compound (SMC), a mixture of chopped fiberglass in a polyester resin. The front and rear facias and front fenders were made from the reaction injected molded (RIM) process in which polyurea is reinforced with mica. Only the hood and rear quarter panels remained galvanized steel.

The Camaro used a windshield raked back to a 68 degree angle. With this angle, the windshield sloped forward enough to cover the rear two cylinders of the LT1 V-8.

In 1993, Chevrolet released two versions of the Lumina. One was a B4C special service package. The other was a 9C3 police package. Both used the 3.1-liter V-6. (Bill Hattersley)

The Salt Lake, Utah, Police joined the St. Louis, Missouri, Police and a growing number of departments that used the 1993 Lumina 9C3. Aluminum wheels were more durable in police use than steel. (Greg Reynolds)

During testing by the Michigan State Police the 1993 LT1 Camaro set four all-time police car records: fastest 0-100 mph, highest top speed, quickest MIS road course times and shortest panic brake stopping distances.

The 1993 275 hp, LT1 Camaro automatic was clearly faster than the 1992 245 hp, B2L Camaro. It was a second-and-a-half faster to 100 mph, which set a new MSP testing record. The LT1 Camaro was almost a half second quicker in the quarter-mile. Around the 1.64-mile MIS road racing course the LT1 Camaro was a full second faster, breaking the record set by the 5.7-liter Camaro in 1992.

The 1993 LT1 Camaro set a new top speed record for police package and special service package vehicles: 154 mph. With four-wheel discs and ABS the Camaro also set an all-time stopping distance record. The deceleration rate of 30.34 feet per second squared works out to a 60-0 mph stopping distance of just 127 feet. And that is after four stops from 90 mph.

The 1993 Mustang was in its last model year as a police car. No changes were made. The horsepower drop from 225 hp to 205 hp was strictly a change in the SAE test methods, which identified numerous subtle changes since the last SAE test six years prior. The Mustang 5.0-liter HO performed the same in 1993 as it had in years past. It ran the quarter-mile in 16 seconds and had a top speed of 135 mph.

The Michigan State Police, as did most enthusiasts, liked the changes made to the fourth generation Camaro. They subjectively rated the ergonomics (human engineering) of the 1993 Camaro higher than the 1992 Camaro and higher than the 1993 Mustang. The Camaro captured five of the six test phases. The Mustang had a better EPA City fuel rating.

The showdown between the 3.1-liter Lumina and the 3.8-liter Taurus was decided once again solidly in favor of the Taurus. The Taurus captured all six test categories. Among sedans, the spunky little front-drive was second only to the 5.7-liter Caprice around the road

The fourth-generation Camaro, such as this Royal Canadian Mounted Police unit, had a new A-arm suspension, anti-lock brakes, rack and pinion steering, dual side air bags and, of course, the 350-cid/275-hp LT-1 V-8. (Bill Hattersley)

The big news for 1993 was the LT-1-powered, fourth-generation Camaro B4C. This set top speed, braking and road course records when tested by the Michigan State Police.

course. While slightly slower to 100 mph, the 3.8-liter Taurus tied with the SOHC Crown Victoria for top speed.

By 1993, the Crown Victoria had plenty of time to complete the performance conversion from a retail car to a police car. Yet the big Ford performed exactly the same as the mid-year version. With the braking problems completely resolved, the Caprice outperformed the Crown Victoria in five of six contests. The LO5 5.7-liter Caprice had the fastest road course time, highest top speed, quickest acceleration to 100 mph, the best interior ergonomics and...the strongest brakes.

The fuel economy from the SOHC 4.6-liter V-8 was a strong advantage for the Ford. However, few police departments buy on fuel economy alone. Those that do would have selected the 5.0-liter Caprice with either the 2.56 or 3.08 gears. For the seventh straight year starting in 1987, the Michigan State Police test method selected the Chevrolet Caprice as the best all-around four-door police car.

The Los Angeles County Sheriffs Department conducted its annual vehicle tests at the same Pomona Fairgrounds used annually for the National Hot Rod Association's Winternationals. In fact, the quarter-mile times for these police cars came from the same drag strip used by NHRA competitors. The 1.85-mile road course is the same flat track used by the Los Angeles County Sheriffs Department to teach emergency driving and pursuit skills to its deputy sheriffs. After the preliminary handling evaluation, the LASD and LAPD test drivers noted:

5.7L Caprice

Slight understeer but predictable, loss of traction through turns occurred quickly, brakes were consistent without problems. Good acceleration, handled well. Vehicle could be made to oversteer by trail braking into turns and accelerate exiting turn, tires (General XP2000AS) were a little slick, transition from traction to loss of traction happened very quickly, brakes functioned well. Brakes were

strong throughout all laps, close to neutral handling, transition from understeer to oversteer occurred quickly.

3.1L Lumina

Very easy vehicle to drive, underpowered which made it very predictable through turns, good brakes on all laps. A little underpowered for its handling potential, some understeer but controllable, moderate body lean and bounce but no control problems, brakes performed well.

5.7L Camaro Six-speed

Moderate understeer, oversteer in turns while trail braking, vehicle felt heavy and had more bounce than sister car with automatic transmission, shift gates very close, some brake fade in later laps, acceleration was quick and required accurate operations to be controllable. Wheel hop while downshifting, had to downshift early approaching turns to minimize driveline effects and wheel hop. Very fast but good handling, fuel starvation in all corners when fuel tank was low, hard riding vehicle but lots of power.

1993 Chevrolet Police Powertrains					
RPO	Engine	HP	Trans	Axle	Model
LO3	5.0L/305cid	170	4-spd AOD	2.56, 3.08	Caprice
LO5	5.7L/350cid	205	4-spd AOD	3.42	Caprice
LHO	3.1L/191cid	140	4-spd AOD	3.33	Lumina
LT1	5.7L/350cid	275	4-spd AOD 6-spd man	3.23 3.23	Camaro

1993 Michigan State Police Patrol Vehicle Test Results				
	Chevrolet	Ford	Chevrolet	Ford
Model	Camaro	Mustang	Camaro	Mustang
Engine	350 cid, pfi	302 cid, pfi	350 cid, pfi	302 cid, pfi
HP, SAE	275	205	275	205
Axle Ratio	3.23	2.73	3.23	3.08
Transmission	4-spd auto	4-spd auto	6-spd stick	5-spd stick
Weight, test (lbs)	3,475	3,243	3,461	3,164
Wheelbase (in)	101.1	100.5	101.1	100.5
Road Course Lap Time	79.52	83.39	80.12	82.28
0-100 mph	15.82	22.34	16.12	18.45
Top Speed, mph	154.0	135.1	147.1	137.0
1/4 mi. ET	14.69	16.24	14.82	15.22
1/4 mi. Speed	95.8	87.6	95.7	92.4
Braking, ft/sec2	30.34	23.76	n/a	n/a
Ergonomics, pts	185.7	170.3	185.7	170.3
Fuel, EPA City	16.6	17.3	16.7	16.6

1993 Michigan State Police Patrol Vehicle Test Results						
	Chevrolet	Ford	Chevrolet	Chevrolet	Chevrolet	Ford
Model	Caprice	Crown Vic	Caprice	Caprice	Lumina	Taurus
Engine	5.7L tbi	4.6L pfi	5.0L tbi	5.0L tbi	3.1L mpfi	3.8L pfi
HP, SAE	205	210	170	170	140	155
Axle Ratio	3.42	3.27	3.08	2.56	3.33	3.37
Weight, test (lbs)	4,141	4,053	4,087	4,131	3,372	3,333
Wheelbase (in)	115.9	114.4	115.9	115.9	107.5	106.0
Road Course Lap Time	85.87	87.57	88.91	n/a	89.95	86.86
0-100 mph	25.86	27.91	35.28	41.56	38.23	29.89
Top Speed, mph	132.0	123.0	110.1 (L)	121.0	115.0 (L)	123.0
1/4 mi. ET	16.75	17.29	18.25	18.70	18.21	17.28
1/4 mi. Speed	82.9	81.8	76.1	75.1	75.8	80.2
Braking, ft/sec2	27.69	27.21	n/a	n/a	24.16	25.08
Ergonomics pts	230.9	207.1	230.9	230.9	173.9	205.5
Fuel EPA City	14.0	16.7	17.4	17.3	18.6	18.8

1993 Los Angeles County Sheriffs Department Tests						
	Chevrolet	Ford	Chevrolet	Ford	Chevrolet	Ford
Model	Caprice	Crown Vic	Lumina	Taurus	Camaro	Mustang
Engine	350 cid	281 cid	191 cid	232 cid	350 cid	302 cid
HP	205	210	140	155	275	205
Trans	4-spd AOD	4-spd AOD	4-spd AOD	4-spd AOD	6-spd man	5-spd man
Axle	3.42	3.27	3.33	3.37	3.23	3.08
0-60 mph	8.89	9.71	10.91	10.36	6.26	9.20
1/4 mi. ET	16.90	17.48	18.12	17.91	14.97	16.93
1/4 mi. Speed	84.1	82.8	76.9	79.1	93.8	89.1
Road Course, sec	100.2	102.2	105.0	102.0	94.2	97.2
Fuel Mileage	16.0	21.6	20.3	19.8	21.5	18.0
60-0 mph (ft)	155.0	155.1	182.6	162.6	147.5	216.3
Engine Temp.	192.3	201.3	226.8	218.2	214.7	211.3

References for 1993

1993 Vehicle Testing and Evaluation Program, Los Angeles County Sheriffs Department

1993 Police Patrol Vehicle Evaluation and Purchasing Program, Michigan State Police

1993 Caprice Police Package, 1993 Lumina Special Service Sedan, 1993 Camaro *Special Service Package*, Chevrolet Motor Division

Chapter 40

1994: LT1-Powered Caprice

The big news for the 1994 Caprice, such as this Seattle Police cruiser, was the 350-cid/260-hp LT-1 V-8. Also new for 1994 was a 265-cid V-8. Both versions used the new 4L60-E four-speed electronic overdrive transmission. (Bill Hattersley)

New powerplants for the 1994 Caprice were two Gen II V-8s, which use the "LT1" engine technology developed for the 1993 Corvette. The combustion chambers, ignition system and fuel systems were all redesigned. The result was improved horsepower, torque, emissions and fuel economy.

The base engine was the new 4300 V-8 producing 200 hp. This 265-cid V-8 was 30 hp stronger than the 305-cid V-8 it replaced. The L99 4300 uses exactly the same block as the LT1 350, and this smaller engine shares all of the Gen III technology.

The 4.3-liter (265-cid) V-8 is a totally new engine. It is not the 4.3-liter V-6 of the late-1980s that had the same bore and stroke as the 350. It is not the 267-cid V-8 of the early-1980s that was a de-bored 350. It is not the 262-cid V-8 of the mid-1970s that had a 3.67-inch bore and 3.10-inch stroke. The L99 is a de-bored (3.75-inch) and de-stroked (3.00-inch) LT1 with the same horsepower per cubic inch as the LT1.

The overall performance of the L99 4300 V-8 Caprice was closer to the SOHC Crown Victoria than the SOHC Crown Victoria was to the LT1 Caprice. The 265-cid Caprice is also much faster to 100 mph than the previous year's 305-cid Caprice.

In 1994, for the eighth straight year, the Caprice won the Michigan State Police tests. The LT-1 Caprice broke the 140 mph barrier and had road course times similar to the 5.0-liter HO Mustang. (Dave Dotson)

The 1994 and newer Caprices, such as this Chicago Police unit, are easily identified by the bolt-on hubcaps. Neither city potholes, nor county washboard roads nor the median between state roads can dislodge these wheel covers. (Greg Reynolds)

Both the L99 4300 V-8 and the LT1 5.7-liter V-8 were upgraded from tuned port fuel injection to sequential port fuel injection. Sequential precisely matches the fuel injection cycle to each cylinder's intake stroke. All else equal, sequential port fuel injection has the same peak horsepower as a tuned port injection engine, but the sequential injection engine has a flatter torque curve.

The 265-cid V-8 was a significant engine for urbanized, metro police departments. The Los Angeles Police ordered its Caprices with the smaller V-8. That is why the joint vehicle tests conducted by the LASD and LAPD included both the 305-cid and later 265-cid engines along with the 350-cid powerplant. The LASD wanted the bigger V-8, while the smaller V-8 fit the needs of LAPD better.

The New York City Police also split its police cars into two engine classes. The small V-8 was fine for the precinct cars, while the "highway patrol" arm of the NYPD got the more powerful V-8s. The Houston Police also became famous for its use of the Caprice with the smaller displacement engine.

For 1994, the L99 265 was available with the KL6 bi-fuel feature. This used natural gas as the primary fuel and gasoline as the secondary fuel source. Chevrolet began this development in anticipation of upcoming legislation for alternative fuels and zero emissions vehicles in California.

The new small-block displacement of 265 cubic inches got bowtie enthusiasts thinking about the first Chevy small-block, circa 1955. Of course, the original bowtie V-8 also displaced 265 cubic inches. And yes, even the bore and stroke were the same.

	1955 One Fifty	1994 Caprice
Engine	265-cid V-8	265-cid V-8
Bore	3.75 in	3.75 in
Stroke	3.00 in	3.00 in
Induction	4-bbl carb	seq. port inj.
HP	180 gross	200 net
Transmission	3-spd stick	4-spd AOD
Axle	3.70	3.23

For the first time, the Corvette-based LT1 was available in a full-size Chevrolet. Rated at 260 hp, the LT1 350-cid V-8 produces 55 hp more than the 1993 LO5 350-cid V-8. Again, LT1 stands for Chevrolet's most advanced small-block engine technology, not any one specific engine. In fact, the Corvette, Camaro and Caprice all use LT1 engines with the same 350-cid size but with three different horsepower and torque ratings.

A number of differences exist between the 260 hp LT1 used in the police Caprice 9C1 and retail Impala SS and the 275 hp LT1 used in the police Camaro B4C and Camaro Z28. First, the heads are different. The Camaro uses aluminum heads compared to steel for the Caprice. Aluminum heads allow more spark advance before detonation occurs. The Caprice's compression ratio is 10.0:1 compared to 10.5:1 for the Camaro. The camshaft and computer logic are also different since the Caprice weighs 650 pounds more than the Camaro. The Caprice uses a true dual exhaust with dual catalytic converters and dual mufflers. The Camaro also uses a true dual exhaust but its backpressure is 10 inches of mercury compared to 13 inches for the Caprice.

Both Caprice engines came teamed with the new 4L60-E electronic four-speed AOD transmission. The 4L60-E compensates for cold transmission fluid, can start off in second gear to maximize traction and has a first gear over-rev protection. It will shift from first to second even with the selector in first gear. The 4L60-E can sense when the engine starts to run hot and then unlocks the lockup torque converter. If the engine does not cool down, the transmission shifts itself from fourth into third.

The 4L60-E for police cars has firmer up-shifts and different downshift points than the 4L60-E used on retail cars. At wide open throttle (WOT), the retail car stays in third and is speed limited to 110 mph. At WOT, the police car shifts from third to fourth at 120 mph and keeps going to its top speed. In the case of the LT1 Caprice, this is over 141 mph.

For the first time, all 1994 police package Caprices came with four-wheel disc brakes. The Caprice had ABS since 1991. Also for the fist time, the 1994 Caprice came with dual side air bags (Supplemental Inflation Restraint). This forced cops to mount shotguns, radar units, radios and mobile display terminals out of the air bag deployment zone.

A Colorado State Patrol 1994 Camaro B4C. The LT-1 now used sequential fuel injection and the six-speed stick cars got the Computer-Aided Gear Selection solenoid. (Greg Reynolds)

The LT1 was so much more powerful than the LO5 350-cid V-8 that Chevrolet took a bold step in the rear gear ratio. The rear gears were lowered from 3.42 to 3.08. This explains the 141 mph top speed and the greatly improved fuel economy. However, it does not explain better road racing lap times and quicker acceleration to 100 mph. The LT1 was such a superior engine in terms of both horsepower and torque that even with a numerically lower gear ratio it still outperformed the LO5 350 in every way that police car measurements can be taken.

The 1994 Camaro B4C was a carry-over from 1993 with four subtle exceptions. First, the LT1 was converted from tuned port fuel injection to sequential port injection. This did not increase horsepower, but it did broaden the torque curve. Second, the Powertrain Control Module now used a Mass Air Flow sensor. This allows a more accurate measure of the air and a more precise fuel to air mixture as conditions change.

Third, the Camaros with the Borg-Warner six-speed stick got the Computer Aided Gear Selection (CAGS) solenoid. The CAGS solenoid blocks the second gear gate when the throttle position is at less than 10 percent or if the Camaro is under 24 mph when shifting from first to second. This second gear blockout can be overridden simply by downshifting. Fourth, the Camaros with the four-speed overdrive automatic now got the new, electronic 4L60-E transmission.

In 1993, the Camaro B4C came with 3.23 rear gears, regardless of transmission. For 1994, the four-speed AOD Camaro got 3.23 gears while the six-speed stick Camaro used 3.42 gears.

A number of changes took place in the MSP test methodology for 1994. First, a minimum rate of deceleration was established. The MSP standard of 24.2 feet per second squared calculates to a stopping distance of 160 feet from 60 mph. They also set a new dual acceleration and top speed standard. The police car had to reach a top speed of 120 mph and do it within two miles. This was the first braking standard and the highest top speed standard set by the MSP.

The MSP also changed the weighting they gave to each test phase. The road course lap times remained the single most important test phase. The braking results were emphasized to now be equal with the 0-100 mph acceleration. Sheer top speed was made slightly less significant. Fuel economy was downgraded to just five percent of the total score. These changes were done to make the testing less of a race and more representative of actual use during patrol. Acceleration, braking and cornering now accounted for 70 percent of the score.

During the annual Michigan State Police vehicle tests, the LT1 was a full two seconds faster around the MIS 1.64-mile road course than the SOHC Crown Victoria. This is a 12 car-length advantage. The LT1 bowtie sedan was also five seconds faster in reaching 100 mph. Police cars accelerate to 100 mph nearly every time they turn around to catch a traffic violator moving in the opposite direction.

While the Crown Victoria picked up a little top speed from 1993, the LT1 Caprice jumped 8 mph to reach 141 mph. This is the first full-size Chevrolet police sedan to officially break the 140 mph barrier. No Ford police sedan has ever reached these speeds. The slick top sedan reaching 140 mph means it will be able to hit at least 125 mph when fitted with twin spotlights and a full size lightbar.

The top speed of 141 mph was an incredible accomplishment for the Chevy small-block V-8. It did what the carbureted big-blocks from the 1960s could not do. This achievement was not just the power of the LT1, of course. Many changes have taken place since the late-1960s including low rolling friction pursuit radials, four-speed automatic overdrive transmissions, and a body style with a drag coefficient of just .329. This makes one wonder what the L29 fuel-injected 454-cid/290-hp big-block would do in a police Caprice!

The best way to put the LT1 police Caprice in perspective is to directly compare it to the 5.0-liter HO Mustang. Even with a 15-inch longer wheelbase and 1,000 pounds more weight, the LT1 Caprice has the same overall acceleration, braking and cornering performance as the police 5.0-liter Mustang.

	1994	1993
Model	Caprice	Mustang
Engine	5.7L LT1	5.0L HO
HP	260	205
Trans	4-spd AOD	4-spd AOD
Axle	3.08	2.73
Weight	4,244 lbs	3,242 lbs
Wheelbase	115.9 in	100.5 in
0-60 mph	8.30 sec	7.98 sec
0-80 mph	13.42 sec	13.18 sec
0-100 mph	21.64 sec	22.34 sec
Top Speed	141.2 mph	135.1 mph
1/4 mi. ET	16.18 sec	16.24 sec
1/4 mi. Speed	86.8 mph	87.6 mph
60-0 mph	149 ft	163 ft
Road Course	83.8 sec	83.4 sec

This side-by-side comparison explains two things. First, it explains the incredible popularity of the 1994 to 1996 Impala SS. These cars gave police Caprice straight-line performance. The Impala SS had a bit better braking and cornering due to 17-inch P255/50 Z-rated radials.

Second, it explains why the police Mustang is no longer needed. It was needed during the 1980s when all the full-size police cars ran 19 second quarter-miles and had top speeds under 120 mph. The full-size, four-door police sedans now ran as hard as the mid-size, two-door police pony cars. The rough ride and lack of prisoner space in the pony cars were drawbacks the cops no longer had to tolerate.

With the 1994 LT1 Caprice, cops got pursuit car performance in a traditional size four-door sedan. The last time that was true was 1976 for Chevrolet and 1978 for Ford, Dodge and Plymouth.

The Caprice narrowly edged out the Crown Victoria in the subjective ergonomic review. In spite of excellent braking performance from the Caprice, the Crown Victoria turned in the shortest stops for a Ford sedan ever recorded by the MSP to capture this category.

The LT1 350-cid Caprice stole all of the fuel economy thunder from the SOHC 281-cid Crown Victoria by exactly equaling its EPA City fuel mileage. Ford had bragged that its Crown Victoria had won the California Highway Patrol contracts based almost entirely on its superior fuel economy. The 1994 LT1 350 was 2.7 mpg more efficient than the 1993 LO5 350. Ford knew the Chevy LT1 in the Caprice would widen the performance gap over its SOHC-powered Crown Victoria. However, Ford could not have known the ultimate bowtie small-block would also steal the Crown Victoria's only true claim to fame.

In the final analysis, with a victory in three of the most heavily weighted tests, a minor weight victory and a tie, the 1994 Caprice was calculated to be the best overall police patrol car under the Michigan State Police methodology. The 1994 LT1 Caprice was also selected by the California Highway Patrol. This was the first bowtie sedan chosen since 1989. In Southern California, the Los Angeles County Sheriffs Department continued its streak of Caprice purchases, which was unbroken since 1985.

Chevrolet was too busy getting the newly styled Lumina ready for its 1995 launch to field a police package for 1994. However, a prototype version of the reskinned mid-size with a 3.1-liter 165 hp Gen III V-6 unofficially ran the MSP tests. At 120.8 mph, the 3.1-liter Lumina still did not have the top speed of the 3.8-liter Taurus. However, the braking was much improved, the road course times were close and the acceleration up to 100 mph bested the Taurus. We would have to wait until 1995 to see how close the production Lumina was to the test mule.

The LT1 Camaro is usually selected with a four-speed AOD for police use. However, the same police agencies that used to select the five-speed in the Mustang still select the six-speed in the Camaro for the same reasons. Transmission maintenance is less expensive with a manual transmission than with a lockup torque converter, electronic overdrive automatic transmission. This assumes, of course, that the pursuit pilots know how to drive a stick-shift car, including how to shift six times while holding a microphone in one hand, a cup of coffee in another, all while driving 125 mph.

The six-speed version of the LT1 Camaro was the record-breaker and record-setter for 1994. It reached an incredible 153.5 mph around the 4.7-mile Chelsea oval. It also accelerated to 100 mph in 17 seconds flat. The four-speed AOD LT1 Camaro was close behind.

The Camaro B4C was the only pure pursuit car available in 1994. It ran a 15 second quarter-mile with a top speed over 152 mph. (Chevrolet)

In mid-1994, the Caprice 9C1 became available with state-of-the-art radial pursuit tires. In the 1970s, the Goodyear Flexten was the police radial. This was replaced in the early 1980s by the Eagle GT, which was replaced in the late 1980s with the Eagle GT+4. In the mid 1990s, law enforcement upgraded to the Goodyear Eagle RS-A and the General XP2000V4. Both of these tires had asymmetric tread patterns.

Asymmetric tires can rotate in either direction, however, a certain sidewall must be mounted to the outside. In 1994, the LASD became the first to use asymmetric tires during their patrol car tests. The Michigan State Police used asymmetric radials during their 1995 tests. The LASD and LAPD police driving instructors had this to say about each of the Chevrolet police cars:

LT1 Caprice

The vehicle displayed moderate understeer. It was difficult to induce oversteer with acceleration through turns. Moderate bounce was experienced but body lean was acceptable. The brakes worked well-no pulling or noticeable fade was noted. Good acceleration out of turns and into straightaways. Consistent brakes. The overall handling of the vehicle was predictable.

4.3L Caprice

Vehicle accelerated well out of turns. Brakes responded well with slight fade experienced after initial laps, but no control problems occurred. The overall handling was predictable with minimal lean and bounce. Vehicle performed very well with this engine. Unable to read speedometer with headlights on in the day time. This vehicle displayed neutral steer handling characteristics and was very controllable. Body lean and bounce was less than that experienced when driving the 5.7-liter Caprice test vehicle. Car handles very good, overall. Neutral in its steering. Accelerated well for its engine size. Brakes worked well.

5.7L Camaro Four-speed

This vehicle accelerated very quickly—very fast out of turns. Low pedal brakes but consistent. Slight bounce experienced in turns with minimal body lean but no control problems. The overall handling was predictable. Moderate understeering occurred frequently. Some brake fade experienced with each driver as brakes heated during laps.

5.7L Camaro Six-speed

This vehicle is very fast, super quick out of turns. Acceleration is continuous on straightaways. The brakes were excellent, with no fading experienced. The suspension was stiff, resulting in a consistent, flat ride for most of the track. The overall handling of the vehicle displayed neutral to understeer and was difficult to force oversteer. Handling was predictable. Body lead was minimal with moderate bounce. Some severe rear wheel hop was experienced on hard braking applications. This vehicle handles, brakes, and shifts better than the 1993 model Camaro. Very impressive car.

1994 Chevrolet Police Powertrains					
RPO	Engine	HP	Trans	Axle	Model
L99	4.3L/265 cid	200	4-spd AOD	3.23	Caprice
LT1	5.7L/350 cid	260	4-spd AOD	3.08	Caprice
LT1	5.7L/350 cid	275	4-spd AOD	3.23	Camaro
			6-spd CAGS	3.42	Camaro

1994 Michigan State Police Patrol Vehicle Test Results						
	Chevrolet	Ford	Chevrolet	Chevrolet	Chevrolet	Ford
Model	Caprice	Crown Vic	Caprice	Camaro	Camaro	Taurus
Engine	350 cid, pfi	281 cid, pfi	265 cid, pfi	350 cid, tpi	350 cid, tpi	232 cid, pfi
HP, SAE	260	210	200	275	275	160
Trans	4-spd AOD	4-spd AOD	4-spd AOD	4-spd AOD	6-spd man	4-spd AOD
Axle Ratio	3.08	3.27	3.23	3.23	3.42	3.37
Weight, test (lbs)	4,244	3,997	4,178	3,463	3,463	3,348
Wheelbase (in)	115.9	114.4	115.9	101.0	101.0	106.0
Road Course Lap Time	83.80	85.79	86.76	79.38	79.95	86.69
0-100 mph	21.64	26.32	30.18	17.37	17.00	31.82
Top Speed mph	141.2	128.2	122.1	152.8	153.5	129.0
1/4 mi. ET	16.18	17.25	18.11	15.02	15.53	17.81
Braking, ft/sec2	25.98	27.27	27.03	29.75	n/a	26.07
Ergo, pts	244.6	243.4	244.6	209.3	209.3	227.6
EPA City Fuel	16.7	16.7	17.6	16.6	16.8	18.8

References for 1994

1994 Vehicle Testing and Evaluation Program, Los Angeles County Sheriffs Department

1994 Police Patrol Vehicle Evaluation and Purchasing Program, Michigan State Police

1994 Caprice Police Package, 1994 Camaro Special Service Package, Chevrolet Motor Division

Chapter 41

1995: Totally New Police Lumina

The 1995 full-size Caprice was almost a total carry-over from 1994. The only real change was larger rear outside mirrors. Mounted on break-away pivots, the mirrors were also moved from the front door panel to the front door window patch.

The Caprice 9C1 powertrains for 1995 were the L99 4.3-liter (265-cid) V-8 and the LT1 5.7-liter (350-cid) V-8. The 265-cid engine proved to be both reliable and economical. The smallest small-block was well received by cops. One-third of the Caprice police cars were powered by this 200 hp engine.

The 1995 Camaro B4C was also nearly unchanged from 1994. The LT1 5.7-liter V-8 rated at 275 hp was available with either a four-speed electronic overdrive transmission or a six-speed CAGS manual shift. The Acceleration Slip Regulation traction control option, announced for 1995, was not available until 1996.

The big news for 1995 was the totally restyled and re-engineered Lumina police package. The Lumina 9C3 was powered by an L82 3100 Gen III V-6 rated at 160 hp. Upgraded to sequential fuel injection, the Gen III changes also included a roller camshaft, better flowing heads, a revised intake plenum, a boost in compression from 9.0:1 to 9.6:1 and a larger volume single exhaust system.

The Lumina's fully independent rear suspension was redesigned for 1995. The new coil-over, rear MacPherson struts have more wheel travel than the original single transverse leaf spring suspension. This eliminated the "loose-lumber-in-the-trunk" sound common to the earlier Luminas when the suspension bottomed out.

The 1995 Caprice, such as this Illinois State Police unit, got larger outside rear view mirrors mounted on breakaway pivots. With five wins and one tie in six tests, the Caprice won the Michigan State Police tests for the ninth straight year. (Jennifer Sturgeon)

The 1995 Camaro B4C, such as this New York State Police unit, continued to be the car of choice for special traffic enforcement. These cars ran a 14 second quarter-mile with a top speed of 155 mph.

New for 1995 was the second-generation Lumina 9C3. Flowed heads, roller cam, higher compression and less restrictive exhaust boosted the 3.1-liter V-6 output to 160 hp. (Chevrolet)

The 1995 Lumina 9C3 got a new coil-over rear suspension replacing the mono-leaf. The police package version was the only Lumina to get rear disc brakes. The top speed was increased to 118 mph. (Chevrolet)

The 1995 police Lumina is different from the retail Lumina and Monte Carlo because it has rear disc brakes. The police package uses 11-inch rear discs from the other GM10 platforms such as the Grand Prix and Regal. However, the Lumina police car is the only GM10 with a MacPherson strut rear suspension and rear disc brakes.

The police Lumina used the same F41 "sports and handling" suspension as the DOHC 3.4-liter Lumina and Monte Carlo Z34. The second generation Lumina also included dual side air bags. As did the 1993 police package, the 1995 Lumina 9C3 included lumbar-adjustable Recaro front bucket seats.

A certified digital speedometer, auxiliary engine and transaxle oil coolers and oversize, 65-series H-rated radials were included in the Lumina police package. The electronic speed limiter on all retail Luminas, even the Z34, was deleted on the 9C3 police package. We got the Lumina test mule up to 123 mph at GM's Milford Proving Grounds.

The 1992 special service package Lumina used retail steel wheels with full wheel covers. The 1993 special service and police package Luminas used the cast aluminum wheels. These were actually more durable and rugged than the retail steel wheels. For 1995, Chev-rolet designed a new, 15-inch heavy-duty steel wheel for all Luminas. The center section used thicker gauge steel and the wheel was vented for better brake cooling. Unique to the 1995 Lumina police car were the full-size stainless steel wheel covers once used on the police Caprice.

With the exception of the newly styled Lumina, all of the 1995 patrol cars tested by the Michigan State Police were carry-overs from 1994. The performance was almost identical to 1994. The 1995 acceleration and top speeds were off from the previous year, however, the road course lap times were generally improved. The asymmetric Goodyear Eagle RS-A was credited with improving the lap times for all cars by more than a half second.

The LT1 Caprice once again had the quickest acceleration to 100 mph, the highest top speed, the fastest road course times and the best interior ergonomics. As a side note, the 132 mph top end recorded by the SOHC Crown Victoria was the first time in more than 25 years that a Ford four-door police sedan broke the 130 mph barrier.

In 1995, the 5.7-liter Caprice stopped from 60 mph, after four 90 mph panic stops, in the record setting distance of just 137.2 feet. The 5.7-liter Caprice again tied the 4.6-liter Crown Victoria in EPA City

A 1995 Caprice used by the Royal Canadian Mounted Police. While the 350-cid LT-1 was the top cop engine, one-third of the departments selected the 265-cid V-8. (Bill Hattersley)

The 1995 Camaro B4C performed very well at the Los Angeles County Sheriff's tests. EVOC instructors described it as having lots of power and speed. It hit 60 mph in 6 seconds.

fuel ratings. With five class wins and one tie, the 1995 5.7-liter Caprice was judged by the Michigan State Police to be the best overall four-door police sedan for the ninth straight year.

The 1995 3.1-liter Lumina was clearly a better police car than the 1993 version. More power. Better suspension. Stronger brakes. It was four seconds faster to 100 mph than the 1993 Lumina and 1.6 seconds quicker around the 1.64-mile MIS road course. The new Lumina closed the performance gap with the lighter Taurus. However, the torque advantage held by the blue oval and mid-size gave it the edge in almost every test. The Taurus even captured fuel economy and ergonomics honors to make it six for six. The Taurus police package would be dropped after the 1995 market year.

The Camaros continued to dominate in terms of sheer performance. The LT1 Camaro four-speed AOD set a new all-time record with a top speed of 155.0 mph. The same pony car broke the record it set last year for the lap times around the MIS road course.

The Los Angeles County Sheriffs Department also tested all the police and special service package vehicles. Here is what LASD and LAPD test drivers said after the preliminary handling evaluation:

LT1 Caprice

Vehicle lean and bounce was minimal until fourth driver, who experienced excessive lean and bounce in laps 27-32 during the turns. Good acceleration through turns and top end. Transition to oversteer was very smooth. Good brakes and predictable tires. Wheel hop was noticed while decelerating in an exaggerated oversteer condition. Mid-range acceleration was good. Transition from traction to loss of traction was very smooth.

4.3L Caprice

Neutral steering-understeered if too fast into the turns. Good/safe vehicle. Moderate mid-range acceleration, with minimum body lean and bounce. Predictable tire traction and dependable brakes. The vehicle handled well and was predictable.

3.1L Lumina

Vehicle handled well. Acceleration was adequate through turns with extended lean experienced through faster

190

turns. Good tire traction. Ergonomically, the driver's seat was very uncomfortable. The vehicle displayed neutral steering through the turns. Body bounce was minimal. Mid-range acceleration was sluggish. Brake pedal became "spongy" in later laps. The tires were predictable. Slight oversteer experiences during high speed cornering.

LT1 Camaro Four-speed AOD

Vehicle displayed slight to moderate understeer through turns. Bounce was moderate and body lean was minimal. Mid-range acceleration was very good. Brakes were good on initial laps but faded moderately on later part of test. The tires were very predictable. Good handling vehicle; positive steering. Good transition to oversteer condition if too aggressive with throttle. Lots of power and speed.

1995 Chevrolet Police Powertrains					
RPO	Engine	HP	Trans	Axle	Model
L99	4.3L/265 cid	200	4-spd AOD	3.23	Caprice
LT1	5.7L/350 cid	260	4-spd AOD	3.08	Caprice
LT1	5.7L/350 cid	275	4-spd AOD	3.23	Camaro
			6-spd CAGS	3.42	Camaro
L82	3.1L/191 cid	160	4-spd AOD	3.33	Lumina

1995 Los Angeles County Sheriffs Department Tests						
	Chevrolet	Ford	Chevrolet	Ford	Chevrolet	Chevrolet
Model	Caprice	Crown Vic	Caprice	Taurus	Lumina	Camaro
Engine	LT1 5.7L	SOHC 4.6L	L99 4.3L	3.8L	3.1L	LT1 5.7L
HP	260	210	200	160	160	275
Trans	4-spd AOD	4-spd AOD	4-spd AOD	4-spd AOD	4-spd AOD	4-spd AOD
Axle	3.08	3.27	3.23	3.37	3.33	3.23
0-60 mph	7.53	8.99	10.33	9.30	9.81	6.19
1/4 mi. ET	15.87	16.88	17.91	17.27	17.47	14.95
1/4 mi. Speed	89.8	85.2	81.7	81.8	80.8	95.2
Road Course	85.9	87.7	89.1	89.3	90.6	82.2
Fuel Mileage	15.7	18.8	19.1	23.4	22.3	19.5
60-0 mph	144.5	149.6	150.0	162.6	185.3	154.8
Eng. Temp.	221.8	193.3	147.4	215.6	225.3	223.5

1995 Michigan State Police Patrol Vehicle Test Results							
	Chevrolet	Ford	Chevrolet	Chevrolet	Chevrolet	Ford	Chevrolet
Model	Caprice	Crown Vic	Caprice	Camaro	Camaro	Taurus	Lumina
Engine	350 cid, pfi	281 cid, pfi	265 cid, pfi	350 cid, tpi	350 cid, tpi	232 cid, pfi	191 cid, pfi
HP SAE	260	210	200	275	275	160	160
Trans	4-spd AOD	4-spd AOD	4-spd AOD	4-spd AOD	6-spd man	4-spd AOD	4-spd AOD
Axle Ratio	3.08	3.27	3.23	3.23	3.42	3.37	3.33
Weight, test (lbs)	4,248	4,005	4,201	3,468	3,445	3,340	3,415
Wheelbase (in)	115.9	114.4	115.9	101.0	101.0	106.0	107.5
Road Course Lap Time	83.07	85.14	86.31	79.20	80.19	87.08	88.30
0-100 mph	22.43	26.71	33.12	16.48	16.46	33.58	34.04
Top Speed, mph	135	132	120 (L)	155	152	128	118
1/4 mi. ET	16.29	17.32	18.46	14.95	15.11	18.15	18.24
1/4 mi. Speed	86.8	82.6	79.4	95.18	95.80	77.9	77.8
Braking fps2	28.4	26.5	28.4	29.6	n/a	26.4	24.4
Ergonomics	234.4	196.3	234.3	162.2	162.2	195.3	158.9
EPA City Fuel	16.7	16.7	17.6	16.6	16.8	18.8	18.7

References for 1995

1995 Vehicle Testing and Evaluation Program, Los Angeles County Sheriffs Department

1995 Police Patrol Vehicle Evaluation and Purchasing Program, Michigan State Police

1995 Caprice Police Package, 1995 Camaro Special Service Package, 1995 Lumina Police Package, Chevrolet Motor Division

Chapter 42

1996: Last Caprice Police Car

The 1996 model year was the 30th Anniversary of the Caprice as a separate series. The Caprice was a trim option on the Impala in 1965, and its own car line in 1966. The first police package for the Caprice was released in 1987.

The powertrain for the 1996 Caprice was a carry-over from 1995. The V-8 engines included the L99 4.3-liter (265-cid) and the LT1 5.7-liter (350-cid). Upgrades for 1996 were minor. The LT1 got composite rocker arm covers and modified piston rings. The only other changes were Dex-Cool engine coolant designed for 100,000 miles, Dextron III transmission fluid intended to triple the miles between changes even under severe use, and platinum-tipped spark plugs. The bi-fuel 4.3-liter engine and the Caprice station wagon police package were no longer available.

For 1996, the 3100 V-6 used in the Lumina was upgraded to roller rocker arms for less friction. The 3100 V-6 already had roller lifters as part of the 1995 Gen III improvements. The Lumina air intake was also improved with a mass air sensor for more precise air to fuel metering under a variety of ambient conditions.

The LT1 used in the Camaros picked up 10 hp to now be rated at 285 hp. This came from improved piston rings, a revised camshaft profile and improvements to both the intake and exhaust.

On the intake side the 1996 engine had a better match between the intake manifold port and the heads. On the exhaust side, the takedown pipe was increased in diameter, while the exhaust pipes remained at 2.75 inches. A second catalytic converter was added. The mufflers were increased from the 4 inch by 19 inch Federal emissions mufflers to the 5 inch by 11 inch California emissions mufflers.

The camshaft profile introduced on the 1995 LT1 used in the Caprice was used on the 1996 LT1 used in the Camaro. The combination of all these changes dropped the back pressure from 17 inches of mercury at 5000 rpm to 12.5 inches at the same engine speed. The result was 10 additional horsepower.

Acceleration Slip Regulation (ASR) traction control was announced on the 1995 Camaros but not actually available until the 1996 model year. ASR is not part of the B4C special service package but is an option on all Camaros. This opens the door to the Camaro B4C as an all-season police vehicle. Some police Camaros are literally used only on sunny days. They are not used when it rains in the southern states and are not used when it snows in the northern states. Really.

ASR changes all of that. The Delco ABS-VI traction control system on the Camaro is similar to the Bosch system used on the Corvette. If one of the rear tires starts to spin, the ABS system on that particular wheel only is activated. A throttle relaxer using spring pressure pushes back on the throttle pedal. If tire slip continues, spark is retarded to reduce engine torque. If the wheel spin still continues, up to three fuel injectors are shut down. It all happens in a quarter of a second.

The ASR does, indeed, affect the vehicle performance when the car is driven to the limit. For this reason, the Camaro's traction control can be turned off and on by the driver. Each time the Camaro is started, the ASR defaults to the "on" mode. A police Camaro with the ASR traction control turned off performs exactly like a police Camaro not fitted with the ASR.

The 1996 Caprice 9C1 on its final lap during Michigan State Police testing. In its last year, the 350-cid-powered Caprice won all six test phases making it the MSP test winner for 10 straight years. (Tom Yates)

The Lumina 9C3, such as this Illinois State Police unit, became the only front-drive police package car for 1996. Its 3.1-liter/160 hp V-6 pulled the Lumina to 122 mph. (Greg Reynolds)

The new Chevrolet police vehicle for 1996 is the four-door Geo Tracker, which has an 11-inch longer wheelbase than the two-door Tracker. The four-door Tracker special service package is actually a response to the two-door Trackers currently in service with the Baltimore, Maryland, police and Huntington Beach, California, police.

The Tracker is an entry level vehicle for police use where speed is not a priority. It is a low cost utility vehicle for airports, campuses and parking control. Other possible applications involve patrol on beaches, in metro parks, shopping malls and hospital complexes.

The Tracker is powered by a 1.6-liter, double overhead cam, multi-port fuel-injected, inline four-cylinder producing 95 hp. It uses an electronic overdrive four-speed automatic. The police version is available only in two-wheel (rear) drive. The police-spec Tracker uses 15-inch steel or aluminum wheels and all-season radials. The brakes are front discs and rear drums with ABS as an option. Chevrolet plans to evaluate the success of the Tracker as a police vehicle after one year of service.

In its last year as a police package vehicle, the Caprice faced a challenge during the Michigan State Police tests from a most unlikely source: Volvo. The Volvo 850 Turbo was a mid-size front-drive sedan with a wheelbase and weight close to the Lumina. However, the Volvo fleet and technical officials bragged that their car was at the MSP runoffs specifically to knock off the LT1 Caprice.

Volvo first splashed on the police fleet scene during the fuel crises of the mid-1970s. *Motor Trend* magazine pushed the Volvo 164E in a series of articles as the ideal police car for the times. *Motor Trend* and the LASD were jointly researching a more fuel-efficient, downsized police car that gave good overall performance. The result of this effort was widespread acceptance of the now-famous Chevy Nova 9C1, circa 1975, followed by the successful, downsized Chevy Malibu 9C1, circa 1979.

Volvo tried the police market again in the mid-1980s with its baseline 240 Turbo equipped with a taxi package. This, too, resulted in only a limited market penetration, and the police package was not pursued.

For 1996, Volvo is back in the police market with an 850 Turbo police sedan and an 850 Turbo police station wagon. Both cars are powered by a transverse-mounted, inline five-cylinder engine fitted with a single turbo. No domestic automaker has ever released a police package on a car powered by a turbocharged engine.

The bitter rivalry between Chevrolet and Volvo started in 1975. The Los Angeles County Sheriffs Department declared the Volvo 164E the technical winner, but instead it was the Nova that was developed into the darling of Southern California police fleets.

A lot was at stake in 1996. Chevrolet wanted to retire the Caprice as a winner. It wanted to extend the Caprice's winning streak to 10 years straight. Volvo had a two decade old grudge to settle. If it could bump the Caprice off the top of the hill, cops would look at the Volvo differently in 1997 when there was no Caprice. A victory over the SOHC Crown Victoria would be meaningless. The LT1 Caprice was the best police car ever made. Volvo wanted to beat the best.

The Volvo 850 Turbo was twice as expensive as the police package Caprice. However, under the Michigan State Police method, a more expensive police car would win the contract if its performance was high enough. The bid price was adjusted by a performance factor based on the six tests. Even if the adjusted bid price was higher than

The incredible 1996 Camaro B4C, such as this Suffolk County, New York, Police cruiser, reached 159 mph during Michigan State Police testing. The 1996 Camaro is available with traction-control.

New for 1996 was the four-cylinder, two-wheel-drive, four-door Geo Tracker. The 1.6-liter DOHC Tracker is intended for parking enforcement.

Brian Tolen has been the B-body police platform engineer for all of the 1990s. He is a part of the team that produced the best police sedan ever built.

the Caprice, to beat the Caprice in heads-up competition would be an immense victory for Volvo.

The Volvo 850 Turbo was bristling with technology. It used a 2.3-liter (142-cid) five-cylinder engine. The 20 valve, double overhead cam fuel-injected and turbocharged engine was rated at 222 hp. Weighing 850 pounds less than the Caprice, Volvo technicians claimed the Volvo sedan would reach 150 mph. With four-wheel discs, ABS and 60-series Z-rated tires, the Volvo promised to be a threat both during braking tests and around the MIS road course.

The LT1 Caprice took to the Chelsea 4.7-mile oval first. Its quarter-mile, 0-100 mph and top speed performance was similar to 1995. It ran the quarter-mile in the low 16s and topped out at 139 mph. The SOHC Crown Victoria was next. The big Ford reached 135 mph, which set a top speed record for blue oval sedans. Remember, that is as fast as the 5.0-liter HO Mustangs ran. As impressive as that performance was, nobody noticed. Cops from 50 states were too focused on the Chevrolet-Volvo showdown. The 4.3-liter Caprice was next. No one cared. All this did was build the anxiety. Rumors circulated among the cops that *Car & Driver* magazine really did get a Volvo 850-T to 150 mph.

Finally, the Volvo 850-T took to the oval. In order, the performance was radioed in. Quarter-mile in the mid-16s. Zero to 100 mph in the mid-20s. Top speed: 126 mph. V-8 torque and LT1 pushrod technology had won the day.

The Caprice kept up the pace by setting an all-time record stopping distance for any four-door police sedan. The big Chevrolet stopped in just 133.1 feet. The big Ford was four inches behind in its best braking performance ever. The 4.3-liter Caprice was next. Then the Camaro four-speed. Then the Volvo, a half a car length back.

By the time the police cars were transferred to the MIS road course, most of the cops had lost interest in the Volvo. It clearly did not have the performance to beat the LT1 Caprice, let alone the performance to justify its vehicle cost. The attention returned to the LT1 Caprice versus SOHC Crown Victoria for the last and most heavily weighted test phase.

The LT1 Caprice captured the road course lap time honors. To commemorate its last appearance at MIS, Chevrolet Fleet personnel piled into the big sedan for a final victory lap. Special Vehicles program manager Bob Hapiak proudly displayed the Chevrolet flag on this final lap. Two weeks later the ergonomics and EPA numbers were available.

In the history of MSP vehicle testing, a single full-size police car has won all six test phases only three times. The 1990 Caprice. The 1991 Caprice. And in its last year, the 1996 Caprice. No other full-size car has done it once. The Caprice did it three times in seven years. Winning the price and performance based MSP contract 10 years in-a-row (1987 to 1996) clearly proved the Caprice was the best overall police car ever made by anyone.

While the 1996 LT1 Caprice marks the end of an era in police vehicles, it also set an incredibly high standard of performance by which to measure future police cars.

The LT1 Caprice was not the only newsmaker during the MSP tests. The LT1 Camaro four-speed and LT1 Camaro six-speed both set new top speed records: 159 mph and 157 mph, respectively. The Lumina 9C3 turned in an overall performance quite close to the 4.3-liter Caprice and also stopped in the shortest distance it ever had. The Geo Tracker was considered a humorous distraction during the great Chevrolet-Volvo showdown. However, the four-door Tracker was well-mannered around the MIS road course.

Larry Stout has been the driving force behind the Lumina police package from the beginning. The rear discs on the 1995 Lumina and a 3.8-liter V-6 on the future Lumina are due largely to Stout's persistence.

Without the flagship Caprice, many cops are uncertain about the future of Chevrolet police vehicles. However, some things are well known.

The Camaro B4C will continue to be available indefinitely. The Ford special service package for the Mustang contained many unique components. This is not true of the Chevrolet special service package for the Camaro. With the exception of the certified speedometer, the Camaro uses Z28 parts to meet the police requirement for durability. This is important. Selling 800 to 1,000 police Camaros per year does not justify a wide variety of police-only components.

With the pursuit power of the LT1 available in the Caprice, major agencies such as the California Highway Patrol and Michigan State Police have stopped buying the Camaro for special traffic enforcement duties. However, other agencies are buying the Camaro for the first time. The police demand for the pursuit pony car has remained at just under 1,000 units per year.

In 1998, the police Lumina will be getting the engine that was planned for the 1995 restyle. This is the 200 hp 3800 V-6 currently used in the Buick Regal. The bump to 200 hp will make the Lumina B4C run like a Monte Carlo Z34. Since the 3800 V-6 has more torque than the Z34's DOHC 3.4-liter engine, the new 3.8-liter Lumina B4C will even be faster than the Z34.

Rumors persist about a stretched wheelbase version of the Lumina, dubbed the Impala, in the 1999 time frame. Rumor has it that a V-8 may be part of the police package for this future front-drive car. Chevrolet Fleet will only say "stay tuned." They have, however, stated that Chevrolet's future four-door police car will have the overall performance of the 1996 LT1 Caprice as a starting point.

One new Chevrolet police vehicle was announced at the Detroit Auto Show in January 1996. Chevrolet's worst kept police secret is the Tahoe police package. The Tahoe is now available as a four-door and it already comes with a 5.7-liter engine. The test mule police Tahoe had the same rear axle and rear discs used on the LT1 Caprice. The production police Tahoe uses rear drums. Lowered by one inch and available only in two-wheel drive (rear), the police Tahoe includes police wheels, pursuit radials, Bilstein shocks and huge sway bars.

The concept police Tahoe was powered by the L31 5700 Vortec V-8. This was cammed and tuned differently than the LT1 5.7-liter V-8 in the Caprice. The LT1 has 260 hp and 330 pound-feet of torque. The L31 has 255-hp and 330 pound-feet of torque. Both use sequential fuel injection and the electronic four-speed AOD transmission. The 4,200-pound 115.9-inch wheelbase Caprice used 3.08 gears. The 4,866-pound, 117.5-inch wheelbase Tahoe used 4.10 rear gears. Chevrolet engineers say the Tahoe will hit 120 mph. The Tahoe test mule driven by the Michigan State Police was powered around the MIS road course in nearly the same time as the LT1 Caprice.

The industry trade journal *Automotive News* was the first to break the story on the demise of the Caprice. In the February 6, 1995, issue, *Automotive News* reported that the Arlington, Texas, assembly plant that produces GM's large rear-wheel sedans would be converted to assemble full-size pickup trucks and sport utility vehicles. The three GM300 platform cars affected by this change are the Chevrolet Caprice, Buick Roadmaster and Cadillac Fleetwood.

The report said the assembly plant would build at least 12,000 Caprice police cars and Impala SS sport sedans (civilian version of the police package) to fill orders that were already on the books. It also reported that Chevrolet had canceled open orders for 4,000 police cars. It normally builds 35,000 police cars a year. The plant was scheduled to build cars through August then convert to truck assembly. The only change for the 1996 models was reported to be the VIN.

Chevrolet's concept of a full-size, rear-drive, V-8-powered replacement for the Caprice is this modified Tahoe. The lowered, two-wheel-drive Tahoe is powered by a 5.7-liter Vortec V-8. (Chevrolet)

The 5.7-liter/255-hp Vortec V-8 pushes this 4,860-pound police Tahoe to 120 mph. Michigan State Police test drivers found it to be as fast around the road course as the 4.6L Crown Victoria. (Chevrolet)

Bob Hapiak has been the police program manager for Chevrolet Specialty Vehicles since the Caprice dominance in the mid-1980s.

In the Money section of the February 6, 1995, copy of *USA Today*, Chevrolet spokesman Bill O'Neill clarified the position. He said the final decision would not be made until April or May. He also said Chevrolet might consider building the Caprice 9C1 and Impala SS at other, underworked plants. However, he added that doesn't mean it will be the Caprice as you see it today.

In 1994, the Arlington facility assembled 156,967 Chevrolet, Buick and Cadillac models. The demand for these cars had been light compared to the heavy demand for light trucks and sport-utility vehicles. The capacity at Arlington was for 250,000 vehicles. GM simply wanted that capacity for the hot selling and profitable light trucks. Industry analysts said Chevrolet could have sold these 250,000 trucks if they had them. The fleet bid, cut-throat profit margins that Chevrolet made on the Caprice 9C1 just made the decision easier. The Impala SS retailed in 1995 for $24,500 while the Caprice 9C1 fetched only $14,700. Mag wheels and leather seats were the only differences.

Police and taxi fleet managers from around the country began a letter writing campaign objecting to the plans to drop the Caprice. Impala SS enthusiasts either bought the car they longed for right then or put the one they owned up on blocks. Ford Fleet rubbed their hands together in glee just waiting for the time to add $5,000 to the bid price of their Crown Victoria. Everyone else just waited.

General Motors made its final decision on May 16, 1995. In a report the next day in the Money section of *USA Today*, GM confirmed its ear-

lier plans. It wanted the Arlington facility to make 1997 model trucks. The GM300 platform would be history after December 13, 1996.

Chevrolet agreed to make up to 25,000 1996 Caprice police cars. It also knew the Lumina 9C3 was not a suitable replacement for the Caprice 9C1, according to nearly all police fleet managers. Chevrolet also agreed to look into ways to improve the Lumina to make it more suitable for a wider variety of police roles. Specifically, this meant a lot more power.

The Texas Department of Public Safety (state troopers) had used the Caprice since 1989. The DPS fleet coordinator, Jerry Newberry, summed up all of law enforcement when he said, "Chevrolet finally got the car exactly as we wanted it."

As early as August 1994, RCI, Inc. expressed interest in buying Caprice body, suspension, engine and frame components to make modified police cars. RCI is owned by Michigan Congressman Richard Chrysler (no relation to Chrysler Corporation). RCI, Inc. and its Cruisers, Inc. subsidiary outfits police cars and performs special, off-line work for all the automakers. RCI's plans were for a Caprice-based vehicle made specifically for cops, much like mail carriers now use vehicles designed specifically for their needs.

After the February 1995 GM announcement, RCI increased the pressure on Chevrolet. Richard Chrysler's plans were now to buy all the tooling and continue to build the Caprice, or a Caprice-like police vehicle at a Canadian auto factory. Chevrolet Fleet had repeatedly told

RCI "no" and in August 1995, GM made it official. It would not sell its GM300 tooling.

Chevrolet General Manager Jim Perkins discussed the replacement for the Caprice 9C1 at the National Automobile Dealers Association meeting in February 1995, shortly after the announcement. He admitted there was no direct replacement currently in place for the Caprice. He spoke of a gap between the time when the Caprice is phased out and a suitable replacement is phased in. Chevrolet officials said the gap will occur in the 1997 and 1998 model years.

The only official word from Chevrolet was "stay tuned."

1996 Chevrolet Police Powertrains						
RPO	Type	Engine	HP	Trans	Axle	Model
n/a	I4	1.6L/97 cid	95	4-spd AOD	5.13	Tracker 2WD
L82	V-6	3.1L/191 cid	160	4-spd AOD	3.33	Lumina
LT1	V-8	5.7L/350 cid	285	4-spd AOD	3.23	Camaro
LT1	V-8	5.7L/350 cid	285	6-spd CAGS	3.42	Camaro
L99	V-8	4.3L/265 cid	200	4-spd AOD	3.23	Caprice
LT1	V-8	5.7L/350 cid	260	4-spd AOD	3.08	Caprice

1996 Michigan State Police Patrol Vehicle Test Results								
	Chevrolet	Ford	Chevrolet	Volvo	Chevrolet	Chevrolet	Chevrolet	Geo 2WD
Model	Caprice	Crown Vic	Caprice	850-T	Lumina	Camaro	Camaro	Tracker
Engine	350 cid pfi	281cid pfi	265 cid pfi	142cid turbo	191 cid pfi	350 cid tpi	350 cid tpi	97 cid pfi
HP, SAE	260	210	200	222	160	285	285	95
Transmission	4-spd AOD	4-spd AOD	4-spd AOD	4-spd AOD	4-spd AOD	4-spd AOD	6-spd man	4-spd AOD
Axle Ratio	3.08	3.27	3.23	n/a	3.33	3.23	3.42	5.13
Weight, test (lbs)	4,249	3,974	4,180	3,399	3,426	3,480	3,457	2,713
Wheelbase (in)	115.9	114.4	115.9	104.9	107.5	101.0	101.0	97.6
Road Course Lap Time	83.35	84.79	87.20	84.97	88.03	79.21	80.57	94.12
0-100 mph	21.47	25.18	32.00	24.14	32.19	16.65	15.99	n/a
Top Speed mph	139	135	120	126	122	159	157	99
1/4 mi. ET	16.14	16.89	18.05	16.65	17.90	14.98	14.99	21.21
1/4 mi. Speed	88.0	83.8	80.2	86.1	79.3	94.9	96.7	66.7
Braking, ft/sec2	29.10	29.02	28.41	26.90	25.03	28.10	n/a	26.53
Ergonomics, pts	217.2	206.1	217.2	160.9	179.6	158.2	158.2	132.2
EPA City fuel mpg	16.8	16.7	18.0	19.1	18.7	17.0	16.4	22.0

1998 Chevy Tahoe Police Package	
Engine	5.700 Vortec, 255-hp V-8
Drivetrain	RWD, 4-spd AOD, 4.10:1 axle
Chassis	117.5 inch wheelbase; 4,866 pounds
Brakes	11.6 inch disc, front; 11.2 inch drum, rear
0-60 mph	9.42 sec
0-100 mph	28.90 sec
Top Speed	121 mph
1/4 mile	17.2 sec @ 81.5 mph

References for 1996

Chevrolet Police Packages, 1996 Specialty Vehicles, Chevrolet Motor Division

1996 Police Patrol Vehicle Evaluation and Purchasing Program, Michigan State Police

"Caprice Future in Doubt," Tom Yates, *Law and Order*, March 1995

"GM Axing Sedans?" *USA Today*, February 6, 1995

"GM Scraps Big Cars," *USA Today*, May 17, 1995

"Caprice Discontinued," Tom Yates, *Law and Order*, July 1995

"Badges?" World News, *AutoWeek*, August 7, 1995

"Chevrolet is Back!" Tom Yates, *Law and Order*, January 1996

Chapter 43

Chevy Cop Cars in California

By John Bellah

The Los Angeles County Sheriffs Department, along with many other law enforcement agencies, utilized Fords during the 1950s. One might assume, knowing the reputation of this professional law enforcement agency that LASD's Fords were Mercury powered. While this may have been true in the early 1950s, by 1955 things were different.

Overhead valve V-8s introduced in 1949 by Oldsmobile and Cadillac were showing that Henry's "flathead" V-8 was becoming rapidly obsolete. To stay competitive, Ford began to develop a new series of engines.

One of the first new engines was a Six. Introduced in 1952, this inline 215-cid Six featured overhead valves and a short stroke design. By the time this engine was in production, performance of this base engine was equal or better than the old flathead. Ford engineers had to increase compression on the V-8s to raise horsepower and keep things in perspective.

The exact reasoning why the department chose to equip its 1955 Ford Mainline four-door sedans with sixes is unknown. Economy, certainly would be one reason. This engine, being somewhat of a "sleeper," gave the county a lot of bang for its buck. Similar cars were purchased for the next year, 223-cid six-cylinder Ford sedans, which now developed 137 bhp, and were equipped with three-speed manual transmissions.

With Los Angeles becoming the "Hot Rod Capital of the World," V-8-powered patrol cars were specified. Ford sedans, powered by 312-cid four-barrel carbureted engines developing 245 bhp and equipped with Ford-O-Matic transmissions, patrolled the county in 1957. The next year, Chevrolet sedans with V-8 engines and automatic transmissions were purchased.

It is unknown exactly what engine/transmission combination these 1958 Chevrolets were equipped with, as records on these cars had long been purged. The best information is that the 283-cid, four-barrel carbureted V-8 developing 230 bhp, or 348-cid, four-barrel carbureted V-8 developing 250 bhp and Powerglide were used. Nevertheless, the same complaints voiced by LAPD officers regarding '58 Chevys were repeated by deputies. One deputy related that he hated to work one day of his work week—a different patrol beat than the one he was usually assigned—because a '58 Chevy was the car assigned to the beat for which he filled in.

The L.A. County Sheriffs Department returned to Chevrolet for 1961. By then some of the brake problems were corrected in the 1959 model year with wider brake linings both front and rear, giving an additional 30 square inches of lining area. Again, best information indicates that the 1961 sheriffs' Biscaynes were powered by 348 cid, four-barrel carbureted V-8s mated to Turboglide transmissions.

Introduced in 1957, the Turboglide transmission featured infinite ratios and extremely smooth operation. There was no Low gear position on the quadrant. Instead, this transmission featured a "Grade Retard" or "Hill Retard" position for engine braking going down hills. In the real world, the Turboglide was far more costly and troublesome than the tried and proven Powerglide. Old-time Chevy mechanics related that in the recession year of 1958, during road tests of customers' cars brought in for routine service, Turboglides were deliberately damaged to generate warranty revenue. It wouldn't take much: race the engine and slam the transmission into the Grade Retard position, and then slam it into Reverse and accelerate.

The Arizona Highway Patrol soon found that its Turboglide-equipped Chevrolet cruisers didn't like high temperatures. Sitting at idle in the hot desert with the air conditioner on for prolonged periods would soon generate enough heat to cause the transmission oil to break down. The trooper would soon realize he'd have a problem when he would put the car in Drive and accelerate—or attempt to accelerate. The next radio call his dispatcher would hear is a request for a tow truck for the stranded trooper.

The LASD migrated to Plymouths for the next couple of years. Ralph Nader, in his book *Unsafe At Any Speed* related that L.A. County purchased vehicles from Chrysler Corporation because they produced fewer exhaust emissions, even though they were not the lowest bidder. This may have been at least partially true, as Chrysler was developing an exhaust emissions package around that time period. It is strongly suspected that the sheriffs' 1962 Plymouths were used to test this exhaust emissions package. Engine photos of the 1962 LASD units show they were equipped with emissions equipment that was not available for another two years. Air pollution was a hot topic in L.A. County at that time.

By the mid-1960s, the automotive-buying public was becoming interested in performance. In this case performance was not limited to

The 1958 Delray was used by the Los Angeles Police. The car turned out to be too heavy for the standard brakes. Moraine sintered metallic brake shoes became a mid-year option. This solved the problem. (LAPD)

a hot engine. The car-buying public, whose views were amplified by automotive journalists, demanded better handling and brakes, just as major fleet buyers demanded for years, these buyers being from law enforcement agencies such as the California Highway Patrol, Los Angeles Police and Sheriffs Departments.

Another problem Chevrolet was addressing was that of automatic transmissions. With the Turboglide being dropped in 1961, Chevrolet stuck doggedly with its Powerglide automatic. The Powerglide being a two-speed affair, was rapidly becoming obsolete. A two-speed automatic behind a big engine would be adequate to commute to work or to the grocery store in areas that are flat and level. Towing a trailer, driving a fully loaded station wagon through mountain passes or even passing another car on a two-lane highway soon reveals the necessity of an intermediate gear.

Part of the problem rested with Chevrolet's reluctance to change. After all, it was the Number One seller! Millions of Powerglide-equipped Chevrolets were sold and were running around, so why change a good thing? Chevrolet engineering staff realized the limitations of the two-speed Powerglide, as the more efficient, four-speed Hydra-Matic had been an option in Chevrolet and GMC trucks for several years. Manual transmissions were subtly recommended by Chevrolet for high performance police work. Chevrolet was losing the police car business on the West Coast, as most agencies were now specifying automatic transmissions with three or more forward speeds. Later, in the mid-1960s, Chevrolet became aware that it was losing sales to the competition that had been offering three-speed automatics for several years.

Chevrolet wanted to build its own three-speed automatic. During the early 1960s the rumor floated about that Chevrolet was going to produce a three-speed Powerglide for 1964. General Motors, however, had different ideas and was looking toward standardization. In the end, GM won, and the three-speed Turbo-Hydra-Matic became a mid-year option in 1965 for full-size Chevrolets equipped with the big-block 396-cid engine.

For 1966, Chevrolet finally had a car that was eligible for the LAPD/LASD vehicle tests. A 325 bhp, four-barrel carbureted, 396-cid engine coupled to a Turbo-Hydra-Matic transmission propelled the Biscayne sedan around the Pomona test track at 84 mph. Moraine metallic brakes and a revised suspension system gave the Biscayne an "Acceptable" rating as a police car, compared to previous models that were not considered acceptable because of poor handling and a two-speed automatic transmission.

The Los Angeles County Sheriffs Department purchased a quantity of 1967 Chevrolets for uniformed patrol. These cars were similar to the Arizona Highway Patrol cruisers purchased that year. They had 396-cid engines, Turbo-Hydra-Matic transmissions, heavy-duty police suspensions, with front and rear anti-sway bars, and power-assisted front disc brakes. It is unknown how these cars were received by the deputies, but most likely, they were better cars than the 390-cid Fords the department purchased the previous year.

Black and white Plymouths wore the sheriff's insignia for the next year, and would continue for several years until the AMC Matador dominated the police car business into the mid-1970s.

In the spring of 1974, two Chevrolet engineers sat down to an informal dinner with members of the Los Angeles County Sheriffs Department. The outcome of this meeting revolutionized the police car as we then knew it.

The Los Angeles County Sheriffs Department was the driving force behind the development and street success of the 1975-1978 Nova 9C1. This was the ultimate urban police car for its era. (LASD)

In some cases, a police cruiser is similar to a taxicab, only with a large engine. The LASD was taking a long, hard look to see if a more economical police car could be utilized, without sacrificing performance. This was even before the famous "Energy Crisis" of 1973-74, which caused long lines of people at filling stations attempting to obtain gasoline. Fueled by this energy crunch, the LASD accelerated its efforts in locating a more economical police package vehicle.

Attending a special meeting were Chevrolet engineers Harry Hammond and Jim Ingle, Lt. Bill Kirtley of LASD, and John Christy, executive editor of *Motor Trend*. What was not published is that John Christy was also a reserve deputy sheriff with LASD. Kirtley and Christy outlined the department's desire for a smaller, better handling and stopping patrol car, which would have equal performance to their current patrol cars, yet be more economical. What the LASD officials didn't know is that the Chevrolet engineers were again kicking around the idea of a Nova police sedan.

About a month after this milestone meeting, the two Chevrolet engineers drove a prototype police Nova from Detroit to Los Angeles for testing and evaluation. To the uninformed this "plain Jane" sedan looked like any of the thousands of Nova sedans produced that year. A closer look at this innocent looking white sedan revealed the a rear anti-sway bar had been mounted just under the differential and that the car was resting on four E-70X14 bias-belted "Wide Oval" tires. Starting the engine clearly revealed that something more potent than a 250-cid Six or 307-cid two-barrel carbureted V-8 rested under the hood.

A test drive revealed this 350-cid, four-barrel carbureted V-8-powered high-performance compact sedan not only had excellent straight-line performance, but had excellent handling qualities and brakes that were almost impossible to fade. After three days of extensive testing, LASD officials were so impressed that an additional 15 of these special Novas were produced for field testing under actual working conditions. Eleven of these cars were purchased by LASD, with the remaining four cars immediately purchased by the Fountain Valley (California) Police Department.

A closer look at the police Nova, or later referred to as the COPO 9C1, showed the Chevrolet engineers dug into various parts bins from the Impala, Camaro, Chevelle and even the truck division to come up with the winning combination. Brake and suspension components came from the Camaro Z28, Chevelle and the full-size Impala. The engine cooling fan and thermal clutch are a Chevy C series truck item.

The next year, 1975 brought about new problems to overcome. It is one thing to build a prototype car, but a finished production vehicle is another matter. First, the 1975 Novas were redesigned. The body was larger and slightly heavier. The suspension was redesigned, using suspension components borrowed from the Chevelle series. Another set of problems was that these cars needed to meet all Federal emissions and safety standards. They also had to meet the more stringent California emissions standards, from which even police cars were not exempt. Also, 1975 was the first year for the catalytic converter. Would this component rob the police Nova of the performance edge that the prototype cars had?

As it turned out, the production 1975 Novas were better than the prototype cars. Ride harshness was gone, while handling improved. Even with the 1975 emission controls and catalytic muffler the Nova consistently produced quarter-mile acceleration trap speeds of 83.5 mph. The front disc brakes with semi-metallic pads and huge 11-inch rear drums were still almost impossible to fade, snubbing the car down at a rate of 1.2g. Was the department sold? Well, maybe not completely, at least that year. The department split the bid and ordered half Novas, and half 360-cid Plymouth Furys. Again, a close watch of the performance and operating expenses of both vehicles was undertaken.

In the meantime, the department held its breath to see how the deputies would react to the idea of a compact patrol car.

As it turned out, the first 33 Novas that left the automotive section after being outfitted were snapped up by members of the Special Enforcement Bureau. The SEB is a mobile group of deputies that handled civil unrest and other problems. This group is similar to LAPD's Metropolitan Division, and is considered a "prestige" assignment. Other deputies soon jumped on to the Nova bandwagon. An initial test drive in what essentially is a Z28 four-door sedan sold most deputies. Even today, deputies who were on the job in the late-1970s reminisce and say, "The Nova was the best police car, ever!"

The LASD switched entirely over to Novas the next year. Other law enforcement agencies followed the department's lead, and purchased Novas. Even the LAPD purchased 16 police-spec Novas in two-door configuration as undercover cars.

Give credit where credit is due. Go back a couple of years prior to the Bicentennial year, when the LASD formed the Automotive Group to research the problem of trying to determine what is the ideal police car. That group consisted of members from within the department and outside automotive experts. Those from outside the LASD were appointed as Technical Reserve Deputies, and donated their time and efforts. Included from the outside were Harris R. Bierman, associate editor, and John Christy, executive editor, of *Motor Trend*. Christy went on to write a series of articles about the development of the compact police car.

The Automotive Group took over the testing procedure from LAPD and revised the vehicle tests to determine the ideal vehicle for police service. In addition to the old test procedures of recording acceleration, handling and braking, the revised procedures used some of *Motor Trend's* testing methods. Fuel mileage, ergonomics, ease of maintenance and reliability were also factored in. These methods are still in use today.

When the dust settled from the revised testing, the top scoring vehicle was not the Nova, nor any other traditional American police car. The top scoring vehicle, by a fraction of a point, was the Volvo 164E. Used by many law enforcement agencies in England and Europe, the police Volvo is specifically engineered for police service. During assembly, Volvos intended for police service are pulled off the assembly line and sent to the Special Vehicle section. There the car is fitted with a police suspension system, heavy-duty electrics with extra relays for police electrical equipment, a special automatic transmission, and heavy-duty interior. The car is then returned to the line for final assembly and for outfitting with whatever additional options the purchaser desires. Operators of Volvos in European police service utilize them in excess of 150,000 miles before retirement.

Powered by a fuel-injected 182-cid inline Six producing 138 nhp, the Volvo ripped through the standing quarter-mile at 84.5 mph; the Nova was 1.5 mph slower. Handling and stopping were about equal. The Volvo proved itself superior in maneuverability, and fuel mileage. Even though the initial cost of the Volvo was higher, when resale value was factored in, the Volvo was more cost-effective. While government agencies normally look for the most "bang for the buck," the Nova was chosen over the Volvo. Perhaps the department felt that it was un-American to have the sheriff's star affixed to the doors of a foreign-built cruiser. Another consideration was parts and service. In Southern California, Chevrolet dealers outnumber Volvo dealers by a considerable margin.

Eventually, the LASD converted its entire marked vehicle fleet to Novas. When Chevrolet stopped offering a police package on the Nova, the Malibu made its debut in police service beginning in 1979. The LASD continued on with Chevrolet until 1982, when it purchased a quantity of 318-cid, four-barrel carbureted Plymouth Gran Furys.

The 1979 Malibu 9C1, such as this Los Angeles County Sheriffs Department unit, picked up on the success of the Nova 9C1. Powered by 305-cid and 350-cid V-8s, the shorter wheelbase Malibu was a widely used police car. (LASD)

By 1984, Chevrolet ceased production of the Malibu, and the LASD purchased a quantity of Ford LTDs. Not to be confused with the Crown Victoria, these mid-sized sedans powered by a fuel-injected, 5.0-liter V-8 exhibited Nova-type performance and handling. In the real world, these "Olympic Fords" had nowhere near the braking capability of the Nova. Interior room, or the lack of, was another problem.

From there the LASD went to the full-size Impala for patrol duties. Part of the reason for the larger car is officer safety. The larger,

The Los Angeles County Sheriffs Department used the Impala or Caprice for most of the 1980s. This is a 1990 LASD Caprice used by a K-9 officer. (Bill Hattersley)

A 1992 Caprice used by the Los Angeles County Sheriffs Department. While the Los Angeles Police selected the 305-cid V-8, the sheriffs' cars all had the 350-cid V-8. (LASD)

body-on-frame sedans offer the deputy more protection in the event of a collision than do the smaller unit-construction vehicles. Another concern is that in the high-tech 1990s, the full-size car affords more room for the deputy, his or her partner, the shotgun, Mobile Digital Computer, security cage for prisoners, air bags and other assorted law-enforcement gear.

As with the Novas, the LASD Impalas and then Caprices were powered by the 350-cid V-8. As time progressed, the Rochester Quad-raJet four-barrel carburetor was replaced by fuel-injection, and the overdrive automatic replaced the Turbo-Hydra-Matic transmission.

Stopping is assisted by ABS. For the 1990s, the Caprice Classics are powered by the 5.7-liter LT1 engine, which produces 260 nhp. The

4L60 overdrive automatic handles shifting chores. To give an example of where the power band is on both the 4.3-liter and LT1 engine, full-throttle 1-2 and 2-3 shift points are set at 6000 rpm, shifting from third gear into overdrive occurs at 4600 rpm.

Like LAPD's Ray Wynne, John Christy was the LASD's man with a vision. Christy attended the University of Miami, receiving a degree in psychology, then served three years as a police reporter in Chicago. Armed with circle track roadster racing experience, he then joined Peterson Publishing Company as managing editor of *Hot Rod*. From there he became the first editor for *Car Craft*. Christy left to freelance and became an editor for *Sports Car Illustrated*, while engaging in SCCA-type racing. He then returned to Peterson as editor

A Los Angeles County Sheriffs Department 1995 Caprice with twin spotlights and a MX-7000 lightbar. In 1995, Chevrolet produced a bi-fuel version of the 265-cid V-8 specifically for the California market. (Bill Hattersley)

for *Sports Car Graphic*, and eventually became executive editor to *Motor Trend*, until he retired in the early-1980s. Sadly, Christy succumbed to cancer in 1993 at the age of 70. Without Christy's dedication in serving as a member of the LASD, and his automotive contacts as a *Motor Trend* staff member, the COPO 9C1 Nova would have never happened. Today's police officer owes a debt of gratitude to men such as G. Ray Wynne and John Christy for their endeavors in producing better and safer police vehicles.

References

"Torture Testing Police Cars," Bill Carroll, *Popular Science*, June 1960

Patrol Administration, G. Douglas Gourley

"What Police Cars Are Made Of," Steve Kelly, *Motor Trend*, June 1966

"M.T.'s Plan to Save The Taxpayers $320 Million," John Christy, *Motor Trend*, July 1974

"You've Got The Wrong Car, Officer," John Christy, *Motor Trend*, August 1974

"Police Nova," John Christy, *Motor Trend*, June 1975

"Super Nova," John Christy, *Motor Trend*, September 1976

"How Hot Are The Police Specials?" Ray Brock, *Hot Rod* , February 1959

"Ranchero vs. El Camino" Ray Brock, *Hot Rod*, February 1959

Unsafe At Any Speed, Ralph Nader

Police Transportation Management, G. Ray Wynne, Coda Publications, 1965

"Police Test The 66's," G. Ray Wynne, *Road Test*, May 1966

"Police Cars-Really That Fast?" G. Ray Wynne, *Super Street*, August 1968

Dodge, Plymouth & Chrysler Police Cars 1956-1978, Edwin Sanow and John Bellah, Motorbooks International (1994)

History Of The Chevrolet Nova, Los Angeles County Sheriffs Department.

Vehicle Log In Book, Los Angeles Police Department

Annual Report, 1955 to current, Los Angeles Police Department

1984 Yearbook, Los Angeles Police Department

1991 Annual, California Highway Patrol

Special Purpose Vehicle Study, California Highway Patrol, 1982

Police Catalogs, 1963 to current, Chevrolet Motor Division

Police Catalogs, 1952 to current, Ford Motor Company

Chevrolet '55-'56 Restoration Guide, Nelson Aregood, Wayne Oakley and Joe Umphenour, Motorbooks International

Standard Catalog Of American Cars 1946-1975, John Gunnell, Krause Publications

Standard Catalog of American Cars 1976-1986, James Flammang, Krause Publications.

The California Highway Patrol...Yesterday and Today, Robert Wick, Phase Three Publishing 1989

"The Twelve Camaros of the CHP," John Bellah, *Pursuit Vehicle News*, January 1995

Chapter 44

Police Car Collecting

by Jim Post

I've been driving cars of all varieties for more than 35 years and have owned more than 150 vehicles. I traded so many times in one year, I could have qualified for my state's "D" (dealer) tags! I retired after 25 years on the Kansas City (Missouri) Police Department. During the last third of my career I began collecting police memorabilia. My collection has now become the basis for a police museum. A natural extension of my police memorabilia collecting, when combined with my love for cars, was police car collecting. A police car is the largest police collectible available!

Compared to street rods, custom cars and exotics, police cars are a cheaper alternative. You're usually talking about a four-door sedan and not a coupe or convertible, basic black or white paint or both and not some exotic candy, pearl, metalflake mix. There's no need for chrome engine and undercarriages, blowers, trick wheels and custom interiors. Cop cars are the best of both worlds. They are interesting head turners and they are inexpensive.

I've got a lot of great memories from my years behind the wheels of cruisers. I spent more time in these cars and drove them more miles than all of my personal cars combined. These cars were my office, restaurant, safety zone and much more. During my career, I developed a real appreciation for these cars, their reliability, handling and impact on the motoring public.

As I began to meet owners of restored and daily driver police cars, I got hooked. I bought my first used police car in 1989. In 1991 I formed the Police Car Owners Of America (PCOOA). The club was formed to promote ownership and enjoyment of police cars, to prevent police cars from becoming taxis and to promote goodwill for the pro-

fession of law enforcement. To my knowledge, there had only been two prior attempts at forming police car clubs and they soon folded.

I suppose I was at the "right place at the right time" because my club took off like a big-block on nitro. With virtually no advertising, other than word-of-mouth, we had 200 members by our first anniversary. We still don't advertise, but we have been featured in several automotive publications, and we now number more than 700 members throughout the United States, Canada and overseas. Our national conventions have been featured in magazines and on television. I am constantly amazed by our growth and proud of this group and our positive impact wherever we go.

As president and founder of the PCOOA, I spend a great deal of time responding to inquiries about police cars. I'm often asked which police cars are the best. I usually recommend cars from highway/state patrols. These units normally have one driver for an eight-hour shift, versus a "big city" car that is operated around the clock by a number of officers.

The highway patrol cars are operated on the "open road" and not subjected to the abuse of their city counterparts. Frequently they are "take-home" units and offer a greater variety of colors. Unmarked cars used by detectives and supervisors make good choices too, but use caution, as some departments buy cars without the police package for this purpose. A quick comparison with a marked unit will reveal the differences. It is possible to find many good cars that saw prior service as marked city or county units. Just take your time.

Regardless of the car you do choose, try to find the car's history. Most departments keep detailed records, and some keep them forever. This record can tell you when it was serviced, warranty work done,

Police car shows are a family affair. This 1955 Two Ten is shown both at police car and classic Chevrolet events. (Bernard Veile)

This 1957 Bel Air is equipped exactly as the St. Paul, Minnesota, police used it. (Dennis Hale)

and if it was wrecked. Once you have determined which department your car came from, you will need the specific unit number. The unit number can usually be found hand painted on the spare, under the hood, in the glove compartment, on the dashboard, on the back of the rear view mirror, etc. The number is usually visible from outside the car. If the department had roof numbers, or numbers on the fenders or trunk lid, you can usually see the number in bright sunlight.

Once you've determined the number, contact the service facility and ask for the fleet supervisor. These requests for information are al-ways best in person versus the telephone. Discovering the history of your cruiser will require patience and some detective work, but that's half the fun! Several members have even tracked down officers/troopers assigned to their cars and their "war stories" can be entertaining.

Agencies dispose of their vehicles in a number of ways: public auction, sealed bid or dealer trade-in. There are several dealers around the country that specialize in used cruisers. They are a good source and can frequently provide service records. You can often buy the cars "as is" or have them painted or equipped to suit your taste. Some of

In 1962, the Pennsylvania State Police used special order Bel Airs, such as this perfectly restored unit complete with radar. (Mike Novatnak)

the nation's largest used police car dealers belong to the PCOOA and their names are listed herein. These dealers specialize in selling cruisers to small departments that can't afford new units, but they will also sell to the general public. The cars are re-conditioned and often have limited warranties.

Occasionally, used cruisers will show up in local papers, or in national automotive publications, but this is still fairly rare, because buyers looking for police cars are still a minority. The PCOOA quarterly publication *The Rapsheet* is a source for used police cars and equipment. Our newsletter is one of the benefits of a PCOOA membership, and classified ads are free to members. There are several cars advertised each issue, from high dollar restorations, to daily drivers and late models.

Another method for locating ex-cruisers in your area is to identify a specific department's cars that appeal to you. Contact that agency directly and ask them how they dispose of their cars. Most state patrol headquarters are located in the state capitol, and most large city or

Most police shows have different classes for restored and in-service police cars and for daily drivers. This 1964 Bel Air is one of the best. (Rick Barnes)

Headquarters for the Police Car Owners Of America is Eureka Springs, Arkansas. Police shows always include a lights-and-siren parade. (Jim Post)

Children of all ages have fun when the emergency lights and siren are used. The laws that cover emergency equipment vary by state. (Greg Reynolds)

state agencies have "Public Information Officers" who can help you, or direct you to someone who can. In smaller departments, check with the chief, sheriff, etc. These inquiries are always best in person. Finally, you can simply call your local taxi company and ask where they buy their cars—you can bet that most of them are ex-police cars!

What is a good used cruiser going to cost you? One preface is necessary when discussing cost. If the first question you ask about a used car is "How many miles has it got on it?" you shouldn't even be looking at police cars. The American motoring public has been brainwashed by car dealers into believing that high mileage is a negative. They use high mileage to further depreciate your trade-in and have developed tables to substantiate these reductions. Remember, police package cars are designed by the manufacturer to rack up high mileage.

I have always believed that the "kind" of miles on a car are more important than the "number" of miles. I would rather have a one-year-old car with 25,000 highway miles than a 25-year-old car with 1,000 "Sunday only" miles. Remember, too, that these cars are not going to get great gas mileage. That's the price we have to pay for wanting a car whose speedometer is calibrated beyond 85!

Another problem with pricing ex-police cars is that there is no category for them in any of the used car guides. Originally, they cost more to make than their "civilian" counterparts, but for a price guide, you must rely on the closest civilian comparison. If a "Tow Package" option is listed, you can figure it in, as it features many of the heavy-duty components a police package does.

Generally speaking, you will spend less for a used police car than you would for a comparable make and model family sedan. Sometimes you can find them for much less. It is not unheard of to find cruisers less than 10 years old for a few hundred dollars. Usually, you can find police cars priced below "wholesale" in the used car guides. Condition should be your determining factor in used police cars instead of odometer miles.

Naturally, expect to spend a little more at a dealer, but chances are that he has already performed necessary mechanical repairs. You'll also be paying for a greater selection, advertising, etc. Sealed bid and auctions can get you better prices, but some state auctions get pretty hectic, as you will be bidding against the taxi companies. As with any major purchase, take your time and research your options thoroughly.

Restoring an older cruiser is really a "bad news, good news" experience. The bad news is that police cars from the 1950s, '60s, and '70s are nearly extinct. This is because of several factors. First, they were never in great demand anyway and, after police service, the majority went to taxi companies that drove them until they dropped. Second, hundreds, perhaps thousands, were parted out for their high performance engines and parts, or they were used "as is" in jalopy races or demolition derbies. I can count on one hand the reports of old police car discoveries in salvage yards.

The good news is the cop cars of the 1950s and early-'60s were not all that different from their civilian counterparts. It is entirely possible to build a correct cruiser out of a civilian model. Through the use of vintage police car photos in this book and factory police package brochures it is possible to identify the necessary heavy-duty equipment.

When deciding upon the restoration of an old police car you have a decision to make. The first option is to locate a car first and then restore it. This can be a genuine police car or a replica. You can do some research to determine who may have used this type of car and then duplicate that department, or build a generic or novelty cruiser. There are a couple of excellent sources available to you to discover who might have used what type of cruiser. A generic car is one simply marked "Police" or "Sheriff" with correct period equipment. Novelty police cars are from non-existent departments, cars from the movies or television or cars with non-traditional modifications such as hot rod engines and customizing. When converting a stock sedan into a police car, factory police brochures will prove invaluable aids, as they provide specs, tire

This kind of police gear is available from a number of private sources. Note the MDT, four microphones and MPH radar unit. Everything except police lights and police radio frequencies is legal on a daily driver.

sizes, etc. The PCOOA has also established a library filled with vintage information and data and it is accessible to all members.

Your second restoration option is to select a department you're interested in first and then locate and build a car used by it. This can be a complex procedure as many smaller departments don't retain much historical data. Contact the department you're interested in and ask for its help. If the agency doesn't have the photos you need, it may be able to refer you to retirees who can help, because many officers have photos of themselves with their assigned cars. Don't forget about police mechanics and body repairmen either. They spend eight hours a day working on these beasts of burden. A final source of information can be your local libraries, newspapers and historical societies. Don't limit your photo search to police cars. Quite frequently photos of local events such as crowds, fires, disasters, parades, etc., will have police cars in them somewhere.

Another popular restored cruiser is one used in police movies or television shows. The best research method here is through modern technology. Obtain a videotape and locate the car you want to build. On "pause" you can usually photograph the image well enough to enlarge it and build your car. I used this technique to complete the final details on a 1974 Dodge Monaco "Bluesmobile" I once owned. Television shows can be more difficult, but videotapes of the more popular shows are starting to appear. Some members have had limited success with contacting production companies directly, but they advise to be patient. Movie and TV cars can be fun to build because the public can

readily identify with them. If your project is that of a long running series or a blockbuster movie, chances are good you can pick up toys, games, posters, etc., to display with the car.

Restoring a police car is both frustrating and rewarding. Frustrations are encountered when attempting to locate body parts and OEM/NOS equipment. Also, reproduction parts suppliers concentrate on the popular models and not the cheaper versions usually used in police packages. Frequently, large salvage yards are your best bet. Vintage emergency equipment and radios are available with some research. Original markings probably won't be available, but usually can be duplicated by local artists or sign painters. Vintage uniforms and equipment can add a lot to a display and can be found at police collector's shows around the country.

As a veteran police officer, I am acutely aware of the problem of police impersonators in this country. I have investigated crimes perpetrated by them and I have inadvertently sold police memorabilia that ended up in the hands of at least one of them. The problem has become so severe in the United States that at least one department (New York City Police) has even had to create a unit just to investigate these crimes. This is the primary reason many police departments may be reluctant to help collectors and restorers. On the other hand, I am naturally defensive about our right to own these cars because of what we are trying to accomplish with them and our club.

What are the laws concerning these cars? This is not an easy question to answer because laws vary from state to state and city to

This 1976 Caprice won first place in the daily driver class at a Midwest car show. Police car shows are held in over half of the states. (Jennifer Sturgeon)

city. The best idea, of course, is to thoroughly research your own city and state laws. Some basic observations, however, can be made.

Without exception, it is illegal to have red or blue lights on anything but emergency vehicles. Some states define that only those that face forward are outlawed. A few states have banned wig-wag (alternating) headlights. Don't panic when you read this however, because (in the majority of cases) you are only in violation if the lights are operating. This is a fine point I realize, but if the lights don't work, you usually won't get busted.

In every car I build, I add an extra fuse block to which I wire all the emergency equipment. The power lead to the fuse block is then connected to the battery with a quick release fitting of some type. En route to parades and car shows the power source is disconnected so all switches, lights and siren are inoperable. Upon arrival at the event, it is then a simple matter to connect the power. All my lights and equipment are permanently mounted in my cars. Because they are only used as show/parade cars, this system has met with the approval of law enforcement officials so far. Another method is to cover external lights en route to an event. There are velcro attached lightbar covers available commercially and some members have custom made light covers. Inside dash and deck lights can be covered as well. Some members have even modified lightbars with quick release wiring and roof mounts, so they can be easily installed at events.

Sirens fall under the same laws as emergency lights. Those traffic laws are only enforced if the sirens are in operation.

Most members like to detail their cars with correct period radios. I recommend installing "dummy" or inoperable radios only. Radios that transmit and receive on police frequencies are illegal nearly everywhere. I usually mount only the radio head, microphone and speaker. For realism at shows, several members have wired police scanners to broadcast through police radio speakers, or external speakers.

Many members have installed shotgun racks in their cars. Displaying these guns is not illegal, since they are not "concealed weapons," but they should be unloaded or made totally inoperable. Mine are in locked gun racks and further secured with trigger housing locks.

There are several different laws governing body markings. For example, California law requires door shields be covered during transport. The car must display "Out of Service" signs in the side windows. Illinois law prohibits the use of State Police markings without written permission. The easiest solution is to mount markings on magnetic sheet materials and install them upon arrival at an event. Magnetic sheet material is available on rolls in widths up to 30 inches and is paintable. The material can be used to mount door shields, fender markings and roof numbers. Some members have used magnetic markings at speeds up to 75 mph. One important note on magnetic markings: Do not leave them on your car too long. Moisture will build under them. Remember to store them flat. The decals are permanently mounted on my cars, so I simply reverse the above process. I cut the magnetic sheets to cover the decals.

Owning a police car is not unlike owning a firearm. Although legal to own, it's how you use it that can get you into trouble. Generally, the newer the cruiser, the more police attention you will attract, particularly if you own a make and model that is still in-service in your area. Twenty- or thirty-year-old cruisers are obviously restorations, but I have even had motorists hesitate to pass my 30-year-old state patrol car on the freeway! A working knowledge of your area's applicable laws, combined with good common sense should ensure a hassle-free ownership. Several members have obtained letters from the agencies their cars represent to keep in the glove compartment. These letters are not "blank checks," but simply state the owner has permission to own and operate the replica and the emergency equipment is only authorized while the car is in a parade or show. These letters seem to appease most traffic officers. Simply put, if you are not a police offic-

This boldly marked 1977 Impala, complete with Aerodynic lightbar, is a real eye-opener on the streets of England. Police car clubs exist in a dozen foreign countries. (John Restall)

er, don't do anything that would be construed as impersonating a police officer.

Despite the fact that restoring a police car is more difficult than restoring classic cars such as 1955 to 1957 Chevys or 1964 to 1966 Mustangs, it can prove rewarding. I've owned all types of cars. I've never had as much fun, and as much positive response to a car, as I have had with my police cars. I'm reminded of a friend who owns a 1957 Ford police car. He first displayed the car a few years ago at a "World of Wheels" car show. To the amazement and chagrin of show car owners with enough money invested in their cars to build his 1957 Ford 10 times over, my friend walked away with the coveted "Peoples Choice" trophy: The one award decided by the show attendees!

Our cars are in constant demand throughout the country for car shows, parades, charity events and movies. The kids love our cars and we have generated a great amount of good will for law enforcement, a profession that gets far too much bad press. If you are considering owning or restoring a police car, I can only quote a 1960's commercial: "Try it; you'll like it."

Chapter 45

1990 Caprice 9C1 Daily Driver

by Bill Hattersley

In January 1994, after seven years of driving a 1968 Ford Custom 500, I was ready for something different. A combination of factors enticed me into a retired cruiser: a fascination with emergency vehicles, the comfort of a well-equipped full-size car, a dislike for wimpy performance and mushy handling from most cars, a need for something durable (I drive 25,000-30,000 miles per year) and a limited budget that dictated something inexpensive.

I started studying my choices. A Washington State Patrol (WSP) cruiser was the obvious choice for several reasons. It was driven by only one trooper. State police agencies, particularly the WSP, are strict about maintaining their cars, while some local police agencies are more hit and miss. It had highway miles instead of city miles. It had cloth seats and power options. Complete service records came with the car.

The February sale was approaching. My choices had been narrowed to a 1988 Caprice, a 1989 Crown Victoria or a 1990 Caprice. Two mechanics advised me that the variable venturi carburetor on the Ford was troublesome. Both agreed the throttle body injection on the 1990 Chevrolet was superior to the QuadraJet of the 1988 Chevrolet.

The week preceding the auction, I made several trips to the state auction in Auburn, Washington, to inspect the cars. There were eight 1990 Caprices to be sold. Study of the car service records eliminated two cars because of bad transmissions, one car with a dead cylinder, one car with noisy differential, and one car with $3,000 in prior body damage. The remaining three choices had 99,000 to 102,000 miles on their odometers. This is typical for used state police cars. Study of the previous sale showed 1990 Caprices selling for $2,800 to $3,200.

Auction day, February 12, I took $3,250 with me. It was a shock when the 1990 Caprices started selling for $3,350 to $3,500. I decided the extra money was worth it and won the bidding on #120, the cleanest car, for $3,500. After a hurried trip to the cash machine, I paid for the car and secured a three day permit.

I was pleased with my purchase. On the way home, I discovered that all the accessories worked and the car ran strong. The following day, I laid out another $500 for tax and license. Evaluating the car further, I discovered a near perfect body and interior and four Goodyear F-32s with 70 percent tread. On the downside, the engine was noisy when cold and surged during warm-ups, the trunk leaked, and the delay wipers did not work correctly.

After a thorough cleaning, I visited salvage yards. The missing spotlight was replaced. Worn sill plates, drip moldings and center post interior trim pieces were replaced. A police option fitted rubber trunk mat, a dome reading lamp and aftermarket cruise control were also installed.

During further study of the repair log, I concluded the car had been driven hard. Based out of Ritzville, a flat area in eastern Washington, the trooper had nevertheless managed to wear out seven sets of front brakes. Transmissions were replaced at 63,000 and again at 85,000 miles. Also, two left exhaust manifolds had warped and been replaced. While taking care of existing problems, the alternator failed with only 20,000 miles on it. The trunk leak was worked on twice and finally corrected. A faulty idle air control valve was replaced to eliminate the surging.

In checking the brakes, I found the original rotors worn way undersize. The police brake rotors are common to many Buick, Oldsmo-

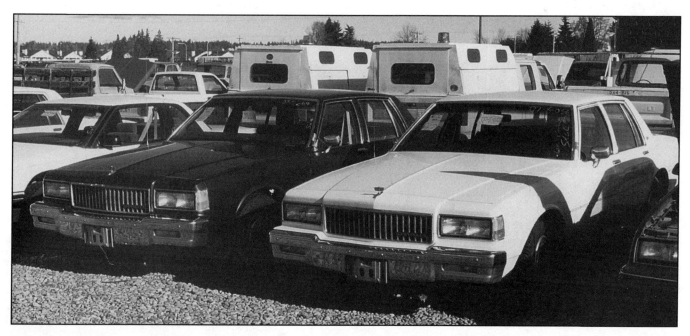

Used police cars are almost always sold at auction. Examples are a brown ex-Washington State Patrol 1988 Caprice sergeant's car (left) and the white ex-WSP 1990 Caprice "spongemobile." (Bill Hattersley)

The bodies on used, late-model police cars are generally good. However, ex-squads have the same problems as all cars with high mileage. (Bill Hattersley)

bile and Cadillac models, so a nice pair was easy to locate. Brake calipers, pads and one wheel bearing were replaced. All together, brake repairs cost less than $300. Front tire wear caused discovery of loose lower ball joints and worn idler arm. With alignment, repairs cost $300.

In May, while checking engine noises, the mechanic I had been using for three years found rod bearing noise under light load. After consulting a friend at the State Patrol, I decided to send the engine to Waterhouse Motors in Tacoma to be rebuilt. They do the rebuilds for the WSP. My mechanic, however, convinced me he could do the job better for the same money, about $1,500. To make a long story short, the final bill was more than $3,000, which included a set of plug wires for $110.

A cracked head and other problems prompted a second rebuild at no charge. The second rebuild was no better and the car was taken to

another shop with the engine being sent to Waterhouse. Their rebuild has been trouble-free. Threat of a lawsuit caused the first shop to re-fund $2,500. During the several rebuilds, the following components were replaced or rebuilt: radiator, all hoses, crossover pipe, water-pump, starter, vibration dampner and several smaller items.

In the meantime, the wiper-washer system failed. I replaced the whole system myself for $246. The washer mechanism lasted 13 months, with a 12-month warranty. Repairs the second time cost $153.

For several months the differential had grown increasingly noisy, whining under light load. The dealer found worn gears and bearings in the center section. Also, a failed wheel bearing had ruined the left axle shaft. A complete rebuild would cost nearly $1,000. Searching a salvage yard yielded a 28,000 mile 3.42 ratio rear end with limited slip for $375. The dealer agreed to swap the parts for $200. After disman-tling my car, the mechanic discovered the new housing was bent and

Expect to replace the brakes and tires on a used police car. Some of the used police car dealers listed in the Appendix also replace belts and hoses before resale. (Bill Hattersley)

unusable. They gave me the choice of putting the bad rear end back in or of setting up the new parts in my housing for about $500.

I was furious that they had not checked the used parts until after taking the rear end out of my car. I called a transmission shop I had used before and they agreed to swap and set up the gear lash in my housing for $300. The service manager at the dealer agreed to reassemble my car for no further charge. The transmission shop finished the job on a Friday afternoon.

Driving the car revealed a bent axle shaft. Saturday morning, when I should have been on my way to Utah, found me returning to the salvage yard for a straight axle, then having another shop install the axle. All told, I spent close to $1,000 on the rear end. At least I upgraded to a limited slip unit and got new wheel bearings.

By the end of 1994, after 10-1/2 months, the car had covered 15,000 miles, spent nearly three months in the shop and cost me just over $6,000 in repairs! This was after the recovered $2,500.

The new year started with exhaust system failure while on a weekend trip. Patronizing a large national muffler chain resulted in a cobbled together system that leaked, rattled and had excessive back pressure. Fortunately, the Seattle store of the same chain replaced the entire system with the correct parts, at no charge.

Continued surging during warm-up prompted another visit to the dealer for a new oxygen sensor, which did not change the problem but cost me $160. Mid-year, a battery and four new Goodyear F-32 tires were installed along with an alignment.

The car ran pretty well until November when performance became sluggish. A tune-up did not improve the performance, but new front brakes and shocks were installed.

In December, after 60,000 miles of use, the transmission failed. Fortunately, I was only a few blocks from home. Getting a little smarter, I negotiated with three dealers to get the best price on the repair. For a GM factory rebuilt transmission with a three-year/50,000-mile warranty, prices ranged from $1,300 to $1,700 installed. With new U-joints and rear end service, the bill was finally $1,600.

Continued sluggish acceleration and now hard starting when cold required another trip to the dealer. A rebuilt distributor solved the starting problem, but the sluggish performance continued. This trip to the dealer cost $400 to solve the problem.

At the end of 1995, a year's driving had added 27,000 miles and cost $3,500 in repairs.

In January 1996, I returned to the dealer because of further deteriorating performance and an intermittent rough idle. Replacement of a sticky EGR valve and a plugged fuel filter did the trick. The performance returned to normal. The bill was $416.

In March, while traveling in Southern California, the "Service Engine Soon" light came on several times and reduced top speed to about 60 mph. A loose connection to the knock sensor resulted in the computer fully retarding ignition timing. This was fixed for free by Alan's Auto Repair in Pasadena, California.

Now after 26 months of ownership, I have put 55,000 miles on the car and spent $14,000-plus on purchase and repairs. When not in the shop, the car has been in constant use, including many long trips around the Western states.

Despite the repair problems, this is the best driving car I have ever owned. The suspension has the perfect compromise between ride and handling. Cornering is near neutral, with just a hint of understeer at the limit. Steering effort is perfectly weighted with excellent road feel and strong self-centering. The brakes are well balanced with no premature rear wheel lockup. Pedal effort is smooth and progressive, not hypersensitive. The car is forgiving of driver error. The 5.7-liter throttle body injected V-8 is strong at low rpm and will wind up quickly and effortlessly. The transmission and rear end ratios are well chosen and shift timing is ideal. Gas mileage varies from 16 to 17 mpg in everyday driving to 18 to 20 mpg on the highway.

My curiosity was aroused by the repair problems I was experiencing so I decided to study the repair records of other WSP 1990 Caprices. Over a 12-month period, I found 18 cars at the auction yard waiting to be sold. The following statistics list the repairs required by the 18 Caprices. All had about 100,000 miles of use and between four and five years of service.

The Washington State Patrol 1990 Caprice as an in-service car. (Bill Hattersley)

215

Engines

1 rebuild
2 valve jobs
3 fan clutches
2 crank pulleys
2 PROM modules
10 left-hand exhaust manifolds
1 right-hand exhaust manifold

Transmissions

2 reseal jobs
14 transmission rebuild/replacements

Driveline

4 differentials
2 rear wheel bearings
1 rear yoke

Exhaust

4 catalytic converters

Cooling

10 water pumps

Suspension-Steering

6 sets of shock absorbers
3 idler arms
3 power steering pumps
1 set of rear springs (sag)

Brakes

6 park brake releases
2 brake boosters (same car)
24 brake rotors
Average six sets of front brakes per car
Average one set of rear brakes per car

Electrical

19 alternators
18 batteries

1 ECM (computer)
4 wiper motors
3 headlamp switches
1 distributor shaft

Climate Control

1 heater core
6 air-conditioning compressors

Miscellaneous

32 wheel covers
16 left front outside door handles
2 headlamp lenses

Most notable for the enthusiast purchasing a used Chevrolet cruiser is the differential. Chevrolet uses a composite case; steel tubes welded to a center section. Hard driving can cause the tubes to sag. This contributes to bearing failure at both ends of the rear axles. Also, the Chevrolet axles use no inner race on the wheel bearing. Instead, the rollers ride directly on the axle shaft and when the bearing wears out it chews up the axle shaft. Because of these weak points, Chevrolet police differentials in usable condition are difficult to locate at salvage yards and expensive when found.

The transmission problems are expensive, but GM's three-year/50,000-mile warranty on factory rebuilt transmissions is reassuring. Most of the other problems noted are easily fixed with the application of lots of money. The wiper system seems particularly prone to failure and when it does, the wipers run by themselves unless the fuse is pulled.

My advice to others would be to carefully consider repair costs before purchase. Making friends with someone in the fleet department of your local police agency can pay off in information on the best sources for parts and repairs. Finding a salvage yard that buys a lot of wrecked cruisers is helpful in searching out used parts.

Another consideration in restoring any vehicle has to do with re-sale value. Money invested in restoring a 1957 Chevrolet convertible will bring a profit when sold. So far, most four-door sedans, including the "plain Jane" police models have not generated high sale prices when sold. Money spent on these cars has to be considered a poor investment. However, enjoyment of the hobby is return enough for many enthusiasts.

Contributors

Benton County, Indiana, Sheriff B.L. "Butch" Pritchett
Bartlett, Dick, police car photos
Boatright, Mark, 1987 Caprice
California Highway Patrol, Commissioner Maury Hannigan (ret.)
California Highway Patrol, Commissioner Dwight Helmick
California Highway Patrol, Reginald "Bo" Bohanan, Motor Transport
California Highway Patrol, Traffic Officer Paul Cresenti
California Highway Patrol, Lt. Greg Manuel, Public Affairs
California Highway Patrol, Traffic Officer Joe Schlelter (ret.)
California Highway Patrol, Traffic Officer John Yeaw (ret.)
Carroll, John, 1963 Chevrolet
Chevrolet Motor Division, Harry Hammond, Asst. Manager-Police & Taxi
Chevrolet Motor Division, Bob Hapiak, Specialty Vehicles-Police
Chevrolet Motor Division, Tom Pyden, Director of Marketing
Chevrolet Motor Division, David Hansen, Engineering & Development
Chevrolet Motor Division, Brian Tolan, Caprice platform engineer
Chevrolet Motor Division, Larry Stout, Lumina platform engineer
Chevrolet Motor Division, Andy Lang, Camaro platform engineer
Chevrolet Motor Division, Mike Collins, brake systems engineer
Chevrolet Motor Division, Leslie Schneider, *PRO* magazine editor
Chicago Police, Lt. Lee Hamilton
Chicago Police, Officer Greg Reynolds
Chicago Transit Authority, Glenn Anderson (ret.)
Christy, John, *Motor Trend* editor, LASD technical reserve (late)
Coffing, Gene, Color Tech photos
D'Andrea, Leo, 1991 Caprice
Evers, Sgt. John, Ankeny, Iowa, police
Frohna, Missouri, Marshal Bob Klaus, 1972 Bel Air
Havelka, Charles, 1955 Old Law One Fifty
Half Moon Bay, California, police, Sgt. Guy Reimche
Harrington, Bob, 1961 Biscayne
Hamilton, Don, 1939 Chevrolet
Hamilton, Judy, custom photos
Hastings, Nebraska, police, Lt. Monty McCord
Hertz, Larry, chief, Wabash Township, Indiana Fire
Illinois State Police, Master Trooper Don McKinney
Indiana State Police, Sgt. Rick Hammer, Headquarters
Indiana State Police, Sgt. Jerry Parker, Lowell Post
Indiana State Police, Sgt. Ed Moody, Lowell Post, 1938 Chevrolet
Indiana State Police, Sgt. Dave Morrison, Lafayette Post
Indiana State Police Museum, Jerry Federspiel, curator
Iowa State Patrol, Trooper Robert Parks
Kemp, Neal, NYPD photos
Kennedy, Mike, MSP photos
Kurz, Eric, 1981 Malibu
Lackman, Jon, 1983 Malibu
Lacy Lakeview, Texas Police, Terry Fiene
Law & Order magazine, Bruce Cameron, editor
Law & Order magazine, Tom Yates, vehicle specialist

Law Enforcement Technology magazine, Donna Rogers, editor
LeBlanc, Patrick, 1956 One Fifty
Los Angeles Police, Sgt. Chuck Shaw (ret.)
Los Angeles Police, Officer Karen Klobuchar (ret.)
Los Angeles County Sheriff, Lt. Donald Green, Fleet Management (ret.)
Los Angeles County Sheriff, Lt. Robert Sedita, Fleet Management
Los Angeles County Sheriff, Sgt. Mike Borges, Fleet Management
Los Angeles County Sheriff, Donald Sachs, Historical Society
Madderom, C., 1985 AFD Impala
Mason, Ken, 1957 Bel Air
Michigan State Police, Lt. Curt VanDenBerg, (ret.)
Michigan State Police, Sgt. Bob Ring
Michigan State Police, Sgt. Dave Storer (ret.)
Michigan State Police, Sgt. Bill McFall
Michigan State Police, Sgt. Denny Steendam
Michigan State Police, Trooper Mark Reaves
Michigan State Police, Trooper Doug Lubahn
Michigan State Police, Trooper David Halliday
Michigan State Police, Shirley Goodson, technician
Missouri State Highway Patrol, Captain Terry Moore
Mt. Prospect, Illinois, police, Officer Tony Halachoulis
Nevada Highway Patrol, Trooper Jeff Leathley, Camaro
North Dakota Highway Patrol, Trooper Jim Benjaminson
Novatnak, Mike, 1962 Bel Air
Old Cars Weekly, John Gunnell, editor
Osbon, Rick, Public Safety Consultants
Painchaud, Neil, Peel Regional Police photos
Post, Jim, KCMO Sgt. (ret.), PCOOA president
Pyewell, Clark, 1984 Impala
Randolph County, Illinois, Sheriff Deputy Butch Weaver
Restall, John, 1977 Impala
Romano, Tony, 1983 Malibu
Russell, Paul, NYC Transit photos
School of Mines, Colorado, police, John Antonelli
Schroedel, Chuck, 1957 One Fifty
Scott County, Minnesota, Don Hamilton
Seaman, Tim, 1949 Styleline
Shakker, Leo, 1982 SDPD Malibu
St. Louis Metro Police, Col. Clarence Harmon, chief
St. Louis Metro Police, Barbara Miksicek, librarian
St. Paul, Minnesota, police, Dennis Hale, 1957 Bel Air
Sturgeon, Jennifer, Illinois photos
Super Chevy magazine, Bruce Hampson, editor
Super Chevy magazine, Terry Cole, editor
Veile, Bernard, 1955 Da Fuz Two Ten
Vermilion County, Illinois, deputy Rick Barnes
Washington State Patrol, PIO Jack Sareault
West Virginia State Police, Cpl. A.W. Robinson

Appendix A

Sources for Cars & Parts

A. *Other police car books:*

Dodge, Plymouth & Chrysler Police Cars, 1956-1978 by Cpl. Ed Sanow and Cpl. John Bellah

Dodge, Plymouth & Chrysler Police Cars, 1979-1994 by Cpl. Ed Sanow and Cpl. John Bellah with Galen Govier

Police Cars, A Photographic History by Lt. Monty McCord

Cars of the State Police and Highway Patrol by Lt. Monty McCord

Modern Police Cars by Robert Genat

Vintage Police Cars by Cpl. Ed Sanow

All books are available from Krause Publications, 700 E. State Street, Iola, WI 54990 at 800-258-0929 or Classic Motorbooks, P.O. Box 1, Osceola, WI 54020 at 800-826-6600.

B. *Police and Car Clubs:*

Police Car Owners Of America (PCOOA)
c/o Jim Post, President
Route 6, Box 345B
Eureka Springs, AR 72632
Newsletter: *Rapsheet* (quarterly) $20

Emergency Vehicle Owners & Operators Assn. (EVOOA)
John Bujosa, President
West 14311 Lincoln Road
Olympia, WA 99204-9398
Newsletter: *Code-4* (bi-monthly) $30

Classic Chevy Club France
c/o Patrick LeBlanc
2 Impasse du Chevy
Mont
79290 Saint Martin de Sanzay
FRANCE

The Andy Griffith Show (TAGS) Rerun Watchers Club
Jim Clark, Editor
9 Music Square South #146
Nashville, TN 37203-3203
Newsletter: *The Bullet* (quarterly) $10

National Association of 1994-96 Impala SS Owners
Troy Willrick, President
1648 Taylor Road, Suite 202
Daytona Beach, FL 32123
Newsletter: monthly, $28

National Impala Association (1958 to 1968)
Dennis Naasz, President
P.O. Box 968
Spearfish, SD 57783
Newsletter: *Impala News* (bi-monthly) $30

5-6-7 Club (1955 to 1957)
2021 Wiggins Avenue
Saskatoon, SAS
S7J 1W2
CANADA

Classic Chevy Club Int'l (1955 to 1957)
P.O. Box 607188
Orlando, FL 32860

International Camaro Club (all years)
2001 Pittston Avenue
Scranton, PA 18505

Late Great Chevys (1958 to 1964)
P.O. Box 607824
Orlando, FL 32860

National Nostalgic Nova (all years)
P.O. Box 2344
York, PA 17405

United States Camaro Club (all years)
P.O. Box 608167
Orlando, FL 32860

C. *Police Badge, Patch & Memorabilia Shows:*

Police Collectors News
Mike Bondarenko, Editor
R.R. #1, Box 14
Baldwin, WI 54002
Newsletter: *PCNews* (monthly) $22

D. *Vintage Police Car Literature:*

Walter Miller
6710 Brooklawn
Syracuse, NY 13211

Ed Faxon's Auto Literature
1655 East 6th Street
Corona, CA 91719

Darryl Lindsay
Code 3 Collectibles
P.O. Box 412
San Carlos, CA 94070
(Also photos, equipment)

E. New/Used/Rebuilt Emergency Equipment:

John Dorgan
The Engine House
7381 E. Stella Road
Tuscon, AZ 85730
(Used police gear)

Jim Post
Police Collectibles
Route 6, Box 345B
Eureka Springs, AR 72632
(New and used gear)

Charles Brooks
Chanute Radar Service
15 South Highland
Chanute, KS 66720
(New and used radar)

Darren Pupo
Emergency Equipment Systems
1429 Maplegrove Drive
Fairborn, OH 45324
(Vintage radar)

Dave Dotson
501 North Vine Street
Sparta, IL 62286
(New and used gear)

Jack Attig
P.O. Box 407
Meriden, KS 66512
(Used police gear)

Rick Osbon
P.O. Box 782
Elmhurst, IL 60126
(Used police gear)

Gall's Inc.
2470 Palumbo Drive
Lexington, KY 40555
(New police gear)

Dennis Sanchez
1205 W. Main Street
Festus, MO 63028
(Used police gear)

F. Used Police Car Dealers:

Cruisers Unlimited
1108 Malvern St.
Middletown, OH 45042

Donna Motors
15 Roosevelt Ave.
Bellville, NJ 07109

Mossberg Specialty Cars
Route 48
Wall, PA 15148

Sun Chevrolet
104-108 W. Genesee
Chittenango, NY 13037

Day Ford
3696 William Penn Highway
Monroeville, PA 15146

Excellent Auto Sales
269 Page Boulevard
Springfield, MA 01104

Pursuit Unlimited
1329 N. Harrison
Shawnee, OK 74801

Veto Enterprises
212 W. Exchange Street
Sycamore, IL 60178

Diversifleet
7150 Kaw Drive
Kansas City, KS 66111

Live Oak Auto Center
34906 Louisiana Hwy. 1019
Denham Springs, LA 70726

Rinto Enterprises
2077 W. Roosevelt Road
Wheaton, IL 60187

Woodside Motors
43-29 Crescent Street
Long Island City, NY 11101

Blue Streak Motors
1703 Cannonsburg Rd
Ashland, KY 41102

	55	56	57	58	59	60	61	62	63	64	65	66	67	68	69	70	71	72	73	74	75	76	77	78	79	80	81	82	83	84	85	86	87	88	89	90	91	92	93	94	95	96
235 I-6	X	X	X	X	X	X	X	X																																		
230 I-6									X	X	X																															
250 I-6											X	X	X	X	X	X	X						X	X	X																	
229 V-6																										X	X	X	X	X												
262 V-6																															X	X	X	X	X	X						
265 V-8	X	X	X																																							
283 V-8			X	X	X	X	X	X	X	X	X	X	X	X	X																											
348 V-8				X	X	X	X																																			
327 V-8								X	X	X	X	X	X	X	X																											
409 V-8								X	X	X	X																															
396 V-8											X	X	X	X	X																											
427 V-8												X	X	X	X																											
307 V-8														X																												
350 V-8															X	X	X	X	X	X	X	X	X	X	X	X	X	X	X	X	X	X	X	X	X	X	X	X	X	X	X	X
454 V-8																X	X	X	X	X	X	X																				
400 V-8																	X	X	X	X	X	X																				
402 V-8																		X																								
305 V-8																							X	X	X	X	X	X							X	X	X	X	X			
265 V-8																																								X	X	X

About the Author

Edwin J. Sanow

Ed Sanow received his Bachelor of Science degree from Purdue University. Sanow raced cars before he got his driver's license. He oval raced Ford stock cars on dirt tracks, drag raced a tri-power Pontiac and ran collegiate go-karts. Sanow raced a SCCA Mustang on road courses in the Midwest for seven years. He is a graduate of the Bob Bondurant School of High Performance Driving, Summit Point's BSR, Inc. Tactical Driving School and SkidCar USA's Vehicle Control Course.

Sanow currently serves as the pursuit driving advisor for the Benton County, Indiana, Sheriff's office. He has been a reserve deputy with the BCSO since 1986 and also serves as its firearms, chemical agents and in-service police instructor. Sanow is the senior reserve officer, holds the rank of Corporal and is one of the most active traffic officers in the county.

During his years of county patrol with the BCSO, Sanow has been issued a number of Chevrolet police cars: 350-cid Impala, 2.8-liter EFI V-6 Celebrity, 262-cid V-6 Caprice, 350-cid Caprice, 350-cid LT1 Caprice and the LT1-powered Camaro.

Sanow's articles on muscle cars and police cars have appeared in *AutoWeek, Chrysler Power, Muscle Mustangs, High Performance Mopar, Super Chevy, Mopar Muscle, MorPerformance, Muscle Cars of the 60s/70s, Law & Order, Police, Law Enforcement Technology, Old Cars Weekly, Chevy Truck, Chevy High Performance, Chevrolet Division PRO* and *Kansas Trooper*. He is the lead co-author of *Dodge, Plymouth, Chrysler Police Cars, 1956-1978*, and *Dodge, Plymouth, Chrysler Police Cars, 1979-1994* and the author of *Vintage Police Cars*.

Sanow makes the police car circuit with his 1972 police package, 402-cid big-block Chevrolet Bel Air and his 1987 police package, 318-cid small-block Dodge Diplomat. He restored a 1976 LM1-powered Chevrolet Caprice Classic while waiting to find a big-block bowtie. Sanow attends the annual police vehicle tests conducted by the Michigan State Police and the Los Angeles County Sheriff. He is the Indiana state representative for the Police Car Owners Of America (PCOOA) and the Emergency Vehicle Owners and Operators Association (EVOOA).

Cpl. Ed Sanow with his 402-cid big-block 1972 Bel Air, which was in-service with the Frohna, Missouri, Police for 24 years.

Contributing Authors

John Bellah

John Bellah was a mechanic for Chevrolet, Datsun and Chrysler-Plymouth dealers from 1968 to 1977. He was the owner of Motor-Medic of Santa Monica, a mobile automotive tune-up and repair service that was one of the first California licensed mobile emission control stations in the state.

Bellah attended the University of Southern California and entered law enforcement in 1977. He is currently with the California State University-Long Beach Police Department where he holds the rank of Corporal. In addition to serving as an investigator and a patrol officer, Bellah developed department policies in patrol vehicle purchase, replacement and maintenance.

Co-author of *Dodge, Plymouth & Chrysler Police Cars, 1956-1978* and *Dodge, Plymouth & Chrysler Police Cars, 1979-1994*, Bellah has been published in *Chrysler Power* magazine, *Newsweek-On Campus* magazine, *Campus Law Enforcement Journal* and *Backup* magazine. He owns a 1963 ex-CHP Dodge 880 413-cid, four-barrel and attends the annual police vehicle tests conducted by the Los Angeles County Sheriff.

Cpl. John Bellah with the 1981 Malibu 9C1 from his days with the San Gabriel, California, Police.

Jim Post

Sgt. Jim Post (ret.) is a 25-year veteran of the Kansas City, Missouri, Police Department. Post holds a B.S. degree in Administration of Justice and a M.S. degree in Criminal Justice Administration. During his 12 years as a sergeant, he served as a field supervisor and as one of the department's driving instructors. Since his retirement in 1990, he has worked for the U.S. Marshal and in private security.

Post formed the Heart of America Police Insignia Collectors Association, the Police Car Owners Of America and, in 1991, hosted the National Police Collectors Convention. He was a regular columnist for *The Thin Blue Line*, a monthly police magazine, and is a frequent contributor to *Police Collectors News*.

Post relocated to Eureka Springs, Arkansas, in 1994 and opened "The Last Precinct," a police museum and gift shop specializing in law enforcement gifts and memorabilia. This is also the world headquarters of the Police Car Owners Of America. Post owns a wide variety of Chevrolet, Dodge, Plymouth and Ford police cars of all vintages.

Sgt. Jim Post with the Kansas City, Missouri, Police 1988 Caprice on the day of his retirement.

Bill Hattersley

Bill Hattersley, a Southern California native, has lived in the Seattle, Washington, area since 1976. A history major in college, Hattersley minored in Traffic Safety Education. He spent 10 years teaching behind-the-wheel and classroom Driver's Education.

A fire engine and police car buff, Hattersley turned his hobby into a business. He currently writes articles and shoots photos for *Fire Apparatus Journal*, takes calendar and advertising photos of fire rigs and sells police car and fire engine photos by mail order.

Hattersley currently owns a 1990 ex-Washington State Patrol 350-cid Caprice that he uses as a daily driver. He lives with wife, Carol, and their cat, Libby, in Seattle. He enjoys collecting and shooting .22 caliber rifles, collects model vehicles and follows NASCAR racing on television.

Bill Hattersley with his ex-Washington State Patrol 1990 Caprice, fondly called the "Spongemobile."

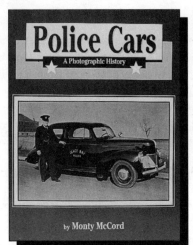
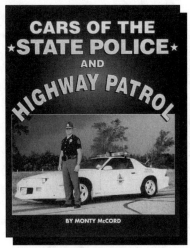

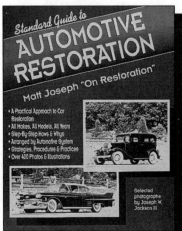